PRAGMATIC PLAGIARISM
Authorship, Profit, and Power

PRAGMATIC PLAGIARISM
Authorship, Profit, and Power

Marilyn Randall

UNIVERSITY OF TORONTO PRESS
Toronto Buffalo London

© University of Toronto Press 2001
Toronto Buffalo London
Printed in Canada

ISBN 0-8020-4814-5

Printed on acid-free paper

University of Toronto Romance Series

Canadian Cataloguing in Publication Data
Randall, Marilyn
Pragmatic plagiarism : authorship, profit, and power

(University of Toronto romance series)
Includes bibliographical references and index.
ISBN 0-8020-4814-5

1. Plagiarism.   I. Title.   II. Series.

PN167.R36 2001   808   C00-932398-8

University of Toronto Press acknowledges the financial assistance to its publishing program of the Canada Council for the Arts and the Ontario Arts Council.

The research for this project was made possible by a research grant from the
Social Sciences and Humanities Research Council of Canada.

This book has been published with the help of a grant from the Canadian Federation for the Humanities, using funds provided by the Social Sciences and
Humanities Research Council of Canada.

University of Toronto Press acknowledges the financial support for its publishing activities of the Government of Canada through the Book Publishing
Industry Development Program (BPIDP).

Contents

Preface   vii
Acknowledgments   xvii

Introduction: What Is Plagiarism?   3

Part One: Authoring Plagiarism
1 What Is an (Original) Author?   23
2 Originating Discourse: Authority, Authenticity, Originality   32
3 Owning Discourse   60

Part Two: Reading Plagiarism
4 Reading the Reader   99
5 Reading the Act   126

Part Three: Power Plagiarism
6 Profit Plagiarism   159
7 Imperial Plagiarism   189
8 Guerrilla Plagiarism   218

Conclusion: Post-Plagiarism   253

Notes   271
Words Cited   299
Index   313

Preface

While the fundamental question addressed in this study could be simply expressed as 'What is plagiarism?,' the proposed answer will radically shift the focus of this investigation, from an author- or even a text-based one to a pragmatic one: not 'Who is plagiarizing?,' as Foucault might have said, but 'Who is reading plagiarism?' In other words: why do some instances of literary repetition become plagiarism, and others become great art?

Plagiarism is a slippery subject because, while almost everyone agrees on *what* it is, few agree on *where* it is to be found. Even a minimal definition such as 'unacknowledged copying for undeserved profit' encounters potential exceptions at every turn. Aphorisms such as 'immature writers imitate, mature writers steal' (T.S. Eliot, Lionel Trilling) or 'copying one book is plagiarism, copying many is research' (Mizner) are evidence that plagiarism is, above all, a matter of opinion, and, as such, it will usually be found to exist – or not to exist – where the most influential opinions claim it to be, or not. Most studies of plagiarism are essentially accounts of accusations of plagiarism against great writers; that is, they are studies of what the literary institution has finally judged to be something other than 'real' plagiarism. This one is no exception. If this work can be read as a contribution to the history of aphorisms describing plagiarism, its two fundamental claims would be: first, that *plagiarism is in the eye of the beholder*, and, second, that *plagiarism is power*.

In other words, plagiarism is pragmatic. The title of this book expresses my double premise by exploiting two different but related meanings of 'pragmatic': plagiarism is a pragmatic category, first, because its existence depends on an act of reception that is itself circumscribed by a variety of contextual features, among which the actual 'fact' of repeated discourse is *perhaps* a necessary, but in reality incidental, feature of the phenomenon. Plagiarism arises less significantly from the intentions of authors than from the judgments of readers. Second, plagiarism is pragmatic because it does something: once discovered – in terms of this analysis I would rather say 'constructed' by the reception of authoritative readers – it inevitably produces effects, some of which are far-ranging and long-lasting. In evoking the terms 'constructed' and 'authoritative,' I have, as well, implicitly oriented my study towards what is commonly known as an *institutional* analysis, although the notion of the literary institution that I develop here is viewed in terms of a *contextual pragmatics*, which is briefly explained in the introduction.

The single most difficult challenge in attempting to write a book about plagiarism is to avoid committing it. Why this should be particularly true about this subject rather than any other may not be self-evident, but how often have I heard, having revealed the subject of my research, this inevitable advice: 'Why don't you plagiarize it?' Why not, indeed? And my search for originality in the field of plagiarism has been further undermined by a series of recent and important publications on the subject, making it more and more difficult to say anything 'new' about a phenomenon that, although probably as old as writing itself, has a fairly limited range of discursive treatments, perhaps corresponding to a rather limited number of practices. Most contemporary studies, ranging from compilations to psychological analyses – and including this one – have in common a lack of interest in discovering instances of plagiarism, and a preference for analysis. This leads to a feeling of *déjà-lu*, in the sense that the received tradition of canonical, that is, interesting plagiarisms, while practically inexhaustible, does tend to reproduce the same source texts, the same major perpetrators, and the same authorities on the subject. Roland de Chaudenay, author of a dictionary of plagiarism, is most eloquent on the difficult task of the compiler, whose work is often undervalued, whereas, in his eyes, 'compilation is an essential vehicle of culture, be it only popular culture' ['La compilation est un véhicule essentiel de la culture, fût-elle populaire' (Chaudenay 22)]. Since I aspire neither to the erudition nor to the bibliographical talents required of compilers and of students of culture, popular or otherwise, I have necessarily had to depend on their research, and have only contributed incidentally to the already existing long list of 'plagiarists.' This work is also, but I hope only partially, a compilation.

Several recent publications signal a renewed interest in the subject. The first, and in many ways the most important, is Michel Schneider's *Voleurs de mots* (1985), a long and fascinating treatment of plagiarism from a psychoanalytical perspective. His principal object is Freud himself, the Vienna Circle, and their encounters with plagiarism and accusations of plagiarism among themselves. As I often cite this work in the course of this study, it is not necessary to deal with it further now. A second study, Thomas Mallon's *Stolen Words* (1989), provides a brief historical discussion of plagiarism, but is mainly devoted to a case-study approach of the details of four different kinds of plagiarism: Charles Reade, nineteenth-century British playwright and novelist (and prolific 'importer' of French theatre to England); Jacob Epstein's plagiarism of Martin Amis's *The Rachel Papers*; historian Jayme Aaron Sokolow's plagiaristic academic career; and the accusations of plagiarism against the producers of the soap opera *Falcon Crest* brought by Anita Clay Kornfeld, author of *Vintage*, a novel dealing with a Napa wine-making family. Mallon's examination of these cases sheds much light on both historical and contemporary uses of plagiarism, and although my own will not be a case-study approach, I will be relying on some of his documentation. A third recent publication, already mentioned, is Roland de Chaudenay's *Dictionnaire des plagiaires* (1990), whose subtitle can stand as its own description: 'a dictionary where one finds classed in alphabetical order writers in French who, by means of borrowings which they appear to have made from the works of other authors, are, or could be considered to be systematic or occasional pillagers, sly copiers, laborious compilers, shameless imitators, conceited literary pretenders, in a word, plagiarists.'[1] At once a precious source of information and a tongue-in-cheek send-up of the criterion of originality, the dictionary treats plagiarism and the process of compilation in which it is engaged with self-reflexive irony, and we will be returning to it.

Another recent book on plagiarism is somewhat outside our domain. Marcel LaFollette's *Stealing into Print: Fraud, Plagiarisms and Misconduct in Scientific Publishing* (1992) is a useful reflection on the ethical and practical issues arising from plagiarism in the scientific world. Her general observations on plagiarism depend largely on the sources that I myself have pillaged, and her contribution to my study is primarily in allowing me not to deal with the subject of scientific plagiarism, and to send the reader interested in this aspect of the field to her book. The subject of plagiarism continues to attract contemporary consideration: recent publications such as Woodmansee and Jaszi's anthology of essays devoted to the history of authorship (1994) and Françoise Meltzer's reflections on the notion of literary originality (1994) make important contributions to the study of plagiarism while situating it in the larger contexts to which the notion is closely related. A recently defended thesis at McGill University (Montreal), 'Le faux littéraire,' is largely devoted to questions of literary plagiarism (Martineau). Most recently, Laura Rosenthal's study *Playwrights and Plagiarists in Early Modern England: Gender, Authorship and Literary Property* (1996) has much in common with this one, from a theoretical perspective, although her subject is Renaissance English theatre from the point of view of the female author and plagiarist.[2]

Two older treatments of plagiarism have become standard reference texts in the English world: Harold Ogden White's *Plagiarism and Imitation during the English Renaissance* ([1935] 1973) and Alexander Lindey's *Plagiarism and Originality* (1951) are invaluable sources of examples of plagiarism controversies – the first from the literary, and the second from a more legal point of view. I use these texts as sources, but many of the stories they recount I do not repeat; for details about specific cases, I refer the reader to these sources.

All of these studies – Rosenthal's excepted – consider plagiarism to be a constitutive *fact* of plagiaristic texts whose discovery provides clues to the biography or psychology of authors, to relationships between texts, to repetition as constitutive of the nature of literature and, indeed, of human beings. Whether understood as a historical or contemporary phenomenon, as a legal or ethical infraction, or as the productive symptom of a psychological complex, plagiarism is usually seen to exist by virtue of the existence of plagiaristic texts produced by plagiaristic personalities for fun or profit. By postulating the radically institutional and reader-oriented nature of plagiarism, *Pragmatic Plagiarism* necessarily parts company with its predecessors, without which, however, it would not exist.

From what precedes, it will be clear that, while this book is 'about plagiarism,' it is not primarily intended to document, much less discover, instances of plagiarism, although some anecdotal description is inevitable. The examples, both historical and contemporary, are chosen for their exemplarity or notoriety, and many will probably be familiar to the reader. My predisposition to consider accusations of plagiarism as significant barometers of literary power struggles necessarily presupposes a selection among the many instances of alleged plagiarism that privileges those having generated a substantial degree of critical controversy: since my object is not plagiarism 'as such' but, rather, its discursive construction and effects, I only discuss those cases that evoked strong – or at least recorded – reactions. As well, the presupposition that some instances of plagiarism are either the cause or the effect of culturally or literarily significant events has biased me in favour of cases entailing, explicitly or implicitly, conflicts that extend beyond the local interests of offended individuals, although this category may in fact comprise the greatest number of accusations of plagiarism.

The enormity of the subject, as well as the principles of selection and analysis that I have adopted, means that many notorious and interesting cases of plagiarism, both historical and contemporary, are not treated here. These lacunae are necessary from a practical point of view: first, my selection aims at being representative rather than exhaustive. A second, more serious category of exclusion is that of the many (post)modern writers and artists who use various forms of imitation, intertextuality, or appropriation that are formally hardly distinguishable from other cases I have included: authors such as T.S. Eliot, Blaise Cendrars, the members of OuLiPo, Malcolm Lowry, Angela Carter, and Raymond Federman are excluded from this study, as are the theoretical questions they generate.[3] The explicit adoption of 'plagiarism' as aesthetic method or the thematization of 'plagiarism' in the theoretical writings of these authors seems *a priori* to define these practices as something other than 'real' plagiarism; but the most important criterion for inclusion in this study is that the authors have been, in some way, accused of plagiarism. If plagiarism is a product of a discourse of reception, these writers are not plagiarists. In the same sense, writers such as Eliot and Carter, who can be shown to have 'copied' in various important ways, have not been accused of 'plagiarism,' as such. Lowry would come the closest to being an accused 'plagiarist,' but, in his case, plagiarism seems to be most significantly of the order of a pathological self-doubt and guilt, rather than of a critical discourse of reception (see Grace).

A second reason for avoiding the fascinating but well-worn paths of intertextuality and allusion is that these various 'innocent' forms of repetition tend to support the position that 'all literature is repetition,' therefore potentially plagiaristic – a generalization that would extend to the entire history of literary art, immediately dissolving my object into non-existence. My corpus includes only authors who have come under the suspicion or accusation of plagiarism, in its strong sense, by members of the literary institution somehow vested with authority on these matters. The choice to keep the word 'plagiarism' clearly in a negative rather than a positive aesthetic category is implied by the incontrovertible fact that, while all texts, literary or otherwise, demonstrate some degree of repetition, their authors are not all equally subject to accusations of plagiarism. What interests me is the fact that some repetitions are judged criminal or offensive and others not, a situation that points again to the pragmatic nature of the category.

My object, in fact, is not primarily the 'plagiaristic' text, but rather the sociocultural conditions of the production of plagiarism as a negative – or positive – aesthetic category, and the discourse that constitutes this production, as it has evolved from early to contemporary times in Western literature. This approach is determined by the notion that plagiarism is a judgment imposed upon texts, and in determining the history and progress of this literary category what is needed is a study not of texts, which are not in themselves *a priori* plagiaristic, but of the judgments that have deemed them so, or that, on the other hand, have absolved them

from guilt. As Bourdieu says, 'the production of discourse (critical, historical, etc.) about the work of art is one of the conditions of production of the
work' ('Field of Cultural Production' 35). The sources of these judgments
are various, ranging from treatises on the subject to letters to the editor in
The Times Literary Supplement. They express or reveal prevailing moods and
modes of aesthetic practice and judgment that certain texts are perceived
to have transgressed.

The history of 'plagiarism' is tentacular, involving not only concepts of
copyright and intellectual property, but also questions of authorship,
authority, originality, and imitation, which, taken together, imply more or
less the entire development of Western literary history. Add to this incomplete list the pertinent historical and cultural dimensions, and the progress
of plagiarism might easily be seen to coincide with that of Western aesthetics.
Needless to say, such a history will not be written here. I deal only with a few
French, British, and North American cases of some notoriety, cases that have
somehow marked the changing frontier between good imitation and bad.
This sporadic approach, which could more kindly be considered 'exemplary,' will of necessity be selective, non-linear, and far from exhaustive.

In the introduction to this book, I attempt to delineate the nature of the
question 'What is plagiarism?,' my object of study and method, by looking
at the *problem* presented by the phenomenon; the *pragmatics* of the approach adopted; and, finally, a *definition* of plagiarism that will serve as a
basis for my analysis in Parts One and Two.

In Part One, I take up the fundamental relationship between plagiarism
and authorship: plagiarism implies the existence of 'authorship' both at a
time when the modern notion did not yet exist, and recently, when it
appears no longer to exist in its traditional contours. 'Authoring Plagiarism' underlines, first of all, the continuous existence of plagiarism, and
therefore of authorship and, on the other hand, situates literary-critical
discourse about plagiarism and authorship in the context of the historical
development of the former. The two principal features of authorship
developed are the function of authors to 'originate discourse' and their
status as 'owners of discourse,' a condition we will see as predating by centuries modern notions of copyright.

Part Two, 'Reading Plagiarism,' develops the premise that *plagiarism is in
the eye of the beholder* by examining the function of the *reader* in *naming, compiling*, and *criticizing* either plagiarism or its critics. While the reader will be
seen as the repressed agent of the construction of plagiarism *qua* plagiarism, it will also be apparent that what the reader is reading, apparently a
text or other kind of cultural artefact, is, necessarily, an authorial *act*, one
that is presupposed to have fraudulent intentions. Various means of accu-

sation and disculpation will, once again, point to the pragmatic nature of the category and its readerly construction as negative or, perhaps, positive. In Part Three, 'Power Plagiarism,' I leave general questions of the history and determination of plagiarism to explore three areas in which the presence of plagiarism has been particularly notable. It is here that my hypothesis of *plagiarism is power*, that is, a discursive act capable of producing effects, is developed. In chapter 6, 'Profit Plagiarism,' I explore the relationship between the perception of unearned advantages and the presumed motivations for plagiarism. The *industrialist* and the *parvenu* are the two figures that dominate this field. I follow them from the time that Balzac and Poe struggled with the burgeoning French and American literary institutions, through Alexander Haley and Martin Amis, to Calixthe Beyala's recent *contretemps* with the French literary institution.

Chapter 7, 'Imperial Plagiarism,' examines one of the most enduring motifs in the history of plagiarism, the 'conquest' metaphor, from its Latin origins to its emergence in contemporary post-colonial criticism. This chapter traces the historical development of the 'conquest' to the case of Stendhal, and then further into post-colonial literature, Martin Luther King, Jr's university 'plagiarisms,' and the controversy surrounding D.M. Thomas's *The White Hotel.*

Chapter 8, 'Guerrilla Plagiarism,' examines some contemporary modes of plagiarism adopted explicitly as a strategy of subversion of the dominant ideology. Within the general frame of 'postmodernism,' I posit 'plagiarism' as a mode of guerrilla warfare directed against an oppressive hegemony. 'Postmodern plagiarism' is also the logical consequence of the (theoretical) 'death' of the author and of the humanist subject, which becomes the contemporary condition of (non)-authorship introduced in the first chapter. In particular, post-colonial and feminist artists are highly self-conscious of their doubly dispossessed condition of subjecthood. In this chapter, I discuss some early post-colonial plagiarists such as Hubert Aquin (*Trou de mémoire*), from Quebec, and Yambo Ouolguem (*Le devoir de violence*), from Mali, in the context of their self-assumed condition of absent subjecthood. Feminist plagiarism, as well, posits a crisis of dispossessed subjectivity within the patriarchal order. I examine in particular the work of Kathy Acker and Sherrie Levine in the context of theoretical justifications for 'plagiarism' and its reception as a mode of aesthetic contestation.

The conclusion examines the *future of plagiarism* in terms of the relationship between copyright law and contemporary aesthetic practice, first, with respect to the 'Art world,' and, second, in relation to the 'information highway.' What are the consequences for the aesthetic and legal status of 'plagiarism' in an age that proclaims not only the 'death of the author' but 'appropriation' as an aesthetic and technological practice?

What has become clear to me through reflecting on some of these historical moments is that, despite shifts in aesthetic norms, plagiarism is a very old and almost continuous phenomenon whose description remains surprisingly stable over time. What is constantly in flux are the kinds of textual practices that count as belonging to the category. This claim in favour of the historical consistency of plagiarism may strike some as anachronistic. The question, for example, of whether or not Shakespeare was a 'plagiarist' inevitably elicits a negative response, for which the standard explanation – beyond that of his genius – is that plagiarism didn't exist in his time, which is a corollary of the argument that 'everybody did it': in other words, what we might call plagiarism was, in those days, the conventional way to write theatre. The well-established fact of the collaborative nature of Renaissance theatre is not at issue here: the question that interests me is not whether Shakespeare 'plagiarized,' but whether he, or any of his contemporaries, *could* have plagiarized, or been seen to have done so, in terms of the aesthetic and market conditions in which they worked. The commonly held belief that not only did Shakespeare *not* plagiarize, but, as a sixteenth-century playwright, *he could not have*, fails to take into consideration the fact that accusations of plagiarism did exist, and that Shakespeare's contemporaries, and some very worthy ones, were apparently moved to accuse him and each other of the crime. The question becomes, then, not whether Shakespeare plagiarized, but what presuppositions are involved when accusations of plagiarism during the English Renaissance were made.

If it is clear, today, that Shakespeare did not plagiarize, it is so only partly because we attempt to apply to his method not our own aesthetic and legal standards, but those that dominated in the sixteenth century. For, in many ways, Shakespeare's method is remarkably similar to some contemporary ones: Kathy Acker is also not a plagiarist by our standards, although her practice is clearly described, both by herself and by literary critics, as 'plagiaristic.' In some quite anachronistic way, Shakespeare and Acker encounter each other in terms of a contemporary aesthetics where, imbued with the ethos of intertextuality, literature is seen to be by nature repetition, and true 'originality' impossible. In a post-humanist, postmodern, postauthorial world, where not only the singularity of authorship, but the originating potential of individual subjectivity, has been much contested; where authors have only recently been resurrected from the limbo to which poststructuralism consigned them; and where technological progress seems to threaten the very foundations of intellectual property law, even the possibility of plagiarism seems fraught with presuppositions about the originality, ownership, and authorship of discourse that are no longer universally shared within the same interpretive community.

Plagiarism clearly does exist, both today and as a transhistorical constant of the discursive field we have come to call literature. But if the fact of the existence of plagiarism is self-evident, the nature of its existence is not: the question is, then – What is plagiarism?

Acknowledgments

This book is dedicated to the memory of my father, Lester C. Randall, who took a lively interest in the subject and the progress of my work up until the end of his life which, at age ninety-five, still came too soon. As the manuscript was being sent to the publisher, he was still able to speak. 'So you're going to put yourself on the line, eh?' was perhaps the last sentence I ever heard him utter. His love of books, learning, and ideas was a constant in my life.

It is impossible to name all those who contributed to this work which is as far from being 'original' as is possible: since there is nothing new under the sun, the degree of my indebtedness to other scholars is total. Peter Nesselroth was responsible for the origins of my interest in literary plagiarism; Max Vernet will recognize his contribution to this text and others over the years; Anthony Wall will remember an early and intense reading of the manuscript. Bernd Frohmann, Alison Lee, Anne-Marie Picard, and Robert Barsky have all contributed actively to the project, as has Yzabelle Martineau, whose interest in the subject of plagiarism is as keen as mine. Among the many who have provided anecdotes, information, and encouragement over the years, I would particularly like to thank Robert Hawkins for his enthusiasm, his stimulating discussion, and his newspaper clippings. Beyond their practical contributions, the interest in my project expressed by these and many other friends convinced me that it was worth pursuing.

Monique Glasgow and Dr Tess Do were invaluable research assistants. And in a more general way, the support and collegiality of the members of the Department of French at the University of Western Ontario – both past and present – have made the years devoted to this book less difficult than they might have been.

I would also like to thank the Social Sciences and Humanities Research Council of Canada as well as the Aid to Scholarly Publications program of the Canadian Federation of Social Sciences and Humanities for their continuing support of my work.

PRAGMATIC PLAGIARISM
Authorship, Profit, and Power

Introduction: What Is Plagiarism?

There is a wealth of received wisdom about plagiarism, transmitted most effectively through countless aphorisms coined primarily by authors, that is, virtual plagiarists, in their own defence. The 'history' of plagiarism can be divided roughly into discourses of apology and of condemnation: the first generally argues that all literature, or art – in fact, all of human activity – is essentially repetitive, and that 'plagiarism,' therefore, is inevitable. The second, ascribing an ethical content to aesthetic activity, defends notions of intellectual property, originality, and individual authenticity, which are seen to be transgressed by certain types of appropriation of intellectual products. These opposing positions meet, however, in their judgment of 'great authors': copying that achieves a superior level of aesthetic approval may escape the negative implications inherent in the accusation of plagiarism. Discursive repetition may be seen either as ubiquitous and essentially benign, producing in some instances great art for which the qualifier 'plagiaristic' becomes inappropriate; or else as exceptional and fundamentally malignant, a transgression of whatever ethical, aesthetic, or legal conventions or laws are available to provide sanctions for it. In fact, the overwhelming consensus about literary plagiarism is that it is bad only when it is not good, and the canonical examples of good plagiarists far outweigh those of the bad variety.

The considerable efforts engaged in by authors to justify 'plagiarism' – or, rather, to recast it in another light – are a significant indication that 'plagiarism' has always marked a definite frontier between the acceptable and the odious, between good writing and bad, between legitimate and illegitimate aesthetic practices. Both the word and the practice have a long and, if not venerable, at least important history, stretching back to antiquity in Western culture and spanning the centuries with a consistency perhaps unknown in any other literary category. Plagiaristic texts ('real' ones), however, are rarely studied, or only inadvertently, precisely because their qualification as plagiaristic automatically excludes them from the domain of appropriate objects of literary attention. Admittedly, a pure and bona fide case of plagiarism, such as Borges imagines in 'Pierre Menard, Author of *Don Quixote*,' would be of little textual significance, and would have mainly artefactual, legal, or biographical interest – in fact, in the real world, plagiarism committed on such a scale would constitute a case of piracy, which is largely outside my domain. In Borges's fictional example, the literary critic's preference for Menard's 'version' of *Don Quixote* over Cervantes's opens up a whole range of fascinating questions to the sociologist or historian of literature. As in so many of Borges's fictions, the hypothetical example is not so far from reality, if one considers the judgment rendered by the Académie française about Corneille's *Le Cid* compared with its Spanish 'original,' or the fortunes of Shakespeare's plays compared with that of their sources. The Borgesian fiction sets the stage for the premise that 'plagiarism' is not, in fact, primarily a textual category, but a *pragmatic* one, principally determined by a wide variety of extratextual criteria that constitute the aesthetic, institutional, and cultural contexts of production and reception of the work. In other words, 'plagiarism' (especially literary plagiarism) does not in fact 'exist' in any positive or objective sense, accompanied by textual criteria that would allow us to recognize it in the same way that we can a lyric poem, a sonnet, or even, however tenuously, a novel.

Far from being controversial, this premise is actually rather self-evident, since disputes about plagiarism and court battles determining breach of copyright depend directly on the undecidable status of explicit repetitions or apparent copies. The question to be answered in such debates is not whether repetition has occurred, but whether, in fact, the repetition that can be seen to have occurred qualifies as one of the sanctionable, unethical, or even illegal forms that we have come to call plagiarism or breach of copyright. The consequence of this evidence is that 'plagiarism' (I use the term, for the time being, in its general sense, to include copyright infractions) is not an immanent feature of texts, but rather the result of judgments involving, first of all, the presence of some kind of textual repetition, but also, and perhaps more important, a conjunction of social, political, aesthetic, and cultural norms and presuppositions that motivate accusations or disculpations, elevating some potential plagiarisms to the level of great works of art, while censuring others and condemning the perpetrators to ignominy. Particular controversies provide clear evidence of the non-textual criteria mobilized in decisions about plagiarism: the status and perceived genius of the authors, both plagiarizing and plagiarized; the status achieved by the plagiaristic text before the discovery of the 'plagiarism'; the national and patriotic interests of accuser and accused; and, of course, the aesthetic and legal norms dominating at the various moments of production, reception, and judgment of the text.

Although the distinction between 'literature' and other forms of discourse is increasingly meaningless as one moves back in history, I have chosen to concentrate mainly on what we now call 'literature' for several reasons, not the least of which is as a means of limiting the field somewhat. The first reason for focusing (primarily) on literary plagiarism arises from my interest in studying the construction of literature *qua* literature, which is what I take to be the fundamental aim of institutional analysis. In this sense, literary plagiarism demonstrates, as do literature and other forms of aesthetic production, certain pragmatic specificities that are not generalizable across the spectrum of discursive or cultural fields, and these specificities arise primarily from institutional differences that are pertinent to the construction of literary plagiarism.

First, non-literary plagiarism – scientific, journalistic, academic, for example – presents particular problems and solutions that can sometimes seem more straightforward than in literary plagiarism, since the institutions in which they occur often have more stringent, or at least explicit, internal standards of behaviour for their members, standards that allow them to judge 'plagiarism' not only as a punctual infraction involving theft of intellectual property, but as an ethical breach of norms or laws that constitute the institution. Student plagiarism, to take one example, is explicitly sanctionable within the terms of the contract of the academy, where it is usually defined and proscribed in student handbooks that lay out the proper use of citations, quotation marks, and other techniques of attribution. The contractual agreement into which students enter is clear, if not always to them, at least to the institution, and when infractions can be identified they are always sanctionable. Academia allows for mitigating circumstances that may attenuate the seriousness of the individual offence, but has no official provision for considering some forms of student copying to be brilliant or inspired, or for considering some student plagiarisms to be indicative of genius, regardless of the fact that some student 'geniuses' may, in fact, plagiarize – the academic plagiarisms of Martin Luther King, Jr, which I examine in Part Three, are a case in point.

The literary institution has a much more difficult time, first, identifying plagiarism, and, second, condemning it. Literary plagiarism is, in fact, not always bad: the brilliant plagiarism and plagiarist-as-genius are much more common in the literary domain than in any other. While the semantic force of the term usually entails negative connotations, 'plagiarism' has often been used to describe the imitative practices of great writers: 'literary plagiarism' is a kind of pleasing oxymoron expressing the transformative power of aesthetic genius and distinguishing between inspired and servile imitation. In postmodernism, 'plagiarism' (firmly framed by quotation marks) has become both a practice and a critical category for which are claimed aesthetic intentions and effects. This blurring of the use of the term 'plagiarism' to describe explicit and intentionally aesthetic forms of repetition is one of the features of contemporary production that I explore.

A second aspect of the institutional specificity of 'literature' is that today, and since what Bourdieu would call its 'autonomization' during the nineteenth century, it is considered to exist quite independently of any extra-aesthetic function to which it may be put, and which many other kinds of writing – academic, journalistic, political, and so on – entail by definition. Modern authorship exists within a market or institutional structure and may serve multiple purposes where the fact of authorship may be only one in a complex of functions defining the writer's role. Professional authors may be engaged by contract or in order to fulfil a specific end; their texts may produce both symbolic and material advantages, the two not necessarily coinciding. Texts produced in a professional academic setting, for example, may have an exceedingly strong symbolic value, and a rather indirect market value, only cumulatively leading to tenure and promotion, and occasionally to financial rewards. Both types of value lead, however, to the fulfilment of a contract that exceeds the condition of authorship. The theft of such professional discourse often not only entails the theft of an individual's intellectual property, but may involve either the legal property or the symbolic values of the institution; such theft is quite often considered a transgression of the explicit institutional norms governing the behaviour of the members.

A third aspect of the specificity of the literary institution is the nebulous nature of its existence. It has no membership lists, no official code of ethics regulating the behaviour of its members, no criteria for legitimacy other than 'authorship' itself; it is a fuzzy and tautological structure whose conditions for inclusion are unregulated and indeterminate.[1] There is no external or institutional necessity requiring literary writers to write literature; the activity and its product are, on the one hand, self-imposed by the author and, on the other, somehow superfluous, or at least autotelic. While literary authors may indeed write under contract, this contract is erected on the expectation of authorship alone, and not on other functions (such as teaching or research) from which it derives or for which it is supposed to account. There are no rules defining the criteria for success or failure to which putative literary authors can adhere. And, as Bourdieu points out, the market and the symbolic value of literary works may be so far detached as to be antonymous. The literary institution lacks, as well, official bodies invested with a legislative role for providing sanctions for internal transgressions, whereas other arenas of professional authorship may have their own internal courts of justice, such as one witnesses within the academic field. The plagiarized literary author seeking justice must ultimately turn to civil law, or else rely on the literary press and other informal means of sanction. In this sense, the discourse surrounding literary plagiarism is itself often the only court wherein the greatest number of putative cases are tried.

While the literary institution is clearly a highly regulated field subject to economic forces and depending for its existence on strongly rule-governed organisms such as the publishing industry and the academic institution, the actual content of the literary, as with any aesthetic domain, is largely constructed from within: the various 'rules' and conventions to which literature has to conform in order to become 'literary' in various historico-cultural situations are normally derived from the constitutive elements of the field itself, which reshapes its contours in a continuing contest for legitimacy that Bourdieu has described: 'There is no other criterion of membership of a field than the objective fact of producing effects within it. One of the difficulties of the orthodox defence against heretical transformation of the field by a redefinition of the tacit or explicit terms of entry is the fact that polemics imply a form of recognition; adversaries whom one would prefer to destroy by ignoring them cannot be combated without consecrating them' ('The Field of Cultural Production' 42).

Once values such as 'originality' and 'authenticity' have been established as constitutive of the nature of an institution like the university, they can be raised to the level of explicit rules that exist not only in the minds of individuals, but in regulative documents that prescribe the behaviour and norms of the members of the institution. These rules exist independently of the actual behaviour of the institutional agents, and their codification lends them relative stability and autonomy. The aesthetic field, on the other hand, despite various degrees of regulation, is much less subject to reification by codification. It has been well demonstrated by theorists, from the early Russian formalists to Bourdieu, that the contours of the literary are continually being reshaped from the inside, most often by forces of contestation and revolution that intend to transgress and overturn precisely those conventions that are perceived to be the most highly codified.[2] In this way, while a concept of 'plagiarism' has always been situated solidly beyond the acceptable limits of the literary, the tolerance for actual literary practices is constantly being reformed by the force of those practices themselves. When techniques of aesthetic 'appropriation,' for example, become so widespread as to be largely conventionalized rather than contestatory, they redefine the limits of the acceptable within the norms of the institution without substantially modifying the proscription against 'plagiarism.' In the aesthetic field, it is the relative weakness of its regulative rules, versus the strong force of its constitutive rules, which results in the fact that the concept of plagiarism, a kind of regulative rule, is fairly stable, while its constitutive features are in constant flux.

If the construction of literature is a function of institutional, that is, extratextual, constraints and criteria, and their intersection – happily or not – with discursive forms, a most compelling reason for focusing on literary plagiarism is its functioning as a barometer of shifting literary norms and aesthetic conventions, and of the power struggles to institute authority that attend the construction of the literary field. What is at one time called 'plagiarism' constitutes, at others, the exact definition of 'good literature,' and an examination and comparison of some of the more radical moments in this history will reveal not only what is 'plagiarism' for a specific historico-cultural period but, perhaps more importantly, what is 'literature' for that same period. In taking debates about plagiarism to be symptomatic of the power struggles inherent in cultural formations, I am in agreement with Foucault, who states:

> Rather than analyzing power from the point of view of its internal rationality, it [a new economy of power relations] consists of analyzing power relations through the antagonism of strategies.
>
> For example, to find out what our society means by sanity, perhaps we should investigate what is happening in the field of insanity.
>
> And what we mean by legality in the field of illegality. ('The Subject and Power' 419)

And, I would add, what we mean by 'literature' through an investigation of 'non-literature': disputes about plagiarism can be seen as instances of power struggles within the literary or, more broadly speaking, cultural field; they can be used to trace its contours, its values, and its institutional formation. Within the literary field, 'plagiarism' constitutes this same otherness that elicits what Foucault describes as an 'antagonism of strategies.'

THE PRAGMATICS

The claim that plagiarism is a pragmatic rather than a textual phenomenon is the corollary of the idea that 'literature' itself exists only as an aesthetic judgment imposed on texts – or authors – and subsequently is taken to be an immanent quality of the work. In this, I adhere to Pierre Bourdieu's sociology of the production of the category of aesthetic objects, when he claims that 'the work of art is an object which exists as such only by virtue of the (collective) belief which knows and acknowledges it as a work of art' ('The Field of Cultural Production' 35). If this claim is valid, as I take it to be, then it is also true of the category of non-literature, of which plagiaristic texts form a particular subset. As the products of judgments rendered about texts that subsequently become exemplary instances of positively or negatively valued cultural objects, literature and non-literature both participate in and arise from complex systems of features. Value – or, in the case of plagiarism, 'non-value' – is, as Barbara Herrnstein Smith says, the result of 'the features of literary and aesthetic judgments in relation to the multiple social, political, circumstantial and other constraints and conditions to which they are responsive' (28). In their analyses of taste and value, both Bourdieu and Smith are concerned with showing the *contingency* of value judgments despite evidence indicating the overwhelming consensus about cultural objects among groups over time. As Smith explains, and as Bourdieu demonstrates in *Distinction* (1979), 'a coincidence of contingencies among individual subjects who interact as members of some community will operate for them as noncontingency and be interpreted by them accordingly' (Smith, 40). In other words, aesthetic 'value' is specific to communities who share presuppositions about what constitutes the appropriate features of the artistic or literary. I will pursue, with examples, this line of argumentation throughout the course of this study.

In Bourdieu's language, the investigation being undertaken here intends to explore the historical shift that has occurred over centuries in the strategies of legitimate symbolic and material appropriation of cultural capital within the specific field of literary production (with occasional exemplary forays into other domains). In the most general terms, this shift will be seen to follow the historical development of literary production from conventions of legitimization by *identification* with authoritative cultural norms, towards an aesthetic of *dissociation* from previous cultural production and an increased emphasis on the value of individuality, as the literary field gains autonomy throughout the eighteenth and nineteenth centuries. And as Bourdieu points out, the twentieth century has witnessed an increasing return to an aesthetics of recycling of past production, but he warns:

In fact, these returns are always *apparent,* since they are separated from what they repeat by the negative reference (when it is not by a parodic intention) to something that was itself the negation (of the negation of the negation, etc.) of what they repeat. In the literary or artistic field at the present moment of its history, all acts, all gestures, all manifestations are, as one painter has well said 'kinds of "*clins d'oeil*" towards the inside of the milieu': these *clins d'oeil*, silent and hidden references to other artists, present or past, affirm, in and by games of distinction, a complicity which exludes the uninitiated, always condemned to miss the essential, that is precisely the interrelations and the interactions of which the work is nothing but the silent trace. Never has the structure of the field itself been as present in each act of production.[3]

While Bourdieu provides us with a structure for understanding the macro-developments of institutional formation, it is the principles of discourse analysis arising from the field of literary pragmatics that allow us to examine the presuppositions embedded in discourses situated in terms of their historical, cultural, and aesthetic determinants. These discourses reveal the contextual conditions at the foundation of perceptions of plagiarism for various historical periods. My method attempts to be transhistorical while avoiding ahistoricity: in crossing vast stretches of time, I endeavour to uncover, despite the historical specificity governing differences in judgments about plagiarism, the transhistorical constants that inform them. This move is motivated only in part by the practical difficulty of performing, for each period of literary history, the kind of specific investigations offered by White, Welslau, and Rosenthal (all centred, significantly, on the Renaissance). While these studies provide essential insights about the social and aesthetic specificity of plagiarism in a particular historical context, I am here less interested in the cultural *differences* and aesthetic preferences that various periods manifest in relation to plagiarism than in the rather more surprising *similarities* among opinions and the stability of criteria for determining plagiarism, despite the variations in cultural presuppositions and the practices that express and produce them. While my fundamental premises are in agreement with the principles of *contingency* in judgments of value (Bourdieu *Distinction: A Social Critique of the Judgement of Taste*; Smith *Contingencies of Value: Alternative Perspectives for Critical Theory*), I assume this position as self-evident, and explore, rather than cultural difference, the transmission of cultural presuppositions that culminate in a certain stability of features characterizing plagiarism, and subsequently literature, for the Western tradition. The exemplarity and excessiveness of plagiarism make it particularly pertinent as an index of these features.

By considering discourse to be of the order of a 'linguistic act,' pragmatics postulates a communicative situation that, while not necessarily intersubjective (as in the case of literary discourse), is perceived by the receiver as an attempt on the part of the producer of the discourse to 'cause the "receiver" to think or do something' (Levinson 16). In other words, it is an act that generates another. It is essential to point out, for the case of written discourse, especially literary discourse, the irreducibly unidirectional nature both of this 'communication' and of the attribution of intentionality to the producer. If, in fact, literary discourse can at all be said to be a kind of communication, it is so only to the extent that the receiver attributes communicative intentionality to the absent subject of discourse. The pragmatic model that I am adopting understands the intentions of the producer to be largely subsumed by the presuppositions of the receiver about those intentions, based on the expectation of discursive conventions similar to those posited by Grice's Conversational Maxims. The pragmatic assumption that felicitous communication requires a minimal level of mutual knowledge is replaced by the notion of *revelance* (Sperber and Wilson, *Relevance*), in which it is necessary for the reader only to *presuppose* the existence or possibility of communal knowledge. Sperber and Wilson provide the example of a question to which the answer is literally or semantically non-sequential. The receiver, presupposing, first, that the interlocutor has understood the question, and, then, that he or she understands and shares the convention of *relevance*, will attempt to repair the apparent deviation by appealing to contextual factors such as encyclopedic knowledge, or discursive conventions such as irony or sarcasm.[4]

In literary discourse, the role of the receiver in constructing meaning and intentionality is crucial, since the intentions of the producer are normally not available for verification (or may be considered irrelevant). The act of reception is, however, inevitably accompanied by a postulate concerning the production of discourse, specifically that at its origin is an author–subject motivated by communicative intentions for which the discourse is the evidence. The construction of meaning on the part of the reader is also often accompanied by a presupposition that the meaning discovered or received was in fact intended by the producer; the receiver might also attribute to the author intentions of an aesthetic or ideological nature, presuppositions derived either from prior knowledge or from textual evidence. While modern literary theory has identified and denounced this communicative illusion under which readers labour by isolating, for example, the 'intentional fallacy' (Wimsatt 3–18) and by turning away from authorially based forms of interpretation, more subtle effects of reading as a communicative simulacrum are still very much with us. The very presupposition of the existence of something like 'literary communication' is a testimony to the continuing power of the notion that literary discourse is a form of intersubjective communication, necessarily entailing the presence of two subjects of intentionality.

Literary discourse is a *linguistic act* in the sense that it entails presuppositions on the part of readers about the communicative intentions of the producer of discourse. These intentions can be minimal ('the author intended to write a novel') or fairly powerful ('the author intended to use a story of a man and a whale as an allegory for the human condition'). In the case of plagiarism, the consequences are evident: first, the perceived presence of plagiarism will be interpreted as an authorial intention to plagiarize; second, the intention to plagiarize will subsequently be seen as an intention that the plagiarism produce specific effects, normally of an illegitimate kind.

A fundamental postulate of the pragmatic approach is that conventions (discursive, literary, social, etc.) are normally invisible precisely because of their conventionality: it is usually only in the event that conventional expectations are flouted that, first, the convention becomes identified, and, second, the discursive act acquires the status of a transgression. The adherence to conventionalized forms of behaviour results from the internalization of expectations that are not easily recognized as such: most particularly in their transgression do they become visible as 'rules' that have been broken. Rarely in the case of literary acts are transgressions of convention liable to be raised to a level involving civil, or even criminal, law: plagiarism is, in this sense, interesting because it is one of the few areas in which aesthetic activity can fall into criminality.

The defining element of pragmatic linguistics is the importance accorded to contextual features in the creation of meaning. The function of *context* is intimately related to the notion of mutual knowledge to which I have alluded: it is presumed that a minimal degree of shared knowledge or presupposition is fundamental to all communication, the most elementary condition being the existence of a code common to producer and receiver. And to the extent that a shared language entails a certain mutual knowledge about the world of reference, about discursive conventions, and about the social behaviour underlying them, the notion of discourse immediately entails contextual features that extend the boundaries of language beyond itself. But if the role of context is considered crucial to pragmatic analysis, it is also sufficiently vague and complex to be fraught with the menace of insignificance.

A brief summary of the varieties of context that are supposed to contribute to the construction of meaning includes both linguistic and nonlinguistic elements. In the first category, which remains relatively manageable for the purposes of discourse analysis, are micro-textual components such as syntax, semantics, and grammar, as well as macro-textual structures such as discursive coherence, narrative schemas, and thematic developments. Notions of connotation and discursive convention are also constitutive of this category. But context most problematically entails non-discursive elements as well, such as the enunciative situation (which, for written communication, normally implies a more or less radical separation between producer and receiver); the context of reference; the personal (autobiographical) situation of the producer and receiver; as well as the social, cultural, and economic conditions of both. Clearly, the non-linguistic context of the construction of meaning is not only potentially unlimited and aleatory, but, to a large extent, inaccessible and, many would argue, irrelevant. Nonetheless, the pertinence of a contextual pragmatics for literary analysis has long been recognized, and is implicit in the developments of literary theories that exploit, each in its own manner, various non-linguistic elements that are seen to contribute to the construction of meaning in the text. Whether it be autobiographical criticism, theories of reception, historical criticism, or various forms of sociological and institutionally based criticism, diverse kinds of 'contexts' are clearly felt to be essential to the understanding of literary discourse.[5] These are the conditions that push pragmatics into the realm of institutional analysis or, perhaps, allow the former to recuperate the latter.

Literary pragmatics has been defined as an 'attitude' rather than as a unified and specific set of methodological procedures, and it is this *pragmatic attitude* towards the phenomenon of literary plagiarism that motivates the present study. The defining features of this attitude are that literary discourse is a linguistic act in which the reader is the most important agent, and in which contextual components are essential elements of the reader's construction of literary signification or, more precisely in the present context, of 'literariness.' Specifically, I postulate that the identification of discursive repetition as 'plagiarism' is an act of reception that, first, imputes a particular form of intentionality to the producer and, second, is itself inscribed in a complex of readerly intentions that may or may not be conscious. *Context* is a determining factor in constructing this web of intentions: among the various contextual features that contribute to the reception of discursive repetition as plagiarism are notably, but not exclusively, the literary conventions and horizon of aesthetic expectations of the historical period in question; the personal, aesthetic, and institutional motivations of producer and receiver; and the position of both within the aesthetic, political, academic (etc.) institutions to which the literary is related, or subject. Repetition becomes plagiarism when it is seen to transgress a set of conventional expectations governing discursive behaviour; the identification of such a transgression is simultaneously an unveiling of these conventions. While, at first glance, the principal convention required to generate accusations of plagiarism might seem to be 'thou shalt not copy,' other expectations, as we shall see, are just as important or, according to the dominant aesthetic conventions of a given period, perhaps even more so.

THE DEFINITION

Of course, plagiarism has never been the only criterion used to discriminate between good and bad literary art. Its value lies, however, in its exemplarity or excessiveness. In the contemporary period – except for contexts in which hate literature, pornography, and sedition constitute discursive crimes – literary theft remains one of the worst possible crimes in a domain that, largely restricted to the symbolic, has a tenuous relationship to the 'real' world in which crimes are normally committed and punished. It will be necessary to divide the field of plagiarism into two distinct realms: the first depends on the symbolic or aesthetic value of a discourse, and the second is governed by its market value, today circumscribed by law.[6] The development of copyright legislation and the commercialization of intellectual property over the course of the eighteenth and nineteenth centuries elicit an apparently easy historical division between pre- and post-copyright notions of plagiarism, the first period corresponding to the symbolic, and the second to the commercial realm governed by legislation. However, the historical divide introduced by the development of modern copyright does not entirely capture the coexistence throughout the nineteenth and twentieth centuries of both plagiarism and breach of copyright as two distinct concepts: as David Saunders points out, 'the legal and aesthetic personalities stand in no general relation one to the other' (15). Heuristically, however, and for purposes of economy, our examination of twentieth-century debates about plagiarism will be preceded by an overview of pre-copyright discussions of plagiarism, where the questions posed are primarily ethical and aesthetic. These discussions will be subsequently useful as a means of establishing the continuity in notions about plagiarism across the historical divide provided by the establishment of modern copyright over the course of the eighteenth century.

As plagiarism is judged by its effects (Schneider 102), the wide variety of consequences it can entail points to the fact that instances of plagiarism, either across history or in any given context, are not always considered to be examples of the same phenomenon. The gravity of the plagiarism problem depends on the structure of the ethical, aesthetic, institutional, legal, or economic contexts in which the alleged act has occurred, as well as on the status of the suspected perpetrator and victim. Its consequences are similarly various. Within the academic institution, for example, plagiarism in a doctoral thesis may be more heavily sanctioned than in a first-year essay; the discovery of journalistic plagiarism may be followed by a reprimand, by firing, or, as in at least one Canadian case, by a suicide.[7] Literary imitators may be praised for the alleged brilliance of their 'borrowings', or may be stripped of their claims to the glory of authorship and expelled from legitimate membership in the literary institution. While plagiarism may be seen to be always a 'problem,' dealt with in different ways by different institutions and individuals, its widely various consequences should be a sufficient indication that the real problem with plagiarism is, in fact, deciding what kind of problem it is.

If plagiarism is necessarily deemed to be an infraction, the realm in which it is historically most consistently located is that of the ethical, rather than the legal or aesthetic. While the terms according to which plagiarism is seen to be an infraction of ethical codes are themselves various, two fundamental features can be distilled from definitions and discussions of plagiarism throughout history. Primarily, plagiarism is unethical because it contravenes the fundamental right to the exclusive enjoyment of and control over one's property, either real or symbolic – that is, it is a form of *theft* – and, second, it is a misrepresentation of one's self in situations where the justified expectations of others entail honesty and authenticity; in other words, it is a form of *fraud*. This definition of plagiarism is immediately problematic in that it presupposes the existence of the two values it appears to contravene: theft entails a notion of *intellectual property;* fraud, a notion of *authenticity* (sometimes confusingly called 'originality'), which is based on the assumption of a necessary and unique causal relation between an author and a work. An obvious difficulty with this definition is that notions of intellectual property and of the originality entailed by authorship are often seen to be modern, that is, eighteenth-century attributes, leading to the common belief that 'plagiarism' did not exist in pre-copyright eras such as Antiquity and the Renaissance. However, concepts of *ownership* and of *authenticity* clearly pre-date the copyright legislation that sets out to regulate them, and they form the basis for the continuing existence of plagiarism since the beginning of recorded history in the West. One of the effects of the history of plagiarism is to modify our understanding of this development, and to show that, far from being a modern invention, the proprietary relationship between authors and the fruits of their labour and/or genius – namely, glory, immortality, fame – is an ancient one, and it is to this relationship that accusations and complaints of plagiarism throughout history point.

The fundamental pragmatic problem involved in questions of plagiarism is not definition, but recognition. Historical descriptions and definitions generally present a rather small and surprisingly stable range of elements to be considered when faced with the possibility that plagiarism has taken place: the issues involved are almost always practical rather than theoretical. While it is relatively simple to agree on the intensional definition of plagiarism, its extensional definition – the actual texts that fit the descriptions proposed – is the problem that all definitions, including legal ones, fail to solve. Plagiarism clearly refers to different practices over time, and sometimes to different practices at the same time; but it is most problematic in the way that it polarizes contemporaneous opinions about a single text. In examining some of these opinions, I do not attempt to distill from them a definitive description of literary plagiarism. My aim in reading the discourse surrounding plagiarism is to consider it symptomatic of cultural norms for literariness and its opposite, as the institution of literature successively constructs itself by processes of inclusion and exclusion.

We have said that the 'What is plagiarism?' question, in so far as it usually elicits either a text- or an author-based response, is not our object. However, descriptions and definitions, proceeding as they inevitably do from readers, constitute the corpus of our study. In order to clear the path for what follows, and to provide a point of departure, we will pursue the 'definition' of plagiarism as it has been provided at two very different points in history. While metaphoric and euphemistic treatments of literary theft characterize the pre-copyright period, more formal definitions of plagiarism arise during the eighteenth century and continue into the present. Not all definitions of plagiarism are equally interesting, nor equally helpful in determining its precise theoretical contours. Contemporary legal definitions are the least interesting for the purposes of identifying plagiarism, since they are restricted to the terms of breach of copyright, which is a small and historically limited subset of the possible types of plagiarism. The French, English, and German eighteenth and nineteenth centuries demonstrated a most fervent interest in the matter, producing some of the most complete and interesting definitions of literary plagiarism; some of these definitions provide the basis for the ensuing discussion, which is particularly intended to underscore the stability of descriptions of plagiarism over time.

The ubiquitous nature of plagiarism, and its occasional ability to produce great literature, often lead to an irreducible ambiguity in the expression of what is, and what is not, properly called plagiarism. Charles Nodier's definition demonstrates such a confusion: 'Let us define plagiarism, strictly speaking, as the action of taking from an author (particularly a modern and national author, which makes the crime more serious) the content of a work of invention, the development of a new idea or one yet little known, the expression of one or several ideas; for there are ideas which can gain from a new expression; established notions which a more felicitous development can clarify; certain works whose content can be improved through the form; and it would be unjust to qualify as plagiarism that which is really only an extension or a useful amendment.'[8] It will be noted that half of the definition is devoted to enumerating what is not plagiarism – namely, imitation by improvement, extension, amendment, what modern definitions call 'significant enhancement.' At the same time, the paragraph presents a convoluted argument, the 'for' in the middle operating a reversal where the list of plagiarisms, 'properly speaking,' is followed by a list of exceptions that coincide closely with the first.

Two exemplary definitions will serve to identify the finer points of taking for one's own the discursive property of another. The first is a product of the encyclopedic endeavours of the eighteenth century, carried on in the wake of the literary debates between the ancients and the moderns, during the transition between classicism and the beginnings of Romanticism, and which took up the definition of plagiarism as a contribution to the literary theories of imitation and originality in the context of the growing importance of the latter. The most complete of these definitions can be found in Diderot's *Encyclopédie*, in Jaucourt's article 'Plagiarism,' which, for various reasons, serves as my point of departure. First, it has the merit of being compatible with more contemporary definitions while at the same time rendering explicit some elements that later definitions repress, but that still inhabit conceptions of plagiarism. It also dispenses with the metaphorical language so common in descriptions of literary theft and is free, as well, of the polemical quality by which many descriptions of plagiarism reveal themselves as apologies for plagiarism or for certain copiers who are not 'really' plagiarists. Here, then, is the definition in the *Encyclopédie*: 'What then is a *plagiarist*, strictly speaking? He is a man who, wanting at all costs to become an author, and having neither the genius nor the talent necessary, copies not only sentences, but even pages and entire passages of other authors, and has the bad faith not to quote them; or who, by means of a few minor changes in expression or a few additions, presents the productions of others as something that he has himself imagined or invented; or who claims for himself the honour of a discovery made by another.'[9]

This is as succinct and complete a definition as is available until the twentieth century, and is more complete than most of these. In particular, it mentions all of the necessary components of 'real' contemporary plagiarism, that is, unacknowledged copying or imitation that is liable to result in moral or legal sanctions against the perpetrator. The essential conditions outlined are: lack of talent; theft of another's property; bad faith and covertness; unearned advantage. Other aspects of this definition will also serve as an inspiration for my analyses: not insignificantly, a plagiarist is a 'man,' but not an author, for he lacks the talent to become one. He copies without giving credit, but the extent of this copying can vary from sentences to whole passages: plagiarism does not seem to be a matter of degree. He usurps property defined according to paternity, therefore accruing to himself the honour due to another. Jaucourt's definition is largely stated in ethical terms: the cause of the theft is lack of 'genius,' its criminal element is 'bad faith,' and its advantage is 'honour.'

Translated into more contemporary and juridical language, the same elements appear in the following contemporary proposal for a definition of plagiarism issued more than 200 years later in an examination of academic plagiarism, *The Melancholy Anatomy of Plagiarism*. The differences between the two are also significant: 'Plagiarism is an *intentional* verbal *fraud* committed by the *psychologically competent* that consists of *copying significant and substantial uncredited* written materials for *unearned advantages* with no *significant enhancement* of the materials copied' (St Onge 101; emphasis added).

The elements retained are 'bad faith' ('intentional ... fraud') and 'copying,' here, as in law, qualified as 'significant and substantial.' 'Unearned advantages' echoes the appropriation of honour due to another, and 'no significant enhancement' returns to the notion of the inadequacy of 'a few minor changes in expression.' So far, the two definitions, taking into account the shift from ethical to legalistic language, are substantially similar. The fundamental and radical difference between them is the suppression in the modern definition of any reference to authorial agency. The author-as-creator or plagiarist has virtually disappeared, and, along with him, the quality of talent and the notion of production resulting in a natural right of paternity. In the eighteenth-century definition, plagiarism has its source in a (non)-author to whom is attributed actions and intentions. In the second, rather than being an infringement of personal rights perpetrated by individuals upon others, plagiarism is seen as a disembodied act perpetrated upon written materials. The human element subsists only implicitly, and is attributed to the plagiarist, a 'psychologically competent fraud.'

There is a significant absence of reference in both definitions to the plagiarizing text itself. What is being judged is not an inanimate object, the text, but rather the agent of a criminal or immoral act. The text is important simply as evidence of the act: as plagiarists are rarely 'caught in the act,' and corroborating evidence in the form of witnesses or other external evidence is rare, the text-as-evidence of plagiarism is substituted for the act itself. In definitions of plagiarism, the focus on acts and agents rather than on the plagiaristic 'text' again indicates that plagiarism is not primarily a textual category, but rather a pragmatic one, involving questions of action, intentions, and consequences, rather than the existence of specific types of discursive objects. The traditional absence of any definition of the 'plagiaristic text,' independently of definitions of the act and the intentions of the agent, is also a feature of contemporary definitions of breach of copyright, where the question to be decided is rarely whether or not similarity exists, since the evidence of similarity is a requisite for the suspicion of plagiarism in the first place. Rather, it is a question of determining whether the intentions and the act that resulted in the similarity constitute infringement of copyright; whether the similarity in question is evidence of a breach of copyright or of a non-sanctionable form of repetition.

The repressed element in both definitions is the pragmatic component of Reader – critic, accuser, or judge – whose authority invests him with the capacity for *recognition* of the repetition, for *naming* it, thereby constructing it as fraudulent or otherwise, and for *judging* the repetition and the perpetrator as being condemnable, excusable, or in some instances praiseworthy. Even in exploring the Author, my true object is, in fact, the Reader, the source of the judgments that form the corpus of the evidence for and against plagiarism.

Several explanations are called for. First, I do not try to distill any kind of positive – either specific or universal – definition of the 'plagiaristic' author or act. These categories are entirely discursive ones relying for their evidence on texts produced about these categories and, as such, they are all, as well, pragmatic categories that have as the Reader the implicit point of origin. Second, in order to avoid the dangers of anachronism, I attempt to avoid referring to plagiarists as 'subjects' of their discourse, since the term has connotations inappropriate to premodern periods. It is in the third part of my exploration, dealing with contemporary uses and accusations of plagiarism, that the notion of the writing or reading 'subject' becomes pertinent for the examination of certain instances of 'plagiarism.' The psychological motivations of individual plagiarists do not concern me directly for various reasons, the most theoretically pertinent one being that such an approach must necessarily consider 'plagiarism' from the point of view of production, thus construing it as a positive phenomenon introduced by the author into the text, and waiting to be discovered by the right reader – or, more accurately, the wrong one. Considering plagiarism as a category of reception entails seeing psychological or other production-oriented explanations of plagiarism as being themselves effects of the judgment of readers, and when we speak of 'motivations' for plagiarism it is always from the perspective of the reader's perception or presumptions of these motives. Contemporary contributions from psychoanalysis and philosophy of language to the understanding of the crucial role played by language in the construction of subjectivity – and consequently of the uses of plagiarism in this complex – are relevant in the third part of this essay. My principal aim throughout is, rather, to unpack some of the cultural presuppositions governing the possibility of literary accusations of plagiarism.

As psychological explanations are themselves culturally determined, they emerge most significantly in the later part of the twentieth century, in concert with the rise of psychologically based literary theories. Psychological explanations of plagiarism belong to a historically delimited discourse of reception that chooses to situate plagiarism in the realm of an authorial act for which motives or causes can be assumed and, perhaps, found.

What is, however, always necessary for plagiarism to be perceived is a notion of authorship entailing concepts of propriety, if not property, over discursive or intellectual products. The author as agent is a social, economic, and cultural construct rather than a psychological one and, as Foucault has taught us, the author's attributes are those of a discursive function, rather than of an individual subject. Plagiarists, as we shall see, are essentially failed or false authors – those who are seen to have transgressed or left unfulfilled the cultural function authorship defines for them. Thus, according to the aesthetic and critical assumptions adopted, the plagiarist may be judged either a thief or a kleptomaniac; an imperialist or a victim of imperialism; a cultural industrialist or revolutionary; the plagiarist is variously seen as a 'subject' striving towards the creation of an 'authentic,' unified identity, or one radically decentred and divided against itself. This is not to say that all, or even any, 'plagiarists' are innocent victims of cultural prejudices or literary correctness. The intention to commit literary fraud exists, as does the intention to produce legitimate works of literary art. But the fate of both intentions rests solely in the hands of readers. In this sense, 'plagiarism' is the result of culturally determined presuppositions governing the role and the attributes of authorship. It is the role of plagiarist as cultural function, rather than as a psychological subject, that I explore now.

PART ONE

Authoring Plagiarism

1. What Is an (Original) Author?

Un artiste original ne peut pas copier. Pour être original, il n'a donc qu'à copier.

Jean Cocteau, *Le Rappel à l'ordre*

The suppression of the author in St Onge's definition does not prevent him from re-emerging as a 'psychologically competent fraud' motivated by the desire for unearned advantages of an unnamed type. In the *Encyclopédie*, however, it is quite clear that these advantages are those bestowed by 'authorship': a plagiarist is a writer who aspires to a position to which his talent is unequal. In this definition, it is important to understand the phrase 'wanting at all costs to become an author' quite literally – authorship and plagiarism are incompatible terms: *authors don't plagiarize*. This might seem counter-intuitive to us today, for it may seem more reasonable to suspect that it is especially authors who plagiarize. The distinction between authors and plagiarists will be seen to be tautological and purely semantic: 'true authors' cannot plagiarize; plagiarists are not 'true authors.' This restrictive tautology turns on a simple syllogism that excludes, as a first principle, 'plagiarism' as an attribute of authorship such that any apparent act of copying on the part of an 'author' must not be plagiarism.

What, then, are the positive attributes of authorship that the *Encyclopédie* presupposes and the plagiarist lacks? In light of our intuition that it may be especially authors who plagiarize, are the distinctions evoked in the eighteenth century still pertinent? At this point, it is conventional to cite Barthes's famous essay 'The Death of the Author' (1968), as well as Foucault's

'What Is an Author?' (1969), in order to argue that traditional notions of authorship are no longer theoretically, philosophically, or pragmatically operative. What both essays signal is the decline of the Romantic and post-Romantic importance placed on the biographical author-person, as well as of the confidence placed in individual agency and control over discourse that involves, inevitably, a belief in the possibility of creative originality. The structuralist and poststructuralist revolution of the 1960s and 1970s in France substituted the notion of *scripteur* for *auteur*, and of *écriture* or *texte* for *oeuvre*, divesting the biographical author of the claim to authority, and returning to language to reassert the Heideggerian principle that 'die Sprache spricht': 'it is language which speaks, not the author' (Barthes 143). Barthes's essay is a call for an intertextual and reader-oriented criticism: the 'death of the author' heralds the birth of the reader as a textual function and allows the text to escape a monologism rooted in authorial intentionality: 'We know now that a text is not a line of words releasing a single "theological" meaning (the "message" of the Author-God) but a multidimensional space in which a variety of writings, none of them original, blend and clash. The text is a tissue of quotations drawn from the innumerable centres of culture [...] [T]he writer [*sic*] [*l'écriture*] can only imitate a gesture that is always anterior, never original. His only power is to mix writings, to counter the ones with the others, in such a way as never to rest on any one of them' (146).[1] (Note in passing the translator's remarkable move of deforming the original by re*authorizing* the dehumanized *écriture* of the French original and substituting the 'writer' as the agent of discourse, imbuing him with an intentionality and a 'power,' however negative or limited.)

The structuralist revolution notwithstanding, and despite the fact that author and writer, *auteur* and *écrivain*, have come to have overlapping or identical contemporary meanings, a long tradition, not entirely devoid of contemporary pertinence, has reserved a rather exalted position for the *author*, preserved in the expression 'authorship.' Despite the perhaps premature announcement of the author's death, not all of the attributes of authorship have disappeared and, moreover, contemporary literary theory as well as common usage still assume the existence of authors and apply to them certain attributes that, although ancient in origin, continue to be relatively stable into the present. Foucault asserts this position when he proposes, in the wake of the author's 'death,' a program of research into 'the modifications and variations, within any culture, of modes of circulation, valorization, attribution and appropriation [...] [T]he "author-function" could also reveal the manner in which discourse is articulated on the basis of social relationships' ('What Is an Author?' 137).

In reminding us that, since the late eighteenth and early nineteenth centuries, the work is defined as an *object of appropriation* of the author, Foucault insists on the relationship between the rise of authorship and the perception of the transgressive value of discourse: 'Speeches and books were assigned real authors, other than mythical or important religious figures, only when the author became subject to punishment and to the extent that his discourse was considered transgressive' (124). He recalls that writing was originally an act fraught with the risks of heresy, blasphemy, and illegality. The codification of discourse as property transformed the 'transgressive properties always intrinsic to the act of writing' such that they became the 'forceful imperative of literature' – a compensatory revival of the 'danger of writing which, on another side, had been conferred the benefits of property' (125). The type of compensatory transgression to which Foucault is referring is largely – and increasingly – restricted to the symbolic field. When discourse has lost its status as action and acquired the nature of 'a thing, a product, or a possession' (124), its capacity for effecting dangerous, that is, punishable, transgression is greatly reduced and, since the Salman Rushdie affair, one would have to say happily so. The exceptional nature of the reception of *The Satanic Verses* as a blasphemous and punishable event attests to the fact that, for most contemporary cultures, the intrinsically transgressive nature of discourse is normally restricted to a specifically symbolic kind: rarely, these days, is 'literary' discourse (as apart from scientific or political discourse) granted the kind of potential power that causes its effects to pass from the symbolic to the realm of the 'real' world. Pornography is a notable exception; plagiarism may be another.

The second point that Foucault contributes to the present discussion is that, while the specific attribution of authorship varies throughout history, '[t]here are, nevertheless, transhistorical constants in the rules that govern the construction of an author' (127). Foucault refers to St Jerome's four criteria for authenticity, which, while they 'might seem largely inadequate to modern critics [...], nevertheless, define the critical modalities now used to display the function of the author' (129). These modalities can be reduced to three: briefly, (1) *interpretive*: the origin of the text with the biographical author has an explanatory function with regard to its nature and contents; (2) *homogenizing*: recourse to the author as a 'principle of unity' provides a source of coherence where none is apparent; his psychology and evolution neutralize unevenness and contradictions; (3) *stylistic*: the author as a 'particular source of expression' is identifiable wherever one encounters manifestations of his discourse. The role of the author as source and origin of the work grounds all of the criteria.

While the attribution of authorship itself is variable, the characteristics of the 'author-function' can be seen to demonstrate certain transhistorical regularities, of which variability is, in fact, an example. Not 'who is speaking,' but what are the attributes of the speaking position: 'Who can fulfil these diverse functions of the subject?' (138). If the transhistorical constants of authorship are pertinent to a discussion of plagiarism, it is primarily because the construction of the plagiarist as non-author is predicated on the presumption of definable criteria for authorship. If the plagiarist is a 'failed author,' what are the functions of authorship that the plagiarist fails to fulfil? If, as we will argue, plagiarism itself appears to be a relatively stable transhistorical constant, and if Foucault is right, then the failure of the plagiarist to become an author will necessarily be a key to the positive attributes of authorship.

Great authors don't plagiarize. As Cocteau says, 'an original artist cannot copy. Therefore he has only to copy in order to be original' (39): in other words, a 'true' author is always original, even if he is copying. This seems to have been profoundly true since the origin of letters, and continues to be believed, or at least expressed, perhaps unintentionally, today. Harold Bloom's *Anxiety of Influence,* for example, is a long lesson in why 'strong poets' are still great in spite of their influences. For Bloom, *origin* and *originality* are closely – and quite appropriately – linked: 'For all of them [Yeats, Stevens, Browning, and Dickinson, the strongest poets of this century and the last] achieve a style that captures and oddly retains priority over their precursors, so that the tyranny of time almost is overturned, and one can believe, for startled moments, that they are being *imitated by their ancestors'* (141).

Bloom is quite adamantly not of the 'dead author' school, and his theory is one of coming-into-authorship, with all of its Oedipal implications. He is quite explicit that the difference between great and mediocre imitation or influence is the quality of 'strength' with which great poets are invested. I say 'poets,' and not 'texts,' because Bloom's is a theory of artists and of individual genius. Michel Schneider's *Voleurs de mots,* a more technically psychoanalytical study of plagiarism carried out by a psychiatrist and 'author' in his own right, also depends on an Oedipal account of coming-into-authorship, which he terms becoming a 'true poet.' While Bloom does not deal directly with 'plagiarism,' Schneider treats it as a psychological condition, sometimes a pathology or a neurosis, which can produce great art as well as great suffering for the poet-victim: the anxiety of influence. Both studies share, however, the tendency to discuss only 'strong' or 'true' poets, the implication in both being that whatever the authors in question did, it was not, in fact, plagiarism in the negative or sanctionable sense. Schneider's focus is the most interesting for us, but by limiting his discussion to 'strong poets,' he constructs plagiarism – or else the fear of it – as a psychological quirk somehow indicative of genius. In any case he signals the unequivocally pragmatic fact that 'it is not the plagiarism which makes the plagiarist, it is the fact that one is a plagiarist or a true author which qualifies the borrowing; influence or plagiarism. A great author remains a great author. He is incapable of plagiarizing mediocre writers [...] Only mediocre writers can be qualified plagiarists, in any case, in the eyes of literary history.'[2]

The belief that great authors don't plagiarize is perhaps the most historically consistent criterion for distinguishing between plagiarism and literature. In *Gradus*, for example, under the heading 'Imitation,' Dupriez refers to the similarity between 'le Cimetière marin' by Valéry and a poem by P.A. Lebrun, 'Cimetière au bord de la mer,' as intertextuality, 'in order to avoid pejorative connotations which would be inappropriate' ['pour éviter les connotations péjoratives, qui seraient déplacées' (248)]. Dupriez does not elaborate the reasons for this inappropriateness. Examples of similar reasoning are too numerous to list, but in order to show that they are not restricted to contemporary judgments, we refer to the nineteenth-century *Larousse* that claims, in a discussion about plagiarism and Racine, that certain of his verses might verge on plagiarism, 'were it but for the respect that we owe to our masters' ['sauf le respect que nous devons à nos maîtres' ('Plagiat' 1109)]. In the same vein, Paul Hazard, in his 'Les plagiats de Stendhal,' cites Paul Arbelet, who, in his *Histoire de la Peinture en Italie et les plagiats de Stendhal* (Paris: Calmann-Levy, 1913), advises: 'Do not disdain Stendhal's plagiarisms. It is necessary to recognize all kinds of superiority. Piracy has it geniuses, infinitely interesting to study' ['Ne méprisons donc pas les plagiats de Stendhal. Il faut savoir reconnaître toutes les supériorités. Le brigandage a ses hommes de génie, infiniment curieux à étudier' (Hazard, 'Les plagiats de Stendhal' 346)]. And Hazard describes with irony the insistence with which Stendhal's admirer's defend his originality:

> They will obstinately continue to recognize the pure Stendhalian spirit in the ideas of Robertson, or Dr Johnson, or twenty others; they will even continue to admire the extreme novelty of the theory of influence [*des milieux*] applied to literature and the arts; even when they are shown evidence that it is to be found in all the great authors of the eighteenth century, beginning with Dubos, they will not be dissuaded from their opinion [...] If one claims to discover in the books of Stendhalian law certain borrowings [*interpolations*], one becomes a heretic and a blasphemer. How, then, dare one speak of plagiarism?[3]

What is first apparent from the preceding examples is that the author is a 'great man,' a 'man of genius,' an 'original,' a 'master'; a plagiarist, on the other hand, is a 'médiocre.'[4] What distinguishes the two, therefore, is not primarily a textual product, but a personal attribute in which great art – or its opposite – originates. Not only does authorship presuppose a causal relation between the originator and the work, but the work itself must demonstrate a kind of spiritual mimesis by which it emulates the life and soul of the poet: great men produce great works, and these works, in turn, guarantee that their authors were great – this is the logic of authority. Such a spiritual mimesis between the author and the work may be the most important traditional attribute of authorship that has been lost in the twentieth century, although it still surfaces in isolated instances, notably in plagiarism cases.

While contemporary notions of plagiarism are largely defined by questions of private property, the continuing belief that 'great authors don't plagiarize' is an index of the survival of the condition of authority with which authors are invested. True authorship is incompatible with plagiarism because authors are by nature – that is, ancient tradition – not only originary, but sincere, that is, authentic. 'Original' authors can't plagiarize, not because they don't copy, but because their signature functions in a tautologous structure similar to that of medieval traditions of authority: since *auctores* authored truth, anomalies discovered in the work of an authoritative author were seen as evidence of a lack of authenticity of the text or as a corruption in the manuscript. Expurgation is no longer a legitimate solution to the discovery of embarrassing lapses on the part of true authors; however, an equally simple and effective expedient has been found: since the true author doesn't plagiarize, his plagiarisms are truly original.

The notion of works *originating* with authors and entailing an intimate link between product and producer continues in the form of requirements of *authenticity* and *originality*. In both the aesthetic and the legal arenas, the *ownership* of a work is determined by the fact that it *originated* with the person who claims authorship of it. And authorship itself is predicated on the condition of authority, which, in the twentieth century, seems a fragile, if not inoperative, criterion. While it is common to refuse *originality* to premodern aesthetics, as it is to reduce the importance of *authority* for modern conceptions of authorship, a history of *authoring plagiarism* will underscore the importance of both of these conditions for the authorial function. In reviewing this history, we will, first, rely on the notion of *originating discourse* in order to capture the essential elements of *authority, authenticity,* and *originality*, which together form the historical constants of authorship. This triumvirate excludes a most crucial fourth element, equally ancient in origin, that of *ownership*, which we will treat independently.

The relationship between plagiarism and a crisis of authority is often at the forefront of disputes about plagiarism: the slippage between the authoritative and legitimizing quotation, and the false appropriation of authoritative discourse are common features of accusations of plagiarism. Compagnon locates this crisis in Montaigne's writing; and in his chapter of Poe's plagiarisms, Kenneth Dauber claims that 'there is, in Poe, a crisis in the relation of the writer to his readers [...] Poe no more than [Franklin, Brown, or Cooper] would either give up all claim to authority or claim as his authority something other than us [i.e., readers] instead' (125). Asking whether 'plagiarism' is symptomatic of a crisis of authority seems to lead directly to a producer-oriented reading of plagiarism as a function of authorial intentionality; but could charges of plagiarism not be instead, or as well, symptomatic of a similar crisis of readerly authority?

From what, in fact, is the authority of authorship derived? And how is it constituted, especially in the twentieth century, when the notion seems so fragile, if not inoperative? In Foucauldian or Bourdieusian terms, it is necessary to see *authority* not as an essential or immanent trait of texts or authors, but as a complex of consensual coordinations among groups of readers who 'agree' to recognize – and thereby invest – authority in the other. If Western tradition unambiguously bestows 'authority' on authors as one of their essential features, it is correspondingly reluctant to recognize that authorizing principles emanate from the readerly tradition and are, unmistakably, a function of readership.

> This writing is all fake (copied from other writing) so you should go away and not read any of it.
>
> Kathy Acker, *Hannibal Lecter, My Father*

Both Jaucourt and St Onge define the act which results in plagiarism as an instance of 'copying,' and it is necessary to unpack the connotations of this word in order to distinguish it from its more noble cousin, 'imitation.' Since artistic production has, historically, been more intimately related to concepts of imitation than to originality, 'copying' refers to the negative forms of imitation that are termed plagiarism. While imitation in art, either of nature or of other models, is never in itself condemnable, the products of imitation may suffer criticism if proper processes of production are not observed. When imitation falls from the merely bad into plagiarism, it is normally because of the presupposition of covertness, entailing the presumption of fraud. Now behind this presumption, whether in the legal or aesthetic domains, are criteria for distinguishing between identity and difference. The 'copy' implies identity: reiteration, transcription, reproduction; its processes are mechanistic; its results devoid of aesthetic value, 'artistry,' or 'genius.' Imitation, on the other hand, implies difference, and while this difference in itself does not constitute aesthetic value, it situates the product of imitation in a contiguous relation with the 'original' or 'model': imitations solicit comparison with their models, beside which they coexist and with respect to which their aesthetic value can be judged as servile, derivative, inspired, or original. 'Copies,' on the contrary, repress their models: they exist in a paradigmatic relationship of potential substitution to their originals (Randall, 'Le faux et le vraisemblable: le cas du faux Chanel').

In the plastic arts, the fundamental criterion for distinguishing between an original and a copy – in the event of the elusive 'perfect ' copy – is that of authenticity, or what Prieto calls 'numerical identity': is this canvas the *very one* to which the artist applied his brush or not? 'Originals' as authentic production are, in this sense, indifferent to aesthetic quality, as a Van Meegern could provide an aesthetic substitute for a Vermeer, but could never substitute for its authenticity.[5] In the literary world, it is necessary to distinguish among fakes, copies, imitation, and plagiarism.[6] The first we consider to be outside our realm: a literary fake is the opposite of plagiarism. Here, an author actually composes an 'original' work, but 'signs' someone else's name, refusing authorship and claiming for the work an exalted provenance and a pedigree that it does not have – such are the cases of Chatterton's Rowley poems and Macpherson's *Ossian*. A literary copy also escapes the definition of plagiarism, being of the order of piracy: an almost perfect, that is, integral reproduction, most often by mechanical means, of a previously existing work, without either attribution to or permission of the 'original' author or, in contemporary times, the copyright holder. It is rare that the kind of imitation qualified as plagiarism demonstrates copying to this degree: various strategies of transformation or 'enhancement' – disguise, translation, paraphrase – tip the scales from identity to difference. Dryden expresses the possible range of imitations available to the poet, and argues that the quality of the model may shift the copy from a servile to a meritorious one:

> Without invention, a painter is but a copier, and a poet but a plagiary of others. Both are allowed sometimes to copy, and translate; but, as our author tells you, that is not the best part of their reputation. *Imitators are but a servile kind of cattle*, says the poet; or at best, the keepers of cattle for other men: they have nothing which is properly their own: that is a sufficient mortification for me, while I am translating Virgil. But to copy the best author is a kind of praise, if I perform it as I ought; as a copy after Raphael is more to be commended than an original of any indifferent painter. (From 'Parallel,' quoted by Aden 138)

Copying is plagiarism when it implies mechanical reproduction, and therefore the absence of talent and work, and the presumption of covertness.

Degrees of identity and difference are both the criteria used to distinguish between copying and imitation and those on which the identification of plagiarism stumbles. Variously defined as 'unacknowledged borrowing' and 'copying,' plagiarism is clearly present in the second case, which is condemnable on its own because of the relationship of identity involved, while 'borrowing' needs to be qualified by the presumption of covertness to be judged illegitimate. In fact, 'copying' implies covertness, because of the relationship of identity, and therefore of the potential for substitution of the copy for the 'original.' The accusation of plagiarism presupposes not imitation, but copying; the existence of a copy presents the potential for a mistaken identity, the erroneous or unethical substitution of one discourse for another. And mistaken identity, in the realm of intellectual production, is a crime against the relation of authenticity subsisting between the author and the work.

2. Originating Discourse: Authority, Authenticity, Originality

Classical and medieval notions of authorship are pertinent to a history of plagiarism for what they reveal about the stability of attributes of authorship over the course of history. In brief, authors *originate* truth; their discourse is *authoritative* in that it expresses truth; and this intimate relationship between author and discourse is the condition of *authenticity* guaranteeing authorship. The tautological nature of this triumvirate is evident: what is less obvious is its continuing power in modern conceptions of authorship.

While classical rhetoric did not formally recognize 'originality' as an aesthetic criterion, an investigation of the rules governing 'good imitation' reveals the negative form of the practice that, today, would count as plagiarism – and that in fact did so during classical antiquity. Classical rhetoric prescribing modes of proper imitation is very clear about the evils of copying and about the work of *transformation* required to shift the imitation from servility to inspiration, the second being found in the happy union between genius and learning. In Latin and subsequently Renaissance rhetoric, the term *inventio* refers to the 'fable' or story, and literally means not invention, but the discovery of something already there, such as a traditional myth or legend. The treatment of the story – *dispositio* – and its stylistic expression – *elocutio* – were the areas in which the natural genius of the author, nourished by his study of the great masters, could enter into rivalry with them in the spirit of transformation with an eye to improvement on the originals.[1] Horace sets out the three principles necessary to avoid bad imitation: 'A subject which has become public by having been already treated, [...] will justly become your private and personal property if you will [1] not waste your time in dilating on a common and obvious round *of trite and trivial incidents,* nor, [2] as a too scrupulously exact interpreter, be over careful to render word for word, nor [3] as an imitator start away into a position in which you are cramped by [reproducing too many details of the original]' (*The Art of Poetry* pp. l. 131ff., pp. 24, 26).

Christian antiquity inherited two different sorts of authority from the classical past: that of *auctoritas* – dependent on the authoritative person – and *authenticitas* – the impersonal authority of discursive tradition which, following Compagnon (219), is derived from the classical *sententiae* – received discursive formulations that, independently of authorship, embody immediately apparent or provable truths. The patristic quotation conflated these two notions: the biblical texts and the Church fathers were *auctoritates* because of their participation in universal truth and the totality of the *Logos*: if the identity of the author guaranteed his authority, the truth embodied in words guaranteed the superfluity of recourse to the name of the author.

The tautologous interdependence of the two authorizing principles – that of personal and discursive authority – is still operative today, and certainly was in the eighteenth century, when it was argued in favour of the medieval authenticity of Chatterton's (forged) Rowley verses, for example, that such a dissolute youth could not have produced such poems. The discovery of their fraud had the opposite effect: the fact of Chatterton's authorship of the verses elevated him to the rank of the 'Golden Boy,' who was to become a symbol of Romantic genius. Similarly, the long controversy about the true authorship of Shakespeare's works was fuelled not only by the absence of substantial biographical data about their putative author, but also by the discrepancy between the known facts and the Victorian preference for equating nobility of soul and condition. As one student of the debate declares, all of the 'anti-Stratfordians' are 'strong believers in the wonders of class distinctions, using the absence of sufficient information about William Shakespeare to paint a portrait of an illiterate, coarse buffoon incapable of even a flash of poetic feeling [...] Denying the role of vicarious experience in artistic creation, they believe, almost to a man, that a writer can describe only those things which he has directly experienced himself. This condition has been defined by one controversialist as "Literary Sincerity"' (Wadsworth 6–7).

In the present day, the continuing controversies over Coleridge's and Martin Luther King, Jr's plagiarisms are witness to the survival of a belief in authenticity as a mimetic relationship between the authoritative work and the great soul imbued with truth and wisdom.

In classical aesthetics, *authenticity* was a crucial element of theories of imitation because of the necessity for the author to effect the transformation of his models. The medieval and Renaissance periods, however, in trying to reconcile the authority of the *auctor* and that of his text as the proper object of imitation, generated many of the rhetorical quarrels that would propel the literary arts up to the Romantic revolution. In order to trace the development from the aesthetics of imitation to those of modern 'originality,' it is necessary to distinguish clearly between the spirit of rules for imitation and their practice. From ancient to neoclassical times, the ideal object of imitation was the same as that pursued by the 'originals' themselves, that is, 'nature,' which meant not textual, but rather something like 'spiritual' mimesis. For Chaucer, for example, 'to be original is not to be "textuel," [*sic*] which [...] means that one cannot imitate one's *auctores* simply by following their texts word by word; rather, to imitate an *auctor* requires that one take words into one's own hand, thus to weave them (or to reweave them) according to one's own sense, design, wisdom, or grasp of the hiddenness of meanings. To imitate an *auctor* means precisely the imitation of authority rather than of a text. To be original in this sense is to transcend textuality (as indeed one is expected always to transcend the letter in [*sic*] behalf of the spirit)' (Bruns 128).

According to Minnis's study of medieval authorship (10), there are four traditional sources for the word: the Latin roots of *agere*, to act or perform; *augere*, to grow or augment (the *New Oxford* adds 'originate'); *auieo*, to tie; and the Greek *autentim*, meaning 'authority.' In the Middle Ages, *auctor* and *auctores* were applied only to such authoritative figures as God, the biblical authors and Church fathers, and, on the secular side, to identifiable ancients such as Homer, Plato, Aristotle, and Cicero. Minnis recounts the gradual emergence of the human *auctor* throughout the Middle Ages, such that, 'at the end of the Middle Ages, *auctores* became more like men, men became more like *auctores*' (216). According to him, the two criteria for the *auctor* were, first, that his writing contain 'intrinsic worth,' that is, both truth (theological) and wisdom (secular) in conformity with Christian doctrine, rendering it worthy of belief and imitation. In addition, the authoritative text must be a 'genuine production of a named *auctor*' (11) – in other words, it must be authentic. The identity of the author and the authoritative nature of his text were intimately interdependent: 'The thinking we are investigating seems to be circular: the work of an *auctor* was a book worth reading; a book worth reading had to be the work of an *auctor*. No "modern" writer could decently be called an *auctor* in a period when men saw themselves as dwarfs standing on the shoulders of giants, i.e. the "ancients"' (12).

If no contemporary writer could aspire to the position of *auctor*, he could, however, fulfil a variety of other functions, notably those of *scriptor* and *compilator*, thereby adding nothing of his own to the text, and that of *commentator*, whose role was limited to explaining the authoritative texts, a function often performed by scribes in the margins of the texts they were copying. Even full-scale exegetes were commentators, not authors, and secular writers of romance and legend such as Jean de Meun and Chaucer claimed for themselves the role of compiler or 'rehearser' of others' stories (197–204).[2] These 'authors' used various strategies of recourse to the *auctoritas* of ancient *auctores* in order to establish authority for their writings as well as to disculpate themselves of responsibility for their contents. Minnis asks whether Chaucer could ever have thought of himself as an *auctor*, and of his work as possessing a degree of *auctoritas*. Whereas Chaucer claimed for himself solely the roles of compiler or translator, Minnis claims for him the status of 'author': 'Indeed, so deliberate was he in presenting himself as a compiler that one is led to suspect the presence of a very self-conscious author who was concerned to manipulate the conventions of *compilatio* for this own literary ends [...] Chaucer was an author who hid behind the "shield and defence" of the compiler' (210). Modern analyses of medieval aesthetics insist on the component of 'invention' in a way that could be generalized to include much Renaissance and classical writing; and it is remarkable how well the following description suits our contemporary, post-structural and postmodern theories of writing as being, inevitably, rewriting:

> Hence for the grammarian there is nothing that cannot be rewritten or enriched by further writing, because no text is closed to him, not even [...] Virgil's. He dwells, it is important to remember, *among* texts, not over and against them, and accordingly he is without anxiety, because his antecedents are great inventories that produce in him the copious mind,.which is a mind capable of endless invention – invention which is, however, textual rather than 'natural,' insofar as its point of departure is always prior writing, not worldly or mental experience. The library (or its mental equivalent, memory) is the grammarian's equivalent of Romantic imagination. (Bruns 126)

Authorship is therefore intimately linked with the authority invested in the person of the *auctor*, repository of truth and wisdom, and entails the notion of authenticity – the author is the originator of the work – as well as a form of originality – the *auctores* were original men. Even as writers evolved, from scribes, compilers, and commentators, to authors in their own right, they continued to invest authority in the *auctoritas* of the ancients, distinguishing between the original source of truth and their own transcribing voice.

But clearly not all authoritative discourse is authored. The capacity of repetition to infuse anonymous discourse with the authority of eternal truth makes some truths available to everyone; repetition is the means by which non-authors – scribes, imitators, compilers – participate in eternal truth by facilitating its transmission. But the *author* has the ability to originate and 'sign' truth: *great authors don't plagiarize* because 'authorship' is precisely that capacity to originate or discover truth, to authorize it *as* truth rather than simply to transmit previously discovered truth. Plagiarism, in this sense, is a kind of authoritative fraud – by usurping either a public discourse, available to all, or the discourse of a proper authority, one claims a personal status to which one is not entitled. It is frequently remarked, quite appropriately, that 'plagiarism' did not exist in the Middle Ages – and this is due to the logic of authority: discourse was either internally authorized by its continual repetition – as general and common knowledge it could only be repeated, not appropriated – or authorized by its source, or *auctor*, and available sources were restricted to a few ancient or Christian names. It is less the logic of property than the force of authority that made plagiarism impossible, or at least unlikely, in the Middle Ages.[3]

Originality is most easily expressed for medieval and Renaissance aesthetics as being the condition of authority – *auctoritas* – embodied in the ancient authors who were 'original' in the sense of being prior and, consequently, in having first said whatever was worth saying, as well as having formulated the best ways of saying it. For succeeding ages, 'originality' was a feature restricted to *auctores* and the function of the post-classical writer was to imitate this 'originality.'

For Renaissance arts, the classical *auctores* had imitated 'nature' directly, and, in so doing, expressed their own authoritative natures. This is the thrust of arguments by Erasmus, Du Bellay, and Montaigne, who, in criticizing the conservative and rule-bound rhetorical arts, point out the folly of imitating only the *discourse* of the masters, without acquiring their *nature*. If, by the end of the Middle Ages, men were becoming more like *auctores* and vice versa, the Renaissance witnessed a continual battle to accede to authority on the part of human authors, a struggle sufficiently exemplified by Montaigne to allow him to stand alone as one of the most modern of Renaissance authors – and as a potential model 'plagiarist.' The difficulty of locating instances of plagiarism in this period is a consequence of the general adherence to practices of imitation and translation, the essential question being whether or not the poet has imitated properly, avoiding servile copying while relying on appropriate models appropriated according to the rules of good imitation. These rules consisted, first, in restricting one's borrowings to ancient and, later, foreign sources; and, second, in not imitating servilely, or translating word for word. Other aspects of the work or the author that opened both to suspicions of plagiarism were evidence of a lack of genius or talent, work, and study, or the manifestations of dishonesty.

David Quint argues that literary originality began to emerge not in the eighteenth century, but in the Renaissance, 'at the moment when a traditional and authoritative canon was historicized and relativized' (220). Imitation, as opposed to scholastic copying, was the result of this historicization by which the Renaissance attempted to establish and reconstruct its continuity with former times, a project that implied, at the same time, the distance between the two periods. It is also a period that sees the birth of the notion of 'literature,' and its simultaneous devaluation as a repository of truth, this function being subsequently taken up by other realms such as philosophy, history, and science. The ancients slowly lose their divine infallibility and become men susceptible to error, especially as a result of their pre-Christian and pre-scientific place in history. Not only. did the individual author fall 'into the realm of historical contingency, at a remove from any timeless or fixed standard of truth' (Quint 7), but, by 'obtaining a cultural autonomy from systems of authorized truth, literature gave up its right to be authoritative' (219).

The classical rules of rhetoric retained in the Renaissance shifted the notion of copying to imitation, while still depending largely on the teachings of Cicero and Quintilian and on the example of Horace. The poet needed talent, culture, and technique: the poet is both born and perfected by work and, for the latter to occur, it was necessary to observe and emulate the immutable principles of art as set down by the ancients. The means to this end were, first, the assiduous study of the rules of composition by means of the reading and interpretation of the works of the masters and, then, their paraphrase and, eventually, translation. In all instances, transformation, applied to the form of the work, was an essential step, for it is in this phase that the genius of the author, prohibited from inventing subjects, was exercised. The reification of and slavish adherence to the form of the discourse of the models, especially in the hands of scholastic and pedantic practitioners, became a common subject of complaints and produced the ossified forms of literature against which the moderns in the eighteenth century and the Romantics after them revolted.

AUTHORIZING PLAGIARISM

Erasmus is an early critic of the vice of servile imitation as manifested by the Ciceronian school. In *Ciceronianus* (1528), he takes the 'Ciceronians' to task in a fictional dialogue between Nosoponus, a defender of the school, and Bulephorus, the voice of Erasmus. The Ciceronians argued that Cicero had attained stylistic perfection, and that all writing could achieve nothing better than his imitation. By using Cicero's rules against his followers, Erasmus refutes their own doctrine in terms that clearly point to the classical importance of individual personality in the business of good imitation. First, Cicero taught, and practised, the emulation of the best in a variety of sources, instead of adhering servilely to one model, be it Cicero himself. Second, Cicero taught that the best art was in the appearance of no art: 'And so, if we want to be successful in our imitation of Cicero, the first thing must be to conceal our imitation of Cicero' (386). Cicero was no servile copier, and so 'it's inevitable that imitation falls short when it tries only to follow a model, not surpass it' (377). The end of imitation is transformation: metaphors of digestion and of the bee's transformation of pollen into honey show that neither memorization nor transcription of one model, but appropriation and transformation of many are needed: 'Bees don't collect the material for making honey from just one bush, do they? [...] And what they bring is not honey to begin with. They turn it into a liquid in their mouths and inner parts, and then reproduce it, transmuted into their own substance; in it one recognizes not the taste of the flower or shrub the bee has sipped, but a creation of the bee itself, compounded from all the contributory elements' (402).

The founding principles guiding these criticisms is also inspired by Cicero, who was great by virtue of his own genius, which, being uniquely his, was inimitable. Surface imitation cannot produce genius: rather than reproducing the product, one must emulate the very process of creation: 'But if you want to express the whole Cicero, you cannot express yourself, and if you do not express yourself your speech will be a lying mirror' (399);[4] 'Minds differ far more than voices and physical features do, and the mirror will lie unless it reflects the true born image of the mind' (440). What is remarkable for our purposes is the emphasis placed by Erasmus on the expression of individual 'genius' in the production of good imitation, and the proscription against formal imitation. In this he is a precursor of Montaigne, in whom the theory of the individual achieves an almost modern sound. But before leaving Erasmus, let us hear a summary of his position with respect to imitation:

> Again, I approve of imitation – but imitation not enslaved to one set of rules, from the guidelines of which it dare not depart, but imitation which gathers from all authors, or at least from the most outstanding, the thing which is the chief virtue of each and which suits your own cast of mind; imitation which does not immediately incorporate into its own speech any nice

little feature it comes across, but transmits it to the mind for inward digestion, so that becoming part of your own system, it gives the impression not
of something begged from someone else, but of something that springs
from your own mental processes, something that exudes the characteristics
and force of your own mind and personality. Your reader will see it not as a
piece of decoration filched from Cicero, but a child sprung from your own
brain, the living image of its father, like Pallas from the brain of Jove. Your
speech will not be a patchwork or a mosaic, but a lifelike portrait of the person you really are, a river welling out from your inmost being. (441–2)

It is crucial to the history of authorship to recognize the coincidence
between the appropriation of authority by the individual author and the
very presence of the possibility of plagiarism, such as is expressed by
the metaphors 'patchwork' and 'mosaic.' By the time we come to Montaigne, some seventy years after Erasmus, we see in this author a full-blown
contradiction between *auctoritas* and individual authority, as well as a
self-consciousness of potential plagiarism. In brief, 'the still living referent
which Montaigne attempted to escape was the great man: the "auctoritas"
who would accord him an identity [...] Montaigne refused the test and the
guarantee of tradition, but he knew of nothing to put in its place.'[5]

Montaigne's attempts to negotiate a path between traditional *auctoritas*
and personal authority earned him the reputation of *copiste* among his
seventeenth-century critics for whom there was no longer any doubt that
the simple faculty of discoursing about the truth of one's self was sufficient
to authenticate the subject (Compagnon 311). Malebranche uses Montaigne as an example of the vice of quotation while giving him credit for
originality: 'One sees throughout his book an original character which is
infinitely pleasing: even though he is an imitator [*copiste*], he doesn't sound
like one: and his strong and daring imagination always gives an original
turn to the things he copies.'[6]

Montaigne is one of my personal favourites in the history of plagiarism
because he at once practised it so flagrantly and defended himself against
the charge so vocally: he is principally important to this study because,
rather than producing a theory of imitation, he has a self-conscious theory
of plagiarism that places him in a rather more modern context than Erasmus. Montaigne has a highly developed and well-known theory of the self,
a problematic self that is both the source of his writing and an obstacle to
his erudition, caught between the Renaissance figure of *auctoritas* and his
own incapacity to know or to say anything about anything but himself. But
this insistence on the self is paradoxically achieved through the rewriting
of others: 'I only quote others the better to quote myself' ('On Educating
Children,' Bk I, 26; 166). Commenting this passage, Delègue declares:

'There is then a way to imitate the models that, under the guise of eternalizing their prestige, aims in fact at freeing oneself from them. One repeats archetypes only to wear them out, to exhaust their reserves, in the hope of ending up elsewhere (*déboucher ailleurs*), if possible.'[7]

Montaigne's project appears modern in so far as it is an explicit attempt to construct an identity in and by writing, a self that is overdetermined by contact with the Other – all the others who have written themselves before him. Among the themes that constitute the identity of the author in the *Essays*, we find the defence of his originality in the face of obvious evidence to the contrary, and an inability to retain learning, which forces him to speak primarily of himself, a fault that is the result of a bad memory putting him above the reproach of plagiarism, since what one cannot remember, one cannot copy. Montaigne's way of learning is to assimilate, digest, and transform the others in his path such that they are now part of him (or he of them). The crux of his argument and practice is familiar from Erasmus: proper imitation is not of product but of process: 'To imitate speech is easy: an entire nation can do it: to imitate judgement and the research for your material takes rather more time! Most readers think similar styles, when they find them, clothe similar bodies. But you cannot borrow strength or sinews: you can borrow mantles and finery' ('On Educating Children,' Bk I, 26; 194).

Montaigne's strategy of writing is sufficiently transparent to appear disingenuous: his own inferiority with respect to learning and genius gives him the liberty not to attempt what is so patently beyond his reach, and to speak, instead, 'only of himself.' But this self, so inferior, is not without its natural talents:

> I undertake to write without preconceptions on any subject which comes to mind, employing nothing but my own natural resources: then if (as happens often) I chance to come across in excellent authors the very same topics I have undertaken to treat (as I have just done recently in Plutarch about the power of the imagination) I acknowledge myself to be so weak, so paltry, so lumbering and so dull compared with such men, that I feel scorn and pity for myself. I do congratulate myself, however, that my opinions frequently coincide with theirs and on the fact that I do at least trail far behind them murmuring 'Hear, hear'. And again, I do know (what many do not) the vast difference there is between them and me. What I myself have thought up and produced is poor feeble stuff, but I let it go on, without plastering over the cracks or stitching up the rents which have been revealed by such comparisons. ('On Educating Children,' Bk I, 26; pp. 164–5)

This is a typical strategy of self-congratulation through self-denegration.

Montaigne's self-proclaimed virtues are twofold: first, he and the great authors of the past often think alike; second, and more important, he does not, when discovering his thoughts to be preceded by those of Plutarch, for example, also steal Plutarch's words to express an idea over which he, Montaigne, chooses to retain the authority. In other words, his weak and feeble expression of an idea common to both him and Plutarch is the proof and guarantee that 'I,' Montaigne, am in fact the originator of this idea, just as surely as Plutarch was in his time.

Although Montaigne is a man of much study, the astonishing weakness of his memory is the reason that he has developed other and higher faculties, those of reason, understanding, and judgment (*sens, entendement, jugement*):

> There is nobody less suited than I am to start talking about memory. I can hardly find a trace of it in myself; I doubt if there is any other memory in the world as grotesquely faulty as mine is! All my other endowments are mean and ordinary: but I think that, where memory is concerned, I am most singular and rare, worthy of both name and reputation! [...] More-over, Nature [...] has strengthened other faculties of mine as this one has grown weaker. If, thanks to memory, other people's discoveries and opin-ions had been kept ever before me, I would readily have reached a settled mind and judgement by following other men's footsteps, failing as most people do to exercise my own powers. ('On Liars,' Bk I, 9; 32–3)

The strategy here is the same: the weakness of his memory is the source of his strength, but his virtue is not presented as a moral one – Montaigne's mind would be as lazy as the rest of the world's if it had the means to be. Montaigne's bad memory is necessary for his individuality, and can be seen as symptomatic of a transition in Renaissance aesthetics from a poetics of memory and memorization, to one of forgetting, a way of conceiving writ-ing that did not really come into its own until the Romantic period. In 'On Educating Children,' he advises young people to read and study the great masters as much as possible, and then to 'forget' as much as they can. By this he means to assimilate knowledge such that it nourishes and enriches one's own faculties of judgment and reason. Metaphors of ingestion and digestion illustrate his point: 'Spewing up food exactly as you have swal-lowed it is evidence of a failure to digest and assimilate it; the stomach has not done its job if, during concoction, it fails to change the substance and the form of what it is given' ('On Educating Children' 169). Montaigne uses his lack of memory (what we later refer to as 'cryptomnesia') both as an excuse to speak in his own name – he 'knows' nothing but himself – and as a ruse to protect himself from charges of 'plagiarism,' that is, from the accusation of intentional and unacknowledged borrowing from others.

The 'cryptomnesia' argument, while neither entirely convincing nor, one suspects, honest, indicates lack of intentionality: what he doesn't remember having read in Cicero, he cannot be accused of copying.

Montaigne's attacks on the 'pedants,' who have simply retention and no learning, are scathing. Pedantism is the ability to quote others without interiorizing their wisdom to enhance one's own soul and understanding: 'We know how to say, "This is what Cicero said"; "This is morality for Plato"; "These are the *ipsissima verba* of Aristotle." But what have *we* got to say? What judgements do *we* make? What are *we* doing? A parrot could talk as well as we do' ('On Schoolmasters' Learning,' Bk I, 25, p. 154). But even from this vice he himself is not free. In an essay criticizing the sterile reproduction of knowledge without understanding, he exclaims: 'Such foolishness fits my own case marvellously well. Am I for the most part not doing the same when assembling my material? Off I go, rummaging about in books for sayings which please me – not so as to store them up (for I have no storehouses) but so as to carry them back to this book, where they are no more mine than they were in their original place' ('On Schoolmasters' Learning,' Bk I, 25, p. 154).

Montaigne would express only himself by appropriating the writings of others and by recasting them with the imprint of his own inimitable (authentic, original) genius – or lack thereof, as he more oftens argues. What is produced is a long meditation on the self as an interpretation of others: 'It is more a business to interpret the interpretations than to interpret the texts, and there are more books on books than on any other subject: all we do is gloss each other [...] How often and perhaps stupidly have I extended my book to make it talk about itself [...] (Book III, 13, 'On Experience,' Bk III, 13, p. 1212).

Antoine Compagnon has written eloquently on Montaigne as a figure of transition from the dominance of *auctoritas* to that of the individual during the sixteenth century. While being greatly indebted to his insights in this area, my present concern is with the transition away from quotation into the nebulous area of assimilation that Montaigne so fiercely defends as his legitimate practice. Montaigne's battle with the great men that preceded him, whose genius surpassed his own both in thinking and in writing, is important in so far as the evident inferiority in these matters, under which he and every other writer of the post-classical period had to labour, was not treated by him as a limitation to his ability to write. Freely inventing, more often paraphrasing, he appropriated the thoughts, ideas, and even words of those past masters and, by writing them himself, made them his own: 'I would rather be an expert on me than on Cicero' ('On Experience,' Bk III, 13, p. 1218). This practice was only plagiaristic in the sense of his explicit intent that it be so, for example, as a trap to ensnare pretentious and foolish pedants (see 'Reading the Reader'). As an intentional aesthetic, it could stand as a model of much modern writing, where allusion and inter-textuality abound, but without attracting either ethical or aesthetic censure for lack of 'originality.' However, Montaigne, as 'original genius,' is a case apart, and cannot stand for what 'real' plagiarism looked like to sixteenth-century writers and critics.

In his *Plagiarism and Imitation during the English Renaissance*, White concludes with the following summary statement:

> Greek and Roman writers during the eight centuries from Isocrates to Macrobius defined and practised a literary theory based on imitation, yet with every safeguard for originality. The Middle Ages adopted this theory in an imperfect form, ignoring these safeguards, burying them beneath an overwhelming reverence for authority. The Continental Renaissance exhumed the ancient principles, but, in its reaction against the dictatorship of medieval tradition, at first set up a new dictatorship of classical laws. Only by degrees were the safeguards for originality restored to their former   ·
> prime importance. (201)

Plagiarism appears to be the equivalent in the sixteenth century of the flouting of the classical rules of good imitation: dishonesty and a lack of talent combined to attract to the usurper of another bird's plumes the accusation of fraud and of attempting to profit from another's property. Those guilty of such infractions were derided, mostly in verse and invective. Yet in the same breath, White claims that, 'although servility, false claims of independence, and outright piracy were more and more hotly rebuked [...], Englishmen from 1500 to 1625 [were] without any feeling analogous to the modern attitude toward plagiarism; they even lacked the word until the very end of that period' (201–2). In this, White seems to ignore his own evidence, for his work is a wealth of stories about quarrels concerning abuses of proper imitation that can only *not* be plagiarism if one applies modern connotations of copyright violation or author's rights to the infraction. And the absence of the word itself is no handicap to the writers that White documents in recounting their many quarrels, accusations, and counter-accusations of improper imitation. White, during the course of his argument that English Renaissance writers 'restored, in its true form, the classical doctrine that originality of real worth is to be achieved only through creative imitation' (202), forgets, or does not realize, that the proper place of plagiarism is not in opposition to 'originality,' which he defines for the period as 'creative imitation,' but rather on the negative pole of that very axis of imitation that so occupied the Renaissance.

The seventeenth century is not without a serious interest in plagiarism from both a practical and a theoretical point of view: ambiguities concerning the legitimate objects of imitation, the practice of translation, and the proper way to imitate generated a number of significant quarrels.

The practice of translation into the vernacular increased the available range of universal truth by allowing for transpositions involving cultural innovations. By the time of the late seventeenth century, the first volley of the *Querelle des Anciens et des Modernes* was in full swing in France, and the great question about the infallibility and perfection of the ancients had been posed. One of the effects of this quarrel was to distinguish between translation and invention: the new historicists such as André and Mme Dacier objected to poetic translations of ancient texts that deformed their historical content, making Homer and his characters into seventeenth-century Europeans. This objection was an attack on universal truth to the extent that it postulated the historical specificity of both the ancients and the modern Europeans, promoting not the immutability of truth as expressed about man and God throughout history, but rather the humanity of the ancients, their fallibility especially as pre-revelation men, and the possibility of progress as opposed to the medieval concept of stasis or its Renaissance counterpart of universal historical decline.

In the field of 'literature' or poetry, such proponents for the vernacular as Du Bellay had already argued that French and Latin verse were not the same, and that French could be in its own way the equivalent to Latin if it were to develop its distinctive specificity. The quarrel between the ancients and the moderns took the argument even farther, by maintaining the superiority of modern poetry over the ancient because of the former's Christian inspiration. Science and philosophy had progressed and, it was argued, literature and poetry were also susceptible to improvement. Paradoxically, this progressive interpretation of poetic invention was to produce the ossification of the rules of taste and rhetoric, for classical norms of composition, distilled into the rules expressed in Boileau's 'L'art poétique,' for example, had become the standard for creation and were substituted for the slavish imitation of models. The notion of universal truth shifted from the particular productions of antiquity to the rules governing those productions: Aristotle had simply codified what Homer had done out of a kind of necessity born of his genius, which could not help but express universal truth. This argument survived well into the eighteenth century and was used in the most inappropriate instances: in defence of the authenticity of Macpherson's forged poetry of the ancient Ossian, for example, which was criticized as being too 'Aristotelian' to have been reasonably concocted by a Celtic bard, it was argued that it was not surprising that Ossian and Aristotle followed the same rules in composing tragedy, since these rules were in nature and were universally true. All genius would necessarily discover or apply them: 'But our astonishment [at finding Ossian's poems so conform to Aristotle's rules] will cease, when we consider from what source Aristotle drew those rules. Homer knew no more of the laws of criticism than Ossian [...] Aristotle studied nature in Homer. Homer and Ossian both wrote from nature. Now wonder that among all the three, there should be such agreement and conformity' (Blair 111).

The most famous of the seventeenth-century quarrels is no doubt the dispute over Corneille's *Le Cid* in 1637, upon which the newly formed Académie française (1634) was called to judge as one of its first significant decisions. Taking exception to almost all of the aspects of *Le Cid*, Scudéry accuses the author, as well, of plagiarizing the Spanish tragedy by Guilhem de Castro, of which it is in fact an adaptation, something that, in itself, is not surprising. But Scudéry's claim is that 'almost all of its beauties are stolen ones' ['presques toutes les beautez sont desrobees' (Gasté 110)]. In spite of his great pains to list them all (they are not all convincing), the Académie ruled that the play was acceptable, and, in particular, that the 'plagiarisms' were not sanctionable on the grounds of 'significant enhancement': first, the 'translations' are not the only merit of the play, and Corneille had, in fact, added many of his own *pensées* (ideas) to his text; second, his enhancements were qualitatively superior: 'Apart from the fact that we notice that in very few of the imitated things has he stayed below the original, and that he has rendered some of them better than they were, we consider as well that he has added many ideas, which owe nothing to the first author' ['Car outre que nous remarquons qu'en bien peu des choses imitées il est demeuré au dessous de l'original, et qu'il en a rendu quelques-unes meilleures qu'elles n'estoient, nous trouvons encores qu'il y a adjousté beaucoup de pensées, qui ne cedent en rien à celles du premier Autheur' (Gasté 413)]. The notion of 'improvement' in the realm of translation is somewhat problematic, since the criteria for deciding between Spanish mediocrity and French superiority are not explicit and may be more chauvinistic than aesthetic. Nevertheless, the intention of the Académie is clear, and corresponds, not unsurprisingly, with the judgment already rendered by the French public upon the play's opening: original or copied, it was a great national masterpiece and popular hit. As one contributor to Corneille's defence claims,

> I have never read Aristotle, and I don't know the rules of theatre, but I judge the merit of plays according to the pleasure I get from them. This one has a charming *je-ne-sais-quoi* in its extraordinary events [...] I am not interested in knowing what is taken from the Spanish Author, or what is not, it is the entire Cid that I defend, and not Corneille; it matters little to me whether it is a translation or an invention; finally, I declare that it is a

very agreable play, whose ideas are extraordinary and spicy, and whose
action is sensitive and amusing.[8]

Despite the play's popular success, contributors to the debate were far
from unanimous on the issue of plagiarism, and much ink was spilled on
both sides of the question. One critic accuses Corneille outright of plagiarism: 'finally, after the confession that you have made, that the Cid has
already been made into a play, there can remain for you no other glory
than that of Plagiarist, and of producing childish rhymes after thirty years
of study. You say however that you are only being charged with sixty stolen
verses in a play of two thousand: those who have read the entire original,
affirm that there is not a word in your work which is not taken from the
Spanish.'[9] In his 'letter of apology' addressed to Scudéry, Corneille rejects
the charge of translation, as well as declaring simply false Scudéry's presumption of his dishonesty:

> You have attempted to pass me off as a simple Translator, under the shadow
> of seventy-two verses that you have marked out of a work of two thousand,
> and which those who know anything about it would never call merely trans-
> lations. You have berated me for having suppressed the name of the Span-
> ish author, even though it was only from me that you learned it and you
> know full well that I hid it from no one, and that I even gave a copy of the
> original in its own language to Mgr the Cardinal, your Master and mine. In
> the end, you have tried in one day to strip me of what it has taken me nearly
> thirty years of study to acquire.[10]

Not only does this dispute hinge on dishonesty, but the source is, as well, of
suspicious value, for we are at the height of the proscription against translation from the moderns, albeit foreign ones. Thus, Corneille's crime is
potentially multiple – choosing an inferior model; copying him 'servilely';
not announcing his model – any or all of which add up to transgressions of
the rules of good imitation.

Corneille's letter attacks Scudéry at his most vulnerable point as a
defender of the ancients, for he essentially accuses Scudéry of being a pedant worthy of Montaigne's most severe censure: someone who, lacking in
understanding, has a certain superficial knowledge gleaned from second-
hand sources, which he neither understands nor can apply correctly.
According to Corneille, Scudéry would consider that good poetry consisted merely in the proper application of rules regardless of the product:

> In order to make me appear ignorant, you have tried to impose on simple
> people, and you have advanced the maxims of theatre on your own author-

ity, maxims from which, even if they were true, you would not be able to draw the twisted conclusions that you have drawn; you have made yourself into Aristotle and other authors whom you have perhaps never read and could never understand, and of whom you don't have sufficient knowledge; you have acted as Moral Censor in order to impute bad examples to me; you have picked apart my verses to the point of accusing me of an absent caesura. If you had known the terms of the profession that you are presuming to criticize, you would have said that the line lacked a pause at the hemistiche.[11]

The Académie's disculpation of *Le Cid* is not without reservation, and in fact vindicates many of Scudéry's complaints while finding others of its own. The turning point for our purposes, and indeed for those of classical French letters, is its final word on the question, which literally throws out considerations of strict and necessary adherence to rules and finds, instead, virtue in the play's more spontaneous, natural, and emotional elements – the *je-ne-sais-quoi* that had so appealed to the play's audiences: 'Nevertheless, the naiveté and the vehemence of its passions, the force and the delicacy of many of its ideas, and the inexplicable pleasure that enhances all of its faults have acquired [for this play] an important place among the French poems of its type that have given the most satisfaction. If its author owes not all of his reputation to his merits, he does not, either, owe all of it to luck, and Nature has been sufficiently liberal with him to excuse Luck, if she has also been generous.'[12] The strongest argument against the accusation of plagiarism that the Académie could muster was the fact that Corneille, for all the faults of his play, was a great author, just as *Le Cid* was, however inexplicably, a masterpiece.

The development of theories of genius and originality throughout the eighteenth century entailed an explicit reversal of previous theories of imitation and of the legitimacy of influence. The shift from a poetics of imitation to a valorization of originality is exemplified by the loss of the connotation of 'discovery' in the term 'invention,' which came to commonly mean a kind of *ex nihilo* creation. Jacinthe Martel has traced through the seventeenth and eighteenth centuries the semantic shifts accompanying the growing importance of the imagination and the production of the 'new' and 'original,' which, as she points out, are 'nevertheless situated within the classical theory of imitation': 'From the time [throughout the eighteenth century] that aesthetic theories put into question the theory of imitation and, consequently, that it is recognized that the poet can find his subject within himself, the term "invention" (in its etymological and rhetorical meanings) is no longer sufficient, and gradually the term "creation" will gain in use until finally replacing that of "invention."'[13] The new aesthetics emphasized individual authorship, where authority was invested in the personality, genius, history, and expression of the poet. As Mortier says, 'the novelty brought about by the eighteenth century was the preference accorded to direct and immediate expression that was faithful and sincere to feelings and ideas. The fact of borrowing images, formal schemas, and existing structures will be considered as an infraction of that sincerity.'[14]

One notable instance of an accusation of plagiarism in mid-eighteenth-century England was the charge against Milton made by William Lauder, who was quickly exposed by John Douglas as having committed forgery. Lauder had produced two pamphlets, the first documenting Milton's imitation of the ancients, and the second, his modern sources, in which he charged Milton with being an 'unlicenced Plagiary.' Douglas exposed the forgery by showing that Lauder had simply falsified the evidence and had interpolated lines from Hog's contemporary Latin translation of Milton into the texts that he then cited as 'sources' for Milton (Douglas). Lauder was eventually persuaded to make a confession by Samuel Johnson, who had been sufficiently taken in by Lauder's claims to have produced a preface and postscript to his text. The brief controversy is interesting primarily for the terms used in the course of the accusation and defence. First, the charge of unacknowledged borrowings from moderns, as opposed to ancients, was deemed sufficiently dangerous (not perhaps by Johnson, but by Douglas) to warrant serious investigation. The revelation of the forgery by Douglas's painstaking tracking down of (false) sources did not diminish the gravity of the charge that Lauder was making against Milton. Douglas's denunciation of the fraud is accompanied by a defence in which he expresses some pertinent opinions on the matters of plagiarism and imitation. Although Douglas is able to show that Lauder's claims are largely false, when he cannot lay his hands on a particular source text, he has frequent recourse to the 'great authors don't plagiarize' defence: even if the charges were true, he reasons, an advocate for Milton might 'yet be able to defend the Genius and poetic Talents of his *favorite Author* to Advantage, that he may grant that he did borrow and yet show that this ought not to detract from his *Fame*; in a Word, that he may allow the Truth of *Lauder's* Charge, and yet deny the Consequences he seems to draw from it' (Douglas 7). Had Milton borrowed in the way Lauder charges, he would have done no more than Virgil. Douglas goes on to make the distinction between genius and originality, imitation and plagiarism: 'For as *one* may be what is called an *original Writer*, and yet have no Pretensions to *Genius*, so another may make use of the Labors of others in such a Manner as to satisfy the World of his own Abilities. There may be such a thing as an *original Work* without *Invention*, and a Writer may be an Imitator of others without

Plagiarism' (8). Douglas also subscribes to the right of genius to appropriate legitimately, by converting 'base metal into *Sterling Coin*': 'A *great Genius* looks upon himself as having a Right to convert to his own Use, and in order to furnish out a more perfect Entertainment, whatever has been already prepared and made ready' (9).

Douglas avails himself of the argument that whatever is already said is available to everyone, although in this he is somewhat misleading, as the domain of public property is more appropriately applied to ancient authors than to the moderns whom Lauder is accusing Milton of imitating. In any event, Douglas counters the charge of the concealment of sources by claiming that 'these Authors were already in the Hands of the World': 'The Books a Man reads, unavoidably give him a Turn of thinking correspondent to them, and the Sentiments he meets with there insensibly become his own; so that, in expressing his own Ideas, he naturally runs into Imitations of his favorite Authors' (21). Douglas also seems to subscribe to a notion of originality involving newness. Endowed with an 'uncommon Strength of *Fancy* and Extent of *Imagination*' (13), Milton is able to dispose and arrange borrowed elements 'as, out of them, to form a regularly digested Plan, which, however some of the Members of it, separately considered, may be borrowed, is as to the Composition of the *whole* entirely new' (13); 'One uniform Design, is a Proof of his Capacity, and makes the Plan an *Original, and his own,* altho' the separate Members of it be *Old, and borrowed*' (13–14). And in a remarkably modern move, Douglas even goes so far as to suggest that one can separate the Man and the Poet. On the charge that Milton deliberately concealed his sources, Douglas maintains: 'This is a Charge of some Consequence: But then, tho' it shou'd prove true, it affects only his moral Character, it may bring him in guilty of *Disingenuity*, but ought not to brand him with *Plagiarism*; it may lessen our Regard to the *Man*, but does not destroy his Reputation as a *Poet*' (14).

The incident is most significant for the vehemence with which Douglas defends Milton of a crime that he shows Milton never committed: in this sense, the argument reveals an interesting double standard. Milton was not a plagiary, and the accusation is severe enough to warrant contest; at the same time, even if Milton were a plagiary, he would still be a great genius.

The watershed moment in the eighteenth-century development of theories of originality is generally considered to be Edward Young's *Conjectures on Original Composition* (1759). In this text, which had a large impact in Germany and France, Young distinguishes between imitation and originality and promotes the second over the first, qualifying originality as the innate nature of man, rather than the acquired capacities that stifle that nature. His famous phrase 'Born *Originals,* how comes it to pass that we die *Copies?*' is supported by an argument that achieves an almost Borgesian tone – or else convicts Borges of unacknowleged borrowing: 'The medling Ape *Imitation*, as soon as we come to years of *Indiscretion* (so let me speak), snatches the Pen, and blots out nature's mark of Separation, cancels her kind intention, destroys all mental Individuality; the letter'd world no longer consists of Singulars, it is a Medly, a Mass; and a hundred books, at bottom, are but One' (24). He prefers originality over imitation but without venturing a precise definition of the terms of the originality in question: '*Imitations* are of two kinds; one of Nature, one of Authors: The first we call *Originals*, and confine the term *Imitation* to the second. I shall not enter into the curious enquiry of what is, or is not, strictly speaking, *Original*, content with what all must allow, that some Compositions are more so than others; and the more they are so, I say, the better' (7).

Among the qualities of the original is its 'vegetable nature,' its spontaneous growth from genius, whereas imitations 'are often a sort of *Manufacture* wrought up by those *Mechanics*, *Art*, and *Labour*, out of pre-existent materials not their own' (8–9). As both originals and imitations are subcategories of *imitation*, he does not proscribe imitation, particularly of the ancients, but reiterates advice already familiar from the ancients, Erasmus and Montaigne: 'Must we then, you say, not imitate antient Authors? Imitate them, by all means, but imitate aright. He that imitates the divine *Iliad* does not imitate *Homer*; but he who takes the same method, which *Homer* took, for arriving at a capacity of accomplishing a work so great [...] Imitate; but imitate not the *Composition* but the *Man*' (13). Young uses the term 'plagiarism' in his essay as the equivalent of 'theft': 'It is by a sort of noble Contagion, from a general familiarity with their Writings, and not by any particular sordid Theft, that we can be the better for those who went before us. Hope we, from Plagiarism, any Dominion in Literature; as that of *Rome* arose from a nest of Thieves?' (15). In the contest between learning and genius, Young declares himself firmly on the side of genius as the higher virtue: genius is compared to virtue and learning to riches; the second are seen to be compensations where the first are lacking (17): 'Learning we thank, genius we revere; That gives us pleasure, This gives us rapture; That informs; This inspires; and is itself inspired; for genius is from Heaven, Learning from man [...] Learning is borrowed knowledge; genius is knowledge innate, and quite our own' (21). The ultimate source of genius, and what distinguishes servile imitation from genuine talent and inspiration, is the sense of self-identity that must precede the productions of true authors: 'Thyself so reverence as to prefer the native growth of thy own mind to the richest import from abroad; such borrowed riches make us poor. The man who thus reverences himself, will soon find the world's reverence to follow his own' (30).

Mortier locates the merit of Young's text rather in the radical nature of the presentation than in the novelty of its ideas (80), and also claims that his argument in favour of individuality is more ethical than purely literary, such that it depends on the Rousseauist dichotomy between the individualizing condition of nature and the uniformizing force of society and education. Mortier concludes: 'Originality assumes here an almost existential character; it becomes confused with *authenticity*. To imitate is to be inauthentic, false, dissembling.'[15]

In fact, the terms of the eighteenth-century notion of the author are significantly similar to Minnis's description of the medieval *auctor* but applied to the human agent: his writings must embody intrinsic worth, and, moreover, they must be 'authentic'; that is, they must have emanated from the genius of a great man. Authorship retains, in the eighteenth century, both the connotations of authority recast in the form of personal genius and inspiration, and the connotations of authenticity, born of the sincerity of expression of the individual and of the intimate connection between product and producer.

The pre-eminence of the writing subject that Montaigne was striving to establish, a double movement in which 'I am therefore I write' coincides with 'I write therefore I am,' was solidly achieved, at least in theory, by the nineteenth century. Which is not to say, of course, that authors in this century neither imitated nor plagiarized: Lamartine, Coleridge, Stendhal, and Dumas are only a few of the notorious 'plagiarists' of which the century of originality is particularly full. What was officially different, however, was the source of authorship and authority. The Romantic poet was the sole source and origin of his discourse, and his authority lay simply in the authenticity of his being and his expression: no recourse to prior models, tradition, or heritage was required to justify and validate his claim to authorship.

By the nineteenth century, 'originality' had acquired the additional meaning of 'new,' in the sense that an individual writer's genius was particular to him: he is his own origin and, as a consequence, his works originate solely with him. The nineteenth-century *Larousse* (1873) negotiates a delicate path between *imitation*, 'the most fertile source of literature,' which 'is also its scourge' ['la source la plus féconde de la littérature,' which 'en est aussi le fléau' (582)], and *originality*, the 'master quality, that which makes the great writer and the great poet' ['la qualité maîtresse, celle qui fait le grand écrivain et le grand poète' (1471)]. In the article on *originalité*, the author is careful to distinguish between the bizarre, the extravagant, on the one hand, and the quality of 'true originality,' on the other, which can be expressed either in new conceptions or new forms, and which is most often characterized by the capacity of the author to become a 'model' for the less original who follow in his footsteps. The article sets up degrees or types of originality in the history of letters: there are those most interested in beauty and in improving on the models provided by original geniuses, a category that includes Virgil, Cicero, Quintillian, Dryden, Racine, and Lamartine; on the other hand, there are original geniuses more concerned with novelty (*nouveauté*): Lucrece, Dante, Rabelais, Shakespeare, and Hugo. Originality can be excessive and fall into abuse if the end is simply novelty, without concern for beauty, and if the writer be not gifted. The source of originality is without doubt the *person* of the artist, variously described as his 'physionomy' or his 'character.' 'Plagiarism' characterizes 'imitation' pushed to its extreme, without benefit of talent – in this context, it becomes an aesthetic, rather than a moral category, affecting works that demonstrate servility with respect to their models, but without overtones of ethical impropriety. Plagiarism is indeed failed authorship, the ultimate absence of originality: 'Some powerful geniuses create or discover; after them, their eyes fixed on these works of art, minds of a lesser genius create similar works, still original in some respect and which are not *imitations*, but for which the authors would not have had the idea without their predecessors. After these, *imitation* becomes servile and falls from degree to degree into plagiarism.'[16]

The article considers imitation to be a necessity imposed by the limited range of human ideas; therefore, it is incumbent on the author to imitate without losing his own originality. Just as there are degrees of originality, so there are degrees of imitation. Predictably, the nineteenth century represents the apogée of originality, first, because of the capacity of modern writers to retain their own individuality, and, second, because of the Romantic preference for literary models originating in national literatures that had 'suffered less from classical influence,' such as the English, German, and Spanish. The nineteenth-century *Larousse* describes the shift in aesthetic values as being nothing short of a revolution: 'The nineteenth century has renewed everything. First, it has proscribed as plagiarism what in the previous three centuries was considered to be a legitimate imitation, a happy theft' ['Le XIXe siècle a tout renouvelé. D'abord, il a proscrit, comme plagiat, ce qui dans les trois siècles précédents n'était regardé que comme une imitation licite, un heureux larcin' ('Originalité' 1471)].

The 'scourge of imitation' (*le fléau de l'imitation*) that was plagiarism was certainly well represented in this most 'original' of literary periods. The epitome in English letters is no doubt Samuel Taylor Coleridge, whose massive imitations, unacknowledged translations, and direct and indirect paraphrase from his German sources were discovered and published shortly after his death by such as Thomas de Quincey and J.E. Ferriar and have been a constant source of dispute ever since. Notably in his *Biographia Literaria*, but also in his poetic productions, Coleridge's compulsive 'divine ventriloquism' has been amply documented and contested. A most forthright attack was launched by Norman Fruman in *Coleridge: The Damaged Archangel* (1971) and the borrowings, called 'plagiarisms,' have been meticulously and objectively documented in Engell and Bate's 1983 edition of the *Collected Works*.[17] More recently, Thomas Mallon has summarized the significant issues. While Fruman's version has not gone uncontested, he clearly recognizes the tenacity of the 'great authors don't plagiarize' theory: 'That most scholars still maintain that Coleridge has no deliberate wish to deny his intellectual obligations to Schelling is surely one of the marvels of literary history' (105).

Both Geoffrey Hartman (1972) and Christopher Ricks (1972) have refuted Fruman's charges by operating an inversion of the 'great authors don't plagiarize' theory, ascribing Coleridge's 'method' to a generalized Romantic agony of influence. Fruman's response to both is to argue, on the one hand, that 'plagiarism' is certainly not limited to the Romantic period, and, on the other, that it is not universally manifested by Romantic writers, who presumably would all have laboured equally under the aesthetic conditions to which Hartman and Ricks attribute Coleridge's plagiarisms.[18]

Most significant and determining, for Fruman, is Coleridge's 'own desperately driven and insecure nature' ('Originality, Plagiarism, Forgery, and Romanticism' 48). Without offering a systematic psychobiographical account of the motivations for this plagiarism, Fruman certainly emphasizes this explanation in his accounts of Coleridge's distressed, fatherless childhood; his crushing 'intellectual self-doubt'; and even his repressed homosexuality. Verging on insanity (for which he was 'officially' discharged from the army) and suffering under his opium addiction, Coleridge was no match for that 'fateful confrontation between a tormented genius, helpless in the grip of overmastering impulses, and the abounding literary riches of eighteenth-century Germany' (*Coleridge* 420). Mallon, who clearly appreciates Fruman's efforts, calls them, no doubt correctly, 'the most wounding and sustained assault ever made on that writer's reputation' (30), and they have indeed generated controversy. Fruman's attack seems largely moral: he does not qualify his judgment of Coleridge as a 'genius,' and admits the incontrovertible fact that his name is now indissolubly linked to the theories that he propounded. Coleridge's reputation is now independent of his 'intent,' which Fruman clearly believes to be of a guilty kind:

> Yet his intent is irrelevant in evaluating his credentials to a place among the important thinkers of his generation, let alone of history. Is it possible to believe that Coleridge had independently arrived at all the ideas in [his] many works? [...] Not even he claimed that. In practically every instance he

simply put forward concepts and theories as his own without reference to sources outside his own private meditations. In every instance, with the exception of Schlegel, coincidence of ideas was not discovered until after his death, and in some instances not until recent years. As a result, many influential formulations have become attached, perhaps irrevocably, to his name. (*Coleridge* 71)

In their introduction to their edition, Engell and Jackson Bate reassert this irrevocable attachment. After citing George Saintsbury's *History of Criticism* (1902–4) – 'So, then, there abide these three, Aristotle, Longinus, and Coleridge' (xli) – the editors go on to claim the abiding interest, even into the 'postmodern' age, of the *Biographia Literaria*:

> This is a strong compliment that we pay to few critics aside from Aristotle, Johnson, and Goethe, and it illustrates the hold that Coleridge has on the literary conscience. Our knowledge of Coleridge's life and character brings him even closer to ourselves. We do not assume we are consulting the Delphic Oracle. Instead we repeatedly experience the surprise that someone so near us in time, someone as flawed as the rest of us, should prove so clairvoyant and put so memorably the insights that seem to tumble from him. Nor can we forget in reading the *Biographia* that it was written by a poet, one of the greatest poets of the last three centuries. (Coleridge xlii–xliii)

Even though one might suspect that Coleridge was, possibly, rather more flawed than the rest of us, his poetic authority remains intact: it is significant that, even today, the attack against his authority is launched in terms of his authenticity. The defence does not reject the notion of authenticity, but judges this to be of a poetic, rather than a personal or ethical type. His importance, as both a poet and a literary theorist, is quite independent of both his literary method and his literary intentions. In particular, the imperviousness of his reputation as a great poet and genius to ongoing revelations about his unacknowledged intellectual debts is a remarkable testimony to the strength of the 'great author' phenomenon.

Where is the notion of authorship situated in the twentieth century? If the criterion of the great soul emitting inspired and universal truths can no longer be considered a fundamental attribute of contemporary authorship (although the testimony to Coleridge by Engell and Jackson Bate cited above may do something to counteract this claim), this is largely in the literary field, as plagiarism in other fields is still an ethical breach that is fundamentally linked to the writer's personal authority and authenticity. The controversy surrounding Martin Luther King, Jr's alleged plagiarisms in his doctoral thesis is testimony to the fact that either great men don't plagiarize, or else plagiarists aren't great men (see chapter 7). And Fruman remarks that in a contemporary context, where the 'word "plagiarism" itself is vaguely discredited' (*Coleridge* 70): 'The worst that Coleridge can be burdened with is failing to make a certain number of formal acknowledgments. This may disturb our ethical view of him, but it does not affect the profundity and originality of his achievement. To view the problem in such a way, however, requires us to believe that Coleridge was sincere in claiming these ideas as his own. Inevitably the question of his veracity and general trustworthiness is raised' (70). Although he raises the question, Fruman never achieves the wholesale debunking of Coleridge's 'genius' that is clearly tempting him.

A minor strain in twentieth-century literary criticism, devoted explicitly or implicitly to defending the ethical value of letters, maintains that, independently of legal sanction, plagiarism is a crime against the 'dignity' of the literary profession. Such is H.M. Paull's argument in *Literary Ethics*: 'Let those who plead that no offence has been committed ask themselves how they would like their own original work to be misappropriated by a rival author. The profession of literature is a high one, and it behoves its members to maintain its high estate by straightforward dealing, the outcome of a sensitive literary conscience' (130). More recently, historian Peter Shaw, in a brief overview of such plagiarists as Coleridge, Baudelaire, Poe, and De Quincey, among others, concludes with the same ethical concerns as Paull:

> At all times, to belittle a breach of professional ethics is to belittle one's profession itself. But in a period such as the present, when there is considerable doubt about the importance and dignity of humane letters, the refusal to render judgment has particularly unfortunate results. Today it is difficult to imagine a plagiaristic act, or indeed any other breach of literary ethics, that would go undefended. It hardly seems an accident that along with this particular devolution, literature, in general, went from a postition where it could claim for itself the highest morality to one in which many are claiming that it is no more than a marginal entertainment. (336)

Although the argument has shifted from the nobility of the literary author to that of the profession, the relationship is clear. And the notion that great authors (as opposed to great men) don't plagiarize survives today in the discourse of literary criticism, such as in Bloom's *Anxiety*, which is an attempt to confront in the works of these believers in individual authorship what previous generations had always known and explicitly practised: that originality is impossible, and that genius may in fact be a flair for creative imitation.

The three founding principles of authorship – authority, authenticity, and originality – can still be seen to be operative, even in this age of 'post-authorship.' In the judicial realm, authenticity and originality are corollary values: originality is the necessary quality of the authentic product of the person (author) having produced the work. And the relative authority of contesting authors may still influence the ability of the court to find in favour of the victim, who is usually the lesser of two lights. In the aesthetic field, originality and authenticity coexist as two parallel but possibly independent values: the virtue of novelty and the virtue of authentic self-expression may coincide, or may be generic indicators, applied in different contexts.

During the middle years of the twentieth century, at a time when when the structuralist execution of the author left academic literary criticism with an intentional vacuum, the question of authorship appeared retrograde; in particular, the intimate relation between the producer and the product was not only incidental to the understanding or the value of the work, but irrelevant to 'textuality' as an object of analysis. But in many cases it was apparent that the 'disappearance' of the author was essentially an ideological move that forced the critic to displace presuppositions of intentionality onto other realms, most notably the text (structuralism) or the reader (reception theory): 'It appears, however, that this concept [*écriture*], as currently employed, has merely transposed the empirical characteristics of an author to a transcendental anonymity. The extremely visible signs of the author's empirical activity are effaced to allow the play, in parallel or opposition, of religious and critical modes of characterization. In granting a primordial status to writing, do we not, in effect, simply reinscribe in transcendental terms the theological affirmation of its sacred origin or a critical belief in its creative nature?' (Foucault, 'What Is an Author?' 119–20).

In later poststructuralist formulations, Foucault's question 'What matters who is speaking?' has become a catchword for literary studies, especially those that turn their attention to literatures originating from traditionally marginalized or 'unauthorized' groups. The notion of the expression of authenticity in 'voice' has gained currency and inspired recent controversies over the misappropriation of cultural experience: authorship and authenticity have been resurrected through communities of identity. 'Appropriating voice' across cultural, gender, or other community boundaries raises significant questions of the role of authenticity as a guarantor of authority in contemporary authorship. In feminist, postcolonial, and gender studies, the debate pits the authorizing authenticity of personal experience against the dangers of the essentialism that authority based on gender, race, or culture and sexuality seems to imply.[19]

The individual writer's voice is also undergoing a renaissance in the form of new autobiographical modes of fiction. Paul Smith (1988) has identified this feature in Roland Barthes's later work. And the literary expression of personal subjectivity is being revisited by writers as disparate as the former French *nouveaux romanciers* and contemporary new feminist writers. This rebirth of authorial subjectivity is accompanied by an apparently contradictory resurgence in practices of imitation and recycling that characterize many postmodern productions. The coincidence of these two modes – on one hand, a kind of nouveau-romantic return to expressivity and, on the other, a sort of neoclassical aesthetic of imitation – could be seen to produce a new Renaissance aesthetic where the personal subjectivity of authorship, challenged by its structuralist erasure, is finding expression in the appropriation of the expression of the Other.

Barthes and Foucault discovered authorship to be a modern concept, produced by the growing value of the individual. As Barthes claims, 'the author is a modern figure, a product of our society insofar as, emerging from the Middle Ages with English empiricism, French rationalism and the personal faith of the Reformation, it discovered the prestige of the individual, of, as it is more nobly put, the "human person" [...] The *explanation* of a work is always sought in the man or woman who produced it, as if it were always in the end, through the more or less transparent allegory of the fiction, the voice of a single person, the *author*, "confiding" in us' (142–3).

Nevertheless, when Barthes, and literary history after him, consecrate the modernity and consequently the fragility and historical contingency of the 'author,' what is being pointed out is perhaps a somewhat tautologous truism: Barthes might have said, more properly but less aphoristically, that 'the *modern* author is a modern personage' in the sense that the author he is describing is the product of a slow historical evolution that 'our society' underwent from the Middle Ages through to the Enlightenment. The notion of the individual 'author' that emerged, and that Barthes and others take to be the one which died – or was put to death – at the end of the 1960s, is only a moment in that evolution, hypostasized as its final – or essential – form. In contradistinction to the particular author that Barthes sees as having died, the function of *authorship* is a historical constant that refers to the capacity of particular writers, or perhaps designated communities of writers in historical contexts, to appropriate the attributes of authority, authenticity, and originality – a capacity that varies and is displaced over time. What appears invariable is that this appropriation is fundamental in all contexts for the determination of authorship. Whether invested in the authority of the ancients or the Church Fathers, or reappropriated by avant-garde revolutionaries such as Montaigne and Kathy Acker, the original and authentic expression of authority has always characterized the 'author.'

I define 'authorship,' provisionally and primarily, as the attribution of a particular set of authorial functions to the agent of discourse. Although many of these functions are historically sensitive, some appear to have a certain transhistorical stability, and it is these that interest me specifically. The attribution of these features to the writer-as-author predicts nothing about the actual system of beliefs or intentions of the authorial agent; these features are purely analytical, deriving from critical or authorial discourse about the practice of authorship. We have seen that the author is always granted authority, originality, and/or authenticity, but that the content of these attributes is the object of changing meanings and values. But beyond these attributes, which could as well be features of the work, are others that accrue more specifically to the function of the authorial figure. Among the supposed attributes of authorship that enjoy a certain stability are, first, the presence of a degree of self-consciousness concerning the role of authorship; second, the notion of the construction of identity through discourse; and, third, the notion of the appropriation of the authority-to-speak.

Self-consciousness, here, is the presupposition that the speaking position entails the responsibility of assuming the ideas expressed as the writer's own, irrespective of their general or specific dissemination; authorship appears to entail less an *originating* moment than an *appropriative* one, in which the author is seen to espouse the ideas expressed through an intentional act of transmission, imitation, transformation, or innovation. While this notion of 'self-consciousness' might seem problematic for pre-Enlightenment authorship, and particularly for societies dominated by ecclesiastical notions of authority, it is not intended as a psychoanalytical category but rather as a category of agency that in fact sets a minimal limit on the function of authorship. The denial of authorship implied in the status of scribe or compiler is simultaneously a denial of responsibility for the ideas expressed; we have seen the play of the attribution of authorial self-consciousness in Minnis's analysis of Chaucer, whom he understands as being a 'true author' intentionally attempting to deny his authorship by his self-proclaimed status as compiler, translator, or scribe. And, in the same way that medieval writers were not granted the kind of authority required to achieve the status of authorship, Latin and Greek literary writers proclaimed it.

The *construction of identity* refers less to the personal or individual nature of authorship than to the qualities of authenticity and originality that are attributed to the relationship between the putative author (be he God) and his work: the attribution of a discursively constructed identity to the author implies that this *identity* is not natural or essential, but can be and is formed through discourse, an insight that is thoroughly pre-modern and only appears modern or postmodern in the light of Romantic presuppositions about the individuality of identity, themselves entailing the forgetting of prior modes of the communal and discursive formation of identities. The notion that identity is constructed through discourse is clear for literary authorship since the Romantic period; in pre-Romantic eras, it can be deduced through experiments such as Montaigne's, and through the prescriptions in favour of the expression of individual authorial identity in the rhetorical lessons of Cicero and Erasmus.

The *authority-to-speak* is also a classical concept, based on the notion of *auctoritas*. It is that which medieval writers, for example, explicitly claim to lack; in the context of the scholastic world, it is precisely this negative claim that allows them to speak; it is also that which Montaigne proclaims, all the while hiding behind translation, imitation, and unacknowledged translation of legitimate authorites. The presupposition of the authority-to-speak exists today in the assumptions that have been uncovered by feminist and post-colonial analyses of marginalized discourses, which point out that authorship is still a privilege that must be acquired (constructed, earned, or appropriated), even in the postmodern, 'post-authorial' context.

The Author is alive and well in contemporary aesthetics, as well as in contemporary literary theory and criticism, surviving as a network of functions that, if one abstracts the historically brief – and illusory – moment of the Romantic fetishization of 'original genius,' are not remarkably different from those traditionally attributed to authorship. At one end of the literary-historical spectrum, the existence of accusations of plagiarism guarantees the presence of the 'author' during those benighted historical times for which contemporary literary history has proposed his not-yet-being. At the other end of the same spectrum, the real death of the author would entail the disappearance of plagiarism that is posited on individual authorship and a proprietary relationship over one's discursive productions. That this death has not yet occurred is a matter of daily experience. But the disappearance of plagiarism is precisely what is predicated, in a contestatory mode, by certain postmodern practices of appropriation that verge on, or intentionally enact 'plagiarism.' The transgressive nature of these practices, and their brushes with legal sanctions for copyright infringement, are sufficient indication that the 'dead author' is a very circumscribed kind of author who is limited to the *biographical individual taken to be an interpretive authority for uncovering the true meaning of the text.* The theoretical impact of this limited death notwithstanding, the reality of contemporary accusations of plagiarism attests to the durability of the attributes of the author: especially to the authority, authenticity, and originality that define authorship both as a privilege and as a transhistorical function.

3. Owning Discourse

Paulus purchases poetry, Paulus recites the poetry as his. For what you purchase you may rightly call your own.

Martial, *Epigrams*, Bk II, xx

PROPRIETY

As plagiarism is predicated on authorship, so does it presuppose ownership. Borges, Barthes, Foucault, structuralism and its 'post,' Ralph Federman, Sherrie Levine, and Kathy Acker notwithstanding, we do not yet inhabit the satirically parallel world of Tlön, where, as Borges tells us; 'in literary matters too, the dominant notion is that everything is the work of one single author. Books are rarely signed. The concept of plagiarism does not exist; it has been established that all books are the work of one single writer, who is timeless and anonymous. Criticism is prone to invent authors. A critic will choose two dissimilar works – the *Tao Te Ching* and the *1001 Nights*, let us say – and attribute them to the same writer and then with all probity explore the psychology of the interesting *homme de lettres* ...' (28).

Although the original plagiarism is no doubt as old and as undiscoverable as the original literature, evidence from as far back as classical Greece indicates that 'literary theft' was both practised and decried. While there is no evidence that there was any mechanism for the legal protection of literary property in Greece, literary clues such as Aesop's fable of the jay masquerading in the peacock's feathers, and accusations of unethical pilfering in Aristophanes' *The Frogs*, attest to the fact that some forms of copying and imitation were often condemned or at least ridiculed. Putnam claims that plagiarism was very general, and while it 'called forth a certain amount of criticism and raillery, especially when the author appropriated from was still living, it did not bring upon the "appropriators" any such final condemnation as would cause them to lose caste in the literary guild or to forfeit the appreciation of the reading public' (73).

At the same time, Putnam provides evidence of the existence of proprietory attitudes about intellectual production, even in the absence of formal protection, as well as of the advantages of prestige attached to authorship. He cites the example of a fragment of the lyric poet Theognis (583–500 B.C.): 'Theognis says he has hit on a device which will prevent his verses from being appropriated by any one else. He will put his name on them as a seal (or trade-mark) and then no one will take inferior work for his when the good is to be had, but every one will say "These are the verses of Theognis the Megarian"' (61–2).

While the concerns expressed by Theognis the 'author' in this fragment are clearly symbolic rather than economic ('inferior work' versus 'the good'), a concept of authorship, and consequently of ownership, is clearly at play: 'These are the verses of Theognis the Megarian.'

Although the evidence for a structure of authorship entailing the possibility of plagiarism in classical Greece is, according to Putnam, not overwhelming, a brief reference to classical Rome is helpful in distinguishing between 'plagiarism' and 'copyright,' especially since the French civil law tradition, in defining the object of author's rights in the wake of the French Revolution, depended heavily on Roman jurisprudence. Roman law, while having no notion of the legal protection of literary property as we understand it, did protect unpublished manuscripts as the property of authors, the rights to which were surrendered once the work was made public.

The word 'plagiarism' has its origins in the second century B.C.: they are found in *plagium*, the Latin word for 'kidnapping,' deriving from the Greek meaning 'oblique.' The crime of kidnapping was a *détournement*, or abduction; the perpetrator of such a crime was a *plagiarius*. The victim of the kidnapping is of some import here: the *Oxford English Dictionary* defines a 'plagiary' as one who abducts the 'child or slave of another,' while the *Dictionnaire étymologique du français* (Robert) defines it as one who carries off and retains slaves owned by another. Older sources, such as the nineteenth-century *Larousse* (1866–70), claim that the term was applied to the capturing and selling of free men into slavery; Diderot's *Encyclopédie* (1777) cites all three, as does Putnam (203). No doubt all of these cases were properly termed *plagium*, a crime that derived its name from the punishment it merited, that is, to be condemned *ad plagia* – to the whip – under the *lex de plagiariis* instituted by Q. Fabius Verrucosus in 209 B.C. (Fiske 27). An examination of the different infractions implied by the Latin meanings of the term yields a clear indication of the ambiguities with which the act of plagiarism was fraught from the very beginning: selling a free man into slavery, kidnapping someone's child (son), and usurping a slave are all instances of improper appropriation, but what is being appropriated in each instance stands in a different relationship to the notion of property.

The poet Martial (A.D. 40–104) was the first to use the term in its literary sense, to condemn another poet whom he accused of passing off in a public reading Martial's poems as his own. Martial seems to have been plagued by plagiarists, and pens many epigrams not only to a certain Fidentinus, but to others, named and unnamed, whom he accuses of the theft of his works. The terms of accusation are usually framed in the proprietary opposition between 'mine' and 'yours': 'That book you recite, O Fidentinus, is mine. But your vile recitation begins to make it your own' (Martial Bk I, xxxviii). This opposition is joined with the accusation of theft: 'There is one page of yours, Fidentinus, in a book of mine – a page, too, stamped by the distinct likeness of its master – which convicts your poems of palpable theft' (Bk I, liii). The relation between the author and his works is couched in terms of master and slave even in the absence of the plagiarism metaphor: 'mutare *dominum* non potest liber notus' (Bk I, lxvi; in Ker's translation: 'A well-known book cannot change its *author,*' the metaphor 'master' for 'author' is lost).[1] Martial mobilizes a variety of other metaphors to condemn both purloined passages and plagiarists: the first are compared to 'crocks [that] degrade crystal glass' and to 'a black raven [...] laughed at among Leda's swans' (Bk I, liii); plagiarists try to 'herd foxes with lions, and to make owls like eagles' (Bk X, c). The plagiarist is compared to the philandering, or perhaps cuckolded, husband: 'Do you ask how it comes that Philinus, who never sleeps with his wife, is yet a father? Gaditanus must answer that, Avitus: he writes nothing, and yet he is "a poet"' (Bk X, cii).

The use of the term *plagiarius* to describe the theft of his literary production is, for Martial, just one metaphor among many; its importance for us is that it has stuck. The epigram in which it appears is an extended metaphor wherein the slave-poems have been pressed into 'grievous servitude' by another, after having been set free by their rightful owner, Martial, who calls upon the patron of the offending poet to intervene on behalf of the poems and restore their freedom. Martial appeals to this patron to proclaim publicly the situation in order to 'shame the plagiarist': *inpones plagiario pudorem:* 'To your charge I entrust, Quintianus, my works – if, after all, I can call those mine which that poet of yours recites. If they complain of their grievous servitude, come forward as their champion and give bail for them; and when that fellow calls himself their owner [*dominum*], say that they are mine, sent forth from my hand [= *manumitere*: to free a slave]. If thrice and four times you shout this, you will shame the plagiarist' (Bk I, lii).

Martial's activation of the slave-thief meaning as a metaphor for the theft of his poetry is a double complaint: the property was originally his, thus its appropriation is a potential theft, but he has set it free, such that its new owner is both a thief and a fraud. This double meaning is useful in pointing out that, when subjected to a contemporary reading, none of the alleged 'property' stolen is genuinely, that is, ethically, the property of either owner. From the point of view of a culture that has officially renounced the ownership of people, the question of the misappropriation of slaves is one to be determined among thieves, the putative owner having no more ethical claim than the usurping one. It is curious to note that the ancient etymology evokes a parallel with some contemporary attitudes towards the notion of discursive property, attitudes that enable some literary theorists, if not copyright lawyers, to suggest that, in fact, individuals have no proprietorship over language that they do not really produce, but of which they are an 'effect': individuals are born into language that is determining of the notion of subject 'because it is a self-contained system which predates any subject and must be assumed by each subject individually' (Grosz 99).[2] Two competing values are thus put into play: on the one hand, language is a common good in continuous circulation and cannot be owned; on the other hand, 'to write is to make language one's own' ['écrire, c'est faire sien le langage' (Schneider 37)]. Language is infinitely appropriable, the 'public domain' *par excellence*, but language once appropriated becomes 'discourse,' which is somehow stamped with the personality of its producer or author. If discourse is subject to social and legal property rights, it is caught up in humanist assumptions about priority, creativity, identity, origins, originality, and individuality, upon which the definition of intellectual property is based. Either individual subjects are creative originators of discourse in their own right, or they are not; either they produce discourse or discourse produces them. It is easy to see that the judicial and certain philosophical or aesthetic factions are, these days, radically opposed on this front. It is in this sense that the Latin etymology is revealing: what – or whom – does one own when one owns a slave?

As well, the ethical question is complicated by the judicial one. Whereas for us there may be no *ethical* grounds for slavery, where slaves constitute property the question is a purely *legal* one. The relationship between the perception of what is unethical and what actually counts as illegal is never simple, such that there may appear to be a disjunction between the letter of the law and the ethics of the practices it sets out to regulate. In the context of contemporary appropriative art, for example, it has been argued that the threat of copyright infringement limits the freedom of expression of artists by restricting their access to the use of copyrighted images and trademarks that they would employ as cultural icons to effect ideological criticism of contemporary society (Carlin). As well, legal restrictions to the terms of copyright may fail to satisfy the ethical demands of persons who feel that a cultural patrimony has been unethically exploited but who have no recourse through copyright law. And in the face of the present prolifer- ation of electronic means of producing, transmitting, reproducing, and 'appropriating' cultural artefacts, the problem of the legal protection of intellectual property is quickly becoming a debate about the cultural rele- vance of copyright conceptions based on outmoded forms of the creation and transmission of intellectual property.

The metaphor of the theft or enslavement of a child (*son*) is also an appropriate description of the perversion of the proper transmission of the 'true' literary heritage that in the Western literary imagination traditionally follows a patriarchal lineage, albeit complicated by Oedipus. This tradition sees a patriarchal form of legitimation in literary descent: the transfer of authority and ownership from father to son activates the stealing-of-the- child meaning of the original 'plagiarism.' In distinguishing between Latin theories of translation and imitation, Rita Copeland situates the theory of imitation in the patriarchal mode, as opposed to the notion of conquest that informed the practice of translation:

> Imitation was figured in metonymic terms, as a patriarchal pattern of trans- mission within the same culture through kinship and legacy, through prox- imity or contiguity rather than through difference. The relationship between model and copy is syntagmatic. The differences that intervene between the two are the products of inventional force, without which imita- tion is a barren act, for 'nothing grows from imitation alone' as Quintilian says [*Institutio oratoria* 10.2.9]. The relationship between model and copy, like the relationship of lineage, is predicated on the act of invention: the model, or ancestor, posits the grounds for future invention. But invention here also creates an interpretive community, and the impulse to rival the model exercises itself within the larger framework of consanguinity and hence continuity. (Copeland 17)

Harold Bloom, in his anxiety about influence, does not neglect to recall the myth of patrilinear genealogy: 'We remember how for so many centu- ries, from the sons of Homer to the sons of Ben Jonson, poetic influence had been described as a filial relationship' (26). According to Bloom, how- ever, the filial metaphor is transformed into one of *influence* in the eigh- teenth century, when 'filial loyalty between poets had given way to the labyrinthine affections of what Freud's wit first termed the "family romance"' (27). When one considers the Oedipal implications of the Freudian family romance, which become explicit in the course of Bloom's essay, and the priority given to the father and son subject positions within the labyrinthine relations governing the quest for the mother-object, one is hardly far removed from the logic of patrilineage. In Schneider's more psychoanalytical version of plagiarism as an Oedipal problem, the theory of masculine genealogy is also expressed: 'Like quotation, plagiarism is taking from the other without asking his permission, except that in plagiarism, one remains in a kind of pre-Oedipal violence, inside of a fusional or a dual relation. The erasure of the proper name of the author indicates a badly addressed Oedipal conflict and a return to the pre-Oedipal. The name of the father has not occurred. The question of the father is probably one of the essential aspects of the psychology of the plagiarist. Absence of the father, falsified filiations, writers subject to plagiarism [...] have often, hidden in their history, a problematic relationship to the father.'[3] The notion that problematic relationships to the father – whether understood in terms of individual psychology or literary influence – produce significant literary effects is sufficient testimony to the continuing pertinence of the filial metaphor for the transmission of literary legitimacy.

The dubious relationships between property and ownership revealed in the etymology of plagiarism suit our contemporary aesthetic because of the theoretical loss of the individual author's claim to ownership of discourse, making literary productions no longer slaves or offspring, but more properly 'freemen,' over whom no one can properly claim ownership. And yet, is this contemporary notion of the free nature of discourse really new? It is commonly and not unreasonably believed that modern plagiarism is a product of the development of copyright laws that depend, in turn, on the rise of individualism and capitalism in Enlightenment Europe. But this socio-economic model is not entirely satisfactory, as it does not explain, as we have suggested, the almost continuous existence of plagiarism as at least a breach of ethics since ancient times.

Again, recourse to Martial is helpful in pointing out that he, at least, understands clearly the role of the author as (economic) proprietor of his works, which, nonetheless, enjoy a symbolic value greater than their economic one. Many satirical epigrams condemn the habit of 'borrowing verses' when they could be bought, or else of copying published books: 'You mistake, you greedy thief of my works, who think you can become a poet at no more than the cost of a transcript and a cheap papyrus roll. Applause is not acquired for six or ten sesterces' (Bk I, lxvi). In other words, while theft is to be condemned, it does not procure a literary reputation. But Martial's complaints do not stop at this legal distinction, whereby an unpublished manuscript was protected as property, and a published one was set free into the world. Charging Fidentinus with reciting his works, he distinguishes between giving Fidentinus his works for free, providing they remain Martial's, and requiring Fidentinus to buy his rights to the work (Bk I, xxix); on other occasions he advises one who would 'borrow' a book of his epigrams, rather to go down to the bookseller and procure one for money (Bk I, cxvii; Bk IV, lxxii).

Latin evidence for the existence of plagiarism is not limited to Martial: Welslau has pointed us to the introduction to Book 7 of Vitruvius' *Ten Books on Architecture* (first century B.C.), where the author defends himself against the suspicion of plagiarism and the unacknowledged use of other's work. Here, as in Renaissance Europe, the absence of the word 'plagiarism' does not indicate an absence of the crime: 'those [...] deserve our reproaches, who steal the writings of such men and publish them as their own; and those also, who depend in their writings, not on their own ideas, but who enviously do wrong to the works of others and boast of it, deserve not merely to be blamed, but to be sentenced to actual punishment for their wicked course of life. With the ancients, however, it is said that such things did not pass without pretty strict chastisement. What the results of their judgments were, it may not be out of place to set forth as they are transmitted to us' (Vitruvius 195). The anecdote that follows describes a literary contest sponsored by Ptolemy in which one Aristophanes was invited to be a judge. The six other judges concurred in awarding the first and second prize to the poets who 'had most pleased the multitude' (196), while Aristophanes reserved his vote for the least popular poet, declaring – and proving by recourse to 'a vast number of volumes brought out from bookcases which he specified' (197) – that the compositions of the other poets were thefts: 'So the king gave orders that they should be accused of theft, and after condemnation sent them off in disgrace' (197). The pertinence of the story to Vitruvius' work is to introduce his own method:

> But for my part, Caesar, I am not bringing forward the present treatise after changing the titles of other men's books and inserting my own name [...] On the contrary, I express unlimited thanks to all the authors that have in the past, by compiling from antiquity remarkable instances of the skill shown by genius, provided us with abundant materials of different kinds. Drawing from them as it were water from springs, and converting them to our own purposes, we find our powers of writing rendered more fluent and easy, and, relying upon such authorities, we venture to produce new systems of instruction. (197–8)

There follow acknowledgments to an impressive number of sources.

To what extent such protestations of intellectual honesty and disapproval of 'plagiarism' are real indicators of a state of affairs is impossible to say. Were Martial, Vitruvius, and others whom we have not cited eccentric exceptions in an economy where 'copying' was rife and acceptable? Or was the kind of copying that they censure itself exceptional, limited to a few isolated instances, and exploited more for rhetorical than for truly ethical or economic ends? Whatever the answer to these questions, accusations of plagiarism point to the belief on the part of (certain) writers that, whether common or exceptional, condoned or condemned, appropriating another's discourse is theft. And where there is theft, there is property.

PUBLIC VERSUS PRIVATE PROPERTY

The notion of property, in contemporary copyright law as in the course of its development, is divided into the two realms of 'private' and 'public.' Copyright deals only with instances of the first kind; public property, or what is considered to be in the common domain, is by definition susceptible to legitimate copying. As well, copyright protection is not available to imitations of works existing in the public domain: only 'original' elements of the new work can be copyrighted. This first distinction is refined by a second, which is the known as the 'idea/expression dichotomy': ideas are public property, whereas their expression is private. Historical evolution in the perception of the origin of ideas, which is found to reside either in nature or in original genius, does not affect the destiny of these ideas, which either 'return to' or are 'released into' the public domain. What counts as an idea, however, as distinct from its expression, is the stumbling block for making the crucial decision.

The etymology of plagiarism as theft of property implies the presence, at least in the minds of victims, of a notion of discursive production as constituting the author's legitimate and private property, in spite of the absence of legal criteria instituting such notions. In order to understand the fundamental distinction between public and private property and its originating relationship to plagiarism, it is necessary to situate the definition of plagiarism not in terms of 'originality' (where it is now located even for judicial purposes), but where it traditionally belongs, on an axis of literary invention that ranges from bad to good forms of imitation. From classical to neo-classical times, public domain was largely situated in the area of content, with the emphasis for transformation placed on the form. Discussing the difference between plagiarism and imitation in classical rhetoric, Fiske points out that the ancient and rhetorical traditions regarded 'the subject matter of an earlier master in any given genre as the common property of posterity. Hence the duty and privilege of the heir to such a noble heritage is, working in the spirit of generous rivalry, to follow in the steps of his master, to preserve unimpaired the essentials of the great tradition, to perpetuate that ordered freedom which conditioned the growth in Greece and the continuation in Rome of all the literary genres' (27).

The same aesthetic condemned as plagiarism 'close verbal imitation or even free paraphrase, especially if the imitator made no direct acknowledgment of his sources, or even deliberately concealed them' (Fiske 27). It is worth remembering that the aim of these caveats, as of those expressed by Horace, is to teach the legitimate appropriation of *public* property – that which has already been released to the world – and the means of its transformation into *private and personal* property. The transformations effected by the imitator are the work/genius by which the act of appropriation becomes legitimate, and this goal is one that is pursued in the same terms throughout the Renaissance and beyond. There is a curious dialectic here between public and private property that it would be useful to explore: authorship, that is, mastery over one's discourse, can be seen as a matter of converting public property into private by means of properly assimilating it and marking it with one's transforming individuality. The public property in question, of course, being the great texts of original masters, remains in the public domain by virtue of its perfection and its expression of universal truth; it is eternally available for reappropriation by another. To quote Fiske again: 'For to the ancients imitation is after all the gestation by the human spirit of all the living elements streaming into its depths from the life and culture of the past, and from the works of the great masters mimetic of that life. From this slow process there is born a work of art expressing that larger vision of the individual spirit, which pierces through the shifting shadows of the world of contemporary phenomena and beholds in undimmed clarity the ideals of beauty and truth, seen *sub specie aeternitatis*' (47).

But what is curious is that the private property thus produced should, as a consequence of the truth it embodies, ideally seek to return to the public domain to become a legitimate object of appropriation by future writers. This logic continues well into the nineteenth century, where 'original genius' is defined in part by its propensity to function as a model for future imitators, that is, to partake of universal truth. The dialectic between public and private property is a recurring theme throughout history, as plagiarized authors often fall into two categories: the great majority who, following Martial's lead, treat their works as private property; and those who, implicitly claiming for themselves the status of an original author, a Homer or a Cicero, see their productions as legitimate grist for other mills, existing naturally in the public domain, and thereby participating somehow in the realm of universal truth. Expressions of such generosity are admittedly rare: more often, of course, it is other writers' property that is considered up for grabs.

Classical and renaissance rules for proper imitation are attempts to nego-tiate the distinction between private and public property by claims to the universality of truth that belongs to all. Seneca is quite clear about this: 'When one writes on topics already treated, he is not pilfering them, as if they belonged to someone else, [...] for they are common property. The best ideas are common property, therefore since what is common to all belongs equally to each, any truth is my own property [and] whatever is well said by anyone is mine' (*Letters*, lxxix, 6; xii, II; xvi, 7; quoted by White 7).

And Molière echoes this sentiment in his famous aphorism 'Je (re)prends mon bien où je le trouve' – or at least, it is commonly assumed that this is the force of the phrase. But a certain confusion results from the occasional disappearance and reappearance of the troublesome prefix, which so radically alters the force of the sentence that was apparently uttered by Molière upon being accused of borrowing an episode of *Le pédant joué* from Cyrano de Bergerac (1654) for his *Fourberies de Scapin* (1671). According to Grimarest, the sole source of the aphorism, Cyrano borrowed the idea from conversations with Molière, who subsequently 'takes it *back*' for his own play.[4]

In Grimarest's account, it is clear that whatever Cyrano borrowed from Molière, the honour was returned to Cyrano without scruple. Subsequent accounts 'deform' the phrase and raise it not only to the level of a quota-tion, but give it a general rather than a specific value: 'Molière, in embel-lishing his petty thefts [*larcins*], had acquired the right to say: "That is good, that belongs to me, one is allowed to acquire one's property [*prendre son bien*] wherever one finds it."'[5]

What is significant and interesting for us, however, is that there are two traditions: the popularly cited, but 'false' one (*prendre son bien*), which seems to justify the wholesale 'borrowing' in which the theatre of Molière, as the aesthetic of the time dictated, was amply engaged, and the lesser known but apparently 'authentic' one (*reprendre son bien*), which seems rather to indi-cate Molière's proprietory engagement with his own ideas, regardless of how he may have treated the 'property' of others. In fact, the 'true' version tends to seem rather anachronistic: while 'prendre son bien là où on le trouve' conforms with good classical theory of imitation, as expressed by Seneca, '*re*prendre son bien' traces a narrative of possession, dispossession, and then legitimate reappropriation of a rightful property, all of which are considered to be anachronistic in 1671, the date of *Les fourberies*. If Grimar-est, in reporting the incident in 1705, that is, some thirty-two years after Molière's death, is the surest source of the aphorism, and perhaps as well its 'true' author, it is difficult to determine whether the phrase reflects Molière's own aesthetic, or that which Grimarest espoused, and considered appropriate for the author. Mongrédien, in glossing Grimarest, notes that many critics – too often substituting *prendre* for *reprendre* – attribute a general meaning to the aphorism and see in it 'an affirmation of the sovereign rights of the artist' ['une affirmation des droits souverains de l'artiste' (Grimarest 39, n. 5)]. Mongrédien argues for the specificity of the statement in the context of Cyrano's borrowing. But whether specific or general, it is the prefix *re* that seems to express 'property' rights over artistic discourse by implying a theft and a legitimate recovery of lost property.[6]

The question of private versus public property is not only a matter of the appropriate objects of imitation and the right set of rules; the distinction between the two is also a matter of having the proper attitude towards the discourses that one 'possesses.' In Bayle's dictionary (1697), the principle of proper appropriation becomes the difference between legitimate and illegitimate possession of knowledge. In much the same vein as Montaigne and Corneille, Bayle distinguishes between false and authentic erudition: the first being the second-hand acquisition of knowledge by reading *about* the ancients in modern texts; the second being recourse to the originals and the direct acquisition of knowledge. The crime of plagiarism is the lack of acknowledgment of those modern sources that have led you to the ancients. Those names you are obliged to cite in the margins of the text, and it is those names that become 'authors.' The name of the (modern) author, according to Bayle, is the one appearing in the margins of the text, and a writer should arrange for his name to be the one that the others cite, along with Aristotle, Cicero, or Virgil:

An author who goes back to *several fountains, and collates* [i.e., *the sources, and verifies;* my translation] all the passages cited by others, becomes a lawful possessor. He has a right to cite only the original authors whom he consulted; and it would be unjust to call him a plagiary, upon pretence that he quotes the same passages as other writers. But, on the other side, it is my opinion that sincerity, equity, and gratitude call upon us to acknowledge the obligation, by which we are bound to those writers who pointed out the sources to us. When, therefore, an author is conscious that had he not read the dissertations of some moderns who have cited the ancient authors, he would not have known to whom he could have applied, in order to find out the original authorities; it would be very decent in him to inform the public of the good office those moderns did him. Having once done this in his preface, he then is at liberty to quote, upon his own bottom, all the antients [*sic*] to whom he had recourse, and act the part of a true proprietor. Let me observe by the way, that those writers who are so conscientious as to cite the very chapters and pages for such passages as they borrow, shew more honesty than policy. They are negligent of vainglory, and deprive themselves of the pleasure of being cited: for they thereby make it so very easy to compare or verify the passages that most writers will do this when they have occasion for the same proofs, or the same incidents that are found in their works; after which, they content themselves with quoting the ancient author. But, if they cited the beautiful incidents without mentioning the authors while they copied them, by only setting down the names of their authorities, other writers would hardly venture to publish the same incidents, except under their authority, unless they were authors of the first class. They therefore would see their own names in the margins of a great number of books; an honour that would be long done them. (Bayle, 'Nihisius,' 1738, p. 818–19)[7]

This principle clearly sets up a distinction between the ancients as belonging to public property – open to appropriation, and the moderns as private property – requiring explicit acknowledgment. The pre-Romantic author exercises a kind of trusteeship over public property to which he acquires certain rights by virtue of his intellectual effort: having discovered a precious (public) commodity that is of benefit to all, he is willing to lend it out, but at a price – the interest accrued on his discovery is the honour of having his name cited in the margins of the text, alongside those of the true authorities. Bayle's distinction is still valid today, particularly in the academic and scientific milieux, and especially since electronic technology has enabled the 'citation index' to weigh the relative 'authority' of an author by counting the number of times others have recourse to him or her in their own margins. The same strategy of false erudition is still considered an illegitimate use of other researchers' knowledge, and the same recourse to citing contemporary authors in the margins is still an indication of their authority, and of one's own honesty and intellectual integrity.

The theme of intellectual production as property is never very far from the concerns of those involved with defending literary ethics and aesthetics. In his *Defense of Poetry* (I, 169), Sidney negotiates a path between the public domain of 'History' and the privatization of this domain by the poet: 'The best of the Historian is subject to the Poet; for whatsoever [...] the Historian is bound to recite, that may the Poet (if he list) with his imitation make his own; beautifying it both for further teaching, and more delighting, as it pleaseth him: having all, from *Dante* his heaven to hys hell, under the authoritie of his penne' (cited by White 61).

In defending the virtue of original genius in the production of literary works, Edward Young attaches individuality to the possession of property: 'His works will stand distinguished; his the sole Property of them; which Property alone can confer the noble title of an *Author*; that is, of one who (to speak accurately) *thinks*, and *composes*; while other invaders of the Press, how voluminous, and learned soever, (with due respect be it spoken) only *read*, and *write*' ([1759] 1970, p. 30).

The conflicting demands of private property and public good are at the heart of the development of copyright law, as we shall see, where they have been largely resolved by a term of protection limited to fifty years after the author's death. This first limitation is complicated, however, by the distinction between idea and expression – namely, that the first is always appropriable while the second (almost) never is. The copying of works in the public domain, or the copying of ideas that escape copyright and therefore cannot fall into legal dispute, are still sometimes the object of accusations of plagiarism as an ethical breach of the literary contract. Outside of copyright, public domain is a vague area largely defined by reader judgment and the notion of common knowledge – but, increasingly, in contemporary Western life, knowledge can be seen to be becoming less and less common. As we move towards a more and more fragmented culture, it becomes virtually impossible to predict what cultural or literary knowledge readers have in common; at the same time, there is a greater tendency on the part of writers to return to an explicitly imitative mode of creation.

Beyond the question of public domain as determined by copyright, we find particular types of texts, about which various ages have demonstrated differing sensitivities. We have already seen that, before the eighteenth century, when imitation was the aesthetic norm, the criterion of legitimate models of imitation rested on the authority of the work. Nodier, in the nineteenth century, distinguishes between works of literature and works of positive knowledge, claiming that the first are open to imitation, but the second are not, constituting properly the private property of their author. In Nodier's treatment, the question of the 'borrowing' of scientific or 'positive matters' falls more easily into the legal realm of intellectual property rights than into the literary, that is, moral, realm of borrowing from literary sources. In his opening chapter, he distinguishes between 'imitation,' a legitimate practice when it is directed to literary texts, and the illegitimate practice of the translation of works that treat 'positive matters' ['des matières positives']: 'This surreptitious translation is a true plagiarism, a definite theft, when it is not accompanied by a formal declaration, or an implicit one, such as is implied by the conformity of the title, and no one has ever judged otherwise.'[8] In Nodier's conception, scientific 'fact,' or positive knowledge, is more closely allied to the realm of intellectual property, susceptible to being owned, than are 'works of the imagination.' This view is in direct contradiction with both the literary tradition and the tenets of copyright legislation, as well as with the practictioners of compilation and dictionary writers themselves, for whom 'knowledge,' as universal truth, belongs more solidly in the realm of public domain.

Roland de Chaudenay's *Dictionnaire des plagiaires* provides us with a contemporary example and ironic treatment of the paradox of compilation. In

his introductory treatment of terms related to plagiarism, one reads the
following:

> A compiler, finding ideas, notions and facts in various sources, sometimes
> little known or forgotten, assembles them, confronts them one with
> another, selects among them and renders accessible to everyone knowledge
> to which normally only specialists have access.
>
> Of course, a compiler who does not cite his sources is no longer a com-
> piler, he is quite simply a plagiarist. It is a compiler who says so.[9]

At the entry for Chaudenay, his (fictional) 'friend' Geoffroy Tory,
charged with justifying the compilation, finds that he must instead accuse
his friend of plagiarism and rails against the disingenuous terms of this
introductory definition, intended apparently to disculpate the author of
what is, in fact, a 'cynical plagiarism.' (Not quite fictional: according to my
encyclopedia, Geoffroy Tory [c. 1480–1533] was a printer, writer, and bookseller who contributed to the spread of roman characters and of modern
typographical conventions. He encouraged the use of the French vernacular for learned works. His *Book of Hours* [1525] is one of the masterpieces
of illumination of the Renaissance.) 'Tory' objects that the simple reference to 'sources' cannot excuse the patent theft and distillation of others'
erudition into a work 'one third of which is composed of quotations from
plagiarisms, another third of quotations from their models, and the rest of
copied commentary' ['composé pour un tiers de citations de plagiats, pour
un autre, de citations de leurs modèles, et, pour le reste, de commentaires
démarqués' (Chaudenay 104)]. This ironic treatment of the dictionary
enterprise provides an able commentary on the traditional dilemma that
the dictionary-writer, as well as the academic 'compiler' in general, must
confront, and that concerns, on the one hand, the existence of a stabilized
corpus of truths ('facts'; 'knowledge') exempt of the necessity for the attribution of the 'source' ('Water freezes at 0 degrees'; 'The sun rises in the
east'; 'All men are mortal') and, on the other, the fixity of their linguistic
expression ('Water freezes at 0 degrees'; etc.). The problem is with the ten-
uousness of the idea/expression distinction, which dissolves when confronted with the tendency to transfer knowledge in reified linguistic form,
producing not only clichés and stereotypes, but genuine pieces of 'universal truth' that are scarcely recognizable outside of their habitual linguistic
formulation.

For us, the situation is somewhat reversed from the one described by
Nodier: in the realm of literary plagiarism it is felt that creative ('original')
products are sacrosanct, while works of positive knowledge, such as dictionaries, encyclopedias, and scientific discourses – those that express and

release 'knowledge' into the world for the public good – are rather less so. Independently of copyright considerations, that is, from an ethical and aesthetic point of view, it is relatively innocuous to copy into one's fiction passages of technical prose ('facts'); however, copying other artists is closer to plagiarism. This distinction is expressed by Zola, who was accused of plagiarizing, notably from *Le sublime* (1870), a documentary work by Denis Poulot on alcoholism among the working class. In response, Zola writes in the *Télégraphe*: 'It is true that I took some information from *Le Sublime*. But you have forgotten to say the *Le Sublime* is not a work of imagination, a novel: it is a book of documents from which the author cites overheard words and true facts. Borrowing something from it is borrowing from reality.'[10]

Zola goes on to enumerate several other of his documentary sources, such as dictionaries of jargon and Valentin Magnan's *De l'alcoolisme* (1874); furthermore, he describes his system of writing: 'All my novels are written in this way; I surround myself with a library and a mountain of notes, before taking up the pen. Look for plagiarisms in my preceding works, Monsieur, and you will make some wonderful discoveries.' Zola also takes the occasion to turn the accusation into a defence of the exactitude of the novel, which had been attacked for falsifying and exaggerating the situations it described: 'Up until now I have been accused of lying in *L'Assomoir:* now I am going to be attacked because it appears that I have relied on the most serious documents.'[11]

The idea/expression conundrum has been significantly raised by cases involving the copying of computer programs that are subject to protection by copyright; the question is to determine which parts of the program are the ideas and which parts the expression. The attempted solution to the problem, known as the 'idea/expression merger doctrine,' provides a distinction that might be relevant to other areas of copyright. The principle allows that substantial similarity is not necessarily an indication of copying if 'there is only one way of expressing the idea in terms of either the program structure or its detailed code' (Bainbridge 163). In other words, 'if the programmer had no option but to write a part of the program the way he did because the task to be achieved dictated its form and content then that part was idea and not protected by copyright' (162). Alternatively, parts of the program that could be written in a variety of ways are deemed 'expression' and are subsequently copyrightable. Commenting on the difficulty entailed by the idea/expression dichotomy, Bainbridge states: 'However, the boundary between idea and expression is a difficult one to draw. Suffice it to say at this stage that judges have been reluctant to sympathize with a defendant who has taken a short cut to producing his work by making an unfair use of the plaintiff's work, especially when the two works are likely to compete' (28).

The confusion between the 'public' and 'private' domains, between ideas and their expression, will be intensely exploited by contemporary aesthetics. The 'real world' of objects, facts, events, people, and language is the modern 'public domain' *par excellence*; since the institution of copyright and trademark laws, it is assumed to be that part of the world which does not consist of privatized commodities. The intentionally perverse levelling of the text-world distinction by postmodern aesthetics points to the contemporary breakdown of the private/public dichotomy entailed by the massive commodification of images, the trend towards the commodification and privatization of 'information,' traditionally situated in the public domain, and even the commodification of bodies both in artistic representation and in the realm of genetic and DNA research and manipulation. As ownership is the crucial element of authorship that has moved into the judicial domain, it will be enlightening to foray briefly into the history of contemporary copyright legislation, at a moment when the crucial distinctions between 'mine' and 'thine' were being forged.

PROPERTY

> What is worth stealing is worth protecting.
>
> Judge Learned Hand

No discussion of plagiarism would be complete without a consideration of the development of copyright laws, because the creation of laws protecting authors and their property intersects with, and sometimes conflicts with, long-standing literary conventions with respect to the relationship between authors and their productions. In fact, the line of development that leads from plagiarism to copyright legislation is much less direct than the one leading from imitation through originality to plagiarism. A brief sketch of the content and development of the legal notions of *droit d'auteur* and copyright will, however, be useful in determining the historical and contemporary contours of what is called plagiarism, in so far as it is distinct from these two judicial traditions.

A review of contemporary intellectual-property cases involving literary works is singularly unrewarding for a study of literary plagiarism, as copyright laws are largely appealed to by corporate enterprises increasingly concerned with computer programs, the vast majority of literary copyright cases being settled out of court. The situation noted by Birrell in 1899 has not substantially changed:

> In reading the cases in the Reports for the last hundred years, you cannot overlook the literary insignificance of the contending volumes. The big

authors and big books stand majestically on one side – the combatants are all small fry. The question of literary larceny is chiefly illustrated by disputes between book-makers and rival proprietors of works of reference, sea charts, Pattesons' 'Roads,' the antiquities of *Magna Graecia*, rival encyclopaedias, gazetteers, guide books, cookery books, law reports, post office and trade directories, illustrated catalogues of furniture, statistical returns, French and German dictionaires, Poole's farce, 'Who's Who?,' Brewer's 'Guide to Science.' This is not by any means an exhaustive list, but it accurately shows the nature of the proceedings. (170–1)

One need only add film companies, the music industry, and especially software manufacturers to bring Birrell's list up to date. If the legal provisions for the protection of literary property are not directly relevant to a definition of the nature and scope of plagiarism, a knowledge of the development of these provisions is fundamental to understanding the distinction between legal and non-judiciable forms of copying. In these matters, however, it is particularly significant that what we have been calling 'literature' is a small part of a huge network of 'print media' that include, among many other things, as Birrell's list shows, university examinations, texts of architectural drawings, accounting tables, and computer programs. Although the Anglo-American and the European (French) traditions have evolved into distinct systems, the first protecting uniquely patrimonial rights, and the second being a dualist system of patrimonial and moral rights, they did so under the same pressures and the same urgency born of the commodification of intellectual products that transformed ownership from a symbolic into a marketable privilege.

The distinction between plagiarism and copyright infringement is worth underlining, since the contemporary conflation of the two masks the historical pertinence and specificity of plagiarism, as well as contributing to an ongoing debate about the literary ethics of borrowing. Plagiarism and copyright have separate histories that invoke two different realms – the deontic and the judicial, respectively – and, while these two are intimately related, the judicial history falls outside of the scope of this study.[12] David Saunders's revisionist view of this history in England, France, Germany, and America is undertaken with the aim of debunking what he considers to be the Romanticist myth that the proper relationship between an author and his work is one of natural and inalienable proprietorship, and that the development of copyright laws enshrines a universal human truth about the individual author's personhood – or at least, that such laws move towards this historical telos, while falling short, in various instances, of achieving the ideal legal protection of this natural right. What is clear in his discussion, and what will serve us as a preliminary distinction between plagiarism and copyright, is that there has been and continues to be confusion between *ownership* as a category of property rights whose protection has been motivated by mercantile and capitalist forces of production and consumption, on the one hand, and, on the other hand, *authorship* as a moral category, entailing inalienable rights over the form of the expression of ideas as they define a moral or ethical persona invested with the identity of creator. As Judge Birrell said in 1899, 'the intent to steal, the unscrupulous determination to benefit by another's labours (that other being a "protected" author) without independent work of one's own, this is to be a pirate at law. If the extraneous matter is not protected property, the offence is the moral offence of plagiary' (Birrell [1899], 1971, p. 172).

These two personae – the 'pirate' and the 'plagiarist,' to use Birrell's terms – are very different, and do not coexist with any consistency either in legal or in aesthetic history. The prior tradition enshrining the existence of proprietary rights of authors over their production has been pointed out by Mark Rose:

> In the early modern period, in connection with the individualization of authorship, the transformation of the medieval *auctor* into the Renaissance *author*, there developed a general sense that it was improper to publish an author's text without permission. The acknowledgment of an author's interest in controlling the publication of his texts is not necessarily the same as the acknowledgment of a property right in the sense of an economic interest in an alienable commodity. In practice, however, the right to control publication has economic implications, and it sometimes becomes difficult to distinguish what we might call matters of propriety from matters of property. (18)

In positing such a distinction between *property* and *propriety*, Rose points to the crucial difference between the modern relation between a text and its owner, and a premodern, although still valid, relationship of propriety between a text and its originator or author: the first is the realm of copyright; the second, of plagiarism.

A positivist account of the legal developments of the notion of authorship, such as Saunders's, does not see the ethical-aesthetic component, that is, in Rose's terms, *propriety*, as a defining force behind the emergence of the author as a legal person, but rather sees the enactment of laws defining the person and the rights of the author as constitutive of his nature and very existence. But since authors have long asserted a proprietary relation over their texts, it is only in a narrow legal sense that the invention of copyright can be said to coincide with the invention of 'authorship.' In order to keep the two accounts separate, it would be convenient to see the victim of plagiarism as an ethical and aesthetic person, and the victim of the infringement of copyright as a legal person. This second person is most notably not necessarily the author, but the owner of the copyright, who is often, in the textual world, the publisher. For our purposes, the victim of plagiarism is always either the alleged creator of the work, irrespective of legal questions of ownership, or else a literary public, when questions of ownership become immaterial. In this way, one can be guilty of plagiarism without falling foul of the law, and suffer important sanctions outside of the courts. Often, of course, the two 'crimes' are indistinguishable, and the same misappropriation can be subject to both legal and ethical sanctions. The point is that while plagiarism and infringement of copyright sometimes coincide, they are not the same phenomenon, nor do they have the same historical development. The failure of the courts to establish breach of copyright does not preclude the possibility that accused authors may continue to be suspected of ethical crimes against institutions whose sanctions lie outside of the law courts. At the same time, not all cases of breach of copyright involve moral persons who are susceptible to incurring ethical sanctions: corporations regularly battle out copyright infringements on purely financial and technical grounds without the slightest trace of ethical sanctions against persons being mustered as elements of accusation or defence. As Normand Tamaro points out, 'it is necessary to understand that the respect for rules of an ethical nature has no influence on the *droit d'auteur*, even if this respect can permit conclusions about the good faith of the [author]. At the same time, the good faith of a counterfeiter is without consequence with respect to the violation of the right to produce or to reproduce a work, although good faith can influence the attribution of sanctions.'[13]

One common assumption in literary discussions about the development of copyright legislation in England and Europe throughout the eighteenth century is that it can be interpreted as a gauge of the rise of the author as a creative agent, possessing individuality that he expresses through his work. While this assumption no doubt has some institutional truth, it seems to deny the ethical and moral reality of the sense of proprietorship existing between authors and their works in pre-modern Europe that we have seen. If the concept of authorship is to be seen purely as a post-Enlightenment attribute, then something else has to account for the existence of clearly proprietary feelings projected by writers in previous ages onto the fruits of their labour and imagination.

The distinction between propriety, the basis of authorship, and property rights, the basis of ownership, can be traced through the assertions of pre-copyright authors about their rights over their productions. Rose points out that, long before copyright, disputes about the misappropriation of texts for the purposes of reproduction were argued in terms of the proprietory relation between authors and works: as early as 1586, the Parlement of Paris decided in favour of the friends of the poet and scholar Marc-Antoine Muret, who contested Nicolas Nivelle's 'King's privilege' to print Muret's work. The terms of their argument, which the Parlement accepted, recall the master/slave relationship between author and work, a form of ownership modelled on God's relationship to his creation: 'In the same way [i.e., as God], the author of a book is wholly its master, and as such he can freely do with it what he wills; even keep it permanently under his private control as he might a slave; or emancipate it by granting it common freedom; giving that freedom either purely and simply, without holding back anything, or else imposing some limits, by a kind of right of patronage, so that no one but he will have the right to print it except after a certain time' (*Muret* v *Nivelle*, quoted in Rose, *Authors and Owners* 20).

The evidence for pre-copyright proprietorship is overwhelming, and comes not exclusively from the eighteenth century when the furious debate over the moral and material issues concerned in the rights of reproduction drew even the attention of the public. Jonson, Milton, Molière, to name a few, were all concerned with securing the proprietory relationship of the author over his work.

It will be necessary to review, however cursorily, the development of provisions for copyright in England and France before drawing some preliminary conclusions. In this, my aim is simply to repeat – or 'compile' – the best-known facets of this history before exploring some of its more interesting relationships to the history of plagiarism. The first distinction that needs to be made is that, regardless of ulterior developments in the directions of personalist notions of authorial rights of ownership, the original issues involved were 'the censorship of the Press and the monopoly of the booksellers, and from these two independent and occasionally clashing interests sprang copyright' (Birrell [1899] 1971, p. 51). Since the time of the Stationer's Company in England, established in 1556, the owner of the 'book or copy' was the bookseller who registered the title in his own name; the 'author's copy' being the manuscript that had to be sold before it could be printed (74). While the protection and regulation of economic rights evolving from the printing and distribution of books was the primary impetus for copyright legislation, these economic questions, originally disputed primarily between contending booksellers, gradually gave way, throughout the course of the eighteenth century, not only to a discourse of authorial privilege with respect to literary property, but eventually to corresponding legislation. It must also be kept in mind that copyright law was essentially aimed at limiting the possibilities of theft deriving from technical advancements: the distinction between piracy and plagiarism is crucial here, for while we may think of copyright laws as having as their general object something called 'plagiarism,' these laws have always been aimed not at the literary tradition of borrowing and repetition, but at the control of the reproduction and circulation of marketable goods.

COPYRIGHT VERSUS DROIT D'AUTEUR

One of the most fundamental aspects of the history of copyright laws as they relate to the question of plagiarism is the development of two distinct types of rights: on the one hand, 'copyright' commonly provides economic or patrimonial protection of the work and the right to its reproduction; on the other hand, the *droits d'auteur*, or author's rights, issue from a personalist conception and definition of authorship and provide 'moral rights' for the protection of the author's person. It is the development of these two types of rights that most clearly distinguishes Anglo-American and Continental intellectual property law, the latter being represented here solely by reference to French history, although German developments were particularly influential in the debate (see Woodmansee; Saunders). The paradigm oppositions are usually taken to be France, 'home' of 'authors' rights' based in civil law, and the United States, where the development of copyright alongside the existence of common law has resulted in strong resistance to the codification of moral rights. The adoption of moral rights into British law dates from the United Kingdom's adherence to the Berne convention in 1887, whereas the United States resisted adherence to Berne until 1989, and then refused to adopt universal moral rights, restricting them to the visual arts.

For historians of copyright, the significant issue evolving from the legal recognition of these two rights is to determine what *kind* of right is at stake in questions of 'intellectual property': whether or not copyright legislation creates such rights by statute, as in civil law, or whether they are personal rights arising from natural or common law. The crucial difference between the Anglo-American and French histories is that, in the English tradition, what was to become in French statutes *le droit moral* relating to personal rights was considered in British law to be already protected at common law. Recht, for example, considers that the evolution of British and French copyright is hardly distinguishable, because of the existence of common law in which personal rights similar to French 'moral rights' have traditionally been protected (20).

In both histories, a central problem consisted in determining whether intellectual products could be equivalent to other kinds of property or whether they are 'property' of a special kind. In the first instance, copyright would be a law regulating the commercial exchange of goods by contract or sale: by assimilating intellectual works to other kinds of property, this argument relies on common law and the principle of personal and perpetual rights over the control of one's possessions. These rights include, somewhat paradoxically, the right to 'alienate' oneself from one's property by selling it to another owner and thus abandoning any rights over it that one has had, in the same way as by the sale of one's real estate.

The evident problem with this argument is that there is something immaterial in an intellectual or literary production such that it is instinctively felt to be different from a field or a house. Two separate arguments arise from this 'metaphysical' view: on the one hand, the recognition of the value of the immaterial aspects of the work – its ideas – supports the case in favour of limited term rather than perpetual copyright, and proposes that knowledge naturally belongs to the public domain for the benefit of all – especially subsequent booksellers; on the other hand, according a different status to the content of the book, as opposed to the vehicle, allows the separation of the two, which led to a distinction between the notion of *author's rights* and *copyright*. The right to publish the work, which is what is ceded by *privilège*, or copyright, to the bookseller or publisher, should not alienate the author's essential rights over the incorporeal aspects of the work, such as the right of paternity over the work and the right to protect the contents from mutilation.

Early copyright laws favoured the material aspect of the creation and were intended essentially as a means of regulating the book trade, preventing the piracy that tended to ruin booksellers, printers, and eventually authors, by reducing the market value of editions to the point where the holder of the privilege was no longer able to finance his business. At the same time, a long tradition favouring the inherent inalienability of authors' proprietorship over their works was used as grist for the mill of those arguing that maintaining perpetual copyright in the hands of the author – eventually his agent or the new owner – was the only way to protect the natural right of propriety invested in the author by virtue of his paternity. Despite much ethical and philosophical discussion, the significant issue at the heart of the eighteenth-century debate became one of financial profit and loss attendant on the reproduction of the work. Paternalist and proprietory notions of authorship, which had always existed, were mobilized in the commercial argument to claim that rights to ownership were indeed found at common law and as such should be perpetual. The short description of the conclusion of these debates is that the privileges of *authorship* are indeed a right at common law, and these rights were not abolished when rights of ownership were found not to exist in common law. *Ownership*, however, was found to have purely statutory origins. Copyright, as it evolved in the British tradition, regulates ownership, not authorship.

PERPETUAL VERSUS LIMITED-TERM RIGHTS

The most significant issue in this debate, both in English and in French history, turns on the question of whether or not the rights to reproduce the work, once ceded in any way to a publisher, were to remain with him in perpetuity, or whether, once a certain term had lapsed, these rights were to fall into the public domain. On the one hand, the debate hinged on an economic argument, pitching the well-being of London and Parisian booksellers against provincial and foreign ones who had to resort to piracy in the face of metropolitan monopolies; piracy, in turn, threatened the economic stability of the privileged booksellers. On the other hand, moral interests were defended, as the monopolies created by perpetual copyright were felt to be detrimental to the advancement of learning and the dissemination of ideas: perpetual copyright in the hands of one bookseller was sometimes confused with perpetual control of the ideas contained within the book. In England and France, influential voices were raised on both sides of the question, each side pleading for its case in similar terms and both claiming economic advantages for their side. According to Rose (*Authors and Owners*), those arguing in favour of perpetual rights tended to view the landscape from the author's point of view, whereas those favouring a limited-term copyright rallied in support of the public good.

The landmark dates in the French and English histories of copyright are significant in that they allowed the theoretical existence of 'author's rights' as opposed to printer's privileges, by permitting the author to register his work *in his own name* (Recht 23). Jonathan Swift is credited with composing the original draft of the first copyright law in England, the Statute of Anne (1710), which introduces the notion of the consent of *authors* as well as of proprietors in the printing of books (Birrell 94). Before Anne, printers and booksellers had traditionally enjoyed perpetual rights to ownership, and thus to reproduction, a tradition more honoured in the breach by the turn of the century. The Statute of Anne announced a twofold aim: first, it was intended to introduce sanctions designed to limit the widespread practice of piracy, which threatened to bring about the collapse of the book trade. This financial situation was detrimental not only to the book traders and printers but, it was argued, to authors, whose remuneration for their intellectual labour was proportional to the expected returns on the sale of their books. The Statute of Anne limited the control of the printing and selling of editions to a specified number of years, breaking the traditional perpetual monopoly previously enjoyed by publishers. Second, the economic motive was joined to a higher interest, that of the development and spread of ideas in terms of both their production and their diffusion. These aims were reflected in the title of the Statute of Anne: 'An Act for the Encouragement of Learning, by vesting the copies of Printed books in the Authors or purchasers of such copies, during the times therein mentioned.' It was felt that piracy, by reducing the pecuniary rewards authors and printers could reap for their labours, would entail the decline of interest in intellectuals and printers alike in pursuing activities held to be in the common good. After a term of years, originally fourteen, which could be augmented by another fourteen if the author were still living, the work reverted to the common domain and its 'ideas' were released into the general public. All Anglo-American copyright acts balance these two aims: the encouragement of production in the form of protected remuneration for authors and printers, on the one hand, and, on the other, the encouragement of the spread of ideas, by limiting the amount of time such protection can be enjoyed, and releasing the knowledge into the public domain, where it can be freely disseminated.

Limited-term copyright was continually felt to be a detriment to the interests of authors and publishers alike and, in spite of the Statute of Anne, was repeatedly overruled by the courts, until the landmark decision in 1774 of *Donaldson* v *Beckett*, in which limited-term copyright carried the day and it was determined that the Statute of Anne was the sole authority upon which copyright depended – in other words, there was no such thing as common-law protection of the right to copy works. The disputes up until this time had turned on the question of whether literary work was property as understood at common law: property rights being inalienable, the rights of authors as owners should be governed in perpetuity by the decisions made by them about their property (including the decision to transfer the rights of ownership). The 1774 decision overturned an earlier (1769; *Millar* v *Taylor*) judgment which had upheld that copyright was indeed a right of property at common law. The 1774 decision distinguished between the perpetual right of ownership of the manuscript or unpublished work invested with the author, and the rights to copy the work, which were for a limited term.

The question was fiercely debated not only in the courts, but in the newspapers and journals, and much ink was spilled on both sides of the question. In attempting to determine the status of literary works as property at common law, the debate centred, first, on the question of whether or not property had to have a corporeal or material form, and, second, on whether or not the incorporeal part of the property, that is, the *ideas* invested in a work, should be limited or perpetual property. If common law were to be applied, the right to own the property would be unlimited, and defenders of this position took pains to argue that there is nothing inherently different about literary property that distinguishes if from any other; or, rather, that as an entirely new creation resulting directly from the fruits of the producer's own labour, literary property should be particularly inviolable. The consequence of this inviolability was that the acquirer of the right to copy the work should enjoy the same rights as the original owner. Most literary contributors to the debate early in the century, Defoe and Addison, for example, argue in favour of perpetual copyright. As Rose says, Defoe activates the etymological origins of 'plagiary' and at the same time, we add, the metaphor of unlawful colonization, which we will examine later on: 'A Book is the Author's Property, 'tis the Child of his Inventions, the Brat of his Brain; if he sells his Property, it then becomes the Right of the Purchaser; if not, 'tis as much his own, as his Wife and Children are his own – But behold in this Christian Nation, these Children of our Heads are seiz'd, captivated, spirited away, and carry'd into Captivity, and there is none to redeem them' (*Review*, 2 Feb. 1710, quoted in Rose, *Authors and Owners* 39).

The 'confusion' between the rights to the copying of the book and the rights to the ideas therein raises some pertinent issues for the ensuing definitions of copyright and plagiarism. While the defenders of the rights of producers and consumers both mobilize economic and 'metaphysical' arguments, the defence of perpetual copyright, based on an analogy with 'real' property, favours the materiality of the property involved, while defenders of limited rights insist on the encouragement of learning by what we would call today the 'free flow of information.' In the first case, 'the right of property in literary works rests on the solid grounds of primary possession and labour' (Enfield [1774] 1974, p. 19); in the second, 'it is inaccurate to say that the author *loses* his property by publication. He only makes his ideas common; he delivers his composition to the public; and puts it in the power of every individual who gets this publication into his hand, to make any use of it he shall think proper' ('Information for Alexander Donaldson and John Wood Against John Hinton' [1773] 1975, p. 11).

The incongruities in the opposing positions are perhaps more subtle than this juxtaposition suggests. Both sides are primarily interested in financial questions: perpetual copyright for authors would imply a 'monopoly' for booksellers over the works coming into their possession, a situation detrimental to provincial booksellers. The financial benefit to authors indeed seems to be on the side of perpetual copyright: defenders of a limited term are obliged to argue, conflictedly, that the greatest writers are only primarily interested in the glory attendant upon fame and disinterested devotion to learning and the public good; and, in any case, that the returns on most works reissued after the fourteen- or twenty-eight-year term are economically insignificant.

An important aspect of the debate for an eventual separation between plagiarism and copyright derives from the arguments made about the distinction between the material book and its immaterial contents. Sir Joseph Yates, the only voice raised in favour of limited rights in the 1769 decision in which these were defeated, maintains: 'From the time of the publication, the ideas become incapable of being any longer a subject of property; all mankind are equally intitled to read them and every reader becomes as fully possessed of all the ideas as the author himself ever was: From these observations this corollary [...] naturally follows, that the act of publication, when voluntarily done by the author himself, is virtually and necessarily a gift to the public' (Yates [1769] 1974, p. 57).

In contrast to this view, the defence of perpetuity, a widely held position that was defeated by only one voice in the 1774 decision, contends that literary production is the property of its author/owner, who has the sole right to enjoy, or dispose of, the financial benefits of his labour. This argument sometimes conflates the proprietorship of ideas and their expressions with the ownership of the rights to the copy; in fact, it is obliged to do so, for in order to establish the existence of a right at common law, it must be shown that this right has existed from time immemorial, which is clearly not the case with copyright. The defence of common law, and hence of perpetual rights, was forced to assimilate authorship and ownership. Rather than argue the separability of the 'composition' and its vehicle, whereby one can maintain paternity over one's ideas while relinquishing the rights over their material dissemination, defenders of perpetual copyright argue that, although authorship and ownership are two distinct rights, the right of authorship, being perpetual, institutes the right of ownership, which consequently should be also perpetual:

> That series of ideas and words which constitute the work, is in itself, an object of property, entirely distinct from the book in which they are written. And out of this right arises another; that of multiplying copies by transcribing or printing; for the work being his own, he may make what use of it he pleases. (Enfield [1774] 1974, p. 26)

> It will be said, that when an author parts with a copy of his work, he must of necessity part with the ideas and expressions, that is, with the composition itself as well as the book which contains it, to the purchaser [...] (28)

> To this I answer, that the original property of the composition residing in the author, it can only become the property of another, so far as he consents to transfer it; and that he cannot be fairly understood, by the mere act of selling a single copy, to give the purchaser a right of multiplying copies. (29)

The confusion generated around the question of the separability of book and idea – from both the practical and the ethical point of view – introduces issues that are more properly relevant to plagiarism, in particular, the difficulty, if not folly, of the notion of treating 'knowledge' as personal property. It is interesting to note that questions we consider today to be the very stuff of literary copyright suits are seen as part of the evils attendant upon the notion of perpetual copyright. Speaking in favour of limited-term rights by pointing out the dangers of perpetual rights, Yates claims: 'Disputes also might arise among authors themselves whether the work of one author, were or were not the same as those of another author, but were only colourable differences; a question that would be liable to great uncertainties and doubts; and of the case of those who should compile notes on a publication, and should insert the text, that author might be liable to an action for it; or if the notes were good, the author might refuse the publication of them' (Yates [1769] 1974, p. 88). Another author in favour of limited-term rights states the case most succinctly: 'If this idea of property, in compositions of the mind, is at all gone into, it is difficult to see where we are to stop. The author of a song, or a piece of music; the person who makes a speech in public, or who whistles a tune, will have the same property in his composition, and may equally insist in lawsuits against every one who pretends to borrow from, or to repeat after him' ('Information for Alexander Donaldson ...' [1773] 1975, p. 19).

It may be that the argument in favour of the fundamental right of possession of one's ideas was simply an expedient that, if accepted, seems logically to lead to the perpetual right of ownership over the vehicle of those ideas. In any case, the argument was not ultimately successful. A more convincing line of reasoning is the one that separates ideas from their vehicle and finds that perpetual copyright does not intend to limit the spread of ideas, but simply to reimburse both authors and booksellers for their labour and expense. Francis Hargrave, an ardent defender of perpetual copyright as a right at common law, argues this position in 1774. Hargrave's point is that retaining rights of ownership over the material aspects of the book is compatible with simultaneously releasing its contents into the world:

> What the author claims, is merely to have the sole right of printing his own works. As to the ideas conveyed, every author, when he publishes, necessarily gives the full use of them to the world at large. To communicate and fell knowledge to the publick, and at the same moment to stipulate that none but the author or his bookseller shall make use of it, is an idea, which Avarice herself has not yet suggested. But imputing this absurdity to the claim of Literary Property, is mere imagination; and so must be deemed, until it

can be demonstrated that the *printing* a book cannot be appropriated, without at the same time appropriating the *use* of the *knowledge* contained in it; or in other words, that the *use* of the ideas communicated by an author cannot be *common* to all, unless the *right of printing* his works is *common also*. If the impossibility of proving such a proposition is not self-evident, I am sure, that there is not any argument I am furnished with, which would avail to evince the contrary. (Hargrave, 1774, pp. 16–17)

In brief: 'the *property* claimed for the author is an exclusive right to the *printing* of his work, and *not* to the *ideas* contained in it, or to the *use* of them; therefore the property is not *ideal*' (18). Unfortunately for their cause, not all defenders of the perpetuity of literary-property rights were as clear-sighted in their reasoning as Hargrave.

Samuel Johnson, for his part, was a strong advocate of limited – but lengthy – rights, a compromise position that recognized the dangers of monopoly attendant upon perpetual copyright, as well as the disadvantages of a term as short as fourteen, or even twenty-eight years. In fact, Johnson's position, which advocated a term of some sixty years or one hundred years, approximates the current term of fifty years after the author's death. According to Johnson's oft-cited passage to this effect in Boswell, he claims in 1773:

> There seems [...] to be in authours a stronger right of property than that by occupancy, a metaphysical right, a right, as it were, of creation, which should from its nature be perpetual; but the consent of nations is against it, and indeed reason and the interests of learning are against it; for were it to be perpetual, no book, however useful, could be universally diffused amongst mankind, should the proprietor take it into his head to restrain its circulation ... For the general good of the world, therefore, whatever valuable work has once been created by an authour, and issued out by him, should be understood as no longer in his power, but as belonging to the publick; at the same time the authour is entitled to an adequate reward. This he should have by an exclusive right to his work for a considerable number of years. (Boswell [1799] 1965, pp. 546–7)

Lord Mansfield, an important supporter of perpetual copyright in the 1769 decision in which it was upheld, argues that the author's rights which common law so clearly upholds *before* publication should for 'the same reasons hold, after the author has published, he can reap no pecuniary profit after the time his works come out; it may be pirated every moment from that instant; it may be pirated on worse paper, and printed in a cheaper volume' (Mansfield [1769], p. 94).[14] The protection of unpublished material is not, however, according to Mansfield, a right at common law found in 'custom,' for before 1732 'the case of a piracy before publication never appeared to have existed' (93). From what source then is the presumption of common-law protection drawn? 'From this argument [...] because it is just that he [an author] should reap the fruits and profits of his own ingenuity and labour; it is just another should not use his name without his consent; it is fit he should judge when to publish, or whether he would ever publish it; it is fit he should not only chuse [sic] the time, but the manner of the publication, how many, in what volumes, what print; it is fit he should chuse to whose care he would trust the accuracy and neatness of the impression; in whose honesty he would confide, not to foist in additions, with other reasons of the same effect' (93–4).

In spite of such compelling arguments, the contrary opinion carried the day (by a margin of one vote: 'the majority of peers in the House [...] listened less to the distinctions drawn by the judges in their reasoning than to their own general predisposition against monopolies' [Saunders 67]) and the right to intellectual property was found not at common law but to be solely sanctioned by the Statute of Anne, and therefore of limited duration as that act had decreed. In deciding against perpetual copyright, the winning side was successful in arguing that there had never been such a thing as a common law regarding intellectual property and that the only precedent in British law governing the property in question was that instituted in the history of the Stationers' Company and intended solely for the protection of that company. If the Statute of Anne was enacted in an effort to break the monopoly of the Stationers' Company in 1710, the same anti-monopoly policy was effective in defeating perpetual copyright. Arguments were made that, during the Revolution – for a period of some fourteen to sixteen years before the Statute of Anne – when the abolishment of prerogative rendered the laws of the Stationers' Company null and void: 'no action was brought, no injunction obtained, although no illegal force prevented it; a strong proof that at that time there was no idea of a common law claim' (Lord Camden, quoted by Saunders, 68). Indeed, common law depends on three criteria that copyright, by its very nature, lacks: it must be immemorial, it must be uninterrupted, and it must not be subject to contention or dispute ('Speeches or arguments of the Judges of the Court of King's Bench in the Cause of Millar against Taylor' ([1769] 1974, p. 128). For these reasons, the defenders of literary property take pains to argue not on the basis of issues seeming to arise from the relatively recent (i.e., not 'immemorial') invention of printing and the commodification of print materials, but rather from the natural rights of ownership devolving from the author's intellectual labour and possession, similar to the criteria defining the ownership of real property.

While copyright legislation as it evolved in the eighteenth century is often construed as an outgrowth of Enlightenment individualism and the spirit of free enterprise, the argument in favour of limited-term copyright relied heavily on premodern conceptions of authorship. In recognition of the fact that limited-term copyright represented a potential financial loss to authors, Lord Camden, an influential and vocal champion of limited rights, resorted in his arguments before the House of Lords to a moral justification that was to plague authors well into the nineteenth century and beyond. As Rose sums it up, 'genuine authors do not write for money' (*Authors and Owners* 104): 'Glory is the Reward of Science, and those who deserve it, scorn all meaner Views: I speak not of the Scribblers for bread, who teize the Press with their wretched Productions; fourteen Years is too long a Privilege for their perishable Trash. It was not for Gain, that *Bacon, Newton, Milton, Locke,* instructed and delighted the World; it would be unworthy such Men [*sic*] to traffic with a dirty Bookseller for so much as a Sheet of Letter-press. [Milton] ... knew that the real price of his Work was Immortality, and that Posterity would pay it' (Camden [1774] 1975, p. 54; cited by Rose, p. 104–5). The pecuniary rewards to which authors are – or are not – entitled is a recurring theme. Since limited-term copyright appeared to be a restriction of the author's (or bookseller's) potential income, arguments were made that 'reputation [...] was of old, and this ought still to be, the true idea of an author's profit; and it is an idea far superior to the modern invention of copy-money: An invention which has tended much to degrade the author's character, and to render him subservient to booksellers and printers' ('Information for Alexander Donaldson ...' [1773] 1975, p.15).

The defenders of perpetual rights are considerably more 'modern' in their opinion, espoused continually by writers from Diderot to Pope to Dickens to Zola, that writing is both a labour and a commerce, and that whether or not the author write for gain, he should not be deprived of it as a consequence of the nobility of his endeavour. Against the 'generosity of the public' or the 'dependence on the patronage of the great' is pitted the value of a product which is offered for sale: '[The author] has a work which his own genius and labour have produced, copies of which he offers to public sale [...] Who would be contented with a vague and indeterminate advantage, under the humiliating idea of a reward, when he has a right to the regular and certain profits of sale?' (Enfield [1774] 1974, p. 37).

In spite of the relative lateness of judicial developments in France (1791, 1793) and the traditional preference for author's rights over copyright protection, a reference to the French situation before 1777 will show that both the arguments and the reasoning were substantially similar. In 1764, the king had granted exclusive privileges only to Parisian printers in an attempt to regulate the practice of piracy. The non-privileged provincial printers and booksellers immediately rebelled and flagrantly disobeyed the law, and a fierce quarrel ensued. On one side, the non-privileged printers argued for a limited term of copyright, after which the work would fall into the public domain, allowing them access to it, which, by virtue of the resulting greater dissemination, would enhance not only the writer's reputation and wealth, but their own pockets, as well as the public good. The debate was fuelled by the 1761 decision in favour of the perpetual right of the author by the granting to La Fontaine's granddaughters the rights to his works, giving them priority over non-privileged booksellers.

In the face of these events, no less a voice than Diderot's argued passionately for perpetual copyright to be invested in the hands of the printer-bookseller, in other words, in the hands of those to whom the author had ceded or sold the rights (Diderot [1764] 1970). Reviewing the history of copyright and the potential for disaster that a time-limited privilege would entail, Diderot compares the fundamental right of property, which inheres in a person's *creation*, to the rights entailed by property, which are inviolable. These inviolable rights include the right to alienate oneself from one's property by selling it to a new owner, who thereby becomes the sole proprietor of the property. Restricting the owner's right to sell his property, and putting limitations on rights over property legitimately acquired, was a violation of the most fundamental liberties of personhood. Diderot recounts at length the confusion and misery into which the whole commerce of literary production would fall when, unprotected, legitimate publishers, having acquired at great cost the limited rights to an edition, find their investment devalued as soon as the rights fall into the public domain. Hack publishers would be left free to produce inferior editions at low prices, and stockpiles of the original edition would be left mouldering in storehouses, preventing the author from profiting from a second edition to correct or improve the work, and driving the whole of culture into a state of financial and scholarly disrepair. Diderot's argument, which is clearly that what is of financial benefit to the material producers of the book is necessarily of benefit to the author, is perhaps coloured somewhat by his own position as both author and publisher. The same argument holds against the reversion of the rights to the author's heirs, as in the case of La Fontaine: Diderot again advances the comparison with other property that one might sell during one's lifetime, and over which one's heirs would not have any legitimate claim.

The evolution of copyright in France, as in England, moved in a direction not recommended by Diderot, as limited-term copyright came into effect there as well, to the chagrin of many writers, including Balzac, an ardent defender of perpetual rights and founding member of the Société des gens de lettres, established for the promotion and protection of authors' rights. His arguments in favour of perpetual rights and against foreign piracy are of the same nature as the ones we have described in England sixty years earlier:

> Over the past two centuries, man has created a new and immense property. In this property, everything emanates from man; he alone has created the ink, he has created the paper; the printed thought comes from him, everything is from him. It is a value which depends only on itself, an anthropomorphic value, for an author pours into it his life and his soul and his nights. And it is precisely the rights to this property that are being contested! This is what will lead to the disinheritance of families without indemnity. The *law* is full of protections for one's gold and one's land, for furnishings acquired by material or commercial work; there are eleven hundred articles in the code for these properties, but there is not one which concerns, in the capriciousness of its transmissions and stipulations, the property created by intellectual work [...] [T]he literary contract is exposed to all the vagueness of random judicial determinations, and judges twist cases in order to force them into the frame of the Code.[15]

In distinguishing between the ownership of property and the ownership of the creations of one's intellect, the debate over the perpetuity of copyright underlined the feeling that there was something inalienable in the owner's rights to his intellectual productions: these rights, known internationally since the Berne convention as 'moral rights,' are not by nature economic but are sanctionable by economic remedies. In France, these rights remain perpetual and unalienable and cannot be waived by contract; in the Anglo-American tradition, before and after the adoption of the Berne convention by various countries, one can waive (but not transfer) one's moral rights as well as one's economic rights.

In British copyright law, the nature of the property in question is only the printing of the book and begs the question of authorship. As Saunders and Birrell distinguish between *piracy* – that which occurs between publishers – and *plagiarism* – the analogous practice between writers – and as Rose distinguishes between *property* and *propriety*, so Anglo-American copyright law is essentially aimed at the first rather than the second of these two types of potential infractions: copyright is an economic rather than a moral protection. The tradition resulting from this decision was to rely on common-law rights such as the right to protection from defamation of one's person or character in order to defend authors whose 'moral rights' had been infringed. Nevertheless, the relationship between authorship and property which emerged from the eighteenth-century conflation of the discourses of originality and of property rights is still with us today:

'By 1774, the year in which the *Donaldson* decision resolved the issue of the perpetuity, all the essential elements of modern Anglo-American copyright law were in place. Most important, of course, was the notion of the author as the creator and ultimate source of property. This representation of authorship was at the heart of the long struggle over perpetual copyright; it survived the determination that literary property was limited in term; and it remains central to copyright today' (Rose, *Authors and Owners* 132).

But, as Recht points out, the apparently clear-cut decision in favour of limited statutory rights that carried the day in 1774, according to which the only rights of ownership where those enacted by legislation, was not so simple. In 1878, a report by the commission created in 1875 to examine existing legislation determined that author's rights depended partly on legislation and partly on common law: 'Legislation is not only arbitrary on certain points, it is incomplete and obscure on others. Thus, the question of whether there exists author's rights at Common law, that is outside of written law, has never been decided and has been the source of several debates.'[16]

According to Recht, whose purpose is to examine the emergence of the *droit d'auteur* in France, and the ensuing new concept of intellectual property, it is futile to search for the origins of such a right, and of subsequent 'moral rights,' in the royal privileges accorded to printers. It is only in the eighteenth century, in conformity with what Recht calls *l'esprit et le goût de la fin du 18ème siècle*, that is, faith in 'individual initiative' (33) that one can trace the emergence of two separate rights: those of the owner of copyright to reproduce the manuscript that he has acquired; those of the author to rewards for his work and his talent. In the preamble of the 1777 French law instituting the first *droit d'auteur* as distinct from the royal privilege of printing, one reads, according to Recht, that 'the privilege accorded to the author is intended to reward him for his work, his creative activity, and it is perpetual. It is not to be confused with the privilege accorded to the publisher, the purpose of which is to repay him for his expenses and this privilege cannot extend beyond the life of the author.'[17]

In this decision, we see a clear distinction between a *privilège* that the law does not create but only recognizes, and, recognizing it, creates means for its protection; and a privilege created by the lawmakers for the protection of their subjects, but existing only by virtue of their decision, not as a preexisting natural right. The clarity of this distinction between the rights of an author over his creative work and the privilege granted to the publisher as remuneration for his expenses is a formulation that seems to have been unavailable to the British in the discussions preceding 1774.

If we accept Recht's uncharitable account, the Revolutionary decisions of 1791 (Le Chapelier) and 1793 (Lakanal), traditionally heralded as the origin of the creation of the modern *droit d'auteur*, did no more than reiterate previously existing laws, while abolishing the *Ancien régime* system of privileges, and limiting the terms of proprietorship, previously perpetual for authors, to a term of ten years (increased to twenty in 1810 and maintained at fifty since 1886) (Recht 36ff.).

Recht's point helps to disentangle the confusion surrounding the British conflation of authorship and ownership: he maintains that the *droit d'auteur* had always existed, as is evident in the fact that the perpetual rights of ownership over an author's unpublished manuscript had never been contested: the debate was limited to the rights of reproduction of a commodity in a market economy. So far, the British and the French systems are comparable. The evolution of a separately legislated *droit d'auteur* was a phenomenon emerging from case law throughout the nineteenth century and culminating in the separation of an intellectual conception of the work from its material support (Recht 25). In Recht's account of this development in France, there were two main factions: those who, like Diderot and Balzac, defended the property rights of authors, and others, adhering to the 'personalist' school, who feared that assimilation of intellectual work to ordinary property would entail a limitation of the author's non-pecuniary rights. The solution was to be what Recht calls a dualist conception of authorship, entailing patrimonial rights over the material support of the work, similar to copyright, and moral rights over the non-material aspects of the work, protected in the British tradition at common law. The final direction of the development in French law was influenced by the Berne convention in 1886, to which France adhered in 1887. The French delegation, dominated by the Association littéraire et artistique internationale founded in 1878 under Victor Hugo, fiercely defended the notion of intellectual 'property,' but was defeated by the members of the German delegation, who argued that assimilating intellectual works to property was counter to their national laws, deriving from a more personalist theory (Recht 67–9).

Ten years after the Berne convention, during an international conference in Paris for the revision of the convention, Zola still complains that limited-term rights subject the descendants of the author to a dispossession of their inheritance: 'However, I have not only given my manual labour, I have given my mind, I have given my heart, I have given my life. And it is for this that we are done the great honour of being expropriated, by invoking the public good, the cause of the whole of humanity.'[18]

The development of copyright legislation decided against perpetual ownership, but in favour of perpetual authorship. In describing the rights of this second persona, the law guarantees paternity, but not exclusive possession. It protects form but not content, that is, not ideas, but rather their particular and individual expression. The notion of 'copying' in contemporary copyright retains a technological bias that has its origins in the evolution of print and subsequent possibilites for large-scale piracy. 'Copying' is not seen primarily as an intellectual, but rather as a purely mechanical operation of reproduction, facilitated by print, then by photography, and most recently by electronic media. The mechanistic foundation of 'intellectual property' law is evident in the fact that it sees the ideas expressed in words or phrases as the unprotectable aspects of intellectual production – that part which, independently of the theory of authorship espoused, is deemed to belong to the public domain.

Premodern notions of authorship and *intellectual* creation construct knowledge or the invention of ideas in a continuum evolving *from* the public domain, the realm in which ideas naturally and eternally exist, *to* individual appropriation. In this economy, authors are never 'owners' but are more properly considered stewards or husbandmen of a common good that is given over to them temporarily and, in the best instances, for improvement. The Romantic and modern concepts reverse the directionality of the process of 'invention,' and situate the origin of ideas within the individual, whose best ideas are ultimately destined to be released to the public. In the modern scenario, authors are seen as enlightened masters, fathers, or landholders – legitimate proprietors caught up in a kind of intellectual communism, where they are expected to relinquish their possessions for the good of society at large, and who should require only that society, in return, recognize their generosity and genius. In both cases, it is to the realm of the common good or the public domain that the essence of intellectual production belongs, whether as its origin or its destiny.

The transition between these two economies received its impetus notably from the Lockean intervention, which placed property rights deriving not only from possession, but also from work, at the heart of the definition of the individual. Ideas appropriated and transformed from the common domain came to be considered property either, because in the process of appropriation they were seen as a kind of reincarnation in which the author-father plays the role of *originator*, whose expression of those ideas reflected his character and individuality intimately; or else, because the production of those ideas involved processes of transformation and formulation representing *work*, the fruits of which must belong to the worker. The conclusion of the debate between perpetual and limited-term copyright was clearly a defeat for the Lockean rationale that can, however, be seen to have dominated the thinking of most parties involved in the issue. The resulting compromise, which concludes that ownership is temporary but that authorship is permanent, maintains the distinction – or perhaps rather the confusion – between real and symbolic, or tangible and intangible goods – that is, between the private but temporary right to economic profits, on the one hand, and the public but permanent right to claim the paternity of ideas, on the other. But the claim to paternity, which specifically does not involve ownership, can profit an author only symbolically or, if economically, then only indirectly.

Plagiarism exceeds the limits of copyright as authorship exceeds those of ownership – it challenges distinctions erected between ideas and their expression, confuses paternity with family resemblance, and origins with originality. With respect to the public domain and the individuality of discourse, plagiarism sits on both sides of the fence at once, on the one hand, proclaiming the individual's propriety over ideas; on the other, seeing discourse as infinitely appropriable in a kind of 'what's mine is mine and what's yours is mine' logic. Plagiarism is often indifferent to economic considerations, and evolves most naturally in a symbolic realm where identity – that is, self-identity – is constructed by a process of indiscriminate projection of self onto the ideas and expressions of others, as if onto one's children. Ultimately, if copyright is a function of the economics of property, plagiarism is rather an index of the intimate and timeless relationship of identity and propriety obtaining between personhood and intellectual activity – a relationship that appears independent of and impervious to institutional and social sanctions or conventions and that surfaces in accusations of plagiarism throughout history. That certain historical periods demonstrate, or at least record, either more or less of these accusations certainly reflects changing sensitivities to and tolerances for the phenomenon. But the very existence of charges of plagiarism – especially in the form of invectives intended as personal insults – is sufficient indication that usurping another's ideas, words, and expressions has always constituted an affront to the integrity of the victim, and a slur on the integrity of the perpetrator. The intense disputes that preceded contemporary copyright laws should provide a stumbling block to theories maintaining the modernity of authorship and of propriety over intellectual work, as well as a stimulus for their reassessment.

PART TWO

Reading Plagiarism

4. Reading the Reader

L'originalité d'un écrit est directement proportionnelle à l'ignorance de ses lecteurs.

Hubert Aquin, 'Profession: écrivain'

Whereas the history of copyright can be reduced, albeit simplistically, to the national laws and their interpretations instituting protection for intellectual property over time, the 'history' of plagiarism is somewhat more elusive, although not for the lack of historians' efforts, as we shall see. It is easier to find accusations of plagiarism than unproblematic examples of it, because the phenomenon itself is constructed by an interpretive discourse of reception such that repetition is not sufficient to condemn a text; it can be, in fact, one of the intrinsic qualities of what is deemed literary. As with any form of aesthetic production, it is analytical discourse itself that is constitutive of value. According to Schneider, 'it is readers' judgment which separates a book from its sources and makes of it an authentic work, even if it is not a new one. Plagiarism is therefore judged by its effects. The evidence of borrowings pales in the face of aesthetic considerations.'[1] He goes on to say that the difference between plagiarism and 'literature' exists in the aesthetic value of the text, and that plagiarism can be excused by the beauty of its results. While the truth of this as a historical account is born out by the very long list of great writer-plagiarists, Schneider does not problematize the notion of 'aesthetic value,' which seems to stand on its own as an intrinsic and objective component of a work to be uncovered by readers, rather as being itself a judgment constructed in and by reception. That some texts are widely accepted as being superior to others is a fact of literary history, and it is unnecessary to have recourse to a theory of aesthetic value in order to recognize the power of readers' judgments in the creation of artistic norms. We do have a notion of canonized works, even if we contest such notions: works attain greater or lesser literary value according to judgments that may change over time, but point to a degree of communal consensuality in the construction of the literary, the non-literary, and even in the revision of literary categories and their contents. As it is the consensual judgment of authoritative readers that 'recognizes' the aesthetic value of texts, and by deeming them literary makes them so, plagiarism is also a result of the recognition of readers, and of a negative aesthetic judgment ensuing from this recognition. The importance of the reader as a feature of the system of literary value is expressed by Bourdieu: 'the apprehension and appreciation of the work also depend on the beholder's intention, which is itself a function of the conventional norms governing the relation to the work of art in a certain historical and social situation and also of the beholder's capacity to conform to those norms, i.e., his artistic training' (*Distinction* 30).

In spite of the importance of the reader in the process of *naming, compiling*, and *criticizing*, instances of plagiarism, it is usually seen as a property of texts arising from conscious or unconscious authorial intentions. Even with the increased importance of the 'role of the reader' in contemporary literary theory, the responsibility for plagiarism has remained solidly with the author: judgments about the existence of plagiarism are decisions about whether or not the author has committed a certain kind of act; in this instance, as in aesthetic reception in general, reader intentionality is disguised as the attribution of intentionality to the author. Thus, the first step in uncovering the 'crime' of plagiarism, the simple discovery of repetition, is not in itself discovering plagiarism – the repetition must be subsequently identified as a fraudulent one. Most cases of recognized repetitions do not become 'plagiarism,' because the reader, having recognized part of his or her own cultural patrimony in the text, does the work of legitimizing the repetition by applying to it available literary terms ranging from imitation through allusion to intertextuality. For the traditional reader, recognition is the counterpart of authorial intention: it not only is a confirmation of the reader's participation in a community of aesthetic expectations that he or she shares with the author, but is construed as the response to an intentional encoding of this mutual knowledge in the text. A more post-structuralist approach would recognize the fatality of repetition and, without invoking conscious authorial intentionality, would see repetition – intertextuality, interdiscursivity – as an inescapable, inevitable part of the cultural, discursive process that may or may not be controlled by the author. The specific details of this horizon of expectations vary according to sociohistorical context, but are indifferent to the actual functioning of the mechanism of identification, which is really a form of self-recognition.

Since all determinations of plagiarism, as we have said, arise from the reader, a brief survey of the history of the positions of the institutional reader/critic is useful to specify the contours of such determinations. This history will begin with the most fundamental aspect of creating plagiarism through processes of naming, and will pursue the critical activities of compilation and criticism – both of plagiarists and of their critics. This history, while necessarily cursory, will take us back to the very origins of the term 'plagiarism' and will underline not only the stability of its determinants, but also the variety of metaphors and euphemisms that have been used to condemn or justify it over the years.

NAMING PLAGIARISM

What's in a name? In the case of plagiarism, a lot. The euphemization of plagiarism is not a new phenomenon but seems to be accelerating in the second half of the twentieth century, corresponding to aesthetic trends that tend more and more, once again, towards imitation as an intentional strategy. An example drawn from Schneider reveals a more than merely semantic confusion that allows him to claim a certain formal identity between what might be labelled either positively or negatively: 'Rehabilitated under the erudite name of intertextuality, plagiarism has, little by little, once again become something which is no longer an inevitability but a technique of writing among others, sometimes claimed to be the only one.'[2]

While his reductionist use of 'intertextuality' should not go unchallenged, he points to a phenomenon that we will often encounter: plagiarism is largely determined by a process of naming.

It is easier to find accusations of plagiarism than definite descriptions of it, and these do not appear until relatively late in time, tacit evidence that plagiarism may be of that order of phenomena which do not need to be defined to be instantly recognized. Countless metaphors pointing to instances of improper appropriation demonstrate many of the elements of later conceptions of plagiarism long before the word is current in English or French, and in the absence of sustained definitions of the phenomenon. In fact, it is essentially from the canon of ancient and perennial metaphors that the modern concept of plagiarism derives its contours. Erich Welslau has compiled an extensive summary of these metaphors in French from the Renaissance until the French Revolution, which, being largely classical in origin, do not differ substantially in the English tradition. I will not repeat here Welslau's exhaustive study; rather, in adopting some of the most important categories of metaphor he provides, I will attempt merely to confirm and enhance them with examples from literatures and periods he does not treat. The facility with which the metaphors he offers are generalizable across cultural and historical periods is evidence of the essential stability of conceptions of negative borrowing, whether described as 'servile imitation' or, later, as 'plagiarism.'

Welslau records the first European usage of the term 'plagiarism' as being by Lorenzo Valla in his preface to Book 2 of *Elegantiae Latini Sermonis*, 1444 (Welslau 97). In French, the *Trésor de la langue française* (1988) cites the first occurrence of the adjective in Charles Fontaine (*Les ruisseaux*, 1555), where, in his polemical presentation of his translation of Ovid, he recalls Vitruvius' anecdote about Ptolemy: 'Now as for those who are such great enemies of all translation, let them believe what they will; but let them not, however, continue to steal (which they call imitate) several verses and periods of ancient poets, such verses, sentences and periods which they attribute wholly to themselves; for they cannot attribute to themselves things similar to the works of certain famous poets, without being referred to the judgment of Aristophance before the king Ptolemy, and to the punishment which the said king visited upon such apelike plagiaristic Poets.'[3]

According to the *Trésor*, the substantive *plagiaire* (plagiarist) is introduced into French in 1584 (A. Thévet, *Les vrais portraits et vie des hommes illustres*) and the same source attributes Bayle's *Dictionary* (1697) with the first occurrence of the word *plagiat* (plagiarism; article 'Leonard Aretin,' note f.). The word appears in English with its current meaning also at the end of the sixteenth century: White (120–1) cites Joseph Hall's line concerning a 'plagiary sonnet-wright' (*Virgidemiarum*, 1598) as the first English use, and Ben Jonson's reference in the *Poetaster IV* (1601) to 'The ditt' is all borrowed; 'tis Horace's; hang him, plagiary' follows not long after (Paull 102).

In considering plagiarism to be the result of a reader's judgment with respect to a perceived ethical or aesthetic infraction, it is first necessary to accept that the absence of the word in the language does not signify the absence of either the concept or the practice. For our purposes, 'thief' or 'jay dressed in borrowed feathers' will do quite as well as a description of someone who is judged to have intentionally misappropriated someone else's intellectual property, or else fraudulently misrepresented himself as an 'author.' Since the existence of plagiarism is primarily a function of reception, much depends on the terms of accusation and defence, for example, the author's (or his lawyer's or critic's) ability to call his 'plagiarism' by another name and get away with it. This is a time-honoured strategy, and has produced a number of euphemisms, ranging from *heureux larcin* (happy theft), to 'conquest,' to 'intertextuality.' Welslau (1976) concludes that, of all the metaphors, from bees producing honey, to the wearing of borrowed feathers, to processes of ingestion and digestion, the only term that is used in a uniquely negative context is 'plagiarism' where it is equivalent to theft. That this constant is no longer strictly true does not reduce the impact of Welslau's study: the difference between good and bad borrowing hinges largely on the terms used to qualify the borrowing. The formal difference between plagiarism and other more legitimate forms of imitation can easily be shown to be non-existent, and two works exhibiting the same formal properties can exist side by side in the same historical and cultural context and be variously labelled plagiaristic or not. Similarly, the same text at different times, or even the same text at the same time, can be construed either as plagiaristic or not, depending on the readers' criteria and interest in judging: temporal distance is not required for inconsistencies in judgments about plagiarism, and disputes support the notion that the 'originality' of the work is constituted less by its formal features, which themselves do not change, than by the judgments rendered about them. The metaphors mobilized to describe textual borrowing or appropriation fall easily into two categories: one the one hand, those intended to vilify the practice and, on the other, those that justify and glorify it. Central to metaphors that defend creative imitation are figures emphasizing natural processes of transformation which produce a new substance from raw materials, processes that are precisely the appropriative and individual work required in order to fulfil the classical tenets of good imitation. Such metaphors include the transformation of food by digestion and the bee's producing honey from pollen. In reference to these terms, La Mothe le Vayer (1662) distinguishes between good and bad imitation: 'In fact, one can steal in the manner of Bees, without doing wrong to anyone; but the theft of the Ant, who makes off with the grain intact, must never be imitated.'[4] The opposition between the method of the bee and the ant underlines the negative effects of simple appropriation without transformation, of which the oldest metaphor is probably Horace's jay wearing borrowed feathers, itself borrowed from Aesop (Fable 47), which La Fontaine popularized.[5] Aesop does not mention plagiarists – his fable is directed against overweening pride and ambition doubled with the fraud of inauthenticity deriving from the imitation of one's betters. In Horace's version, however, the allusion is directed specifically towards an imitative writer: 'What is my Celsus doing? He has been advised, and the advice is still often to be repeated, to acquire stock of his own, and forbear to touch whatever writings the Palatine Apollo has received: lest, if it chance that the flock of birds should some time or other come to demand their feathers, he, like the daw stripped of his stolen colours, be exposed to ridicule' (*Epistles*, Bk I, 4, Horace, *Works* 235–6).

A familiar and related figure is that of the imitative ape. In the *Deffence* (II,3), Du Bellay advises the writer to 'diligently listen to his nature and to compose in imitation of him to whom he feels himself closest. Otherwise his imitation will resemble that of the ape.'[6] Similarly, Robert Greene is commonly credited with an early charge of plagiarism directed against Shakespeare in *Groatsworth of Wit* (1592), Greene's 'swan song' or deathbed 'repentance.' Here the accusation of fraudulent disguise is doubled with that of the imitative ape: 'there is an upstart Crow, beautified with our feathers, that with his *Tygers hart wrapt in a Players hyde,* supposes he is as well able to bombast out a blanke verse as the best of you: and beeing an absolute *Johannes fac totum,* is in his owne conceit the onely Shake-scene in a countrey. O that I might intreat your rare wits to be imploied in more profitable courses: and let those Apes imitate your past excellence, and never more acquaint them with your admired inventions' (Carroll 84–5). While the allusion to Shakespeare is not contested, the nature of the accusation is, as is, in fact, the authorship of *Groatsworth,* which may be a literary hoax (see Carroll, Introduction and Appendix G). But these questions of attribution are of less importance than the general reference to imitative apes and the advice to playwrights to keep their 'inventions' to themselves for fear of pillage by less-talented authors. Regardless of the authorship and the intention with respect to Shakespeare, unlicensed and uncondoned imitation seems to have plagued the Elizabethan stage, and Greene in particular. In his discussion of Greene's text and its Shakespearian allusion, Carroll points out that 'the passage is now read more as an index to a state of mind, Greene's, than as a clue to Shakespeare's moral sensibility or early methods' (141). As much as we would concur with Carroll, on general principles, that 'plagiarism' is more significantly a state of the accuser's mind than a state of texts or authorial intentions, one needs only to subtract the problematic reference to Shakespeare from the general complaint to conclude that some form of 'plagiarism' was recognized among the Bard's contemporaries.

With this conclusion, however, Carroll does not concur. In discussing the context of the accusation, one in which the University Wits were being upstaged by uneducated playwrights such as Shakespeare, who were supplanting – and profiting from – their elders and cultural betters, Carroll says: 'To this line of argument *Groatsworth*'s slur against Shakespeare is the culmination: this common player is an ignorant, egotistical imitator of a bad style [...] The general thrust of the attack, when one considers this matrix, would appear to be otherwise than against plagiarism as such' (Carroll 143).

One wonders what kind of plagiarism Carroll has in mind when distinguishing between this attack and 'plagiarism as such,' that is, 'real' plagiarism as it could have been identified and attacked at the end of the sixteenth century in England. Subtracting the name of Shakespeare from the equation leaves us with the opposition between 'Apish imitators' profiting from the inventions of 'rarer wits' – why this is not 'plagiarism as such' Carroll does not explain. Ben Jonson, in *On Poet Ape* (1616), similarly accuses another writer, whose identity also is either Shakespeare or not, in the following terms:

> Poor Poet-Ape, that would be thought our chief,
> Whose works are e'en the frippery of wit,
> From brocage [illicit dealings in old things] is become so bold a thief,
> As we, the robb'd, leave rage, and pity it.
> At first he made low shifts, would pick and glean,
> Buy the reversion of old plays; now grown
> To'a little wealth, and credit in the *scene,*
> He takes up all, makes each man's wit his own.
> And, told of this, he slights it. Tut, such crimes
> The sluggish gaping auditor devours;
> He marks not whose 'twas first: and after-times
> May judge it to be his, as well as ours.
> Fool, as if half eyes will not know a fleece
> From locks of wool, or shreds from the whole piece? (Jonson 164)

Even in the absence of the word, and regardless of the object of the epigram, the presence of something very like 'plagiarism as such' is clearly indicated.

The natural world is also evoked in the form of organic metaphors, of planting borrowed seeds or plants in one's own garden, or of grafting a branch onto one's own tree. Less dynamic images of borrowing as recombining of elements in a new form produce metaphors of mosaic and the making of new garments by patchwork: such metaphors recall the etymology of the *cento,* which is linked to 'patchwork' in Latin, just as modern descriptions of intertextuality as a text woven of other texts have recourse to the etymology of text as *tissu* (Fr: cloth). A similar metaphor involves the gathering of flowers into a bouquet, which gives us the *florilège,* a compendium of *fleurs de rhétorique,* or famous and beautiful sayings from the ancients.

A notable class of metaphors draws its dynamism from the irony of oxymoron. These involve variations on the theme of theft or larceny, and are designed not only to justify the means by the end, but to demonstrate in their own way the transformative nature of imitation. The coupling of a negative substantive, usually denoting 'theft,' with a positive qualifier indicates that the negative potential is positively transformed by the intervention of genius or creativity. In the French tradition, 'larcin,' meaning small or petty theft, is often used to qualify an instance of good borrowing. Welslau cites 'larcin [...] noble et industrieux' (Pasquier sur Ronsard, *Les recherches de la France*, éd. 1607, 878; Welslau 97); a '*larcin* [...] *honneste et legitime*' (Deimier sur Ronsard et Desportes, dans *L'académie de l'art poétique*, 213; Welslau 98), and from the *Larousse* we have already quoted *heureux larcin*. Other terms such as *contrefaire*, *usurper*, and *emprunter* can be used with positive or negative connotations (Welslau).

Another category of metaphors involves the discovery of something formerly hidden, as in the defence against an accusation of plagiarism attributed to Virgil, who claimed that he was uncovering gold from a dunghill, which is often repeated in the form of the metaphor of buried treasures that would otherwise be lost if some genius had not saved them from oblivion. Pope provides an ironic version of this metaphor in his satirical imitation of Longinus: *Peri Bathous: Of the Art of Sinking in Poetry* (1728). In 'Of Imitation and the Manner of Imitating' (chap. ix), Pope advises: 'As Virgil is said to have read Ennius, out of his dunghill to draw gold, so may our author read Shakespeare, Milton and Dryden for the contrary end, to bury their gold in his own dunghill. A true genius, when he finds anything lofty or shining in them, will have the skill to bring it down, take off the gloss, or quite discharge the color by some ingenius circumstance or periphrase, some addition or diminution, or by some of those figures the use of which we shall show in our next chapter' (61).

A significant category of metaphors involves the conquest of foreign lands, which is originally related to the theft metaphor through the action of 'pillaging,' recommended by both Du Bellay and Ronsard. Significantly, the land to be pillaged was ancient Greece and Rome, a legitimate source of literary treasures, situated in the premodern equivalent of the common domain: authoritative texts embodying universal truth. The defence and justification of theft from foreigners, specifically the Greeks, dates back at least to Terence, who, in the second century A.D., excuses himself from plagiarism by pointing out that his model was not Latin but Greek (Welsau 110–11). This tradition governing borrowing becomes a genuine rule for later Renaissance and classical Europe, for whom imitation was strictly circumscribed to translation from foreign sources, preferably ancient ones. The terms of the metaphor justify borrowing from foreign sources as a form of conquest, itself seen as a positive activity. The history of this metaphor is long and prolific, and it is interesting because of its tenacity: it is one of the few traditional metaphors that have continued to be active into the present, albeit transformed from the virtue of conquest into the crime of imperialism and cultural appropriation (see chapter 6).

COMPILING PLAGIARISM

One index of the relative importance of the perception of plagiarism across history is without doubt the time and effort spent by literary critics and historians in documenting the phenomenon, and in the place given to it in encyclopedia and other compendia of knowledge. According to this criterion, the French nineteenth century constitutes the great era of interest in plagiarism (apart, perhaps, from our own), although the preceding two centuries were not without their important contributions to the ferreting out of literary offenders. This development seems to coincide with the growing importance of the value of originality versus the aesthetic of imitation and, although interest in plagiarism in France predates copyright laws (1791–3), the most extended efforts of analysis and compilation are situated in the nineteenth century. The existence of copyright laws, coupled with the growing emphasis on subjective originality, meant that certain types of repetition became more susceptible to accusations of plagiarism. Schneider situates the turning point in the interest in plagiarism as a form of sanctionable literary 'crime' around the beginning of the nineteenth century, from 1810 to 1830, and cites Nodier's *Questions de littérature légale* as a signpost: the text, re-edited in its definitive version in 1828, was originally composed in 1812. This opinion seems to be borne out by other evidence that will come to light later in the discussion, but does not answer the question of why these particular years constitute a turning point.

The earliest important work on the subject is Jacques Thomasius' treatise *De plagio litterario*, first published in Leipzig as a dissertation in 1673, and later augmented in 1679 and 1692. This work is a major source for Bayle's *Dictionnaire historique et critique* (1695–7), in which he undertook to 'correct' the *Grand dictionnaire historique* of Louis Moréri (1674) by the historical examination of received dogma and traditions. Although Bayle's subject is not 'plagiarism,' his studies of classical and contemporary philosophers and men of letters are often nourished by insights on plagiarism furnished by Thomasius, whom he undertakes to translate in significant contexts. Bayle becomes, in turn, an important source for Diderot's *Encyclopédie* (1747–66), whose article 'Plagiat,' signed by Jaucourt, is indebted to Thomasius quoted by Bayle.

The very act of dictionary-writing itself was early recognized by its practictioners as an exercise in virtual theft, imitation, and compilation, and the eighteenth- and early nineteenth-century *encyclopédistes*, who undertook the new and daunting task of amassing and reproducing the state of knowledge of the arts and sciences for the time, also took explicit pains to legitimize their enterprise and to shield it from the potential accusation of plagiarism. In the familiar psychological twist of 'protesting too much,' these defences against virtual accusations of plagiarism can often point to a guilty conscience. In Abraham Rees's 1819 *Cyclopaedia*, we read under the entry 'Plagiary':

> Dictionary writers, at least such as meddle with arts and sciences, seem in this case to be exempted from the common laws of *meum* and *teum;* they do not pretend to set up on their own bottom, nor to treat the reader at their own cost. Their works are supposed, in great measure, compositions of other people; and whatever they take from others, they do it avowedly. In effect, their quality gives them a title to appropriate every thing that may be for their purpose, wherever they find it, and they do no otherwise, than as the bee does, for the public service.
>
> Their occupation is not pillaging, but collecting contributions; and if you ask them their authority, they will produce you the practice of their predecessors of all ages and nations.

The argument is a familiar one and, so far as it goes, that is, in the historical context, justified. But the apology is curious in that it is rather too long, constituting more than half of the entire entry on plagiarism. In fact, this apology, and the accompanying definitions of plagiarism, including its etymology, are translated almost verbatim from Jaucourt's entry for *plagiaire* in Diderot's *Encyclopédie*, an established authority in the field of dictionary-making. By expressing what is true, the *Encyclopédie* has also fixed that truth in language, and it is not clear, in Diderot, whether the proper domain of the *encyclopédiste is* the *fond* or the *forme* of this truth. The text is ambiguous about the status of the truths expressed, but the selection in Rees's translation renders his version of the apology less convincing. Rees's overstated concern with legitimizing his role as compiler, or virtual plagiarist, is a clear case of self-accusation, of which another indication is that one of the most significant changes introduced into the translation is the use of the third-person pronoun to designate those dictionary writers who should not be accused of plagiarism. In the *Encyclopédie*, the author assumes his position as compiler and uses the first-person plural to refer to his activities: '*nous* empruntons'; 'la qualité de compilateurs *nous* donne un droit'; '*nous* dérobons,' and so on. Where Rees claims that 'whatever *they* take from others, *they* do it avowedly,' Jaucourt's text reads: 'what *we* borrow from others *we* borrow openly, in the light of day and quoting the sources *we* have used' (my emphasis, ['ce que nous empruntons des autres nous l'empruntons ouvertement, au grand jour et citant les sources où nous avons puisé']). The nature of the encyclopedic endeavour not only justifies the 'pillage' of other sources, but seems to thrust the encyclopedia naturally into the public domain:

Jaucourt sets himself and the *Encyclopédie* up as original sources, by claiming: 'Would it be possible to fulfil the plan [of the encyclopedia] without
this freedom [to borrow from others] that the judicious reader will not
refuse us, and which we accord to those who will write after us?' ('Seroit-il
possible d'en remplir le plan [i.e., of the encyclopedia] sans cette liberté
[i.e., borrowing from others] que le lecteur judicieux ne nous refusera
pas, et que nous accordons à ceux qui écriront après nous?'). It is difficult to say whether Jaucourt would have considered that Rees accepted
his offer a bit too willingly and more literally than it was meant. In any
case, Rees, by omitting this passage, either considers it a dangerous invita-
tion to other thiefs or is using the *Encyclopédie* as public property by virtue of its authority, part of which includes its priority. Rees does not feel
the need to quote his sources, and Diderot and his collaborators were not
unfailingly scrupulous in this respect either.

Nodier's major work, *Questions de littérature légale. Du plagiat, de la supposition d'auteurs, des supercheries qui ont rapport aux livres* (1828), remains today
one of the most interesting. It is a fascinating study of a panoply of literary
crimes by an author who has been – as is so often the case – accused of
many of them. Most commentators on plagiarism quote in this context his
famous apology for lack of originality from *Histoire du roi de Bohême et de
ses sept châteaux* (1830), a burlesque 'pastiche' of Diderot and Sterne in
which the author rails against imaginary accusations of plagiarism by align-
ing himself with a lineage of plagiarists stretching back to Rome, and
which ends: 'And you want me, I repeat, to invent the form and the content of a book! heaven help me! Condillac said somewhere that it would be
easier to create a world than an idea.'[7] In *Questions de littérature légale*
(1828), which is a version of 'literary curiosities,' Nodier deals with much
more than plagiarism. Most of the first part of the book, before the entry
on 'plagiarism' and the subsequent chapter on 'literary theft' (piracy), is
devoted to types of repetition that, when appropriately practised, constitute proper rather than improper appropriation. Forms of repetition
treated are 'Imitation,' 'Quotation,' 'Allusion,' and 'Similarity of ideas and
subjects.' Nodier also relies on Bayle and cites, among other Latin treatises,
Thomasius' dissertation, although there is little evidence in the text that he
has referred to it other than through Bayle. (In fact, the original version of
Nodier's text was apparently written 'completely without books' – 'dans un
dénûment absolu de livres' [*Questions de littérature légale* i].) Nodier's
work has become a major source for all studies following it: Ludovic
Lalanne's *Curiosités littéraires* (1845) and Quérard's treatise *Les supercheries
littéraires dévoilées* (1845–53) both quote him liberally. The nineteenth-
century *Larousse* article 'Plagiat' is little more than an updated compilation
of Diderot quoting Bayle quoting Thomasius, so that, in the French tradi-

tion, there is an almost unbroken line of authority and received knowledge – one might say serial plagiarism – on the subject.

In his chapter on 'plagiarism,' Nodier treats *encyclopédistes* rather unsympathetically. He qualifies dictionaries, in general, as being 'plagiarisms in alphabetical order' ['plagiats par ordre alphabétique' (*Questions de littérature légale* 37–8)], where all the elements of positive knowledge (i.e., the 'facts') must necessarily be repeated, even if they are given a new and elegant expression. Nodier considers that in the enterprise of compiling works of this sort, it is only the gathering of knowledge, and not its expression, which represents real labour, but to this *industrie vraiment laborieuse* the public is often indifferent, and is easily charmed by a work 'which has no other real merit than to dress up in modern form previously explored riches' ['qui n'a d'autre mérite réel que d'habiller à la moderne des richesses anciennement explorées' (38)]. He exempts Diderot and Panckoucke from these charges, the first having effected immense expansions to his model (Chambers's *Encyclopaedia*, 1728) and the second having improved the form by substituting the philosophical for the alphabetical order (*Encyclopédique méthodique et par ordre de matières*, 1772–1832). But since Nodier's interest, as ours, is largely literary, he renounces finally the need to draw definitive conclusions, for 'it is a particular type of question to know whether it is permitted for the editor of any work to enrich himself through the work of a rival, thereby destroying the latter's property, even should science benefit from this action; it is a question, I say, which appears to me to belong less to the realm of literary criticism than to that of morality.'[8] Or, we would say, less to literary criticism than to the courts.

In Nodier's preface to the second edition, addressed to 'M.C. Weiss, bibliothécaire de la ville de Besançon,' he claims that his purpose is solely to discuss 'those learned trifles which have amused our lives until now' ['ces doctes bagatelles qui ont amusé jusqu'ici notre vie' (v)]. In his conclusion, however, he achieves a moralistic tone, claiming to have 'sufficiently demonstrated that literary laurels have often been bestowed on men devoid of delicacy and of honour, who considered the career of talent to be only one of the roads to riches.'[9]

Disenchanted with contemporary society and the success of the young romantics, he turns against Hugo on the eve of the success of *Hernani* and taxes him with having achieved celebrity through industry ('une célébrité d'industrie' [Boisacq-Generet 25]). Nodier maintains such a fervent belief in the natural conjugation of talent and virtue that he proposes the censorship of the works of men devoid of virtue: 'The examples of great geniuses who have been spoiled by great vices are extremely rare, and it is to be wished that they didn't exist at all, even at the price of the beautiful works that we would be obliged to lose.'[10]

Joseph-Marie Quérard follows Nodier's moralistic example, but pursues his aim much more virulently. His three-volume work *Les supercheries littéraires*, compiled between 1845 and 1853, is the work of a literary historian and bibliographer. As distinct from Nodier's earlier work, which was the product of an artist-critic exercising a properly pre-nineteenth-century function of the writer as reader and judge, Quérard writes not as an artist, but primarily as a professional critic, whose aims are not purely aesthetic; or rather, for whom aesthetic value is allied with larger cultural concerns that link literary production to the political, social, and economic. Quérard's work coincides with the career of Sainte-Beuve, another of the early 'professional critics' later to become the academic critic, embodied in Brunetière, Thibaudet, and Lanson.

Already a bibliographer and literary historian of renown, Quérard's role is to judge and arrange the literary field according to what he sees as its essential and worthy elements. His studies had revealed to him the growing number of literary frauds and pretenders that by the middle of the century appeared to threaten the nobility of French letters and signal its decline into mediocrity or worse. Literary 'pygmies' enshrined in the annals of the national literature, plagiarists, and above all 'literary industrialists,' concerned solely with financial profit and uninterested in and incapable of the pursuit of literary genius, all plagued modern French letters. Quérard's aim is to purge the noble house of letters of these sundry imposters, accumulated over centuries, but becoming more serious since 1830, because of the rise of what he calls 'les industriels littéraires': 'By what necessity, one might ask us, do we unmask so many people? By a very noble one: that of easing, as much as possible, the difficulty of writing the literary history of our times: of ridding our archives of the confusion into which they have been thrown. While industrial biographers daily overload our historical dictionaries with literary pygmies, whose titles posterity will have to discard, should we leave to this posterity even the difficult burden of inquiring into imaginary personages? It is this consideration which has prompted us to unmask the vast majority of writers who presently occupy the public's attention.'[11]

Quérard does not himself offer a definition of plagiarism, except to qualify it as 'one of the most shameful transgressions; that which the courts pursue' ['l'un des plus honteux délits; celui que les tribunaux poursuivent' (69)]; he quotes at length the definitions by the Baron de Reiffenberg and Nodier. His position is somewhat contradictory, claiming, on the one hand, that 'all nations, ancient and modern, have practised plagiarism' [toutes les nations, anciennes et modernes, ont pratiqué le plagiat' (70)]; and, on the other, that the contemporary phenomenon is a sign or an effect of the degradation of the times: 'The dignity of letters has disappeared. Especially since 1830, literature, in general, is no longer a mission for contemporary writers. Writing has become a business, a way for upstarts to succeed (*parvenir*), a means of acquiring money: from the moment that each man no longer needed anything but money to achieve consideration, the man of letters has not wanted to be considered below green grocers and vendors of rabbit skins, who have become eligible electors: intelligence has tried to do battle with riches.'[12]

Quérard here aligns the industrialization of literature with the July Revolution of 1830, which installed a bourgeois monarchy and a parliamentary system based on suffrage determined by capital. He does not pursue this theme explicitly, however, and it is undermined by the long list of plagiarists from the Middle Ages to the present, which includes the most illustrious names in French literary history. His real aim seems to be to reveal the unworthy writers of the present age, who risk passing unwarranted into the annals of legitimate literature if he does not do for the nineteenth century what others have done for previous ages. Alongside famous names of the past, there are revelations intended to have a moral impact on the present: 'It is a book which contains some very spicy revelations. It is perhaps a mean book; but the fault is less mine than that of our times; I have had so many frauds and so many examples of charlatanism to reveal! this book is nonetheless that of an honest man.'[13]

The moral and political underpinning of Quérard's mission are not always echoed in the projects of other students of plagiarism and literary curiosities, particularly in the twentieth century. A notable example is Georges Maurevert's *Livre des plagiats* (1922). Beginning with the ancients and ending with 'Quelques petits et gros plagiats typiques de nos temps,' Maurevert's book includes chapters on many of the greatest names in French and European literature. In his 'Avertissement,' he explains that although he had conceived and begun the work in a 'rather frivolous spirit,' as the research progressed, the subject appeared to him more and more serious. His first objective had been simply to amuse his readers; ultimately he hopes to 'make them think' (5). Maurevert considers the times propitious for the publication: 'Never has plagiarism been so much discussed as in our day' (6). Faced with the overwhelming quantity of matter available to him, he chooses to study separately 'the cases of our most well-known plagiarists, that is to say most of our great writers' (7). Maurevert's position is that 'plagiarism' is as old and as durable as literature, and his subject ranges from various forms of classical imitation to contemporary accusations of plagiarism without any trace of moral condemnation. His purpose – beyond the revelation of the details of the 'plagiarisms' he recounts, which entails an enormous erudition – seems to be to conflate imitation, influence, and 'plagiarism.' He does not offer a definition of plagiarism and, in applying the term indiscriminately to the 'great authors' throughout history whom he discusses, he places himself solidly within the tradition that defends the ubiquity of literary repetition. Seen in this light, his work amounts to a series of 'source studies' to which the application of the word 'plagiarism' seems destined more as a strategy intended to pique the curiosity of the reader, an ironic way of reading literary influence that implicitly condemns the contemporary flurry of accusations of plagiarism to banality.

Compared with the French interest in compilations of 'plagiarism,' the English tradition is remarkably poor in the genre. While accusations of plagiarism are not lacking, there are few examples of a sustained interest in the question, and most sources are in the form of 'curiosities' such as published by D'Israeli ([1791–3] 1971) and Walsh ([1892] 1966). The tradition that, in France, stretches in an unbroken line from Thomasius to Chaudenay is non-existent in English, and only really appears in the twentieth century in the form of scholarly studies such as White's and Ogden's and, more lately, those of Mallon and Lafollette. One can only speculate about this indifference. It is certain that the relative rigidity of the French literary institution – the presence of the Académie française, the stronger, more formalized commitment to classicism and the subsequent intensity of the Romantic revolution – made the literary oppositions between imitation and originality appear more trenchant in France than in England. The relative lateness of copyright legislation in France, followed closely by the effervescent years of political revolution and literary and theatrical 'industrialism' in the first half of the nineteenth century, certainly contributed to heightened awareness of questions of originality and property in the literary field. And it may perhaps be that the 'encyclopaedic' tradition of compilation and classification is itself less developed in the English tradition. For whatever reasons, plagiarism-hunting in the English tradition has generally been a function of source studies focused on individual authors or on studies of literary periods, and has rarely been carried out for its own sake.

CRITICIZING PLAGIARISM

Compared with developments since the nineteenth century, previous literary readership constituted a relatively homogeneous family sharing a common cultural background and heritage – writers reading readers writing and so on – in a continuing contest for legitimate inclusion in the family. A version of the elite and restricted nature of literary authority survives today in the academic literary institution, especially in the person of the academic critic as this function became professionalized in the nineteenth century. The explosion of literacy in the eighteenth and nineteenth centuries, which entailed a growing distinction between readers and the culturally literate, progressively invested the specialist with the task of providing the lay reader with the equipment needed to recognize the lineage from which a work was born; source studies and critical editions proceeded to supply the reader's missing erudition. As Thibaudet will say: 'The works of the past can only be understood and judged by those who know the past. This is the domain of the professional critic.'[14] Invested with the authority to discover sources, the critic's function was not only to identify the work's patrilineage, but also to recognize the genius and beauty of originality when it was present.

I have argued elsewhere that the nineteenth century was in some sense responsible for the 'invention' of plagiarism (Randall 1992). This argument, which appears to contradict the historical evidence confirming the continuity of plagiarism from the beginning of letters, plays on a distinction made by Thibaudet between 'criticism' and 'critics': before the nineteenth century there were *critics*; the nineteenth century, however, saw the birth of *criticism* as a discipline.[15] The institutionalization of *la critique* as an autonomous discipline, carried out by a professional corps of specialists devoted exclusively to the function of criticism, coincides historically with a growing consensus on a practice of illegitimate repetition. The attention paid to plagiarism at a time when the literary institution was to achieve its professional form can be seen as an indication of the stabilization of the contours of the literary, and of explicit attempts to legislate appropriate membership in the ranks. But before discussing the nineteenth century, it will be instructive to evaluate the role of the critic in identifying plagiarism as it appeared before the modern form of literary criticism was institutionalized. On a general view of things, this role is not exalted. William Walsh, author of *Handy-book of Literary Curiosities* (1892), expresses a common long-standing feeling when he claims: 'On the whole, as between the plagiarist and his accuser, we prefer the plagiarist' (899).

Montaigne is relentless in his attacks on pedantic critics, taxing them with having memory but no judgment, learning but no understanding. In his hands, 'plagiarism' becomes a method of catching out false pedants by the use of unacknowledged translation: it is an early instance of 'guerrilla plagiarism,' which we examine in Part Three. The most revealing passage comes in 'Des livres,' where he expresses the conflict between the ancients and the moderns and defends his use of the vernacular for the expression of eternal truth:

> I do not count my borrowings: I weigh them; if I had wanted them valued
> for their number, I would have burdened myself with twice as many. They

are all, except for very, very few, taken from names so famous and ancient that they seem to name themselves without help from me. In the case of those reasonings and original ideas which I transplant into my own soil and confound with my own, I sometimes deliberately omit to give the author's name so as to rein in the temerity of those hasty criticisms which leap to attack writings of every kind, especially recent writings by men still alive and in our vulgar tongue which allow anyone to talk about them and which seem to convict both their concept and design of being just as vulgar. I want them to flick Plutarch's nose in mistake for mine and to scald themselves by insulting the Seneca in me. ('On Books,' Bk II, ch. 10, 458)

The failings of the false critic are also outlined in Pope's *Essay on Criticism* (1711, ll. 610–19):

> Such shameless bards we have; and yet 'tis true,
> There are as mad, abandoned critics too.
> The bookful blockhead, ignorantly read,
> With loads of learned lumber in his head,
> With his own tongue still edifies his ears,
> And always listening to himself appears.
> All books he reads, and all he reads assails,
> From Dryden's Fables down to Durfey's Tales.
> With him, most authors steal their works, or buy;
> Garth did not write his own *Dispensary*. (18–19)

Most eighteenth-century interest in the practice of plagiarism spends at least as much time denouncing plagiarism hunters as plagiarists: a most eloquent summary of this position is proferred by Marmontel in his *Elemens de littérature* ([1787] 1968) in the article 'Plagiarism,' which is largely a diatribe against the hapless critic who, just as Montaigne's pedant is the repository of much knowledge but no wisdom, thinks that every case of repetition is a case of plagiarism: 'It is a kind of literary crime, for which the pedantic, the envious and the foolish never fail to put famous writers on trial. *Plagiarism* is the name which they give to a petty theft of ideas, and they rail against this theft as if they themselves were being robbed, or as if it were essential to public order and peace that the properties of the intellect be inviolable.'[16] And Marmontel also provides an explanation for this ignoble behaviour: 'Why then are the pedantic, the half-cultivated, and malicious critics more scrupulous and more severe? Here is why. Because pedants have the vanity to want to display their erudition by discovering a literary theft; the small-minded, in reproaching this theft, have the pleasure of believing that they humiliate the great; and the critics of whom I speak follow the unhappy instinct that nature has given them, that of pouring out their venom.'[17] In other words, 'great authors don't copy,' and the accusation of plagiarism is a sign of pedantry, or worse.

Other sources tend to give more credit to the critic, by attributing to the 'true critic' the faculty to distinguish between imitation and plagiarism. According to Diderot's *Encyclopédie*, 'Nothing is more common in the republic of letters [than plagiarism]; the truly erudite are not taken in; these disguised thefts rarely escape their perceptive [*clairvoyant*] eyes.'[18] The powers of insight that enable the true *érudit* to detect the hidden theft are an instinctive and natural part of the cultivated reading process, thus differentiating genuine literary knowledge from the pedantic kind – Diderot does not go on to say whether or not it is praiseworthy or ignoble to extend one's authority into the realm of denunciation. On the same subject, the nineteenth-century *Larousse* is more or less in agreement, and quotes from Ludovic Lalanne (119), who introduces a subtle double bind into the process: 'all those men who appear at different times to dominate their century are related to their generation and to previous generations, not by invisible threads, but by strong and powerful links which can be easily perceived as soon as one takes the trouble to see them.'[19]

In this argument, the insightful critic is able to distinguish between plagiarism and the legitimate heritage of letters on which great authors depend and which they naturally exploit from 'generation to generation,' in a version of the patrilinear metaphor. Here the double bind is a result of the simultaneous adherence to the tradition of imitation and to the newer tenets of originality: the relationship between great writers is at once 'easily perceived' – thereby exonerating these writers from the suspicion of plagiarism – and difficult to see: it is necessary to 'take the trouble' to recognize them. That is, the ease with which certain readers are able to identify the heritage of the past is a result of the work and study by which the true critic acquires facility of perception. It follows that the vast majority of borrowings identified by true critics in the work of great authors are not plagiarisms: not because the great writer never copies, but because the 'plagiarisms' of great writers get renamed, and because the genuine scholar, who presumably deals in great literature, distinguishes himself from the pedant by recognizing that such borrowings are not theft. According to Marmontel's reasoning, to denounce plagiarism would be to identify one's self as a pedant, a simple, mean-minded and/or envious critic: if true plagiarism is an activity carried out by talentless men masquerading as authors, then to turn one's attention to it is not only a waste of one's erudition, but risks turning the weaknesses of the plagiarist back onto the critic. The disdain for the pedantry involved in accusations of plagiarism is expressed by de Quincey, himself a 'plagiarist' of some notoriety, in an 1827 note on 'plagiarism': 'It is undeniable, that thousands of feeble writers are constantly at work, who subsist by Plagiarism, more or less covert. It is equally undeniable, [...] and partly it arises out of this very fact, partly also to shew their reading, and partly because it is the cheapest way of writing criticism, without any expense of thought, that thousands of feeble critics [...] subsist by detecting plagiarisms or imitations, real or supposed' (Letter to the editor of the *Edinburgh Saturday Post*, 3 Nov. 1827, in de Quincey 181). And, after citing Tennyson and Walter Scott on the same theme, Branders Matthews declares: 'It was the original owner of King Solomon's mines who asserted that there was nothing new under the sun; and after the lapse of hundreds of years one may suggest that a ready acceptance of the charge of plagiarism is a sign of low culture, and that a frequent bringing of the accusation is a sign of defective education and deficient intelligence' (26).

The difficulty in distinguishing between plagiarism and legitimate imitation puts the critic in danger of exposing his ignorance by mistaking as plagiarism those repetitions that the insightful, from their vast warehouse of the history of letters, recognize as imitation, an act of homage directed towards one's literary ancestors, or else as a case of improvement. Walter Scott makes this point with regard to an accusation of plagiarism levelled at Lesage: 'Lesage's claim to the title of original author of this delicious work [...] has been stupidly, I would say almost ungratefully, contested by those half-critics, who imagine that they have discovered *plagiarism* as soon as they perceive any kind of resemblance between the plan of a good work and that of another of the same nature, previously developed by an inferior writer.'[20]

Needless to say, such authorial attacks on the attackers of plagiarists might be construed as acts of self-defence generated by a guilty conscience.

The rise of professional criticism in France throughout the nineteenth century has been seen to coincide with the autonomization of the literary field: criticism and literature are mutually interdependent. Brunetière announces that the birth of modern literature was a result of the emancipation of criticism (414). This relationship is confirmed by more recent studies: except for the fact that Brunetière situates this double 'birth' in the Renaissance and the modern point of view situates it in the nineteenth century, the relationship between the autonomization of the literary field and that of the rise of criticism is confirmed by studies such as those of Gérard Delfau and Anne Roche (1977) and Jacques Dubois (1978). According to these authors, it is between 1830 and 1880 that two important developments will lead to the corollary professionalization of literature and criticism: first, the emergence and enormous popularity of journalistic criticism, and, second, the institution of the study of literature in the universities, giving rise to academic criticism.

The professional critic will eventually supplant the artist-critic in prestige and influence; his expertise is no longer merely a matter of refined and superior taste but is based on the erudition acquired by long and intense study: natural discernment must be honed and informed by a good dose of historical knowledge. Indeed, the professional critic will attempt to rival even the artist in importance. The battle between artist and critic is not new, and in order to understand the role of this conflict in shaping the literary field, it is necessary to recognize that these two apparently pitched camps are both part of the same institution. The debate between the 'artist-critic' and the professional critic continues the conflict that Montaigne identifies as being between himself and the 'pedants.' Reformulated by Thibaudet, this relationship is characterized as a 'state of battle [which] is part of a rhythm incorporated into the very life of literature' ['l'état de lutte [qui] fait partie d'un rythme incorporé à la vie même de la littérature' (92)]. In this battle, the professional critic aims at a function no less important or exalted than the writer himself, a function justified in terms of its objectivity: 'Criticism, by granting [to great writers] its disinterested support, has more or less assured that their works and their reputation will outlast their lifetime.'[21]

In 1865, Matthew Arnold makes the same argument for 'disinterestedness' that, in the larger sphere of 'life and the world' with which he is concerned, is the 'keeping aloof from what is called "the practical view of things"' (Arnold, 'The Function of Criticism at the Present Time' 18). But the criterion of 'disinterestedness' claimed for criticism becomes thoroughly suspicious, not only on the personal level, but also on those levels that escape the consciousness of the most diligent critic. If there is one area in which the most disinterested of critics *is* interested, it is in defending the necessity of his own function and of the institution on which he depends. Plagiarism was 'invented' in the nineteenth century in the sense that the professionalization of academic criticism defined the critic's role as that of judging and explaining the great works of the past, as well as of identifying the great works of the present. Not only is criticism necessary, but it is difficult, and can be properly practised only by specialized individuals. As 'a distinterested endeavour to learn and propagate the best that is known and thought in the world' (Arnold 29), the critical power, for Matthew Arnold, rather than being 'of lower rank than the creative' (10), is a very high and demanding one, requiring its practitioners both to 'possess one great literature, at least, besides his own; and the more unlike his own, the better' and to consider Europe as 'one great confederation, bound to a joint action and working to a common result; and whose members have, for their proper outfit, a knowledge of Greek, Roman, and Eastern antiquity, and of one another' (29).

Brunetière announces the function of criticism as explication, classification, and judgment; following him, Lanson will insist on the study of sources as being an integral part of literary explication. As the ability to speak of 'works of the past' will become limited to those who know and understand that past, the academic critic will become indispensable for his specialized knowledge, an important part of which will be the ability to recognize literary sources and allusions, and to construct the patrilineage of the great work. Recognizing sources, not denouncing plagiarism, is the true task of the academic critic.

It is here that the notion of 'plagiarism' gets circumscribed as a crime against the profession, in which only the untalented engage – the perfect harmony between great writer and great critic assures that the great may practise any manner of imitation and not suffer, while the true crime is relegated to those lacking talent, who are in any case unworthy of consideration. If the nineteenth century 'invented' plagiarism, it is by defining it as a moral and literary 'crime' distinct from legitimate 'influence,' and engaged in only by unworthy authors, represented in a circumscribed domain of texts that lack, *a priori* and *a fortiori*, literary legitimacy. The canonization of literary authors entails that their borrowings fall outside the realm of plagiarism, and that they demonstrate, rather, the noble influences that guarantee their ancestry. The emerging literary institutions of the nineteenth century, both in France and in England, were concerned with establishing the legitimacy of literary tradition in the face of the preference for originality. The knowledge of past literatures was construed as essential to contemporary literary production. Arnold insists on the immaturity of some nineteenth-century writers because they 'did not know enough' and 'should have read more books' (12); Eliot later counters the argument that modern writers know more than past writers with a pithy 'Precisely and they are that which we know' ('Tradition and the Individual Talent' 16). Both the role of true criticism and the 'maturity' of literary art depend on the fundamental literary-historical knowledge that informs them and joins the individual artist and the critic within a common tradition.

If professional literary critics are hesitant to engage in accusations of plagiarism, it is, in part, because of the suspicion with which accusers of plagiarism are treated. Despite the moral purpose and the righteous indignation expressed by defenders of the virtue of letters, accusations of plagiarism are often met with scepticism, with the suspicion of envy or of faulty or mean-spirited judgment. The most condemning aspect of accusations of plagiarism is the suspicion of self-interest that is often seen to accompany them. A widespread version of this is petty jealousy, of which less successful writers are unfailingly accused when they claim to discover the seeds of their own imagination flourishing in someone else's apparently more fertile soil. The same suspicion can also be levelled against the successful writer who, being robbed of something like an excess of possessions, is too petty to bestow on the poor that which he could generously afford to give up. Tradition, since Virgil, deems that great writers perform a service to the world by uncovering for its benefit gold previously buried in a dung-hill. However, the well-established writer as victim of plagiarism might consider him- or herself already so well endowed with riches as to be able to afford to give up some of the wealth that, partaking in universal truth or beauty, is by nature destined to go out and enrich the poor or less talented. A rare twentieth-century example is provided by André Schwartz-Bart, who, upon being informed that Yambo Ouologuem's novel might contain some borrowings from his *Le dernier des justes,* replied to the Seuil editor in the following terms:

> I am in no way worried by the use that has been made of *Dernier des justes* ... I have always looked on my books as appletrees, happy that my apples be eaten and happy if now and again one is taken and planted in different soil.
>
> I am therefore deeply touched, overwhelmed even, that a black writer should have leant on *Dernier des justes* in order to write such a book as *Le Devoir de Violence.* Thus it is not Mr. Ouologuem who is in debt to me, but I to him. (Schwatz-Bart; quoted in Flamand 129)

In examples of plagiarism embedded in larger institutional structures, the identification of self-interest is more difficult, but is clearly important if we are to seriously consider the notion that battles about plagiarism are exemplary of power struggles in the construction of the literary field, battles waged by and in favour of the dominant institution against threats to its hegemony and authority. One of the most convincing and important examples of the presence of institutional self-interest in these debates is probably the newly formed Académie française's favourable judgment of *Le Cid.* The strategy of the Académie was to acknowledge the justice of many of Georges de Scudéry's objections to the play, but to throw out the charge of plagiarism, and essentially to maintain that, in spite of its many or alleged faults, *Le Cid* was still a great French work of art. In this judgment, the Académie did little more than ratify public opinion, which had already expressed its overwhelming approval of the play. The decision of the Académie in favour of *Le Cid* coincided with its own interests to the extent that these were necessarily allied with those of the development of French letters. In exonerating *Le Cid* in spite of its faults, the Académie was promoting its own interests by protecting those of French dramatic poetry.

Contemporary literary critics have inherited the belief that genuine originality is impossible, that all literature is somehow repetitious, and that intertextuality is everywhere; the latter has in fact been held to be the defining characteristic of literariness. In the face of such well-entrenched literary principles, which by no means date from the invention of 'intertextuality,' the accusation of literary 'plagiarism' may strike the literary critic either as hopelessly naïve or as seriously beside the point. There are many aesthetic euphemisms available to the literary critic to legitimize repetition: from imitation to source to allusion to pastiche to parody, to intertextuality and appropriation, no literary generation is bereft of a rich arsenal of more or less sophisticated terms to describe what might just as well amount to plagiarism, if the reader-critic in question were susceptible to the temptations of literary purism, to the demands of ethics, and to the moral outrage that accompanies the feeling of being 'had.'

In an essay on academic plagiarism, Neil Hertz analyses the rhetoric proscribing plagiarism in the Cornell English department's pamphlet entitled *A Writer's Responsibilities* (Hertz 144–59). Hertz's suspicion is that the moralistic tone of the discourse betrays it as a form of scape-goating that the dominant members of the culture, the professors, visit on student victims as a 'response to a perceived threat' (145): the fear of plagiarism suffered by the professors, the fear of being discovered to have themselves, however unwittingly, 'plagiarized,' is projected onto the hapless student. While not intended as an argument in favour of student plagiarism, Hertz's reasoning seems intuitively sensible. He points out, as Schneider also does, that most professional writers will inevitably and innocently commit small pecadillos of unintended 'plagiarism' – better termed, probably, 'palimpsestic syndrome,' or 'periodic cryptomnesia' – and that a certain investment of time and more effort than it is worth would probably turn up evidence of unfortunate lapses of absolute originality among one's colleagues' publications. According to Hertz, 'the plagiarizing of students can focus their teachers' anxieties about writing in general, more particularly about the kind of "writing" involved in teaching – the inscription of a culture's heritage on the minds of its young. A teacher's uncertainty about (to quote the pamphlet again) "whose words he is reading or listening to" begins, in the classroom, with his own words – and this would be true not merely for those colleagues we think of complacently as less original than ourselves' (149).

Academia is much prone to internal accusations of plagiarism, carried out from time to time in the public eye, as cleansing rituals in which the mechanism of scape-goating, raised to the level of purging the internal ranks of the elite, guarantees the honesty, or the appearance of honesty, among the ranks of the virtuous.[22] Although accusations of plagiarism in academia are not my focus, the field is sufficiently linked to the literary to be of some use, if only by contrast. While honesty in academic and scientific pursuits is deemed essential to the functioning of the institutions that support them (the pamphlet cited by Hertz claims that 'one of the principal aims of a college education is the development of intellectual honesty' [146]), the same is not true of the literary profession. During the course of the nineteenth century, with the emergence of the literary bohemian, the romantic 'poète maudit' and such scandalous literary figures (and 'plagiarists') as Baudelaire, de Quincey, Valéry, and Rimbaud, the quality of personal virtue became less important, and even started to acquire an inverse relationship to genius. Genius came to be seen not only as a source of inspired art, but also a potential cause of moral or psychological depravity.

Whereas academic plagiarism is an explicit contravention of criteria, such as honesty and originality, that constitute the institution, the same attributes seem no longer to play any significant constitutive role in literature. While academic plagiarism may be treated as evidence that the perpetrator is morally unfit for membership in the institution, the condition of intellectual dishonesty uncovered in potential cases of literary plagiarism is not fraught with the same consequences. The literary field is one of the few – if not the sole – to tolerate T.S. Eliot's paradox – appropriated by Lionel Trilling – that 'immature writers imitate, mature writers steal.'

The delicate question of reading plagiarism – or of reading *as* plagiarism that which can be construed in another light – is aptly illustrated by a case of academic plagiarism in which the purely discursive nature of 'knowledge' provides both the source of the alleged crime and the terms of the defence. A controversy over a text of historical biography pits the academic against the non-academic writer, and not only reveals different reading tolerances for 'honesty' and 'originality' but focuses issues of public versus private property, idea versus expression, and the inevitability of 'intertextuality' in what Nodier would call the treatment of 'matières positives.'

The controversy entails an accusation of plagiarism made by the academic historian Robert Bray against Stephen Oates's 1977 biography of Lincoln, *With Malice toward None*. In a paper presented to the American Historical Association (AHA), Bray claimed that Oates had suppressed his use of Benjamin Thomas's *Abraham Lincoln* (1952), for years the 'standard one-volume life' which 'remains an important Lincoln book nearly forty years later' (Bray 9). Bray documents his evidence in standard 'parallel passage' form, and attacks, as well, Oates's historical accuracy and general scholarship. Bray's conclusion that 'plagiarism is absolute intertextuality' is not intended to excuse Oates (22), although he does indeed offer an intertextual theory of biography, and of historiography in general:

> So why, to conclude, did Oates plagiarize Benjamin Thomas? Because of intertextuality, Lincoln biography is a palimpsest, a text 'written over' with the ghosts of countless earlier subtexts [...]; and because of the historical and

popular fascination with the subject, Lincoln is also 'over written.' Thus a genuinely *new* life is impossible. These constraints are givens for any aspiring writer on Lincoln. Add to them, in Oates's case, a literarily and philosophically naive commitment to 'realism' and the prospect is all the more difficult, if not a sure recipe for failure. Oates tried hard to create the illusion of the 'real Lincoln,' but he relied too much, as biographies of biographies will do, on mostly stale secondary materials – an imitation of an imitation. With the authority of Thomas ever-present, Oates must have had an anxious struggle. He *had* to stand on his Lincoln father's shoulders, but he could not admit to the reading world that that was what he was doing. On the contrary, Thomas, as the threatening precursor, must be banished. (21)

In spite of his apparent affection for intertextual theory, and his appeal to a kind of Freudian (or Bloomian) inevitability, Bray's charge was intended seriously, and was subsequently taken very seriously, notably by Cullum Davis, the chair of the session, who took the matter to the AHA.[23]

In his denial of the charges, Oates challenges, first, the jurisdiction of the AHA, of which he was not a member, and, second, the objectivity of his critics, whom he characterizes as being 'academicians with axes to grind' (26) – imputing to them not only pedantry, but also small-mindedness and jealousy. More important, he takes up the legal argument that 'historical facts and events are in the public domain. Not even the interpretation and order of presentation of historical information and events are copyrightable by law' (27). Oates essentially concurs with Bray's notion of historiography as 'intertextuality,' but charges that equating such intertextuality with 'plagiarism' is a deliberate perversion:

> Lincoln literature itself constitutes 'a single network' of writing. It consists of a common body of knowledge about Lincoln, particularly his well-known early years, that has accumulated for more than a century and is in the public domain. If there are similarities between my book and Thomas's, it is because both biographies draw from that common 'text' or body of writing and information. As I will demonstrate, there are also similarities between Thomas's work, which my accusers so admire, and the Lincoln biographies and studies that preceeded his book. In other words, Thomas did the same thing I am accused of doing. This is a crucial point, one that Bray and my other accusers miss completely. In truth, there are intertextual similarities among Lincoln books as a whole, for the simple reason that they derive from and are part of a common body of recorded knowledge. (27–8)

One recognizes in this defence, apart from a general appeal, through intertextuality, to the notion that 'all literature is plagiaristic,' the justification by the great-authors-of-the-past argument, and a hint that 'I may have copied, but if I did, it wasn't only from Thomas' (in other words, copying from one book is plagiarism, copying from many is research). But the crux of the argument is that not only are there 'facts' associated with Lincoln's life, but these facts are framed in language such that the repetition of this language not only is unavoidable, but constitutes itself part of the canonical 'knowledge' to be transmitted. In support of this defence, Oates demonstrates the presence of parallel expressions in other Lincoln biographies, supporting the fundamental point made by Bray himself in the course of his accusation, that 'one's words in a Lincoln biography are inevitably the echo of the many books about Lincoln one must read in trying to prepare another' (Oates 30). The many examples of parallel phrasing show convincingly that many of the expressions that Bray accused Oates of copying from Thomas were in fact not 'original' with the latter. Oates's defence conflates two standard principles: (1) there are only a certain number of ways to express received truth; and (2) the expression of 'fact' is in the public domain and as such is not copyrightable. His prime example is the sentence 'On March 24, 1836, Lincoln was proposed to the bar as a man of good moral character,' of which he provides nine variants, including his own and Thomas's, each of which closely resembles all of the others.

The AHA eventually declared that 'plagiarism had not occurred, but rather an insufficiency of acknowledgment of one particular source' (Oates 41), a decision to which we will return. In the meantime, the controversy continued. Oates was subsequently accused of plagiarism for his biographies of Martin Luther King and William Faulkner by a historian who submitted his findings to Peter Shaw, Gore Vidal, William Styron, and other notables, all of whom concurred with the accusation (Burlingame 49). The evidence is much more convincing than is Bray's initial accusation, and the apparently repetitive nature of Oates's 'plagiaristic' method tipped the scales for some of his former supporters (recidivism being a mark of the 'real,' that is, the intentional plagiarist).

Most contributors to the controversy represented in the *Journal of Information Ethics* publication range themselves on the side of Bray (the accuser) against Oates (the 'plagiarist'), but the terms of their judgment are clearly mitigated. One asks a series of rhetorical questions: 'Is it possible to compose the umpteenth biography of Lincoln without saying some things as predecessors have said them? Are there canonical events by now that must be recounted – and canonical formulations for doing so? Do voices merge, not only in sermons in the tradition of the black churches, but also in other fields where the same stories are told again and again [...]?' (Wollan 63–4). On the other hand, the same author continues, 'is copying to be condoned in a field where it seems to be customary, so that

practices unacceptable elsewhere are acceptable in the Lincoln field? [...]
Have authors so disappeared, once 'their' text is composed, that they have
no claim upon the passages that make their way thereafter, by copying,
into the text of another?' (64). One decidedly unsympathetic contributor
answers these questions, and the terms of Oates's defence: '[If such practices were allowed] three things must follow: undergraduate and graduate
students would develop into mindless scribes; English Departments could
promptly rename all "Composition 101/102" courses "Copying 101/102";
and everyone could abandon the belief that scholarship emanates as a creative act, an original contribution, from the mind of an author fully in
command of pertinent data and sources' (Zangrando 66).

We will refrain from commenting on this last passage, and will leave the
last word to a lawyer invited to comment on the question of academic plagiarism and copyright in general. Viewing with dismay the confusion and
range of opinions preferred by the contributors to the case, she has this to
say with respect to the AHA's 'vindication' of Oates: 'What else is plagiarism
if not the failure to adequately attribute source materials [...]?' (Kozak 75).

Although the question of the appropriation and transmission of 'knowledge' may seem to take us away from the field of literary plagiarism, it is an
act of particular relevance to documentary fictions such as social realism,
the historical novel, and its more contemporary or 'postmodern' version,
'historiography.' In this case of the 'inevitable' rewriting of previous texts in
an area closely related both to literature and to what Nodier would call *les
matières positives*, it is clear that the intertextual biographer both plagiarized
and did not plagiarize. The readers of the case, caught between the aesthetics of intertextuality and the ethics of academic honesty, chose to apply to
Oates the standards their own institution claims to uphold – the comparison between Oates's practice and 'English 101' courses is clear evidence of
the confusion of institutional categories. The AHA's disculpation of Oates
while at the same time finding him guilty of 'lack of proper acknowledgment of one source' is a transparent retreat from the conclusions of their
own investigations, and is an illustration of Hertz's notion of the academic's
fear of plagiarism as well as of the time-honoured principle that there may
be more danger in reading plagiarism than in 'plagiarizing.'

As plagiarism is constructed by the judgment of readers, it is not the text
itself that is the object of accusation but the intentions behind the authorial act that produced it. Readers of plagiarism, ostensibly recognizing
repeated discourse, are actually, as we shall see, readers of an act in which
they recognize the absent, but presumably dishonest, intentions of a failed
author.

5. Reading the Act

Is plagiarism a crime? For ourselves we confess that we hold it only a venial offence – unless, of course, it is found out.

William Walsh, *Handy-book of Literary Curiosities*

The best way not to be accused of plagiarism, as is the case for all crimes, is not to get caught, but, in the case of plagiarism, avoiding detection does not necessarily entail the invisibility of the crime; it consists, rather, in showing that an evident discursive repetition does not fit the criteria defining the transgressive variety, but is of an innocent, or better yet, positive form. Most defences against plagiarism are not denials of discursive borrowing, or even of copying, but attempts to cast the repetition in an innocent light.

Identifying plagiarism entails ascribing to an agent a series of guilty or fraudulent intentions. The necessity to show intent, in order to establish guilt, or at least degrees of it, is by far the most important of all criteria for establishing plagiarism, in the sense that it presupposes all the rest. The criterion of authorial intention, while perhaps not traditionally considered problematic, has become so today for aesthetic judgments that often still maintain, in the wake of structuralism, the irrelevance of the author's intention with respect to aspects of the text's meaning. But intending to copy is presumably to intend consequences of the copying. Intentionality is relevant to copyright infractions, where it can affect the gravity of the offence and its sanction, but 'unintentional' breach of copyright is still an infringement. Plagiarism, however, always implies self-consciousness on the part of the alleged plagiarist, as well as knowledge of the conventions and ethical norms that the act, if discovered, will also have contravened. As Schneider says: 'In the moral sense, plagiarism describes a deliberate act, intending to use the efforts of others and to appropriate illicitly the intellectual results of their work. Plagiarism in the strict sense is distinguished from "cryptomnesia," the unconscious forgetting of sources, or involuntary influence, by the fact that the borrowing and erasing of sources were performed consciously. It is dishonest to plagiarize. The plagiarist knows that what he is doing should not be done.'[1]

Plagiarism is not then merely intentional copying, but also the intention to pass off the copy of another's text as one's own, presumably to benefit unjustly somehow. If plagiarism implies intent to defraud, then it is covertness or deviousness that implicitly condemns the offender. Admitting the act and self-inculpation rank highly among forms of disculpation used by accused plagiarists. For what is shown cannot at the same time be hidden and what is not hidden is not plagiarized. The sole evidence of the potential plagiarist's intention is usually, however, the offensive text itself, from which both the act and the agent's intention are necessarily absent. The intent to hide the imitation is thus often inferred from its apparent initial invisibility: the blindness of the reader is projected as deviousness onto the writer. There seem to be no rules allowing us to distinguish between innocence and deviousness in this respect: disputes about plagiarism presuppose one or another of these intentions, which, residing presumably in the author, are not normally visible in the text.

The ascription of motives – whether used to establish guilt or innocence; whether presumed to be conscious or unconscious – is a fundamental criterion of plagiarism, for motives always imply that the act itself has taken place, and that it participates in a network of intentions attributable to the agent. Intentional copying can be for fraudulent or aesthetic motives, and only in the first case does one properly speak of 'plagiarism.' A large range of copying, although undisputed, may escape charges of plagiarism by the denial of intentionality, or else via the claim to aesthetic intentions.

IDENTIFYING INTENTIONS

If borrowing is clearly not stealing, the modalities for proper borrowing are sufficiently unstable that the distinction is a fundamental and ancient problem for determining cases of improper 'appropriation.' Hiding the source is closely linked to a fraudulent intent, and the standard tests for determining intention hinge on the proper use of conventional strategies for identifying repeated discourse. But the complaints by writers protesting against dishonest imitation or proclaiming their own honesty are evidence that citational practices, while constituting an ancient and essential element of authorship through the appeal to honesty and authenticity, were so often transgressed that to respect the conventions of attribution becomes a virtue worthy of notice. John Donne, in the *Progress of the Soul* (1601), claims: 'Now when I beginne this book, I have no purpose to come into any man's debt; how my stocke will hold out I know not; perchance waste, perchance increase in use; if I doe borrow any thing of Antiquitie, besides that I make account that I pay it to posterity, with as much and as good: You shall still finde mee to acknowledge it, and to thanke not him onely that hath digg'd out treasure for mee but that hath lighted mee a candle to the place' (cited in White 127). Oliver Goldsmith (1728–74), for his part, is not so sanguine about the practice of Donne's contemporaries. In the *Life of Dr. Thomas Parnell* (1970), he claims: 'It was the fashion with the wits of the last age to conceal the places whence they took their hints or their subjects. A trifling acknowledgement would have made that a lawful prize, which may now be considered as plunder' (cited in Paull 115).

The historically evolving norms governing the appropriate attribution of quotation and other borrowed discourse have a constant ground, which is the identification of the source of the discourse primarily in order to guarantee its authenticity and authority. In modern and contemporary literary discourse, however, the criterion of ownership has all but replaced notions of authenticity and authority in the use of quotation and borrowed discourse. The post-romantic presupposition of literary 'originality' proscribes signalling the presence of borrowed discourse, and the practice is sufficiently marginal that it reveals a specific aesthetic stance with respect to originality or other literary conventions; indeed, footnotes in contemporary fiction are largely used either in a wholly fictional or a parodic vein, intended to foreground or undermine conventions of textual authority and originality, and the recognition of unsignalled repetition, either as allusion or as a one of many forms of 'intertextuality,' is often part of the self-reflexive game of reading (Benstock 205).

The shifting standards of attribution imply less that different periods had different tolerances for plagiarism, than they indicate differing conventions concerning the proper signalling of borrowed discourse. In pre-modern vernacular texts such as Montaigne's, borrowed discourse was normally signalled by the change of language from French to Latin or Greek: while the author of the quotation was to be recognized by the erudite reader, the locus of the borrowed discourse was unmistakable. Montaigne's strategy of paraphrase into French approaches some contemporary writing in that it put the greater onus on the reader who was required not only to identify the source, but also to recognize the presence of 'quotation' without benefit of any textual signalling. Mistaken attributions or the absence of recognition may or may not diminish the impact of the work in question; it is certainly the case for any extended parody or rewriting that complete ignorance of the pre-existing work significantly changes the potential of the appropriative aesthetic.

Theories of intertextuality and allusion become pertinent here as contemporary discussions are still grappling with questions of attribution and of the signalling of borrowed discourse.[2] Early formulations of intertextuality as a 'new' mode of writing/reading took great pains to distinguish it from the traditional use of sources, on the one hand, and, on the other, from accidental reminiscences arising from the reader's cultural encyclopedia, which were not a strategic part of the textual strategies. Globalizing definitions of intertextuality, such as that initially furnished by Kristeva, saw every text as being an inevitable rewriting of other texts, where 'text' was granted an extension to make it include the 'world.' Later refinements are more explicit about the distinction between accidental and significant intertextuality. Michael Riffaterre attempts to distinguish between 'weak' or 'aleatory' and 'strong' or 'obligatory' intertextuality: situated in the first category are unintentional echoes that form part of the common culture of reader and writer; in the second are the functional aspects of the text's appeal to another discourse, which Riffaterre claims are always signalled by 'agrammaticalities' in the text, requiring decoding by the reader. The crucial moment is the reader's recognition of the *presence* of intertextual interference, inescapably marked by semantic agrammaticality; the exact source and locus of the intertext can remain unknown: 'there is obligatory intertextuality when the meaning of certain words in the text is neither that which the language permits nor that the context requires, but the meaning that these words have in the intertext. It is the unacceptability of this meaning in the language or the context which forces the reader into a presumption, a hypothesis of a solution offered in a formal counterpart of the text which he is trying to decipher. Consequently, the intertext is not an object of quotation, it is a *presupposed* object.'[3]

In the same tradition, Carmila Perri's essay 'On Alluding' (1978) claims that allusion is 'always marked' in the text, thereby distinguishing the functional (intentional) allusion from the insignificant (unintentional) one, invented or constructed by the reader, rather than written into the text. While strictly text-oriented discussions have largely been surpassed by more reader-oriented criticism and Derridian-inspired versions of 'deconstruction,' it is still the case that the textual marking of borrowed discourse is deemed to be a necessary criterion for distinguishing intertextuality or allusion from plagiarism.

In his recent work, *Allusion*, Allan H. Pasco espouses this distinction, but his demonstration reveals a tension resulting from the conflation of a reader-oriented theory with a more structurally inspired one. Caught between classical structuralism, which endorses the complete submission of the reader to the authority of immanent textual structure and content, and theories of reading promoting the liberation of the reader from textual constraints by underlining the indeterminacy of meaning in the actualizing processes of reception, Pasco wisely adopts a middle ground. For him, the 'alluding textual term' is an explicit component of the textual surface, but allusion itself is a relationship established in the mind of the reader between the alluding text and the referent text, which, moreover, 'must be known to the reader' (18). The desire to reconcile both text and reader in the act of reading leads Pasco to 'posit as a working ploy that allusion exists in the text, whether or not it is recognized by a reader and completed' (191, n. 38); at the same time, 'allusion that is not recognized does not function' (18). Allusion, in this view, is an element of meaning deriving from authorial intention, the evidence for which is clearly visible on the page, but is liable to fail, become insignificant, in the hands of the wrong reader.

Pasco further subscribes to a theory of aesthetic intentionality in distinguishing between plagiarism and allusion. The plagiarist's intention 'must be to prevent [the two texts] from coming together' (15); allusion, on the contrary, strives to evoke a relationship between them. While admitting that plagiarism and allusion are frequently mistaken for each other, Pasco argues that 'the key rests in whether the subsequent text has gained more from a source through unacknowledged repetition or whether it has used the source as an element in a new creation that would be enhanced by the reader's recognition of the previous creation [...] The test is in whether or not the two texts work together within the reading experience, and if so how' (45). The fact that this 'test' is solely a function of reader intentionality is evidence of the circularity of the argument in favour of the criterion of the textual explicitness of the alluding term.

The attempt to establish textual evidence or 'markers' for allusion is partially, at least, motivated by the desire to reduce the unbridled indeterminacy of potential significance that threatens to destroy, if not literature itself, at least the parameters of literary study that consist in the organization and mastery of a circumscribed field of knowledge. Gérard Genette, possibly the most formalist of the intertextualists, expresses this position: 'I can [...] track down, in any work, partial, localized and fugitive echoes of any other work, past or future. Such an attitude would have the effect of including the totality of universal literature in the field of hypertextuality, which would render its study uncontrollable; but above all, it seems to me that this attitude gives an unjustified credit and function to the hermeneutic activity of the reader [...] I envisage the relation between the text and its reader to be of a more socialized nature, more openly contractual, as if arising from a conscious and organized pragmatics.'[4]

If lack of recognition of 'intertexts,' the arbitrary assignment of meanings, or the identification of incorrect or merely mistaken allusions produced readings equally valid as those deriving from informed recognition, then a large part of the literary academic institution would be left bereft of its *raison d'être*. Pasco and Genette join a long tradition of authors and critics, exemplified by Montaigne, who, believing that, in literature as in life, knowledge is better than ignorance, situate knowledge within the writer who then solicits an equally informed reader as his or her ideal addressee. But this contest of intentionalities – authorial versus readerly, fraudulent versus aesthetic – breaks down when it becomes ultimately the reader's function first to recognize authorial intentionality and then to judge it. The potential invisibility of allusive markers enhances the importance attached to what is essentially authorial intention disguised as textual functioning and then offered up for recognition by the informed reader. Since the elitist nature of literature has always depended on the accumulated erudition of the appropriate reader, identification of allusion depends less on the attribution of credit to an original author than on the signalling to the reader of the 'unoriginality' of the discourse in question. The consensus seems to be that, while it is up to the reader to be smart enough to identify the source, the onus is on the writer to give the reader sufficient clues that there is a source to find.

The functioning of plagiarism is derived from this logic of intentionality invested, first, in the author and, then, assumed by the reader as his alterego: if the author intends the reader to 'get it,' the 'right' readers will, and allusion will occur. If 'allusion' becomes invisible to these same readers – inevitably popping up by accident at an inappropriate moment – the initial invisibility of the 'allusion,' potentially attributable to a lack of erudition on the part of the reader, may be projected onto the author as deviousness, and a fraudulent intent may be supposed. In constructing a pragmatic 'theory' of plagiarism, it seems to be more consistent to recognize the purely reader-oriented nature of this process, and to dispense with presuppositions about authorial intentionality. As the history of plagiarism amply shows, one reader's 'allusion' is another reader's 'plagiarism' and vice versa.

The ascription of fraudulent intentions purely for financial gain is by far the least interesting suspected motive for plagiarism: simple theft seems not to generate the aesthetic and ethical ambiguities that generate controversy. What is significant in such cases is less the motivation for the plagiarism than the motivation for the accusation. We will leave the discussion of the most interesting cases of presumed fraud for financial or symbolic profit to our consideration of *profit plagiarism*. The present discussion summarizes some of the more common presumed motives for plagiarism and the responses they generate, on the part of either authors or critics in their defence.

GUILT WITHOUT INTENTIONALITY

Mea (non) culpa

Faced with indisputable evidence of repeated discourse, the most common defence against charges of plagiarism is to admit the fact of the copying, but to deny intentionality. Probably the most usual version of this claim is to plead that one is a victim of the 'note-book' syndrome, in which sloppy and/or obsessive note-taking on the part of the author is blamed for the fact that, somehow, unacknowledged passages taken from writers end up without quotation marks in a new context – in other words, 'I didn't mean to do it,' or, better, 'I didn't know I was doing it.' Québécois author and 'plagiarist' Hubert Aquin has borrowed a term from medieval scribal practices to describe this unconscious textual misplacement: he uses the term *inserendes* to describe his own practice of writing from the margins into the text.[5] *Inserendes*, as he defines it, is the accidental transfer of a marginal comment made by a scribe into the text that is being copied, where it appears as if it is of the text itself. The term can be applied to the 'note-book syndrome' in which discourses shift from their site of origin and slip into new contexts where they appear to be 'original.'

Academics and writers of documentary fiction requiring much research are particularly prone to this malady. Jean Prévost has recourse to this defence in his discussion of Stendhal's creative method, which involved copying out large segments of texts into bound notebooks. Comparing this method to the later practice of using file cards, Prévost explains: '[Beyle's] preferences for paper and binding, his taste for the continuous note-book, contributed to his involuntary plagiarisms. It is difficult to break up a long text that one has copied from a single author.'[6]

A more recent example is the accusation of plagiarism directed against the Québécois writer Paul Ohl for his best-selling historical novel *Soleil noir/Le roman de la conquête* (1991) wherein were discovered disturbing similarities with a Larousse publication, *L'Amérique des Andes*. The evidence was such that Ohl was forced to fall back on the *inserendes* argument particular to the note-taker and documenter. Protesting lack of intention ('But plagiarism? – It's out of the question!'), he alleged that somewhere in the forty-five files containing notes, photocopies, and various other documents, he 'probably found these passages without being able to determine where they came from' (Roy A1). A variation on the note-book syndrome, one that is fragile in that it verges on an implicit renouncement of authorship, is the 'plagiarism-by-proxy' defence used by Alexander Haley against charges of plagiarism in *Roots*. His claim was that borrowed passages had in fact crept into his notes, but that he was innocent of any intention to plagiarize, the passages having been supplied to him by students or other researchers hired to undertake the massive documentation required to write the novel.

The 'note-book syndrome' is a dodge of intentionality akin to what Michel Schneider calls 'cryptomnesia.' Here, the author is present, but also without intentionality: he has 'forgotten' what he has read and has reproduced it unconsciously. On this defence, there is equally no attempt to deny the fact of repetition, only the intention to commit fraud and therefore plagiarism. Outside of the legal arena, where lack of intentionality can reduce the gravity of the offence, the argument may be unconvincing, since it will not be subjected to the intense scrutiny required to establish proof of the claim to innocence; readers may also suspect that someone who forgets that he is stealing may suffer from a variety of other weaknesses, notably a lack of talent or originality. But 'cryptomnesia' as a mode of writing has a long and venerable tradition identified by Montaigne as both the scourge and the inspiration of his own writing; Schneider has elaborated at length the self-conscious fear of plagiarism that has haunted the greatest artists. Arguments proposing inadvertent imitation born of the practice of unconscious assimilation are most effective in that they activate the personal experience of readers and writers over the ages as well as the demonstrable practice of some of the greatest authors. Such imitation appears justified not only by its antiquity, but also by its inevitability: all literature is somehow repetitive, and plagiarism that is everywhere is no plagiarism at all (Schneider 29).

Akin to claims of innocence via unintentionality are a series of phenomena in which specific and individual agency is replaced by a more generalized and de-subjectivized agency. The 'palimpsestic syndrome' and 'OBI' are terms coined by Robert Merton in his fascinating and entertaining study *On the Shoulders of Giants: A Shandyean Postscript* in which he attempts, in pseudo-Sternian fashion, to trace the origins of the aphorism, commonly but erroneously attributed to Newton: 'If I have seen farther, it is by standing on the shoulders of giants.' In his meanderings through the history of science and letters, Merton recounts, by means of the transfers and transformations of the aphorism, the ways in which 'knowledge' (and 'disknowledge') are transmitted across time, cultures, and disciplines. In the labyrinth of 'OTSOGism' (on-the-shoulders-of-giants-ism), Merton has several brushes with plagiarism and other forms of textual repetition that are germane to the question of how to 'plagiarize' and get away with it.

The 'palimpsestic syndrome' is Merton's term for a phenomenon common in the transmission of 'information,' in which 'each succeeding repetition *tends to erase* all but one antecedent version' (218). The palimpsestic syndrome can be an innocent and intentional borrowing without intention to hide it, or else an argument designed to disculpate the guilty. This phenomenon is a subcategory of a more general one which Merton calls 'OBI,' or the 'obliteration of the source(s) of ideas, formulations, methods, or scientific findings *by* incorporation in current canonical knowledge' (311):

> In the course of this hypothesized process, the number of explicit references to the original work declines in the papers and books making use of it. [In due course] users and consequently transmitters of that knowledge become so thoroughly familiar with its origins that they assume this to be true of their readers as well. Preferring not to insult their readers' knowledgeability, they no longer refer to the original source. And since many of us tend to attribute a significant idea or formulation to the author who introduced us to it, the altogether innocent transmitter sometimes becomes identified as the originator [...] In the successive transmission of ideas, repeated use may erase all but the immediately antecedent versions, thus producing a historical palimpsest in which the sources of those ideas are obliterated. (311–12)

Whether OBI is always in fact as innocent as Merton here pretends it to be is a matter for the courts, or interested readers and critics, to decide: the point with respect to claims about plagiarism is that the phenomenon clearly exists in a benign and innocent way. Unintentional obliteration or palimpsestism, while producing textual forms of repetition virtually indistinguishable from plagiarism, may escape, through claims to innocence via lack of intentionality, charges of plagiarism.

Mea culpa – tu quoque

Name-calling and plagiarism have gone together since the earliest times, when there was little other recourse in defence of one's wounded pride or proprietorship. From Martial's time to ours, the accusation of plagiarism is useful for vilifying one's rivals, quite independently of the justification of the charge. An effective defence against the insult is to accuse your accuser, a claim that has the advantage of probably being provable if anybody had the time or interest to look into the matter. In his history of plagiarism from the Renaissance to the Revolution in France, Erich Welslau treats vilification as a category of accusations of plagiarism not worthy of much importance. A review of this category would be worthwhile: just because one is accused of plagiarism for reasons of enmity doesn't mean one isn't guilty. One example is Langbaine's pursuit of Dryden in the *Momus*, where he berates the poet not only for plagiarism, but 'for taxing others with stealing

Characters from him [...] when he himself does the *same*, almost in all the Plays he writes; and for arraigning his Predecessours [*sic*] for stealing from the *Ancients*, as he does *Johnson;* which [*sic*] tis evident that he himself is guilty of the same' (Langbaine, 'The Preface,' [10]). Merton coins (?) the phrase *tu-quoque-ism* in his description of Newton's counter-attack against Hooke, who had claimed that Newton had stolen his ideas from him. In a letter to Halley, Newton writes: 'This carriage toward me [i.e., Hooke's accusation of plagiarism] is very strange and undeserved; so that I cannot forbear in stating the point of justice, to tell you further, that he has published Borell[i]'s hypothesis in his own name; and the asserting of this to himself and completing it as his own, seems to me the ground of all the stir he makes' (cited from Brewster, in Merton 95).

Newton points out a psychological commonplace, remarked upon by many and explored by Schneider, that there is a protesting-too-much aspect about accusations of plagiarism that often points to the guilt of the accuser, or else, in Schneider's psychological account, to the fear of plagiarism as a complex suffered by the writer. Coleridge has been cited as the most extreme case of *tu-quoque-ism*: 'It is doubtful whether any other writer in the history of letters has accused so many writers of plagiarism and so many so falsely. That this circumstance should coincide with the fact that Coleridge has been charged with having perpetrated the most extensive plagiarism in the annals of literature (for a writer of any fame) is not without its own psychological interest' (Fruman, *Coleridge* 98–9).

Fruman analyses an early (1796) case of such an accusation, for which Coleridge was moved to 'apologize,' issuing the following statement in the 'Advertisement' of the 1797 edition of 'Lines on an Autumnal Evening.' In the previous edition, Coleridge had defended himself against an accusation of failing to acknowledge a poem by Samuel Rogers, and accused Rogers, in turn, of having purloined a poem by Michael Bruce. In his subsequent apology, Coleridge alleges a temporary lapse of judgment brought on by psychological causes: 'No one can see more clearly the *littleness* and futility of imagining plagiarisms in the works of men of Genius; but *nemo omnibus horis sapit* [no man is wise at all hours]; and my mind, at the time of writing that note, was sick and sore with anxiety [...]' (cited in Fruman, *Coleridge* 51).

Psychological (in)competence

Recourse to psychological explanations to excuse such lapses is particularly useful in the case of Genius, which is sometimes considered, especially since the era of Romantic bohemianism, to harbour a certain incipient insanity. Despite Fruman's apparently ruthless attack on Coleridge's intentions and honesty, he urges such mitigating circumstances as the writer's mental and physical condition: 'In later years, when, it is true, Coleridge was sorely afflicted both physically and mentally, he charged plagiarism against Hume, Schelling, Hazlitt, and Erasmus Darwin, men generally considered possessed of as much genius as Samuel Rogers. He chided Sir Walter Scott for a 'pilfering imitation of Goethe's *Mignon*'; he also accuses James Mackintosh, Horne Tooke, Voltaire, and many others of plagiarism' (*Coleridge* 51).

The notion of psychological competence, which appears in St Onge's definition as a necessary component of sanctionable plagiarism, is a relatively recent addition to the list of criteria for determining the existence of plagiarism, and one that obviously depends on 'sanity' being considered a necessary condition for assuming the legal responsibility for one's acts.

Defences of breach of copyright on the grounds of mental incompetence are to my knowledge non-existent: what is not lacking, however, are frequent references to the act of plagiarism as being a symptom or manifestation of various psychological maladies. This analysis is in direct contradiction to the eighteenth-century one, which attributed the crime to a simple lack of talent. The modern introduction of a psychological component dispenses somewhat with the concept of 'talent,' and replaces it with the notion of compulsion. As a thief, the eighteenth-century plagiarist is simply a poor man who steals what he cannot afford to buy, and which, by virtue of his poverty, he does not deserve to own. In the contemporary psychological version, the plagiarist steals not because he is needy, but because he cannot help himself: in other words, plagiarism is a form of kleptomania, where the victim of the illness is driven to want to steal what he could buy, or what he does not need: 'The plagiarist resembles the kleptomaniac both in his evident wish to be detected and in the circumstance that what is stolen may not be needed. (With kleptomania, lack of need, we are told, is absolutely central.) Because kleptomania so evidently issues from an uncontrollable compulsion, furthermore, it tends, like plagiarism, to inspire understanding and sympathy. The comparison, though, stops here. For kleptomania does not result in any confusion over whether or not goods were stolen' (Shaw 332).

It is not the need to possess the object that is the cause of kleptomania; rather, something in the fraudulent nature of the means of acquisition of the object is itself the object of desire. The kleptomania analogy is useful for explaining the inexplicable: why writers who would otherwise be considered 'authors,' having within their grasp the ability to be 'original,' or at least to be judged so, resort to plagiarism. Plagiarism as disease is not, however, taken very seriously by defenders of literary ethics, perhaps because 'psychological competence' has never been a criterion of authorship.

While the analysis of plagiarism as a form of kleptomania is largely metaphorical, a recent exposé of more serious pathological motivations has been undertaken by the American poet Neal Bowers, the victim of a lengthy and bizarre plagiarism episode. His account of the case uncovers a plagiarist formerly convicted of paedophilia. Says Bowers:

> An additional liability of revealing Jones's criminal past is implying that all plagiarists are pathological. Unmask a plagiarist and find a child molester is not the message I want to send, knowing that plagiarists are often driven by much more pragmatic urges [...] At the same time I can't help feeling that the concept of the respectable plagiarist is at least oxymoronic. That we harbor such a notion at all indicates how uncertain we are about those who steal the words and ideas of others. Ironically, Jones's personal history may be his best defense against charges of plagiarism, simply because it deflects attention and gives those already squeamish about the subject of literary ownership an easy way out. 'Jones is not your typical plagiarist,' they say. Indeed, but then who is? (1997 124)

The psychological-incompetence theory is demonstrated at length by Schneider (1985). For him, a whole list of literary obsessions such as quotation, pastiche, and plagiarism are the results of varying types of Oedipal trauma resulting in neuroses, psychoses, or other psychological conditions. While all these conditions are somewhat 'aberrant' from a psychological point of view, they invariably, in Schneider's view, produce genius, or at least great or interesting art. His is a version of the theory that, while everyone has an Oedipal complex of some kind, some are more productive and interesting than others. Plagiarism, for Schneider, is a benign form of psychological incompetence suffered by Baudelaire, Stendhal, Freud, and a host of others. Benign, in the sense that, although some of its victims may have had difficult or tragic lives – Schneider cites the 'pathetic' case of Malcolm Lowry, for example – their 'sickness' may not have been sufficiently dangerous (at least to others) to warrant being qualified as a case of 'psychological incompetence.' Schneider distinguishes between 'plagiarism' of the creative kind, and plagiarism (without quotation marks) of the pathological kind. The difference depends on the successful passage of the artist through his Oedipal situation: 'the writer kills the plagiarist in himself [...] This work will take the form of an appropriation, of a style, somewhat in the way that normal sexuality is related to and derives from deviant sexuality in the specific way that it detaches itself from it, by transposing, repeating, contradicting it, through a symbolic structure, that of Oedipus.'[7]

As an explanation of plagiarism, psychological causes and motivations presuppose the existence of the act, and short-circuit the central question of how the evidence of discursive repetition came to be construed as a case of plagiarism in the first place. This is not to say that excessive, recurring, or blatant instances of repetition may not have their origins in psychological conditions – simply that these conditions and their consequences do not in themselves necessarily result in accusations of plagiarism. A study of the psychology of the plagiarist, such as Schneider's, taking the point of view that plagiarism is an obsessive intentional or unintentional act of production, does not contribute to explaining the literary 'success' or 'failure' of the obsessive act or to outlining the criteria of reception that push the repetition from the category of good imitation to bad. A psychology of plagiarism might more profitably investigate the psychology of the reader than that of the author.

AESTHETIC INTENTIONS

'Divine Ventriloquism' and Plagiarism as a Fine Art

The most sophisticated defence against the suspicion or charge of plagiarism, and one that is particularly successful in the case of 'great authors,' is to allow for the intention to copy, but to shift it from a fraudulent to an aesthetic arena. Internal clues pointing to the existence of borrowed discourse in texts are thus highly valued as signs of authorial aesthetic intention, revealing not 'plagiarism,' but rather 'allusion,' 'parody,' 'imitation,' 'intertextuality' – any number of borrowings for which aesthetic intentions can be claimed. This claim can, however, always 'fail' if the artist is not sufficiently well-reputed to overcome the suspicion of lack of genius, or if other institutional reasons intervene in the decision. The contemporary irony surrounding the strategy of intentional copying for reasons of aesthetic significance is that it presupposes recourse to authorial intentionality as a criterion for aesthetic decisions – an intentionality whose pertinence is often denied by literary theory. The efficacy of the claim to intentionality normally depends on the perceived 'success' of the intent, which may be determined solely by the prior literary reputation of the perpetrator. While it is obviously not sufficient that only the author claim for his or her copying an aesthetic status, having recourse to a theory of literary creation that justifies the practice does help to shift the question of intention from the criminal to the aesthetic domain.

The best early example of intentional aesthetic copying is probably the *cento* (Latin, patchwork), a composite work made entirely of lines from other poems, and practised from the time of the ancient Greeks on. It was always a humorous and devalued form, at best a literary parlour game. As a recognized genre, it perhaps most approaches some forms of contemporary creation relying explicitly on collage, appropriation, and recontextualization of other texts. Adaptations – reworking of previous literary matter without parodic intent – are often confused with plagiarism, or else 'plagiarisms' are recast in the light of the 'adaptation' in order to jusify borrowings on aesthetic grounds. Corneille's *Le Cid* could most effectively be seen as an adaptation of the Spanish play for the French stage; Régine Deforges's *La bicyclette bleue* could be seen as a French adaptation of *Gone with the Wind* – the problem being, of course, that adaptation is only legal on copyrighted work with the permission of the owner of the copyright.

In the same vein, Coleridge's 'translation' of Schelling, whatever his intentions concerning his acknowledgment of sources, can be argued to be founded on an 'aesthetic' principle: at the end of the passage where he acknowledges his debt to Schelling, Coleridge makes the famous claim: 'I regard truth as a divine ventriloquist: I care not from whose mouth the sounds are supposed to proceed, if only the words are audible and intelligible' (Coleridge 164). Fruman, however, considers the claim to 'divine ventriloquism' an example of insincerity and he contrasts it not only with Coleridge's many accusations of plagiarism against other writers, but also with his protestations about the importance of intellectual honesty. Fruman cites, for example, the following claim: 'I regard, and ever have regarded the obligations of intellect among the most sacred of the claims of gratitude. A valuable thought, or a particular train of thoughts, gives me additional pleasure, when I can safely refer and attribute it to the conversation or correspondence of another' (Coleridge 15).

Whether it is significant that Coleridge omits published works from the short list of potential sources of valuable thoughts is a matter of opinion. What is significant is that the 'divine ventriloquist' theory, when applied to what could be considered a translation or adaptation of a foreign work for a national audience, reverberates with aesthetic legitimacy dating back to Latin times and continuing until at least the eighteenth century: the free translation from foreign sources required no more attribution than the type that Coleridge had effected. That this practice was no longer quite as acceptable in 1815 when Coleridge composed the *Biographia* does not detract from the fact that the appeal to this kind of aesthetic principle, which Fruman ironically refers to as a 'fine phrase surely express[ing] a noble ideal' (*Coleridge* 91), is a common manoeuvre to admit intentional copying (in case plagiarism might be suspected) and to attempt to reconfigure the borrowing as a legitimate strategy.

The most overwhelmingly popular argument used to buttress claims to aesthetic intentionality takes the form of flattering comparisons between one's own imitations and well-known great-author practices of the past – most notably of those pasts where imitation was a legitimate aesthetic. This defence depends directly on the assumption that all literature is 'plagiaristic' and furnishes as evidence the 'great authors don't plagiarize' theory in the form of *ad hominem* arguments claiming that the suspected plagiarist is simply doing what great writers (Shakespeare, Molière, Corneille, etc.) throughout history have done. The literary instances of such disclaimers often take the form of polemical counter-attacks against direct or indirect accusations of plagiarism and constitute much of the corpus of received assumptions and aphorisms about plagiarism – most 'great' authors have expressed an opinion about the relationship between 'plagiarism' and literary creation. Recourse to the 'famous plagiarists' defence also solicits the view that 'plagiarism' is an ubiquitous feature of literary production, thereby not attempting to diminish its importance or presence, but, on the contrary, glorifying it while at the same time implying a criticism of those misguided false critics and pedants who lack the ability to recognize genius and to distinguish between inspired and uninspired imitation. The paradigm case of this argument has been proffered by Dumas. In the course of a well-known defence that we will have more than one occasion to cite, he claims: 'It is true, for my consolation, that I have at least this resemblance with Shakespeare and Molière, that those who have attacked them were so obscure that no memory has conserved their names.'[8]

The artist-as-copier is not only a traditional but a familiar figure; the artist-as-plagiarist has only recently achieved a status less than oxymoronic, and only within a contemporary theory of artistic contestation, which we explore in Part Three. And even within these subversive aesthetics, 'plagiarism' must be qualified by quotation marks – copying is not *really* plagiarism from the moment that it corresponds to an intentional and formulated aesthetic – whether expressed by the author, or subsequently 'discovered' by the critic.

Discreet Acknowledgment and Clandestine Credit

Naming the source and admitting to the crime ahead of time are both strategies designed to deflect or diffuse potential accusations of plagiarism, and are particularly valuable as evidence of an aesthetic intention. In the examples of D.M. Thomas's *The White Hotel* and Régine Deforges's *La bicyclette bleue*, the authors signalled in the acknowledgments their debts to the borrowed authors in question, but the attribution was done discreetly enough that it either escaped the notice of readers or else was deemed to be intentionally clandestine, like the 'small print' in a slightly shady contract. The details of these cases differ sufficiently that it is difficult to generalize from them. It is significant, however, that neither author was finally found guilty of breach of copyright (Thomas, in fact, was never actually charged), and the signalling of the sources played an important role in the eventual innocence of both authors.

The most notorious example of crediting one's sources and 'plagiarizing' at the same time is no doubt Coleridge's *Biographia Literaria*. Fruman notes that 'the reference [to Schelling] itself has been seized upon to demonstrate that Coleridge's failure to acknowledge Schelling was not complete, but rather a matter of degree. This result itself suggests that the parenthetical and murky reference (which no one seems to have followed up for some twenty years) was intended precisely to blunt possible charges of plagiarism' (*Coleridge* 103). And this seems to have been, in general, the result. The reference in question is the following:

> With exception of one or two fundamental ideas, which cannot be withheld from FICHTE, to SCHELLING we owe the completion, and the most important victories, of this revolution in philosophy. To me it will be happiness and honor enough, should I succeed in rendering the system itself intelligible to my countrymen [...] Whether a work is the offspring of a man's own spirit, and the product of original thinking, will be discovered by those who are its sole legitimate judges, by better tests than the mere reference to dates. For readers in general, let whatever shall be found in this or any future work of mine, that resembles, or coincides with, the doctrines of my German predecessor, though contemporary, be wholly attributed to *him*: provided, that the absence of distinct references to his books, which I could not at all times make with truth as designating citations or thoughts actually *derived* from him; and which, I trust, would, after this general acknowledgment be superfluous; be not charged on me as an ungenerous concealment or intentional plagiarism. (Coleridge 163–4)

This acknowledgment is murky indeed, not least because Fichte and Schelling are far from being the only source-texts for the *Biographia*. The wholesale giving over to Schelling of the responsibility for any resemblance or coincidence between his thought and Coleridge's – the 'general acknowledgment' – is offset by the prior appeal to the work's 'sole legitimate judges,' those who are capable of judging its true source and originality. This sentence is remarkable in the context of a paragraph wholly devoted to a statement about Coleridge's indebtedness to his German predecessor, especially since, other than by implication, Coleridge does not prejudge the judgment of these 'sole legitimate judges,' and does not make any direct claims for the *Biographia* as being the 'offspring of *his* own spirit.' A few pages prior to this apparent blanket acknowledgment of his debt to Schelling, Coleridge sets the stage for the contrary scenario, in a move that is reminiscent of Montaigne's claim that an identity of thought between himself and a previous author does not reduce his own originality:

It would be but a mere act of justice to myself, were I to warn my future
readers, that an identity of thought, or even similarity of phrase will not be
at all times a certain proof that the passage has been borrowed from Schelling, or that the conceptions were originally learnt from him. In this
instance, as in the dramatic lectures of Schlegel to which I have before
alluded, from the same motive of self-defence against the charge of plagiarism, many of the most striking resemblances, indeed all the main and fundamental ideas, were born and matured in my mind before I had ever seen
a single page of the German Philosopher. (Coleridge 161)

Fruman spends several pages (85ff.) taking apart the claims made by
Coleridge in these two passages, including the veracity of the chronologi-
cal priority of the maturing of his own ideas before his encounter with
Schelling. Fruman's fundamental argument is that Coleridge was an inveterate liar and self-mythologizer, and that the blind spot in Coleridge studies is the crediting of the author's own claims about himself. In any event,
what is clear is that Coleridge's 'murky' disclaimers are sufficiently explicit
to have done the work they were apparently intended to do, and allowed
his defenders to claim unintentionality for the 'plagiarisms,' that is, to
credit him with acknowledging his debts, and to defend the intellectual
honesty that he claimed for himself.

Such dodgy attributions are more effective in aesthetic and ethical battles than in legal ones, primarily because permission and payment, rather
than attribution, are at stake. Parody and pastiche, for example, are legitimate literary forms which depend for their effects on an explicit relationship with another text, but which can contravene both patrimonial and
moral rights.[9] Claims about aesthetic intention and overt signalling of textual borrowing, however cursory and furtive, may be effective defences
against accusations of plagiarism because of the criterion of covertness
necessary to constitute the crime. In the literary field, the presumed or perceived overt nature of a parodic or otherwise 'intertextual' relationship is
often seen to be less a function of the reader's erudition than of the
author's intention. This defence was used in the appeal that overturned
the original decision to accuse Régine Deforges of plagiarism: first, she
cites Margaret Mitchell in the acknowledgments; and, second, there is an
explicit reference to *Gone with the Wind* in the fiction. The court of appeal
judged these clues to be sufficient evidence that the borrowing was done
with explicit intent that the reader not only recognize the reference, but
recognize as well that the author *intended* her reader to 'get it.'

Luce Irigaray uses the same technique of discreet acknowledgment in
The Speculum of the Other Woman (1985), where, on the final page of the
book, that is, in a paratextual comment situated outside the text, she

acknowledges having quoted many unnamed sources without quotation marks, a technique she justifies on theoretical and feminist principles (see *infra*, Chapter 8). This strategy is similar to a typical postmodern strategy of rewriting used by other 'plagiarists' such as Acker and Cotzee: the 'copied' text is in both cases an integral and necessary component of the new text, but, in fiction, the intertextual relationship is clearly an aesthetic move, while, in Irigaray's work, it is motivated by strong political and theoretical considerations. The lack of scientific references common to an academic work such as Irigaray's is in itself a subversion of conventional norms; the subsequent signalling of this absence indicates that the strategy has significant subversive, but not fraudulent, intentions.

Another subtle way to signal the presence of borrowing without naming the source or resorting to paratextual commentary is to thematize plagiarism within the work. In this way, many plagiarizing authors are assumed to have left clues at the scene of their crime that could point the suspicious reader, if not to the source of the plagiarism, at least to its possible existence. The paradigm case of this type is probably Sterne's famous passage on plagiarism in chapter 1 of the fifth book of *Tristram Shandy* (1761):

> Tell me, ye learned, shall we for ever be adding so much to the *bulk* – so little to the *stock*?
>
> Shall we for ever make new books, as apothecaries make new mixtures, by pouring only out of one vessel into another?
>
> Are we for ever to be twisting, and untwisting the same rope? for ever in the same track – for ever at the same pace? (Sterne 355–6)

This most 'sardonic piece of plagiary' (Merton 163), in which Sterne rails against plagiarism by plagiarizing Burton's *Anatomy of Melancholy* (1621), was pointed out by Ferriar in his *Illustrations of Sterne* in 1798, in which he lists not only 'ludicrous' (comic) authors 'from whom Sterne probably took general ideas' (among them Rabelais, D'Aubigné, Swift), but also 'other writers imitated by Sterne,' the most notable being Burton and his *Anatomy of Melancholy*. Ferriar provides an extensive list of passages by juxtaposing Sterne and Burton, and uses this source as an explanation for what appear to be anachronisms in Sterne's satire and 'the pains bestowed by [him] in ridiculing opinions not fashionable in his time' (Ferriar 57). Textual repetition in Sterne's works is not limited to *Tristram Shandy*, as Ferriar and many others have shown. What concerns us is the evolution of the judgments about such repetitions, a development outlined by Thomas Mallon. Essentially, this history is divided between interpreting them as intentionally covert, genuine plagiarisms, and considering them to be intentional allusions, 'adding an ironic dimension to the novel'

(H.J. Jackson, cited in Mallon 19). Mallon's point is that modern commentators go to great and sometimes unconvincing lengths to read as an aesthetic 'method' a dishonest use of textual sources that, in Ferriar's eyes, was due simply to a lack of learning. The ignorance of Sterne's contemporaries about the *Anatomy of Melancholy*, Rabelais, and other of his sources guaranteed that, until Ferriar, Sterne's brilliant satirical discourse was read as being brilliantly Sterne's. Whether it be the need to rescue Sterne's reputation from himself, or the force of contemporary thinking on rewriting, modern commentators raise his intention from a dishonest to an aesthetic one, such that Sterne becomes a model of the postmodernist aesthetic as well as a model of modernist narrative devices. Mallon leaves no doubt that, in his opinion, Sterne was a 'plagiarist' (without overtones of moral condemnation), while those whom he has inspired may not be. Mallon's criticism is less of Sterne than of modern critics who insist on attributing to the latter a clever aesthetic, or at least a ludic intent, in this case of what Ferriar claims to be, and Mallon concurs that it is, a simple palliative to a simple lack of learning.

The history of the critical appreciation of Sterne's 'plagiarisms' is also a case in point of the notion that thematic 'clues' left by plagiarizing authors should be treated as indications of an aesthetic intent with which to offset any suspicions of fraud or guilt. Internal indications of the presence of 'plagiarism' normally achieve the status of 'clues' to a crime or aesthetic purpose only after the discovery of some kind of copying has been made: the choice between constructing them either as evidence of a guilty conscience, or else as clues to the presence of a clever literary game or intentional aesthetic transgression, is left to the reader or critic.

It is generally considered, for example, that Isidore Ducasse (Lautréamont), author of the *Poésies*, has thematized his plagiaristic method in the famous 'le plagiat est nécessaire' passage, signalling not only his extensive *détournements* of Pascal, Vauvenargues, and others, but, more particularly, his wholesale plagiarisms in Chant 5 of *Les chants de Maldoror* from *L'encyclopédie d'histoire naturelle du Dr. Chenu* (Nesselroth 193). Much more extensively, Hubert Aquin thematizes plagiarism, apocryphal writing, inauthenticity, and appropriation as the central problem of *Trou de mémoire*, his self-conscious 'detective' novel. The several writer-readers in the book are constantly accusing each other of inauthenticity, and accusations and admissions of plagiarism are explicitly made in the fiction. In one notable passage, the fictional editor accuses the fictional author of plagiarizing a passage from a work by Blanchot (Aquin, 'Note de R.R.,' *Trou de mémoire* 86). The work cited by the editor does not exist, but one critic has claimed that the source is in fact a letter addressed to Hubert Aquin by Roland Barthes (J.-P. Martel 75). This letter does not now exist and the 'truth' of these claims is not established. What is established, however, is that this fictional self-accusation of plagiarism, occurring in a context of fictional plagiarism, is interpreted as a thematic clue to the strategic functioning of the novel, in which it is supposed that borrowed discourse performs an aesthetic function.

Yambo Ouologuem, accused of plagiarizing in *Le devoir de violence*, also has recourse to a strategy of apparent self-accusation in his 'letter to (black) ghost-writers of famous authors' ('Lettre aux Pisse-copie nègres d'écrivains célèbres'), where he promotes a method of wholesale plagiarism designed to enable African writers to produce best-selling mystery novels, a second-class type of literature for which the essay ironically maintains that the African is eminently suited. Propounding an elaborate pseudo-scientific system of plagiarism to produce works compiled from passages of the best mystery novels of the century, the essay is wonderfully tongue-in-cheek: reread in the light of the discovery of his 'real' plagiarism in *Le devoir de violence*, the self-accusation did, in this case, nothing to alleviate the crime. Since Ouologuem was pursuing doctoral studies in Paris at the time the plagiarism was discovered, his *Lettre à la France nègre* prompted one sardonic critic to hope that, in his doctoral thesis, Ouologuem would not follow his own advice as he so apparently had in his prize-winning novel (see *infra*, Part Three). Despite claims to aesthetic intentionality and textual evidence to support these claims, the charge of plagiarism stuck and the author's promising career was ruined. It is reasonable to postulate that the African's vulnerable position, coupled with the considerable embarrassment which the French literary institution had caused itself by not recognizing the borrowed elements, were justification enough for the charge of plagiarism.

What emerges from the critical reception of borrowing by 'great authors' is that the intention to signal literary borrowings is easily either invented by the critic or else, when that is not possible, the 'disguised' imitation is interpreted as ironic, satirical or aesthetic, intended to delimit a field of readers who are 'up to the challenge' of the game being played. The explicit signalling of borrowed material in literature (fiction) is simply not a convention that has generally survived the Romantic period, the dominant aesthetic since Romantic times espousing a notion of originality that dispenses, superficially at least, with the imitation of former discourse, and produces itself spontaneously. This presupposition, while demonstrably false, is one that governs the surface strategies of the text and precludes explicit attribution of sources of inspiration.

A variation on self-accusation by means of internal evidence is the recourse to extra-fictional (hence, 'true') claims to intentional and, therefore, presumably, aesthetically motivated copying. Kathy Acker invokes this strategy when she claims on the back cover of the Semiotexte edition of *Hannibal Lecter, My Father*, that 'this writing is all fake (copied from other writing) so you should go away and not read any of it.' At the same time, she makes a clear distinction between 'plagiarism' and what she calls 'appropriation': 'To be guilty of plagiarism, according to the law, is to represent somebody else's material as your material. I haven't done that. I have been very clear that I use other people's material. I haven't quite listed sources in my later books not to sound like an academic, but in many interviews, in many theoretical texts, I said where each section came from. [...] I've always talked about it as a literary theory and as a literary method' (12–13).

Michel Tournier engages in the same strategy with, evidently, considerable success. Roland de Chaudenay reports that, after an explanation of the role played by Flaubert in *Le roi des aulnes*, Tournier adds: 'I am like the thieving magpie. I gather from here and there everything which pleases me and store it in my nest. The problem is to stir around all of these heteroclite things until out of them comes a book.'[10] The argument apparently carries weight with Chaudenay, who comments: 'Bravo! Here is talent doubled with a forthright honesty which cuts short any suspicion of clandestine literary appropriation. Those who thought to make important discoveries by sifting *le Roi des aulnes* through the sieve of Flaubert will be wasting their time.'[11]

The admission of copying is obviously an ineffectual defence against accusations of breach of copyright, although it is a strategy that has been employed. In Deforges's case (*La bicyclette bleue*), the court was obliged to argue not only that the imitation of *Gone with the Wind* was intentional, and therefore part of the aesthetic value of the text, but also that the borrowed material was quantitatively insignificant and, moreover, that substantial 'enhancement' or reworking of the borrowed elements had taken place. The original finding of guilty had relied on detailing the *similarities* between the two novels; the appeal court's decision reversed exactly this judgment by stressing the importance of the *differences* between the two works. At no time did the defence argue that the borrowing had not taken place. In fact, among the claims to innocence based on intentional borrowing was the fact that the idea had been suggested to Deforges by her editor. The radical reversal of the original decision by the appeal court is an exemplary instance of the pragmatic nature of plagiarism: the fact of the textual repetition was not in question, merely whether or not it fit the categories of intention to defraud and to gain unearned advantage without significant enhancement of the materials borrowed. It has been suggested, not unreasonably, that a large part of the appeal court's motive for reversing the decision of guilty depended on the important role played by Deforges in the French literary institution (Gallays 198). This argument looks even more plausible when one compares her fate to that of others not so well placed, such as Yambo Ouologuem.

COPYING RIGHT

Public Ideas / Private Expressions

The first rule of plagiarism – or of copying without getting caught – is to exploit the idea/expression dichotomy that has moved from the realm of ancient tradition into copyright law. If it is safer to copy an idea than its expression, this is the case not only because ideas are considered 'public property,' but because spotting an identical idea is somewhat more difficult than spotting an identical expression. Both literary tradition and copyright laws make the saying-well of something more individual than what is said: if nothing is new under the sun, there are almost endless new ways of saying old things; plots are fewer in number than are possible combinations of words. While, for legal purposes, copyright is clearly a matter of expression rather than content, the separability of form and content is not, however, entirely self-evident, especially in many aesthetic productions where the vehicle is virtually indistinguishable from the content, and where the distinction may be considered, at best, artificial. While, on the one hand, 'art' may seem to escape the domains of 'knowledge' and of 'truth' altogether, on the other hand, the notion of 'ideas' is most easily understood in contemporary literature by considering such elements such as plot, character types, themes, and situations that demonstrate a certain perennial or archetypal frequency, and much legal effort has been expended in making these determinations.[12] There has never been, and there is not now, consensus on the difficult question of how to distinguish between ideas and their expression, but opinions range from the 'what oft' was thought but ne'er so well expressed' school to one promoting a philosophy of 'what oft' was expressed but ne'er so well expressed.' In the first case, ideas are by their nature in the public domain, and it is their expression that is the result of genius, work, originality, or whatever else is deemed to qualify the resulting text as private property. In the second scenario, it is the form of the expression itself that becomes the object of appropriation, and, here, questions of 'significance' and of 'enhancement' become crucial.

We have seen that many non-legal accusations of plagiarism have fallen into ridicule for the misapprehension of the fine distinction between an 'idea' and its 'expression.' And this distinction is clouded by another, which is the wealth of stereotype and cliché existing both in the popular and literary imagination and in language. The public nature of language is such that a large body of cultural goods either have no 'author' or have come to be perceived, irrespective of copyright law, as belonging to the cultural common domain. The Baron de Reiffenberg, collaborator with Quérard in his *Supercheries*, and victim in this same text of numerous accusations of plagiarism, is nevertheless quoted by Quérard in his introduction:

> We must agree on the word *plagiarism* and not confuse the petty theft of ideas or style with the use of this common stock of banalities to which the most original intelligence is condemned, as the body is to the laws of movement, whether it has the proportions of the Apollo of Belvedere or those of Thersite. An imbecile claimed one day that Voltaire copied him, because he ended his letters, like him, with 'your very humble and very obedient servant.' There is no lack, in fact, of small minds who have neither ideas nor talent, and who imagine that others have so little self-esteem as to borrow from them. These poor people forget that one only borrows from the rich.[13]

Within this large grey area consisting of those 'inevitable banalities' to which even the most original mind is condemned are situated most of the debates about the existence of plagiarism. Defences against the charge of plagiarism often have recourse to demonstrations that the ideas in question are so common as to circulate freely throughout history, such that for every plot one has copied, one can demonstrate its existence in multiple other texts from which one has clearly not copied. Or, by invoking the 'great writers don't plagiarize' argument, one points out the long tradition of borrowing: Dryden uses this defence in his preface to *Don Sebastian*, soliciting the ancients and their practice of treating the 'fable' as common property: he *didn't* copy the story, but, even if he *had*, 'though, if I had taken the whole story [from the French novel *Don Sebastian*], and wrought it up into a play, I might have done it exactly according to the practice of almost all the ancients, who were never accused of being plagiaries for building their tragedies on known fables ...' (quoted in Aden 106). He goes on to exploit the common domain distinction between idea and expression: 'It is the contrivance, the new turn, and new characters, which alter the property, and make it ours. The *materia poetica* is as common to all writers as the *materia medica* to all physicians' (106). Similarly, in his essay 'Apologie pour le plagiat' (1892), the Nobel Prize–winner Anatole France asserts unequivocally: 'A mind caring only about literature is not interested in such contestations [i.e., accusations of plagiarism]. Such a person knows that no man can reasonably flatter himself for having thought of something that no other man has thought before him. He knows that ideas belong to everyone and that one cannot say: "This one is mine" [...] He knows, finally, that an idea is only as good as its form, and that to give new form to an old idea is the whole of art, and the only creation possible to humanity.'[14]

Georges Maurevert, in his *Livre des plagiats* (1922), goes on to devote a chapter to the 'borrowings' made by France, most of which were divulged not by his critics, but by his 'fanatics,' who, 'with great salutations, with protestations of admiration and respect, continually present to the public the latest "borrowing" of their idol' ['avec de grands saluts, des protestations d'admiration et de respect, présentent à chaque instant au public le dernier "emprunt" de leur idole' (225)].

Victorien Sardou, a French playwright of the late nineteenth century, was so often accused of plagiarism that he produced a work entitled *Mes plagiats*, in which he denies the charges. In the course of his demonstration, Sardou promotes the theory that there exists only a certain number of dramatic situations available to an author, and that, inevitably, the same plots will be recycled. To demonstrate his argument, he retells the plot of the *Barber of Seville* by Beaumarchais and *L'école des femmes* by Molière in a single paragraph. As Maurevert points out, 'the reader will doubtless notice that, in this analysis, Sardou manages to recount the entire *Barber of Seville* without once mentioning the name of Figaro, who is its protagonist.'[15]

The idea/expression dichotomy is also delicate because it seems to imply that ideas are completely separable from their expression, and that the intentional theft of an idea, disguised in a different expression, would be legitimate. The infamous seventeenth-century example of how to copy an idea and get away with it by changing the words – disguising one's imitation – is the oft-cited case of Professor Richesource, about whom Quérard says that plagiarism was so accepted in the seventeenth century that it actually deserved a university chair ['Le plagiarisme fut tellement à l'ordre du jour au dix-septième siècle qu'il eut jusqu'à une chaire' (*Supercheries*, vol 1, 74)]. Quérard reports, after Ludovic Lalanne who cites D'Israeli,[16] that Richesource published his course on rhetoric under the title *Le masque des orateurs, ou la Manière de déguiser toutes sortes de compositions, lettres, sermons, panégyriques, oraisons funèbres, dédicaces, discours etc.*, in which he teaches the 'fine art' of *plagiarisme*, 'an ingenious and easy mode, which some adroitly employ to change, or disguise, all sorts of speeches of their own composition, or of that of other authors, for their pleasure, or their utility, and in such a manner that it becomes impossible even for the author himself to recognise his own work, his own genius, and his own style, so skilfully shall the whole be disguised.'[17]

The method is simple, and known at least to most undergraduates (and graduates, and professors, and probably everyone else who is required to write professionally): one simply changes the syntax and lexicon of the original. For example, in place of the sentence 'An ambassador must possess three qualities: honesty, talent and courage' ['Un ambassadeur doit posséder trois qualités: la probité, la capacité et le courage'], Richesource recommends: 'An ambassador must be strong, virtuous and capable' ['An ambassadeur doit être ferme, vertueux and capable' (Lalanne 148)]. Richesource is frequently mentioned in compilations and lists of literary curiosities, chiefly as a figure of ridicule. There is little evidence that his teaching, or his method of *plagiarisme*, was taken seriously as an important moment in the history of rhetoric, or in the plagiaristic arts.

Contemporary copyright law, however, has addressed the strategy of *plagiarisme à la Richesource* by sanctioning 'disguised imitation' in order to render the distinction between idea and expression less opaque. According to the principle that 'an original work is never founded on fraudulent bases' (Tamaro, *Le droit d'auteur* 44), Richesource's method is explicitly condemned: 'there exist situations where a person might try to disguise the borrowing from an anterior work. This is the notion of the "disguised imitation." And disguised imitation of a work is the case when one intends fraudulently to reproduce an important part [of another work].'[18]

Insignificant and Insubstantial Copying

The criterion of 'significant and substantial materials' is the modern copyright formulation of Jaucourt's expression 'copying sentences, pages and entire passages.' In his view, plagiarism is not a matter of degree; neither does he distinguish between copying essential passages and copying whatever might be considered 'insignificant' or 'insubstantial.' In terms of copyright, 'significant and substantial' in the field of unacknowledged borrowing is designed to protect against borrowing that might be deemed *quantitatively* insignificant. The category of significant materials is a case-by-case determination based on the *qualitative* importance of the elements of the borrowed work in the new work, when evidence of a purely quantitative kind is insufficient. To be judged 'significant,' the borrowed elements must essentially be those that permit an 'ordinary' reader or observer to establish a relationship of identity or derivation between the two works, something like what we might recognize as a distinctive feature. In this way, the borrowed or 'plagiarized' elements might constitute a mere detail of either the original or the derived work, but this detail may be seen to be so characteristic of the identity of the original work as to contribute significantly to the interpretation or understanding of the new work.

In non-legal situations, the distinction is equally problematic, but often depends on the perceived quality of the borrowed material and its function in its new context: in the literary tradition, the more 'significant' the borrowed elements, the nobler the imitation – as Dryden has said, a mere imitation of a Raphael is to be preferred over a mediocre original. However, current copyright law legislates in direct conflict with this tradition: the more outstanding and distinctive the features of a work (the more 'original'), the less legitimate their appropriation.

Since plagiarism depends on the reader's recognition of repeated discourse, the copying of a little known or obscure, that is, insignificant, source rather implies that the perpetrator counted on not being found out, which goes a long way to establishing fraudulent intent. Laurence Sterne, Lautréamont, and Hubert Aquin can stand for examples of the copying of the obscure, and all 'got away' with their plagiarisms sufficiently well that their posthumous discovery had no negative impact on the reputations they had already achieved; in fact, the 'plagiarisms' eventually contributed to an alleged aesthetic theory of which their work appears as the realization. The obscure sources that they plagiarized were in all cases scientific or encyclopedic texts that, to the extent that they could be seen to participate in the realm of 'knowledge,' could be considered in the 'public domain.' In the case of Lautréamont, if one excepts the verses rewritten from a variety of well-known authors such as Pascal, Vauvenargues, and La Rochfoucauld (which, because of their visibility, hardly qualify for serious plagiarism), one can cite the famous passage concerning the flight of the cranes, and other descriptions from the fifth song in *Les chants de Maldoror*, copied word for word from Chenu's *Encyclopaedia of Natural History*. This discovery was not made until the 1950s, by Viroux ('Lautréamont et le Dr Chenu,' *Mercure de France*, 1 Dec. 1952), and it is natural that the obscurity of the source, which is not so much hidden as improbable, contributed to its invisibility. François Caradec argues that the documentary character of these plagiarisms 'permit Lautréamont to substitute for direct observation a scrupulous indirect observation ... by the faithful copying of works of scientific vulgarization' ['permettent à Lautréamont de substituer à l'observation directe une observation indirecte scrupuleuse ... par la recopie fidèle d'ouvrages de vulgarisation scientifique']. And Chaudenay, to whom we are indebted for this summary of Caradec's remarks, adds 'Pourquoi pas?' (Chaudenay 184). The argument is similar to the defences proffered in favour of Sterne's plagiarisms: lacking direct knowledge, he substituted that of others.

In the case of Aquin, similar types of 'documentary' sources are used to nourish the scientific or erudite discourses concerning psycho-pharmacology, baroque theatre, and art. In many cases, these passages are copied whole hog from scientific and encyclopedic sources of a rather specialized nature, not in the reading repertoire of the general, however well-educated reader. There is something transparent after the fact about these passages:

once alerted to their presence, it is an easy matter to spot them simply on a matter of style and content even when the source, and thereby the proof, remains hidden. The effect of these 'plagiarisms' on the reception of Aquin's work has been somewhat paradoxical. Upon the publication of *Trou de mémoire*, detractors of the work criticized its 'erudition' on many grounds, from *taedium* to pretentiousness, reacting to the effective difficulty of reading a text so full of esoteric or technical language. None, however, reacts with charges of plagiarism. In one remarkable instance, one of the most virulent critics of the text praises the beauty of an isolated passage that describes the painting *The Ambassadors* by Hans Holbein, which is a central figure in the fiction (Bosco). Ironically, the passage in question is copied almost word for word from Jurgis Baltrusaitis's treatise *Anamorphoses ou perspectives curieuses* (Paris: Oliver Perrin, 1955), and owes very little to Aquin himself. It is probable that the duped critic would, in this instance, feel vindicated in her criticism of Aquin's prose by the discovery of the 'plagiarism'; Aquin, at the same time, would probably also feel a sense of triumph. The copied passage has produced two different but positive effects: as an unrecognized borrowing, it has enhanced his reputation as a stylist; as an uncovered one, it is assimiliated into a network of aesthetic intentions in which formal imitation, the inevitable reiteration of 'variants,' replaces the artist's quest for the elusive, if not impossible, 'originality.'

The opposing strategy is paradoxically somewhat safer: copying something well-known (significant) verges on pillaging the public domain, which is legitimate, and further protects the copier by the presumption of overtness. This practice is usually explained by the assumption on the part of the writer of cultural knowledge shared with the reader. Whether considered genuine or fraudulent, the assumption may be judged unfounded or misplaced, generating either accusations of pretentiousness, as in some of Aquin's critics, or outright plagiarism. As Robert Merton points out, writers do not want to insult their readers by referring them to well-known sources; less learned readers (i.e., in Merton's expression, 'most of us') 'attribute a striking idea or formulation to the author who first introduced us to it' (218). Or, to remain with Aquin: 'The originality of the work is directly proportional to the ignorance of the reader.' The apparently innocent practice of alluding to something presumably well known can be misinterpreted as intentional covertness, or it can actually be an attempt to hide one's sources. The convenient defence in the second case will then be the claim on the writer's part that he was delving into the common domain.

The sheer obviousness of some potential 'plagiarisms' and their substantive nature is sometimes used as proof of innocence, as in the cases of Stendhal's appropriation of Carpani's *Life of Haydn*, and Coleridge's 'translation' of Schelling The same holds true for Régine Deforges: the similarity between *La bicyclette bleue* and *Gone with the Wind*, joined to the notoriety of the second (it has been very popular in France), puts the author above the suspicion that she was trying to hide her source: in this case, we again see the distinction between 'plagiarism' and breach of copyright. From a literary point of view, most alerted readers might consider the relationship between the two texts as a form of 'intertextuality,' ranging from adaptation to transposition, and constituting part of the pleasure of the French text. The court, however, was clearly interested in questions of property: copyrighted texts are protected from unauthorized adaptations.

Significant Enhancement

Much depends on significant enhancement or, in Jaucourt's terms, on the fact that something other than 'a few minor changes in expression or a few additions' must have occurred. Modern cases of copyright infringement turn not only on whether or not the repetition in question constitutes a significant and substantial part of the old work or the new but, as well, on whether or not, in borrowing, the author has significantly 'enhanced' the borrowed materials. This was one of the arguments that won the case for Régine Deforges; it is also the argument the Académie française used to justify Corneille's rewriting of *Le Cid*, since he had 'rendered some of the imitated things better than they were' ['il en a rendu quelques-une [des choses imitées] meilleures qu'elles n'étaient' ('Les sentiments de l'Académie française,' in Corneille 820)]. 'Significant enhancement' implies both imitation and transformation, and descends directly from the classical tenets of appropriation by transformation and, ideally, 'improvement' of one's model.

If the question of enhancement by improvement is difficult enough, that of enhancement by simple repetition is even more so. The idea is expressed in the common cliché of bringing to light that which had been buried, or finding a treasure in a dunghill, where an author who saves from oblivion a moment of genius buried in the works of a non-author is doing humanity a service. This logic goes back to Seneca's position that 'whatever is well said by anyone is mine,' and the author who repeats what was once well said by someone unknown has added to truth. A small but exemplary case might be Lamartine's famous line 'Un seul être vous manque, et tout est dépeuplé' ('L'isolement'), copied whole hog from Nicolas-Germain Léonard, a minor Creole poet who was one of Lamartine's strongest – and most suppressed – influences (see Maurevert, 140ff. and Chaudenay, 'Lamartine'). The line is apparently 'enhanced' by the change of pronoun from the original *me* to *vous*: this transformation is considered sufficient to save the line from banality and thrust it into the realm of genius. At least, this is Chaudenay's opinion: 'The creation of Lamartine, which is perhaps not negligeable, consisted in substituting *you* for *me*, and in then replacing this beautiful alexandrine in a context where it really shines.'[19] May the reader be the judge.

The category of 'significant enhancement' is itself significant for positioning plagiarism not in terms of originality, but rather in terms of imitation, for what is significantly enhanced is by definition repeated or imitated. All agree, it would seem, that imitation is acceptable if changes, usually deemed 'improvements,' are effected on the original text or idea. The difficulty obviously lies in measuring the degree of change deemed to be 'significant.' In contemporary courts of law, where such decisions are necessarily made on a case-by-case basis, the degree of 'enhancement' achieved may be proportional to the relative astuteness of the opposing lawyers. The question is related to that of intention, as we have already seen with respect to *La bicyclette bleue:* aesthetic imitation, the kind that depends on recognition by the reader, entails a certain close fit between the original and the imitative text, a similarity that may call into question the significance of the 'enhancement' effected.

In cases of unmistakable textual identity, where the degree of similarity seems to thrust the repetition beyond the realm of coincidence, the accuser is required to show, first, that the accused could reasonably have had access to the purloined property, and, second, that there was no 'significant enhancement' of the copied text. If Pierre Menard's fictional critic were the defence counsel, he would inevitably argue that the recurrence of an identical text in a new context is sufficient enhancement in and of itself to counter the accusation of plagiarism, and he would be joined by a certain number of contemporary theorists who would argue that every utterance is a new one by virtue of a different time, place, and identity of the speaker. Obviously, lawyers usually have to argue significant enhancement on more concrete grounds. How many different words constitute significant enhancement? Is translation a version of enhancement? Does the change of context from, for example, a scientific text to a fictional one sufficiently reorient the text? Is it the text itself which must be different, or its 'significance'?

Significant enhancement in the realm of ideas is an even cloudier area, first, because of the general consensus that ideas are rather fewer in number than possible combinations of words, and, second, because they properly fall into the realm of common domain or public property. Régine Deforges's version of *Gone with the Wind* is a case in point: 'Boy meets girl' is hardly suitable for copyright, while 'headstrong young woman in love with the wrong man in the middle of a war (etc. etc.)' is less likely to be a pure coincidence. But is a headstrong young American woman of the Civil War era *different from* or *similar to* a headstrong young French woman during the Second World War? (Lucas 209). And if there are differences, are they 'significant,' do they constitute a new work or a repetition of the old one? In terms of content or ideas, the judgment of significant enhancement is always relative and is open as well to the defence of public domain.

In this area, one aspect of the common-domain theory that goes beyond simple copyright infringement is the notion of the proliferation of ideas. If the 'boy meets girl' plot is public, it is because at this level of generality it is found everywhere since time immemorial (literally) and no protectable source can be claimed. The more specific the repeated elements, the more likely the suspicion of direct influence. The problem for protection of copyright becomes one of proof that one specific text was used as a source and not another. In a landmark Canadian case of musical plagiarism involving unconscious plagiarism (*Gondos* v *Hardy*), the defence introduced to the jury, as well as the two melodies in question, eleven other melodies containing various degrees of similarity in order to show, first, that *if* the accused copied someone, it was not necessarily the plaintiff, and, second, that the proliferation of the theme was such that its recurrence could constitute coincidence (Carruthers).

Reconstructing authorial intention from the presence of textual evidence is the essential moment in the determination of plagiarism. But, as we have seen, this reconstruction is most often a projection of the reader's intentionality onto the author. Not only authorial claims to innocence, but also critical arguments for the innocence of 'great authors,' manifest the opinion that accusations of plagiarism are founded on a misapprehension of intentions. Now this misapprehension – the reader's mistaking of legitimate imitation as fraud or theft – can always itself be suspected of fraud. As it is always the reader who identifies and judges plagiarism, such readers are necessarily motivated by their own intentions, which are rarely admitted or even recognized, except for the single ethical motivation of defending the honesty or integrity of the literary profession – or one's own property.

In the final part of this study, in which we examine the uses to which plagiarism – or accusations of it – can be put in the struggle for power within the literary institution, we will often be encountering instances of the strategies here enumerated. However, the cases of 'profit,' 'imperial,' and 'guerrilla' plagiarism that follow illustrate charges and presumed motivations and intentions for plagiarism that move us out of these personalized types of argument into larger social, cultural, political, and institutional realms.

PART THREE

Power Plagiarism

6. Profit Plagiarism

Je travaillerai comme un Dumas.

H. de Balzac, Lettres à Mme Hanska

Plagiarism without profit – or without the perception of it – is hardly conceivable. It is only when repetition results in advantages to the author that suspicions of fraud become plausible. Thus, while authorial intentions may be indeterminable from textual evidence, they may be deduced from the effects or consequences of the alleged act: a profitable 'borrowing' will easily be shifted to the category of theft. As the example of Martial's coining of the metaphor 'plagiarism' implies, it is a constituent and original part of the definition of plagiarism that someone lose and someone gain, and that what has unjustly changed hands be of some value. However, the question remains as to what, exactly, is lost or gained in the appropriation of intellectual property, and what role the notion of *unearned advantage* plays both in accusations of plagiarism and in copyright legislation.

The two most important and intuitively evident contenders for undeserved profit are money and reputation (honour), which can be either intimately associated or completely separate: honour or reputation divorced from significant financial considerations can still be valued as an object of desire in its own right, as in many artistic instances, especially where a minor or 'unsuccessful' artist accuses a 'successful' one. In these cases, there is little question that the accused has deprived the accuser of profit, for the stolen property is usually considered to be of the order of a treasure recovered from a dunghill. It is often not financial loss, or even the loss of potential fame or reputation, that is contested, but the unearned gain, either financial or symbolic, acquired by fraud on the part of the plagiarist.

In concert with Jaucourt's definition, where plagiarists are those who 'wish at all costs to become an author' but fail, one of the most cited motives for plagiarism is specifically the wish to profit from the celebrity and glory attached to authorship. Erasmus, in *The Praise of Folly*, considers the foolishness of authors who 'buy an empty reward, namely, praise – and that the praise of a handful. They buy it with such an expense of long hours, so much loss of that sweetest of all things, sleep, so much sweat, so many vexations. Add also the loss of health, the wreck of their good looks, weakness of eyes or even blindness, poverty, malice, denial of pleasures, premature old age and early death – and if there are other things like these, add them' (74). In contradistinction to these fools, he praises 'wiser writers': 'those who put out the work of others as their own. By a few strokes of the pen they transfer to their own account the glory which was the fruit of much toil on another's part, drawing comfort from the thought that even it if should happen that they are publicly convicted of plagiarism [*plagii*], meanwhile they shall have enjoyed for a period the emoluments of authorship. It is worth one's while to see how pleased authors are with themselves when they are popular, and pointed out in a crowd – "There's a celebrity!"' (74–5).

Examples of literary plagiarism enacted primarily for the *expectation* of financial gain as a separate motive from honour are rare, and often involve the more corporate aspects of the literary institution since its autonomization throughout the course of the nineteenth century. In the artistic field (excluding industries such as film and rock music), financial gains and losses are often negligible, or at least indeterminable, and one has to have a reputation before it can be lost to someone else. Plagiarism is most economically advantageous in modern periods where there exists no legislation covering a particular practice, as in the case of 'cross-border' copying before the internationalization of copyright legislation, or during the fervent period of literary 'industrialism' in nineteenth-century France, England, and America, as we shall soon see. However, financial gain as a *consequence* of discursive repetition inevitably gets recast as intention. While contemporary cases of copyright involving works of creative literature are rather few in number for the simple reason that the costs involved in pursuing the action usually far outweigh the potential financial benefits, twentieth-century 'literary industrialism' has motivated plagiarism suits for purely economic interests. Alexander Lindey recounts the story of 'plagiarism rings' operating in America at the beginning of the twentieth century. In a kind of reversal of the tradition of piracy, over a third of the plays performed on Broadway between 1910 and 1930 were confronted with fraudulent plagiarism suits; after considerable legal expenses, all were held blameless. The motive behind the false allegations was to get the defendant to settle out of court, thereby profiting the blackmailers directly.[1]

The 'failed author' of Jaucourt's definition often falls into one of two categories of profiteer: the *parvenu* or the *industrialist*, both of which presuppose lack of talent. As 'authors don't plagiarize,' a significant strategy in constructing plagiarism is to construe the potential plagiarist as something other than an author. This is most easily done with contemporary writers whose reputation, however successful, is not yet sanctified by time: dethroning a (dead) great author for his plagiarisms is nearly impossible, and of little advantage to the accuser. However, since unsuccessful bad writers necessarily attract little attention either from critics or from any other type of reader, the writer who is particularly susceptible to the judgment of being either an 'industrialist' or a *parvenu* is inevitably the *successful bad* writer, that is, one whose success is judged to be inexplicable, undesirable, and, most important, undeserved.

The *parvenu*, or literary upstart, is an untalented writer bent on rising above the level of 'Grub street' and on achieving fame – or notoriety – by virtue of a genius to which he can, however, only pretend. The accusations against Yambo Ouologuem clearly point to the suspicion that, were it not for his plagiarisms, the author would never have achieved his success; his critics point to his other significant work, *Lettre à la France nègre*, to demonstrate the inferior quality of his talent. Accusations against D.M. Thomas for his use of the Babi Yar holocaust story in *The White Hotel* and for his translation of Pushkin's poetry sometimes fall back on the assessment of lack of talent or opportunism, especially since outright accusations of outright plagiarism seem literally inappropriate.[2]

Deluded rather than dishonest, the *parvenu* claims a higher motive for his art. In the 'inverted world of art' of the nineteenth century described by Bourdieu, he may even use popular failure as a gauge of his own genius, but the instances of legitimation usually consider his talent to be no less mediocre for the rarification of his readership. The *parvenu* is immemorial and appears everywhere from the moment that Aesop immortalized him as a jay wearing borrowed feathers. Greene's 'upstart Crow' is a case in point, regardless of the real target of the insult. And because authorship turns out to be a competitive enterprise, the championing of one author often entails the denial of authorship to a rival. Pope has summarized the critical competition between the defenders of Shakespeare, the natural genius, and Ben Jonson, the pedantic imitator, who out of all his learning could not squeeze the talent that overflowed from Shakespeare's untutored nature: 'It is ever the nature of Parties to be in extremes; and nothing is so probable, as that because *Ben Johnson* had much the most learning, it was said on the one hand that *Shakespear* had none at all; and because *Shakespear* had much the most wit and fancy, it was retorted on the other, that *Johnson* wanted both. Because *Shakespear* borrowed nothing, it was said that *Ben Johnson* borrowed every thing' (Pope, from preface to vol. 1 of *The Works of Shakespeare*, [1725], quoted in Craig 378).

The competitive nature of even premodern literature points to the Manichaean aspects of the power struggles involved in legitimate inclusion in the ranks. If it is difficult enough to reconcile the art of Shakespeare and Jonson within the same aesthetic, these struggles will become acute during modern periods of the commercial industrialization of literature and its developing capacity to generate not only symbolic but financial profit.

The *industrialist* is a kind of *parvenu* born of nineteenth-century literary commercialism. He writes purely for popular success and the ensuing financial advantage. His economy supposes quantity, rather than quality, of production, according to the principle that the lowest forms of work will be the most palatable to the greatest number. At least since Horace, the higher the work the more rarified its audience: 'You that intend to write what is worthy to be read more than once [...] take no pains to make the multitude admire you, content with a few [judicious] readers' (Horace 181). Financial success due to prodigious production, and equally prodigious popularity, are the most notorious indicators of the industrialist: the image of the noble and disinterested artist has traditionally proscribed both financial gain and popularity as being incompatible with true genius. In the industrial economy that supplanted the pre-commercial reliance on patronage or the activity of writing as an aristocratic pastime, financial need forced the artist to adopt methods designed to promote speed and quantity of production; the same methods can be seen as a means to palliate a lack of talent.

During the eighteenth and nineteenth centuries, the autonomization and commercialization of literature led to a double system of conflicting values: the more traditional and conservative view maintained the nobility of letters and its necessary separation from interests of profit, while the growing mass of popular writers attempted, more or less successfully, to make a commercial living from their efforts and to demand remuneration for their work and production. Of course, the two systems are not distinct and they coexist in the most successful authors, of whom Balzac, constantly torn between the necessity of production and the demands of true literature, is no doubt the pre-eminent example. The coincidence of these two value systems led to the division that we know today between popular and 'high' literature: the romantic bohemian figure of the *poète maudit* – the starving unappreciated genius, destined to die in poverty only to be discovered by future generations – gained an aura of disinterested nobility as a counterpart to the commercialization of mass literature. As Bourdieu's analyses of the nineteenth-century French literary institution have shown, the absence of financial success became a hallmark of the self-styled literary elite, while mass popularity, accompanied by financial success, became the mark of the lack of aesthetic distinction that made the work accessible to the mediocre and badly educated masses. As Bourdieu says:

> Certain writers, like Leconte de Lisle, go as far as seeing in immediate success 'the mark of intellectual inferiority.' And the Christ-like mystique of the *artiste maudit*, sacrificed in this world and consecrated in the next, is doubtless no more than the transfiguration, into a professional ideal or ideology, of the specific contradiction of the mode of production that the pure *artiste* aims at founding. This is, in effect, an inverted economic world: the artist can only triumph in the symbolic field in so far as he loses in the economic (at least in the short term) and vice versa (at least in the long term).[3]

It is often said that many accusations of plagiarism are examples of failed authors airing their petty jealousies at the expense of great ones. Nevertheless, accusations of plagiarism levelled against the *parvenu* or industrialist are a notable example of the contrary situation and constitute a defensive strategy against the encroaching of the margins upon the institutional centre: whether it be Shakespeare's (alleged) plagiarisms, Dumas's methods as described by Quérard, or Ouologuem's practices as decried by his detractors, this category of plagiarism, where it is the established literary tradition that accuses a challenger from the margins, is one that reveals the weak points of a besieged literary institution. The denunciation is a last-ditch form of institutional self-defence.

The conflicting figures of the profiteer and the genius are recurring themes in nineteenth-century fiction: Balzac's Rastignac of *Illusions perdues* is probably the best-known example of the first; an exemplary genius is Vigny's Chatterton in the play of the same name. Chatterton became a powerful mythic figure since his early and impoverished death at the end of the eighteenth century. Long after the fraud of the purportedly medieval origins of his 'Rowley' verses was exposed, the influence and popularity of his poetry, as well as his mysterious and youthful demise, made the 'Golden Boy' into a tragic Romantic hero representing the unrecognized and unappreciated genius.

In nineteenth-century France, at the time of the crystallization of these distinctions, two opposing principles determined the difference between the genius, on the one hand, and the industrialist or *parvenu*, on the other. First, the genius was 'original,' both in his person and in his productions; the *profiteer* owed his relative success to nothing other than imitation. Second, while genius did not exempt an author from the necessity of genuine work and study, an opposition developed between the notion of 'work' and that of 'industry,' with all of the negative implications of the latter term that we will explore. The link between imitation and industry was entailed by the large amount of production required to sustain one's income by meeting the demands of journalistic or theatrical production: Dumas is the prime example of this kind of successful industrialism.

BALZAC VERSUS INDUSTRIALISM

The opposition between genius, implying honest work, and industry, implying speed and quantity of production, is a recurring theme throughout the nineteenth century. Nodier, as we have seen, deplores the fact that contemporary letters have been delivered into the hands of 'men devoid of refinement and honour, who considered the career of talent as only one of the paths to wealth' ['hommes dénués de délicatesse et d'honneur, qui ne regardoient la carrière du talent comme un des chemins de la fortune' (152–3)]. He distinguishes between past generations of true genius and originality, and the present one, which must substitute industry: 'we must appreciate their efforts to replace, by an innocent industry, the resources of which they have been deprived by their predecessors' ['on doit leur savoir quelque gré d'avoir essayé de remplacer, par une innocente industrie, les ressources qui leur ont été ravies par leurs devanciers' (99)]. 'Industry' is clearly inferior to genius, but a necessary evil in the inferior historical moment of the early nineteenth century.

The nineteenth-century *Larousse*, in the article 'Imitation,' expresses with respect to the industrial mode of production an attitude which is generalizable to literary industrialism. The principal goal of 'industry' is 'not to create products of great value and originality, but to produce as abundantly and as cheaply as possible [... O]ne rarely sees industrials taking the time for study and research [... ;] they must get on with the job quickly.'[4] As Quérard will later do, Sainte-Beuve (1839) links industrialism and democracy as threats to the nobility of letters:

> It is necessary however to resign one's self to new practices, to the invasion of literary democracy as well as to all other democracies. It matters little that the problem appears more evident in literature. Writing and publishing will become less and less a matter of distinction. With our electoral and industrial manners, everyone, at least once in his life, will have had his page, his speech, his prospectus, his *toast*, and will be an *author*. From there to publishing a novel (*feuilleton*), there is but a step [...] What could be more honourable, more worthy of interest than the assiduous work (be it a

bit hasty and badly done) of an impoverished writer, living by his pen and supporting his family?[5]

Sainte-Beuve's essay is largely directed against the formation of the Société des gens de lettres, an association intended to promote the protection of author's rights, that is, what Sainte-Beuve calls 'le démon de la propriété littéraire' ('De la littérature industrielle' 201), a contributing cause of the industrialism into which literature had fallen. Some seventeen years later, as a judge for the same society for the awarding of a literary prize, Sainte-Beuve appears to be somewhat reconciled to the notion of literary property, but still rather cautious:

> From the moment, moreover, that wealth is produced in a society, it will have a proprietor, and it is just that the wealth produced not mistake its owner, that it not go almost entirely to he who has least merited it. Given this situation, material questions become mixed up with moral ones, questions which involve the future state of the man of Letters and the reality of his financial independence. These complex questions were perhaps broached in your program: they will remain mere proposals for a long time still; we like to hope that they will be resolved little by little, and in a way that will not be a permanent disadvantage either to the honour of Letters, nor to freedom of thought.[6]

Balzac's role as a founding member of the Société confirms his status as an 'industrialist,' for in the eyes of Quérard, for example, the Société has forgotten 'everything that is noble about the literary culture' ['tout ce qu'a de noble la culture des lettres'] and, instead, constituted 'a commercial association, substituting speculation for morality' ['une association commerciale, substituant la spéculation à la morale' (Quérard, *La littérature française contemporaine*, vol. 1, 140–1)]. And literature is not the only victim of industrialism. The scourge of literary industrialism was also taken up as a challenge by the professional academic critic. According to Sainte-Beuve, 'Industrial literature has managed to suppress criticism and to inhabit the territory without contradiction as if it existed alone' ['La littérature industrielle est arrivée à supprimer la critique et à occuper la place à peu près sans contradiction et comme si elle existait seule' ('De la littérature industrielle,' in Sainte-Beuve, *Pour la critique* 202–3)]. He ends his essay with a call for a renewed critical vigilance: 'let us try to advance and to mature this judgment by separating out good [literature] and by firmly limiting the other' ['tâchons d'avancer et de mûrir ce jugement en dégageant la bonne [littérature] et en limitant l'autre avec fermeté' (222)]. In the eyes of the defenders of literary nobility, the situation continues to deteriorate, so that towards the end of the century, Ferdinand Brunetière (1880) rallies to Sainte-Beuve's call and asserts the importance of criticism as a bastion against the invasion of literary industrialism: 'Ever since art and literature, which formerly brought the writer or artist only esteem, now lead him to wealth, and since letters or painting have become "careers" like commerce or administration, many people who see only a business opportunity or money to be made have thrown themselves into artistic pursuits. It is important that one recognize such people, and it is the role of criticism to denounce them.'[7]

On the other side of the ideological fence, Zola, as Balzac before him, defends the commercial rights of the author not only as being just remuneration for work, but as a condition of the emancipation of literature:[8] 'With money, he [the artist] has dared to say everything, he has examined everthing, including the king, including God, without fear of losing his livelihood. Money has liberated the writer, money has created modern letters' ['Avec l'argent, il [l'artiste] a osé tout dire, il a porté son examen partout, jusqu'au roi, jusqu'à Dieu, sans craindre de perdre son pain. L'argent a émancipé l'écrivain, l'argent a créé les lettres modernes' ('L'argent dans la littérature,' [1880] in Zola 71)]. And he advises young writers in the following terms: 'Next, have respect for money, do not fall into the childishness of ranting like poets against it; money is our courage and our dignity, we writers, who need it in order to be free to say anything and everything; money makes of us the intellectual leaders of the century, the only possible artistocracy. Accept the present era as one of the greatest in human history, believe firmly in the future, without pausing to worry about such fatal consequences as the excesses of journalism, the mercantilism of low literature.'[9]

Among writers of the century whom Zola cites as proof that literary work can produce financial success – Sue, Dumas *père* et *fils*, Hugo, Sardou – he is most attached to the example of Balzac, whose literary talent lent honour and dignity to 'industrialism':

> It would be necessary to study the prodigious case of Balzac, if one wanted to explore in depth the question of money in literature. Balzac was a true industrial, who produced books to do honour to his signature. Burdened by debts, ruined by unsuccessful endeavours, he took up his pen as the only tool he knew, the only one that could save him. Here the question of money is posed directly. It is not only his daily bread which he asks of his books; he asks them to make up the losses incurred by him in the industry. The battle lasted a long time, Balzac did not earn a fortune, but he paid his debts, which was already quite something. We are far removed, are we not, from good old La Fontaine, dreaming under trees, passing the evening at

the table of great seigneurs, paying for his dinner with a fable. Balzac [...]
did not look only for glory in Letters, he found there dignity and honour.[10]

It is in fact necessary to follow Zola's advice and to examine, however
briefly, the career of Balzac, his 'industrialism,' his battles with plagiaries
and his accusers, as well as his competition with that other literary giant,
Alexandre Dumas (*père*). While jealous of Dumas's success, Balzac nevertheless defended himself from the charge of industrialism often laid at
Dumas's door. Balzac expresses the critical distinction between himself
and Dumas as of that between *work* and *industry*. In comparing himself to
Dumas, Balzac is at pains to distinguish his own type of frenetic labour
from that of his rival: 'In the furore of necessity, I write three pages an
hour. That's what Dumas does. But afterwards I have to correct them ten
to twelve times, which Dumas doesn't do' ['Dans la fureur de la nécessité
j'en écris 3 [feuillets] par heure. C'est ce que fait aussi A. Dumas. Mais il
faut après, ce que ne fait pas Dumas, les corriger 10 à 12 fois' (Balzac 203)].
Commenting this passage, Delattre concurs: 'Thus the clever technique of
Dumas, either on the stage or in the novel, can in no way make up for the
weaknesses left by the absence of profound work, the speed of execution
and above all the absence of an original vision which, for Balzac, quite correctly, marks the true work of art.'[11]

And Quérard is also in full agreement. Recounting Balzac's early career,
he remarks that 'by study and by work, M. de Balzac prepared himself to
become a distinguished man of letters' ['par l'étude et par le travail, M. de
Balzac se formait à devenir un littérateur distingué' (*La littérature française
contemporaine*, vol. 1, 139)]. But featured in his long list of Dumas's weaknesses, or worse, one finds the accusation of excessive industry and little
true work: 'Whatever of interest he is able to put into his stories, they
always lack, as do all of his works, the polish, the unity, the perfection
which only study and work can produce' ['Quelque intérêt qu'il sache
mettre dans ses récits, ils manquent toujours, comme toutes ses oeuvres, de
ce fini, de cet ensemble, de cette perfection que l'étude et le travail peuvent seuls donner' (J. Cherbuliez, *Revue critiques* [sic] *des livres nouveaux*,
1838, 247–8; quoted by Quérard, *Supercheries littéraires dévoilées*, vol. 1,
1095)]. Dumas is the opposite of the 'original genius' described by Vigny
in his preface to *Chatterton* (1834): 'he needs to *do nothing*, in order to do
something in his art. It is necessary for him to do nothing of a utilitarian or
routine nature in order to have the time to listen to the harmonies that
form slowly in his soul, harmonies that the coarse noise of productive and
regular work interrupt and inevitably drown out.'[12]

The 'crimes' of which Dumas was accused are numerous: hiring ghost
writers and unacknowledged collaborators, 'stealing' plots and ideas and

'adapting' them to the stage, and various other kinds of plagiarism – although Balzac, too, suffers accusations of industrialism and self-plagiarism.[13] As one critic cited by Quérard exclaims: 'It is physically impossible that Dumas write or dictate everything which he publishes under his own name' ['Il est physiquement impossible que M. Dumas écrive ou dicte tout ce qui paraît signé de lui' (M. de Loménie, 'Notice sur M. Alexandre Dumas,' in Quérard, *Supercheries* 1023)].

In his battle with Dumas, one of Balzac's principal difficulties was with the latter's theatrical success, a genre which Balzac never mastered. Dramas were more popular than novels, and the financial returns were greater; the popularity of the theatre demanded a high rate of production, and the practice of 'adapting' novels to the stage was common. In 1840, in an effort to stem the tide, Balzac proposes to the Société des gens de lettres a 'Literary Code' designed to regulate some of the practices of which writers were victims. One section of the code is devoted to 'plagiarisms not anticipated by the Civil Code' ['plagiats non prévus par le Code civil']: 'The translation of the subject of a book or of any literary work whatsoever into a play, and reciprocally, [...] without the express written consent of the author, constitutes plagiarism.'[14] However, the force of this clause is somewhat attenuated by the intervention of the criterion of 'work,' which is seen as a legitimizing condition of the 'translation,' shifting the result away from plagiarism: 'Since a certain kind of literary work can remove the plagiarism, the action of a complainant will be accepted only after the report of a commissioner declaring that there is cause to admit the charge' ['Tel travail littéraire pouvant enlever le plagiat, l'action d'un plaignant n'aura lieu devant le comité qu'après le rapport d'un commissaire disant qu'il y a lieu d'admettre la plainte' ('Code littéraire,' in Balzac, vol. 23, 715)]. Thus, the problematic distinction between a legitimate imitation and a sanctionable plagiarism hangs on the criterion of 'a certain kind of work,' of which it is not said whether this is to be of the industrious or the studious variety.

In his personal evaluations of his own production and that of those around him – Dumas and Sue in particular – Balzac is clear about the difference. In his letters to Mme Hanska, references to his obsession with money (his lack of it), the financial success of others, and his superior talent meet constantly. The worst example of lack of talent is the novelist Paul de Kock: 'I am jealous of nothing, not even money, for Hugo is not envious of Paul de Kock, even though he earns more money and sells better' ['Je ne suis jaloux de rien, pas même de l'argent, car Paul de Kock ne fait pas envie à Hugo, quoiqu'il gagne plus d'argent que lui et se vende à un nombre supérieur' ('Lettre 241, Monday, 11 Nov. 1844,' in Balzac, 1968, p. 535) *Lettres à Madame Hanska*]. Balzac's expressed goal is to succeed by literary talent and work, where parvenus or industrialists gain undeserved success and popularity by means of financial deals, cheap imitations, and empty noise. If he measures success largely in financial terms, it is partly a simple matter of need, and partly out of a sense of justice:

> Moreover, I cannot, I must not, I will not suffer the depreciation which weighs on me because of the deals made by Sue, and by the noise made by his two works, I must show, by means of *literary* successes, by works of art, in a word, that his watered-down works [*oeuvres de détrempe*] are like cheap tin in front of a fireplace [*des devants de cheminée*]; I've got to exhibit Raphaëls alongside his Dubufes. You know me well enough to know that I harbor neither jealousy nor bitterness against him, nor against the public! Thank God, my rivals are Molière, and Walter Scott, Lesage and Voltaire, and not this Paul de Kock in satin and sequins; but [...] it is a matter of paying off 120 000 fr. in debts, of having a lodging and a decent life, which, for a man like me, at forty-five years of age, is a necessity, and if I have no envy at all for this triumphant two-bit poet [*triomphateur à mirliton*], you will permit me to deplore that he is paid 10 000 fr. per volume while I only get 3 000 for mine. Well, in striking two great blows – in being literary in the grand style and, which is more interesting, in being true – if I succeed in stifling, for my own benefit, this *furia francese* that has been unleashed by the *Mystères* [*de Paris* by Eugène Sue] [...], I will get 200 000 fr. for 10 volumes of the *Scenes of Military Life*, and I will have bread.[15]

If Dumas is notorious for the plagiarisms occasioned by his industrial modes of production, Balzac, as we have seen, is not altogether exempt from similar accusations. Quérard, although he is generally sympathetic to Balzac as a man of true talent, does not neglect to note in passing that a large number of his publications after 1830 were of previously printed works. Balzac's fall into this industrial mode, which is bad enough as a market-driven procedure of booksellers, is inexcusable on the part of a true author: 'One could, it seems to us, justifiably reproach M. de Balzac with having often made a new book by assembling sketches or studies already long known: such means are too often employed by booksellers to induce booklovers to buy a book which they already own for a second or third time a book; but when it comes to a true man of letters, such means must not be excused.'[16]

In his annotations to Balzac's bibliography, Quérard gives the history of these reimpressions, commenting with respect to subsequent publications of *Le livre mystique:* 'Eh! Mais c'est trop de transformations' (art. XXXII, 145). Annotating *Le livre des douleurs* (Paris: H. Souverain, 1840), he adds: 'Here again are five volumes the publication of which we would like to believe that M. de Balzac was ignorant. What is the *Livre des douleurs*, if not a new edition of the *Livre mystique*, which was itself nothing but the reunion of two works which had already been reprinted four and five times [...] In truth, M. de Balzac should firmly object to this disgusting mercantilism.'[17]

Quérard's annotations include one case of plagiarism of a story titled 'Jésus-Christ en Flandre,' 'copied word for word from the abbé Dulaurens [...] in a little book entitled, I believe, *Vérité et cérémonie de catholicisme* [...] M. de Balzac did not hesitate to draw from it' ['copié textuellement de l'abbé Dulaurens [...] dans un petit livre intitulé, je crois, *Vérité et cérémonie de catholicisme* [...] M. de Balzac ne s'est pas fait faute d'y puiser' (*La littera-ture française contemporaine*, vol. 1, 143)].

If Quérard has rather less sympathy with Dumas, he is still willing to see him as a victim of industrialism. In spite of a promising beginning, Dumas 'unfortunately, [...] allowed himself to be led on by great profits, and as his name was an excellent advertisement for the bookstore, he responded to the often considerable offers of publishers with hasty productions [...] Dumas has been reproached so often and so severely for what one calls his literary industrialism, that we will not insist on this fact. But admitting, as it is said, that M. Dumas buys his novels ready made and passes them off as his own, is it only he who is to blame, and is the mercantilism of the sellers not equally as condemnable as his own?'[18] In the course of his bibliograph-ical annotations, which include documentation of Dumas's 'plagiarisms' and his self-defence, Quérard comments: 'All that is well and good; but M. Dumas will never convince anyone that it is permitted for a writer to copy word for word entire pages written by others, and to give them out to the public as his own.'[19]

It is in the *Supercheries* that Quérard's most scathing attacks appear. He seems to have lost any vestiges of sympathy he might have had for the young Dumas, since become 'one of the most active traffickers in litera-ture' ['l'un des plus actifs trafiquants en littérature' (1023)]. In defending himself against potential critics for including this *maréchal littéraire* in a rep-ertory dedicated to literary fraud, Quérard claims that Dumas is guilty of a large number of transgressions, and refutes the contention that the detrac-tors of Dumas are simply jealous of his success. Instead of accusing Dumas in his own name, he cites the critics opposed to Romanticism who recog-nize Dumas's talent and wish him to employ it in more dignified ways.

In the end, Dumas's undeniable success and the financial profits atten-dant on his popularity are a problem for his critics. Wishing, as perhaps in the case of Corneille, to preserve the dignity of the literary institution that so enthusiastically embraced Dumas, the critic and defender of the nobility of letters has to negotiate the difficult path between genius and industrialism. Thus, in spite of the 'disgusting' methods employed by

Dumas (and to a lesser extent by Balzac, not to mention Sue and many others), the view of Dumas that Quérard propounds is of a potential genius, led astray by his own greed into victimization and exploitation by the literary industry. On the one hand, the newly important value of originality, dependent upon the authentic, individual productions of genius, and, on the other, the demands of industry, emphasizing speed and volume of production, were placed in direct and conflictual opposition. In a commercial context, it was painfully obvious, to Balzac for instance, that the demands of art and those of industry were difficult to reconcile: money was a product of the second, rather than the first. The progress of literature as an industrial market commodity, in which serial rather than singular, artisanal production was the key to success, lends to Lautréamont's later aphorism a new and unexpected meaning: 'Plagiarism is necessary; progress implies it.'

POE VERSUS *PARVENUS*

In some ways, the American publishing scene of the 1830s and 1840s resembled the French battle of the theatres of the same period. It is a time which sees the call for a distinctive national literature, and during which 'literary industrialism' took the form of a struggle between American writers and the publisher-booksellers who largely preferred the 'legal' piracy of reprinting British works which were unprotected in the United States until 1891: 'American publishing, exploiting both native and foreign writers, was emerging as Big Business by 1836' (Moss 21). As Moss describes the situation, this piracy was constantly decried by British authors, such as Dickens, and Americans alike, who understood that the lack of international copyright benefited only the publishers, and remained a detriment to American authors and to the development of a national literature. The difficulty of finding a publisher forced American writers into the magazine form, which subsequently flourished in a spirit of 'sectional' rivalry: the New York and Boston 'cliques' establishing themselves as a closed circle against the Southern and Western writers and the magazines which promoted them. In this battle, Edgar Allan Poe, Southern magazine owner, editor, and author, took up the struggle against the scourge of industrialism, waging a fierce battle against the *parvenu* plagiarists who were attempting to make an undeserved name for themselves. Moss has recounted the whole story in detail and we will not repeat it here: Poe's attacks on those he suspected of plagiarism, particularly Longfellow, are well known in the field and are widely considered to be one of his more unfortunate moments, contributing to his reputation for psychological instability. They can be seen as a paradigm case of the ridicule that returns to the accuser of plagiarism, or of *tu-quoque-ism*. Nevertheless, in the course of these 'literary battles' (Moss), Poe has occasion to make some salient critical pronouncements and to develop a theory of plagiarism that, rife with contradictions and inconsistencies, underlines the ambiguous nature of the distinction among originality, imitation, and plagiarism.

The search for an American national literature was undermined not only by the preponderance of pirated works but equally, according to some critics, including Poe, by the colonial tendency towards the imitation – or plagiarism – of British works and styles, a practice identified and denounced not only by Americans, but, more embarrassingly, by British critics such as John Forster, who commented: 'True poetry imitates nature: that which imitates poetry ought to have some other name' (quoted in Adkins 170). According to Adkins, American poets 'stand convicted [by Forster] of "petty larceny," which "forms a prominent and ostentatious feature of their productions"' (quoted in Adkins 170). As a literary critic, Poe is much in agreement on the general principle, and virulently pointed in his accusations of particular practices. With respect to Morris Mattsons's *Paul Ulric*, he pronounces: 'The book is despicable in every respect. Such are the works which bring daily discredit upon our national literature. We have no right to complain of being laughed at abroad when so villainous a compound ... of incongruous folly, plagiarism, immorality, inanity, and bombast, can command at any moment both a puff and a publisher' (quoted by Moss 77–8).

Puffing was the editorial practice, in the absence of advertisements, of placing 'highly laudatory, essentially uncritical reviews in magazines and newspapers which favored books coming from the proper presses and written by the proper authors, generally those authors who contributed to the journals that publicized their works' (Moss 22). The system of puffing was made worse by the sectional cliques and coteries already mentioned, and which Poe constantly opposed in both his critical essays and publishing practice, although such fierce opposition often led him into an anti-cliquism that appears to be as biased as the cliques themselves. Moss describes the situation:

> Now, the reviews published by editors engaged in this traffic were, for the most part, superficial and, far worse, misleading, acclaiming or denouncing the work of an author in unqualified terms, depending upon whether the author was in favor with the clique. To entertain the notion of success, writers had first to come into the good graces of editors – a process that involved toadying and quackery, the current words of contempt for the truckling and charlatanry on the part of contributor to editor and editor to the public. Authors and editors who preferred to remain independent and

self-respecting were, by and large, marked for failure. The occasional writer or editor who clashed with the cliques was practically doomed. (Moss 30)

'Puffing' threatened the integrity not only of criticism, but of literature itself, as it led to the promotion of the untalented, especially those supported by the most powerful cliques. A second reason for the preponderance of the *parvenu* was the lack of international copyright laws, which promoted piracy, making it impossible for all but the leisure class to indulge in writing. Thus it is not industrialists but *parvenus* – 'gentlemen of elegant leisure' – who are the only ones who can afford to write. Unfortunately, according to Poe, 'mere gentlemen of elegant leisure have been noted, time out of mind, for the insipidity of their productions. In general, too, they are obstinately conservative, and this feeling leads them into imitation of foreign, more especially of British models. This is one main source of the imitativeness with which, as a people, we have been justly charged ...' (*Godey's Magazine and Lady's Book*, XXXI, 121 [Sept. 1845]; quoted by Adkins 183).

There seems to be no doubt that Poe's long-standing obsession with the denunciation of plagiarism was at least in part due to his nature and to what Adkins, in concert with a certain critical tradition, calls his 'pedantry.' There seems to be little disagreement that in the worst cases he was guilty of charging others of plagiarism for the purpose of pure unjustified vilification, especially where he perceived himself to be the victim. On other occasions, he retracted from his hard-line stance of conflating imitation and plagiarism, and rallied to the idea that, while all poetry is plagiaristic, 'no true poet can be guilty of a meanness' ('Reply to Outis,' in Poe, Works, vol. 6, 196–7), and that 'all literary history demonstrates that, for the most frequent and palpable plagiarism, we must search the works of the most eminent poets' (197–8).

The link between the *parvenu* and the plagiarist was clear for Poe, as demonstrated in his evaluation of Longfellow as 'a man of property and a professor at Harvard' (*Literati* 6; quoted by Adkins 202). Longfellow belonged to that class of *dilettanti* who, as well as manifesting a tendency towards imitation born of the innate conservativeness of the monied class, are quite simply lazy: 'we must observe that to imitate is a matter of less effort than to originate; and we must not expect effort as a general thing, certainly not as a continuous thing, from those whose condition is affluence and else' ('Imitation-Plagiarism'; quoted by Adkins 202). However, Poe's understanding of plagiarism, as is apparent from the many examples of it that he offers in his critical reviews, is of a particular and curious brand: most instances imply something of the order of the theft of ideas; many appear to be hackneyed or clichéd poetical commonplaces dressed up in something that might qualify in court as 'significant enhancement.' His assessment of what qualifies as plagiarism is in direct contradiction not only with classical literary theory, but also with legal norms. For Poe, the

> most barbarous class of literary piracy [is] that class in which, while the words of the wronged author are avoided, his most intangible, and therefore his least defensible and least reclaimable property, is appropriated. Here [...] there is nothing of a visible or palpable nature by which the source of the American poem [Longfellow's 'Midnight Mass for the Dying Year] can be established. But then nearly all that is valuable in the piece of Tennyson ['The Death of the Old Year'] is the first conception of personifying the Old Year as a dying old man, with the singularly wild and fantastic manner in which that conception is carried out. Of this conception and of this manner he is robbed. ('Reply to Outis' 185–6)

This frequent lack of 'visible and palpable' evidence for Poe's charges of plagiarism – his construal as plagiaristic that which might appear to be simply literary imitation, even if it is judged indicative of a lack of talent – can be seen as proof that Poe was using the charge in a misdirected double attempt at vilification and self-aggrandizement. On the distinction between proper and improper borrowing, however, his theory is consistent, if somewhat quirky. In *The Literati*, he is moved to defend Charles Anthon, an academic classicist who had been accused of plagiarism for his *Classical Dictionary*. The convoluted argument, which stretches the proscription against 'disguised imitation' to the limits of plausibility, is clearly an attack against the Boston cliques:

> There are very few points of classical scholarship which are not the common property of 'the learned' throughout the world, and in composing any book of reference recourse is unscrupulously and even necessarily had in all cases to similar books which have preceded. In availing themselves of these latter, however, it is the practice of quacks to paraphrase page after page, rearranging the order of paragraphs, making a slight alteration in point of fact here and there, but preserving the spirit of the whole, its information, erudition, etc., etc., while everything is so completely *re-written* as to leave no room for a direct charge of plagiarism; and this is considered and lauded as originality. Now, he who, in availing himself of the labors of his predecessors (and it is clear that all scholars must avail themselves of such labors) – he who shall copy verbatim the passages to be desired, without attempt at palming off their spirit as original with himself, is certainly no plagiarist, even if he fail to make *direct* acknowledgment of indebtedness – is unquestionably *less* of the plagiarist than the disingenuous and contempt-

ible quack who wriggles himself, as above explained, into a reputation for originality, a reputation quite out of place in a case of this kind, the public, of course, never caring a straw whether he be original or not. These attacks upon the New York professor are to be attributed to a clique of pedants in and about Boston, gentlemen envious of his success, and whose own compilations are noticeable only for the singular patience and ingenuity with which their dovetailing chicanery is concealed from the public eye.

('Charles Anthon,' *The Literati*, in Poe, *Works*, vol. 8, 36–7)

In spite of this singular and rather contestable claim, the nature of the plagiarist is clear: he is a contemptible quack who has earned for himself an undeserved reputation by virtue of his disingenuous concealment of his 'dovetailing chicanery,' which is, for Poe, a particularly odious combination of talentless imitation and dishonesty. In 'How to Write a *Blackwood* Article,' and 'The Literary Life of Thingum Bob, Esq.' (Poe, *Works*, vol. 4), Poe has satirized the magazine publishing industry and the quackery of the *parvenus*, the paradigm among whom is 'Thingum Bob,' the untalented and bombastic son of a wealthy merchant who enters the literary scene and succeeds through a series of chicaneries. Thingum's success is due not only to his own dishonesty, but also to the self-interested idiocy of the contesting cliques and magazines, through which he ascends to literary and financial power, and universal fame. Thingum first fails in his attempts at poetry by plagiarism, not because he is discovered, but because the editors accuse his work, which is purloined from Homer, Dante, and Milton, of being 'balderdash,' 'unmeaning rant,' and 'ineffable nonsense.' Thingum is led by degrees to assume the role of literary critic, where he succeeds by adopting a wholesale method of cut-and-paste plagiarism.

In 'How to Write a *Blackwood* Article' an aspiring lady editor/writer is advised by Mr B— on how to write a successful magazine article. The most important aspect of his method is the 'filling-up.' Says Mr B— :

> 'It is not to be supposed that a lady, or gentleman either, has been leading the life of a bookworm. And yet above all things it is necessary that your article have an air of erudition, or at least afford evidence of extensive general reading. Now I'll put you in the way of accomplishing this point. See here!' (pulling down some three or four ordinary-looking volumes, and opening them at random). 'By casting your eye down almost any page of any book in the world, you will be able to perceive at once a host of little scraps of either learning or *bel-esprit-ism*, which are the very thing for the spicing of a 'Blackwood' article.' (Poe, *Works*, vol. 4, 206)

We have discussed Poe's attitude to plagiarism without alluding to his own, predictable, failings in this regard, which are probably no more plagiarisms than many of the other instances that he himself identified. What is significant for our purposes is the link he establishes, throughout his campaign against the quacks, between the literary industrialism of the day and the means by which the untalented rise to unmerited fame, the foundation of which is dishonesty, and the principal strategy of which is plagiarism.

As an independent writer and editor, excluded by sectionalism from participation in the literary centre, Poe may be seen as a 'minor' writer crying plagiarism after a major one – whether it be Longfellow himself or the representatives of the northern cliques. His expressed motives were, nonetheless, to defend the purity and nobility of literature from the encroachments of unscrupulous profiteers, from talentless imitators and dilettantes. I will not examine his propensity for plagiarism-hunting in the context of his theories of originality and genius, which Adkins has outlined, concluding that: 'Any examination of Poe's principles touching the problem of plagiarism leads, it seems to me, to one conclusion: the man's essential sincerity in the charges which he was continually making. In art, Poe stood for *genius*, and what must inevitably be the product of genius, *originality*' (183).

Regardless of the peculiar and sometimes perverse judgments about plagiarism to which he was prone, it seems evident, first, that a good deal of American writing of the period indeed suffered from the colonial propensity towards imitation and, second, that the competition for recognition in the magazine publishing industry and the 'quackery' involved led writers and critics into modes of production and judgment founded less on disinterested literary values and talent than on market considerations. I will not argue, with Poe, that 'plagiarism' actually flourished in this climate, but, rather, use his obsession to point out that what he called 'plagiarism,' which we might rather call 'uninspired imitation,' was a direct result of the American brand of literary industrialism and of the associated means of promotion of the untalented.

Was Poe besieged by a crisis of authority, a crisis that led him not only into 'plagiarism' but, more significantly, into obsessive plagiarism-hunting? Kenneth Dauber argues in this vein, claiming that 'whether the self does in fact steal from the other or only seems to, the issue of stealing must arise because the oppositional pair of self and other has been conceived of *as* in opposition. There is a crisis in the relation of readers and writers. Reading and writing, properly one, have been separated' (134). Dauber holds this separation – or alienation – to be a phase in the American Renaissance, of which Poe is an exemplary incarnation. For Dauber, Poe's peculiar relationship to plagiarism is, however, an idiosyncratic manifestation of this crisis of authority and of the 'relation of readers and writers.' Seen, however, less in terms of Poe's psychology than in the literary market context that Moss describes, the suspicion of plagiarism – regardless of the excessiveness of Poe's denunciations – seems rather more predictable than otherwise. If there is a crisis of authority, it would appear to reside less in the relation between writers and readers (Dauber refers here to the alienation of the writer from the reader-public) than in the one that existed between competing writers – that is, between the multiple functions that professional writers were required to assume. Poe appears as a canonical example of the artist-critic in a transitional phase moving towards the professional separation of the writer-reader functions. In his case, the reading and writing functions were both profoundly conjoined in the traditional figure of the artist-critic, and pragmatically separated by the market structure in which he assumed simultaneously the roles of aspiring writer, commercial entrepreneur, and literary critic. The crisis of self and other that he faced – of writer and reader – looks more like an internal conflict of interest leading to a multiple-identity complex. Poe was face to face with himself as other in the fiercely competitive industry in which he was called upon to be simultaneously judge and judged.

If plagiarism is linked to industrial modes of literary production during the formative years in the development of the French and American literary institution, the same relationship is still seen to exist in the twentieth century, when the market determinations of literary production are so solidly entrenched as to have become all but invisible. The production and consumption of 'low brow' literature is no longer a concern of the defenders of literary purism, for whom the line between 'literature' and 'pulp' is more clearly drawn. In particular, it is no longer expected that the market successes of 'genre' writers, of romance, mystery, and detective novels, and so on, will be free from the imitations that the very nature of formula writing demands. At the same time, such imitations are no longer seen as a threat to 'real' literature. It is, rather, on the well-populated border between 'popular' and 'high-brow' contemporary writing, in an area currently referred to as 'popular culture,' that charges of plagiarism founded on 'industrialism' or *parvenu-ism* are most likely to arise.

The tensions that Bourdieu outlines for the period of the autonomization of the literary field in France during the nineteenth century, and which can be identified during the American Renaissance, are no doubt less well defined in the late twentieth century: although commerical success may still stand in an inverse relationship to the criteria of literary elitism, the grey area of 'popular literature' is no longer the oxymoron that Bourdieu describes, no doubt because the very potential for financial fortune that leads to literary industrialism has largely been eclipsed by the production of other forms of cultural commodities, notably cinema and television. Nonetheless, charges of plagiarism motivated by the perception of unfair, dishonest, or inauthentic modes of production still attempt to distinguish between legitimate members of the literary field and unwelcome pretenders to a status that their talent or labour does not justify.

Commercially successful writers taxed with plagiarism represent, since the nineteenth century, the paradox of the inverted artistic world that Bourdieu has described, wherein financial rewards were both sought after and despised. Whereas in Bourdieu's model, the cultural elite is not in competition for the rewards of popularity enjoyed by the writer of popular fiction, Balzac is the epitome, and Zola after him, of the attempt to reduce the contradiction between the two fields. The democratic principle of legitimate financial rewards for honest labour intervened in opposition to the notion of the disinterested nobility of art: according to the developments that we have seen, financial reward came indeed to be seen as compatible with true authorship. The inverted world postulated by Bourdieu was clearly felt by many of its inhabitants, such as Balzac and Zola, to be rather a perverted one.

PROFITABLE MARGINS

While charges of plagiarism against commercially successful modern authors reveal the antinomies inscribed within the structure of the literary field, in the contemporary literary industry, popularity and success are often not sufficient to condemn an author to inferiority. It must also be shown that success is undeserved. Today, although 'literary' (highbrow) authorship still occupies the lower end of the scale of economic returns – at least in the short term – and the biggest commercial rewards are still reserved for best sellers of the 'popular' type – the Stephen Kings and Danielle Steeles – international communications and modes of dissemination such as movies and television adaptations enlarge both the economic and the symbolic rewards available to the literary elite. If authorship is no longer falsifiable on the basis of popular and economic success, other discrediting means must be found to delimit, in the literary industry, the frontiers of the field. One of these strategies is the charge of plagiarism.

Contemporary literary industrialists appear as successful writers who have the rare ability to be judged 'literary' and, at the same time, to achieve wide popular, and hence financial, success. They resemble a modern-day Balzac, torn between the necessity of producing in quantity (the industrialist not only produces a large number of books, but tends, at the same time, to make them big) and in quality: their books must be sufficiently 'literary' or 'highbrow' to escape the determination of 'pulp fiction,' even though the 'masses' read them. Their distinguishing characteristic is that the *lite-*

rati read them as well, and take them seriously: they often appear on university courses in contemporary literature. The contemporary industrialist as great author participates both in 'popular' and in 'culture': popular success is the necessary prelude to accusations of plagiarism, while a certain cultural status provides protection from the damage such attacks would inflict on less successful authors. This category seems largely to exclude contemporary industrialists such as Stephen King and Danielle Steele – perhaps because the popular type of writing in which they are presumably engage escapes the criteria of 'authorship.' As 'industrial plagiarism' was a child born of nineteenth-century necessity, so does it – or the perception of it – seem to be on the wane. Accusations of industrialism and *parvenu* plagiarism are, these days, often conjoined, and the perpetrators may rather seem to take on the face of victims, inhabiting margins other than the ones defined by financial profits.

Such is the case of Alexander Haley, whose 'great author' status was not divorced from his cultural role as an African-American hero: a popular and literary writer, having achieved legitimate international fame on the strength of great books. Arising from a background of obscurity and social marginality, Haley achieved the Black version of the American dream as the author of the highly acclaimed *Autobiography of Malcom X* in 1965 and subsequently of the Pulitzer Prize–winning historical work *Roots* in 1976.

Two separate suits for plagiarism were launched shortly after the publication and ensuing success of *Roots:* the first, by African-American writer Margaret Walker, claiming plagiarism from her best-selling novel *Jubilee* (1966), was dismissed; the second, more notorious claim by Harold Courlander for his historical novel *The African* (1967), was eventually settled out of court. As well as accusations of plagiarism, Haley was also taxed with accusations of fraud. *Roots* recounts Haley's personal journey into his African background and his eventual identification of his ancestors through first-hand research. The work was marketed – although perhaps not created – as non-fiction. Historians quickly identified many factual errors in the work, and investigations into Haley's papers, held in the Special Collections Library at the University of Tennessee, uncovered evidence of a hoax which has been documented in a long exposé in the *Village Voice* (Nobile 31–8).[20]

In the course of the exposé, the authors insist on what appear to be the meager literary talents of the author, whose manuscripts were qualifed by then Doubleday editor-in-chief as 'a mess' (37) and whose reliance on editorial corrections apparently included the use of ghost-writers. The story suggests that both the plagiarism and the fraud were the results of a mediocre talent confronted by the market exigencies of commercial success: 'Haley was a writer of modest talents, as a number of editors would say, who required enormous editorial support. But his prose needed more than polish; as Haley admitted under cross-examination, he lifted passages from several books [...] to fill up the pages of *Roots*' (32). Margaret Walker, one of Haley's putative victims, whose plagiarism suit against him was unsuccessful, is quoted as saying that Haley was a 'hack' who 'needed professional help' (37). The professional help in question, long-time collaborator Murray Fisher (*Playboy*), was reluctantly coaxed into an 'admission' of the extent of his contribution by the *Voice* interviewers, who apparently jogged his memory by supplying him with documents from the University of Tenessee archives: 'Confronted with the contents of these folders in a later interview, Fisher admitted he rewrote the African section – more than a fifth of the book – because Haley was trapped in a quagmire of Africana. "Finally, we ran out of time and I just simply decided to take the bull by the horns and finish them [the African chapters]"' (Nobile 38). This confession directly contradicts Fisher's testimony in the introduction to *Alexander Haley: The Playboy Interviews* in which he states that 'the last 200 pages [went] directly from [Haley's] desk to the typesetter after the book was already in galleys' (Fisher xvi). At the same time, Fisher states that Haley's book had cost him 'no small portion' of his own life: 'I had left *Playboy* in 1974 to devote my full time to helping Alex finish. Alex's wife, My, and his lifelong friend and researcher, George Sims, were equally devoted' (xvi).

The *Voice* styles Haley as an enigmatic and charming figure whose 'public image was noble, heroic, even sainted,' and who had achieved the reputation of the 'most acclaimed author of colour in the world' (32). At the same time, he appears as an inveterate liar, constantly plagued by financial problems and seeking advances for books and projects that were never completed. He was also, apparently, the benefactor of inverse racisim, both in the judgment of the all-male all-white Pulitzer Prize jury and in the reluctance of Judge Robert Ward, who, in spite of evidence of copying in 'sufficient and compelling amounts to be substantial,' chose not to pursue an affidavit charging perjury: '"Haley had written *The Autobiography of Malcolm X* and young black writers looked up to him," Ward said. "I did not want to destroy that, especially if the plaintiff was inclined toward a settlement"' (Nobile 36).

Was Haley an 'intentional' plagiarist and fraud, as The *Village Voice* and his out-of-court settlement seem to imply? Was he the victim of jealous writers in the same field whose success he far outstripped, and who claimed 'plagarism' where there was nothing more than the use of historical facts embroidered with enough significant enhancement and contextual changes to justify the borrowing? Was his out-of-court settlement ($650,000) with Courlander motivated by the desire to avoid further expenses, to avoid a guilty verdict, or, rather, as one defender has it, was it less a defeat than the surrender of 'a man weary of the continuous assaults upon his dignity and scholarship' (Boyd 33)? The question which really concerns us, however, is to what extent the climate of literary industrialism in which Haley was an undisputed success was a contributing factor either to his apparent apparent plagiarism and fraud, or to the accusations against him. In a comparison with Mitchell's *Gone with the Wind*, which was also taxed with charges of plagiarism, Herb Boyd declares: 'It is not unusual that the phenomenal success of *Roots* has brought a rush of serious and scurrilous claimants to Haley's door demanding to share in both the author's fame and his soaring capital gains' (31).

Haley will not be unseated – he was both a 'great author' and a cultural hero by the time the accusations of plagiarism and fraud were brought forward, and claims against either his literary or historical authenticity, or his personal integrity, will not negate the popular impact of the legend of *Roots* and its importance in contemporary African-American culture. There is no doubt, however, that his success was due to industrial modes of literary production, both in his own use of researchers and 'editors,' and in terms of the marketing strategies – such as the television miniseries of the novel – which were applied to his work. At the same time, there is equally little doubt that the commercial success of his work contributed to the origin of the accusations of plagiarism and fraud levelled against him.

At this advanced stage in the evolution of literary industrialism, it is more tempting to see a phenomenon like Haley as a victim rather than as an exploiter of the publishing industry. Whereas Dumas's methods can be seen as innovations in a developing economy which he contributed to creating, Haley appears more like a cog in a well-oiled machine than an intentional agent perpetrating fraud for his own gain. It is difficult to say whether 'literary industrialism' produced him, but it is clear that the demands of the industry preceded him. Reminiscing about the writing of *Roots*, and his feeling at the time of being swept along by forces greater than himself, he declares: 'It was like, I guess it was sort of like riding a tiger ... you always remember, you ride this tiger and the crowds cheering, always remember if you fall off the tiger, you's eaten' (quoted in *Village Voice*, 38). And the costs of success are clearly expressed by Haley in his essay: 'There are days when I wish it hadn't happened':

> Like so many who've made it big – financially as well as professionnally –
> I've become a sitting duck for lawsuits. Six have been lodged against me
> since *Roots* came out (Fisher 451).

> Perhaps it will serve as a reminder that our great god 'success,' with its
> omnipotent trinity of fame, wealth and power, is something we should learn
> to *respect* rather than to worship – lest it enslave us (452).

As opposed to the 'industrialist,' the contemporary *parvenu*-plagiarist is easy to spot – he is often to be recognized as a one-hit wonder, whose demise is implicit proof not that charges of plagiarism are sufficient to wreck a career, but of the meager talent that led the *parvenu* into plagiarism in the first place, a talent entirely spent on the first and only unfortunate attempt, the success of which must be credited to his plagiarism. The *parvenu* must, by definition, be identified in the early stages of his career, and have no literary reputation by which his success can be justified or his 'plagiarism' excused. Such are the cases of Jacob Epstein (*The Wild Oats*, 1979) and Yambo Ouologuem. The *parvenu* plagiarist might arise 'out of nowhere,' as in the case of the African studying in Paris, whose eccentricity with respect to the Parisian literary scene was at first an exotic attraction and, subsequently, a source of vulnerability. Or he might, as in the case of Epstein, be a 'gentleman of the leisure class' – one whose background provides him with advantages which his talent cannot match.

This is the implicit conclusion at which Mallon arrives in his discussion of Jacob Epstein's *The Wild Oats*, which had been accused of being a plagiarism of Martin Amis's *The Rachel Papers* (1973). Each is a coming-of-age novel recounting the college experiences of a young and aspiring writer, American and British, respectively. Both authors are sons of well-known literati: Amis is the son of British novelist Kingsley (*Lucky Jim*), and Epstein the son of prominent New York editors Jason and Barbara. In spite of the controversy surrounding the accusation, the case appeared to be open-and-shut, depending for its final outcome on Epstein's apology for having fallen victim to the 'note-book syndrome.' The plagiarism was a 'most awful mistake, which happened because I made notes from various books as I went along and then lost the notebook telling where they came from. The first edition should never have been published. I wanted to write to Martin at the time, but was advised against it. I shall certainly be writing to him now to explain' (Epstein, in Susan Heller Anderson, 'New Novelist Is Called a Plagiarist,' *New York Times*, 21 Oct. 1980, C7; quoted in Mallon 110).

Mallon offers primarily an Oedipal explanation for the plagiarism, citing the parallelism between the situation of the victim and that of the perpetrator, both sons of highly successful literary figures. He suggests that although Epstein clearly did plagiarize Amis, the affair was blown out of proportion because of the notoriety of the players – or, rather, of their parents. He considers, as well, that the expectations concerning Epstein's novel were unfairly inflated. Citing the *Saturday Review*'s judgment that Epstein showed 'tremendous future promise,' Mallon comments: 'There were some followers of New York literary life who would say, of course, that Jacob Epstein could hardly have shown anything else, that he had, after all, been born in belletristic clover [...] It was certain that *Wild Oats* would be seen as the first novel by the Epsteins's son – and in this respect young Jacob was not so much a hostage to fortune as a potentially sacrificial lamb' (Mallon 102).

Mallon cites the glowing reviews about the American novel, with which he does not concur. In proffering his own judgment about the two novels, his preference for the 'original' is clear. In a description reminiscent of Montaigne's characterization of bad borrowing, he comments:

> If one were to read *Wild Oats*, unaware of *The Rachel Papers*'s existence, one would be left with a certain puzzlement: how is it that Epstein's workman-like prose will take those occasional trampoline bounces into the realm of real style before dropping back down to the mat – and staying there for an awfully long time between leaps? Amis's exposé clears up the mystery, and after reading it, the style-conscious reader who goes back to *Wild Oats* without a copy of *The Rachel Papers* will have little trouble finding other plagiarized lines, ones left unmentioned in the article. All he really need do is look for the passages that whistle instead of hum. (Mallon 104–5)[21]

For Mallon, Epstein is clearly a *parvenu* of the cultural aristocratic type, whose talent was not up to the challenge of becoming the author for which his background seemed to have prepared him. And this analysis leads in turn to a psychological one: he is construed as a failed author compelled by his Oedipal complex to join literary suicide with the killing of the father.

If plagiarism implies authorship, the charge of plagiarism could be seen as being something like an 'ascension to authorship' in the sense that the accusation implies authorial potential and importance. Cameroonian writer Calixthe Beyala represents a case that unites various aspects of *profit plagiarism* of the *parvenu* rather than the 'industrial' variety – but with a difference. She has authored no fewer than ten novels between 1988 and 1998, two of which have won important awards, most notably the Grand Prix de l'Académie française for *Les honneurs perdus* in 1996. Beyala is the perfect writer to cleanse the French literary institution of its notorious misogyny and racism. Beautiful, young (her first novel was published at age twenty-five), talented, and an outspoken if self-appointed defender and promoter of African women's rights, Beyala is courted on television and in the media as the quintessential new generation of French writers who allow the national institution to prove its liberalism – and African writers their Occidental coming-of-age: 'Beyala is the prototype of the new generation of writers who have succeeded in the West because she clearly distinguishes herself from the authors of "Negritude" and of post-independence. Because of this, it is herself that she sells by selling her novels, a way all her own of making a name for herself' (Dunton).

Three years after the publication of her 1992 novel *Le petit prince de Belleville*, the French journal *Le canard enchainé* accused her of plagiarizing the American author Howard Buten's *Burt*; she was eventually convicted in the high court of Paris. Upon her winning of the Prix de l'Académie française for *Les honneurs perdus* (1996), Pierre Assouline, publisher and editor of the literary magazine *Lire*, exposed a second case of plagiarism, this time of Anglo-Nigerian writer Ben Okri's 1991 Booker Prize–winner, *The Famished Road*, which had been translated as *La route de la faim* (Julliard 1994). After an initial television exposé, Assouline details in the pages of *Lire* – in parallel-passage fashion – 'borrowings' from no fewer than four novels, including Alice Walker's *The Colour Purple* in three of Belaya's works. He implies that this is the tip of the iceberg. The similarities are convincing.

Assouline's declared motives are literary ethics: he is particularly disturbed by the Académie's awarding the prize to a previously convicted plagiarist, thereby 'consecrating' plagiarism as a literary method (Assouline 8). He himself seems to have forgotten *l'affaire Corneille*, which marked the Académie's debut, and he accuses certain of the *académiciens* of justifying their choice according to the noble French literary tradition of 'plagiarism' extending 'from LaFontaine to Proust' (10) – a tradition to which he evidently does not subscribe. Despite his claim that his principal object is the Académie, his main complaint against this body seems to be one of favouritism, which, in the context of the tradition of the French literary prize, is a rather weak accusation, suspicions of favouritism being more usual than otherwise (Do). His denunciation includes thinly veiled innuendo of inappropriate interest between jury members and the author: 'As soon as the vote had been taken, one of [the jurists], no longer able to contain his joy, got out his portable telephone in front of some of his dumbfounded colleagues in order to announce the news directly to the most interested party.'[22]

While Assouline's attack on the Académie could be seen as an example of the internecine quarrels to which the institution is prone – in this case, pitting the journalist against the elite critic – his real target seems to be Beyala herself. The inexplicable choice of the jury is even more so since her prose is 'insipid and *passe-partout*' and her cut-and-copy method results in 'a patchwork,' a 'disjointed style, an incoherent narration, a gratuitous story' ['un style disloqué, une narration désunie, un récit sans nécessité' (Assouline, 11)]. The affair is complex and interesting because of Beyala's position which is both marginal – she is a Black African woman writer in Paris – and privileged – she has become the 'pet' of that notoriously patriarchal institution. Her 'seductive' effect on the male-dominated literary circle is often close to the surface of journalistic discourse.

In a special section dedicated to cultural plagiarism on the occasion of Assouline's exposure, the magazine *L'événement* implicitly, but ironically, accuses Assouline of obsession (*acharnement*) in his pursuit of the case, while simultaneously finding the author's 'cryptomnesia' defence (in her terms, 'reminiscence') improbable, given the textual similarities. Nevertheless, the article is clearly a defence of the author in the form of the 'everyone plagiarizes' theory. The article also plays on Beyala's 'seductive' reputation, referring to her as *la belle* and describing, in typical (French?) literary journalism fashion, her decidedly atypically unseductive wardrobe and appearance during the interview (implication: adopted for the occasion). While the irony of the article is clearly not all directed at Assouline, it ends with a jibe at the latter, who is styled as the 'Sherlock Holmes' of French literature: 'One might think that all this is without importance,' Assouline is quoted as saying. The article ends with a Sherlockian: 'Quite so ...' (Liebaert 65).

The evidence of unacknowledged borrowing provided by the 'obsessed' Assouline seems incontrovertible, if the author's previous conviction were not sufficient proof of the pudding. But what astounds him even more than the act, is her refusal to confess; a refusal so brazen that it apparently opened his eyes to her guilty conscience: 'Accused with proof in hand, confronted with documentation, she never replies directly to the charges of plagiarism, but always beside the point. Off topic, as it were. But she does it so consistently that it really becomes suspicious. That was all it took [for me to] delve into her novels.'[23]

What, moreover, disturbs him is her refusal to avail herself of the 'aesthetic intention' defence, implying that she suffers from a lack of literary humility: 'Calixthe Beyala has never claimed any such *potpourri* method. And she denies all voluntary inspiration in order to rely essentially on "the divine"' ['Calixthe Beyala n'a jamais revendiqué un quelconque potpourri. Et [...] elle nie tout inspiration volontaire pour s'en remettre essentiellement "au divin"' (Assouline 11)].

Beyala's defence, in the face of the evidence, shifts from 'reminiscence' to evoking the African 'oral tradition' to, eventually, charges of racism, in a move that may be more astute than it first appears. In a defence related to *tu-quoque-ism*, she has directly accused her critics of ethical crimes potentially worse than plagiarism – of 'racial hatred' and of sexism: she has attacked 'left-wing journalists' for trying to discredit her 'since I'm not part of their club being a woman and black' (Alberge and MacIntyre). Her counter-attack, while not constituting a defence *per se*, strategically situates the responsibility for condemning 'borrowing' as 'plagiarism' clearly in the reader's court, and shifts the terms of the argument from the author's to the reader's motivations. Her accusations designate her as a victim of the presumption of *parvenuism* for which, moreover, she possesses all the requisite traits: she is young (and not dead), extraordinarily prolific and popular, and, as she says herself, 'a poor black come from nowhere' (Paris 9) – *nowhere* being frequently the origin of the *parvenu* – affirming for her supporters her victimization.

The plagiarism and Beyala's reaction have been commented and condemned by fellow Cameroun author Mongo Beti. In an article published in *Génération* (April 1998) and reported in *Cameroun actualité* (Mani), Mongo Beti accepts as self-evident or 'habitual' (*coutumière*) Beyala's plagiaristic practices and cites her reactions as an indication of her guilt. But what is most interesting in his commentary is his questioning of the 'complicity' of the French literary establishment in the fiascos (*déboires*) of Black African writers. Comparing Beyala to Ouologuem, he wonders not only whether plagiarism would be specific to French African writing, but also whether it is supported by France, which awards literary prizes to such writers as a way of 'reinforcing mediocrity in Black African literature.' In his comparison with Ouologuem, Mongo Beti broadens the horizon of culpability to include a certain number of francophone African writers who 'feel psychologically obliged to plagiarize, gripped by an *arrivisme* [i.e. *parvenuisme*] which entails a great vulnerability in the face of the temptations of easy success' ['Ils se sentiront psychologiquement obligés de plagier, aux prises d'un arrivisme qui entraîne une grande vulnérabilité face aux sirènes de la réussite facile' (Mani)].

Having been previously convicted of breach of copyright – a decision she left uncontested – and in light of the evidence provided by Assouline, Beyala shifts the ground of her defence from her own intentions or lack thereof and directly accuses her accusers, appealing to the guilty conscience not only of the institution but of the nation and, as well, of her natural allies, the 'left wing' whom she has alienated by her lack of first-world political correctness. The target, which combines sexism with racism, is a large one. For Mongo Beti, however, 'the racism and sexism alleged by Calixthe Beyala in her defence are examples of intellectual terrorism' ['le racisme and et le sexisme qu'évoque Calixthe Beyala pour sa défense ne relèvent que du terrorisme intellectuel' (Mani)].

Her case interests us because the beautiful and talented African 'feminist' displays a clear understanding of her position as being one of privilege bestowed on a marginal by a white male–dominated hegemony. While her accusations of racism and sexism against her accusers may appear heavy-handed, they are effective because the opposite of being accused of plagiarism for reasons of bias may be receiving privilege for the same reasons. Beyala is obviously sensitive to the possibility that there may be an element of 'tokenism' present in her institutional success, and she intends to use it in her own defence. In the same breath that she attacks Assouline, she foregrounds the institutional suppression of the glaringly obvious: as a Black African woman writer she is not a 'neutral,' or even a natural, choice, and Assouline may be right in pointing out the exceptional nature of awarding such a prize to a convicted plagiarist: as *The Independent* declares: 'It is hard to imagine what Calixthe Beyala and the *Académie française* could possibly have in common' (Paris 9). Assouline is 'obsessed' by trying to explain the inexplicable, but, by attacking Beyala, misses the mark. She, however, may have put her finger on it: 'I am a black woman.' If 'I am a black woman' can be used to counter accusations of plagiarism, it is also an unanswerable challenge to the Académie to deny that these same conditions may have motivated their choice. In his attempts to explain this choice, Assouline does not consider what Beyala's accusation seems to imply: that the jury may have been haunted by the consequences of *not* awarding the prize to a (seductive, beautiful, prolific, popular, and outspoken) Black African woman (feminist).

Assouline's judgment of her writing would support the theory that he is attempting to style her as a *parvenu*. But *parvenuism*, in the hands of Beyala, is exposed not as a condition of the (non)-author for which plagiarism is the evidence, but, rather, as a bias visited upon the outsider by virtue of her marginality. Beyala has clearly understood the delicate nature of her position and, in attacking her attacker, simultaneously opens her supporters – essentially members of the same 'club' – to the suspicion of bestowing 'privilege' where they should be rewarding merit. Reacting implicitly to the charges of racism, Assouline's article begins: 'In fact, the biography of the accused author is of little consequence (and the quality of the publisher even less so). It is the principle and not the person which is in question. In the past, *Lire* has had other occasions to denounce, in the strongest terms, plagiarism committed by authors coming from different horizons.'[24]

'I am not a misogynist-racist' is clearly inscribed in this disclaimer. By defending the disinterested neutrality of his own literary judgments, while attacking the objectivity of the prestigious Académie française, Assouline may have fallen into his opponent's trap. If Beyala 'sells herself by selling her novels,' this self is very explicitly that of a Black African woman, and it is precisely that which Assouline pretends not to have noticed. His suppression of the 'biography of the author' is disingenuous – not only in the context of the French literary prize, where biography is often foregrounded, but in literary judgments in general: in the various contexts in which it is inscribed – whether it be contemporary literary theory, racial and sexual politics in France and the West, or the politics of the literary prize – the claim to objectivity is no longer the solid or legitimate foundation that it once was.

Both work and talent continue today to be requisite attributes of author-ship, and where one or the other is perceived to be lacking, plagiarism may be sought or suspected as an explanation for inexplicable success, whether it be of the symbolic or the financial kind. The cases of Haley, Epstein, and Beyala are all couched in contexts where institutional merit is considered to have been undeservedly bestowed on otherwise untalented writers. Charges of plagiarism are attempts on the part of the institution to explain this success to itself by discrediting the author while preserving intact its own inviolability, despite the paradox involved in the institutional promo-tion of the apparently undeserving. Preserving authority in the face of apparent grave errors in judgment is a delicate matter and, as we have seen, charges of plagiarism are not always effective in bringing the sus-pected *profiteer* to heel. But maintaining the authority of the literary institu-tion is not, in the end, particularly difficult: the literary institution will always succeed, because it is a closed circle without an exterior. Outside of inside, there is simply nowhere.

7. Imperial Plagiarism

Captive Greece captured the savage victor and brought the arts into rustic Latium

Horace, *Epistles* II, i, 156

CONQUEST AND CULTURAL IMPERIALISM

Commenting on the passage that introduces this chapter and the Latin practice of translation, Rita Copeland says that, for the Latins, the 'aim of inventional difference in the replicative project of translation is founded on a historical agenda of conquest and supremacy through submission' (17). This relation between the conqueror/translator and the submissive, conquered nation/culture has a reciprocal structure: the military and political superiority of Latium is matched by the cultural supremacy of the ancient Greeks. By the translation and latinization of Greek culture, the act of conquest becomes at the same time a recreation of Latin culture in the image of the conquered – a double conquest, in which the conquerer assimilates what is superior in the conquered culture and becomes transformed in the image of the vanquished. If Greece is to become Latin, Latium is nonetheless to become Hellenic.

I have been arguing two major premises: first, that while there is considerable historical consistency among definitions of plagiarism as to its essential elements, there is a significant lack of consensus as to what discursive objects correspond to the definition: *plagiarism is in the eye of the beholder.* Second, that accusations of plagiarism can be mobilized to discredit unwelcome players in the field, or plagiarism games can be used against instances of power to undermine their authority, as in the example of Montaigne: *plagiarism is power*. As literature articulates the larger social, historical, political, and economic structures in which it is embedded and which are determining of the field, so, too, plagiarism expresses structures of and struggles for power that implicate far more than the individual agents or victims.

While plagiarism is in the eye of the beholder, the beholder is not a timeless and objective judge, but is inscribed in a complex context of social, aesthetic, economic, and political determinants that govern the reception of texts and the judgments made about them. Understanding the role that context plays in defining literature or art in general entails understanding the presuppositions of the instances invested with the authority to identify both art and non-art. Plagiarism, like literature, cannot be found in a text, or even in an intertext. It exists only in the space circumscribed by texts, readers, and their cultural presuppositions, that is, in the pragmatic space of the literary context.

One way to track the evolution of the practice and theory of plagiarism is to examine the metaphors that have been mobilized to describe it, as well as the connotations inherent in the choice of descriptors. If the concept of plagiarism is to be granted a certain historical stability, then this should be reflected in a corresponding stability of its metaphoric field. We have seen that one of the ways in which plagiarism maintains its slippery yet stable identity over time is through a process of euphemization or renaming, in which the same practice/product acquires different ethical or aesthetic characteristics, depending on the connotations of its qualification. Among the various and colourful metaphors condoning or condemning plagiarism, none is more enduring or pervasive than the ancient metaphor of *conquest*. If one traces the avatars of plagiarism-as-conquest throughout history, two things become clear: on the one hand, plagiarism has continuously been seen as a form of conquest, therefore explicitly as a form of exertion of power over others; but, on the other hand, 'conquest' has not, historically, always been seen in the same ethical light, and is certainly not seen in the same way by victors and vanquished. The metaphoric migrations of the term 'conquest' and its semantic derivations, its application to various types and forms of imitation, trace a historical development within which the practice of imitation inhabits a conceptual field circumscribed by the notion of cultural wealth as a source of power. While the significant cultural and political differences with which the act of imitation is invested are underlined by the variants within the metaphoric field, at the same time a certain degree of stability of the field reveals that acts of cross-cultural imitation have been, throughout history, continuously invested with values that are consistent with political and economic theories governing

national identity. What begins as a positive metaphor describing the benefits of translation as a form of cross-cultural imitation will be transformed
into a form of imperialism, and eventually colonialism, each form of the
metaphor being invested with the positive or negative values corresponding to these activities in the political realm.

At the origin of the metaphor of plagiarism-as-conquest is a relationship
of opposition. As the opening quotation indicates, the original metaphoric
relation equates not *plagiarism* but, rather, *translation* and *conquest,* both
terms of positive connotations in which the political dominance of foreign
territories was accompanied by the civilizing effects of the foreign culture
on one's own linguistic and cultural identity. Whereas the Latin conquest
of Greece and the European cultural 'conquest' of the ancients readily recognized the cultural superiority of the foreign civilization, which was assimilated into a re-creation of the conqueror's identity, later European
colonization of the New World established the hierarchy of the civilized
conqueror over the savage conquered in the imposition of a culture/lan-
guage on the other: 'translation was, and still is, the central act of European colonization and imperialism in the Americas' (Cheyfitz 104).[1] The
metaphor of conquest has traditionally expressed the legitimacy of translating foreign works: translation and conquest were good; plagiarism was
bad, being negatively applied to the usurping of national property, that is,
theft. From classical through neoclassical aesthetics, the imitation of
national and modern literatures was precluded in favour of the imitation
or translation of ancient and subsequently foreign ones. From the time of
the Roman conquest of Greece, the importation of the foreign culture was
an extension of the imperial victory; translation was 'invented' by the
Romans as a strategy for transforming the superior culture of the conquered nation into the culture of the conquerors: 'Roman theory of translation emerges from a disturbing political agenda in which forcibly
substituting Rome for Greece is a condition of acknowledging the fundamental status of Greek eloquence for *Latinitas.* Translation can scarcely be
theorized without reference to conquest as a component of rivalry, or
aggressive supremacy in the challenge to Greek hegemony' (Copeland 17).

The distinction between legitimate translation from a foreign language
versus the imitation of national writers is a very old defence against the
accusation of plagiarism, and is recorded as given by Terence (second century B.C.), who, when accused of plagiarism, proclaimed his innocence by
saying that he had not imitated his Latin compatriots, but rather the
Greeks (Welslau 110–11).[2] In Saint Jerome's *De optimo genere interpretandi,*
inspired by Cicero, the theory of translation expressed, according to Hugo
Friedrich, 'sounds even in his words like a declaration of power by a
Roman emperor: "The translator considers thought content a prisoner

(*quasi captivos sensus*) which he transplants into his own language with the prerogative of a conquerer (*iure victoris*)'" (Hugo Friedrich, 'On the Art of Translation' [1965], in Schulte and Biguenet, 1992, pp. 12–13).

The Roman theory of translation-as-conquest resurfaces with particular pertinence during the Renaissance, as the European nation-states develop national identities and boundaries, national cultures, and vernacular languages defining differences. Whereas the latinate Middle Ages conceived of the universality of the Christian community, and practised the *circulation* of truth across cultural boundaries by the common use of Latin, the fifteenth and sixteenth centuries witnessed the growth of nationalisms and national boundaries, the solidification of political entities and the implantation of the vernacular – the creation of cultural specificity as an index of national identity and, subsequently, of territorial property. The establishment of political boundaries and differences transforms the medieval ethic of the circulation of a common culture into a growing ethic of separation, entailing the possibility of the transgression of cultural as well as political boundaries. Cross-cultural appropriation in this context retains more than a metaphorical link to foreign conquest; as well, both are seen as positive means of enriching the national storehouse.

The proscription against the imitation of moderns and of nationals was a central feature of Renaissance poetics: as vernacular French, for example, began to gain respectability as a literary language, translation and adaptation from the ancients were deemed to be legitimate forms of imitation, while intra-linguistic imitation was not. The terms used by Ronsard and Du Bellay to describe their practices where freely bellicose: Ronsard *pillaged* Thebes and *ransacked* ancient Italy ('A sa lyre,' *Odes* Bk 1), and in the *Deffence* Du Bellay recommended: 'Pillez moy sans conscience les sacrez Tresors de ce Temple Delphique' ('Conclusion à toute l'oeuvre,') while simultaneously protesting against the 'odious' practice of imitating moderns and compatriots: 'And certainly, just as it is not a fault, but rather worthy of great praise, to borrow sentences and words from a foreign language, so is it greatly to be criticized, even odious to every reader of a liberal nature, to see such an imitation within a single language [...].'[3]

The rule of imitating only ancient texts was later relaxed to include contemporary foreign ones, which could be imitated by translation into the national tongue. The proscription against intra-cultural and linguistic imitation continued well on into the seventeenth century, and even into the eighteenth. But it has been remarked that, even in the seventeenth century, this 'rule' was more often breached than respected, as theft from native and modern texts simply developed into a clandestine version of what was officially legitimate (Welslau 115).

Unlike the Roman conquest of Greece, the Renaissance pillage of the ancients was pure metaphor, but the desired effect was the same: the consequence of such a conquest was a moral and aesthetic improvement of the national spirit and letters. During the succeeding centuries these metaphors become more concrete and elaborate, following, apparently, the progress of conquest and then colonization essential to European mercantilism. The expression of translation as conquest is repeated well into the nineteenth century, where it is usually employed with reference to the ancients. Humboldt, for example, reminds us in 1816 that the impetus for translation is improvement through imitation: 'To the same extent that a language is enriched, a nation is also enriched. Think how the German language, to cite only one example, has profited since it began imitating Greek meter. And think how our nation has progressed, not just the well-educated among us but the masses as well – even women and children – since the Greeks have been available to our nation's readers in authentic and undistorted form' (Wilhelm von Humboldt, 'From the Introduction to His Translation of *Agammemnon*,' 55–9, in Schulte and Biguenet 57). The perception of an imperial impulse underlying the Roman attitude with respect to translation is nowhere more succinctly expressed than in Nietzsche's famous phrase 'In those days, indeed, to translate meant to conquer' (Friedrich Nietzche, 'On the Problem of Translation,' from *Die fröliche Wissenschaft* [1882], in Schulte and Biguenet 69).

The most repeated source of the conquest metaphor used to distinguish between plagiarism (theft) and translation (conquest) is J.-B. Marini, an Italian poet of the sixteenth and early seventeenth centuries, who is reported by Scudéry in the preface to *Alaric* as having said that to take from one's compatriots is theft, but to steal from foreigners is conquest. And La Mothe le Vayer (1588–1672) gives us a version of the same: 'To take from the Ancients and to profit from what they have written is like piracy beyond the equator (*au delà de la ligne*); but to steal from those of one's century [...] is like stealing coats on the pont Neuf.'[4] Commenting on this passage in his *Dictionnaire* (1695–7), Pierre Bayle confirms the notion that the rule was more honoured in the breach than in practice since the distinction between translation and plagiarism was really between legitimate and illegitimate pillage. Adherence to these scruples was rarely innocent, and perhaps more apparent than real: 'I believe that all authors agree on this maxim, that it is better to pillage the ancients than the moderns, and among these, one should spare one's compatriots, rather than foreigners [...] All plagiarists, when they can, follow the distinction that I have claimed: but they do so not by any principle of conscience; it is rather in order not to be recognized. When one pillages a modern author, prudence requires that one hide one's loot.'[5]

The legitimacy of pillaging foreign treasures to enrich one's own storehouses is founded in good mercantile political economics:[6] the sixteenth and seventeenth centuries are the great era of European exploration and conquest of foreign territories. The pillage-model of conquest is centripetal, wealth being drawn into the sphere of the conquerer from the outside. During the eighteenth and nineteenth centuries, this model gives way to the centrifugal movement of colonization, where conquest is by expansion of the national boundaries and by the exertion of influence over foreign territories and peoples. While the first implies transformation of the conquerer by the importation of external wealth, the second implies transformation of the foreign territories and peoples under the influence of the conquerer.

Marini's distinction between foreign conquest and native theft is repeated in English by Gerard Langbaine in his *Momus Triumphans: or The Plagiaries of the English Stage* (1687). This catalogue of plays 'both Ancient and Modern, that were ever yet Printed in English' contains in its preface, alongside a denunciation of Dryden's plagiaristic plays, 'a view of Plagiaries in general, [...] that we may observe the different proceedings between the Ancients and our Modern Writers' ([7]). The argument is mainly that the ancients proceeded to imitate and appropriate properly, an art largely lost to the Moderns, excepting 'Shakspear and Johnson' [*sic*]. From the list of plagiarists, Langbaine exempts translators, 'or those who *own* what they borrow from other Authors,' reasoning that they contribute to 'the Knowledge of the *Unlearned*': 'Yet at the same time I cannot but esteem them as the worst of Plagiaries, who steal from the Writings of those of our own Nation. Because he that borrows from the worst *Forreign* [*sic*] Author, may possibly import, even amongst a great deal of trash, *somewhat* of value: whereas the former makes us pay extortion for *that* which was our own before' (Langbaine, 'The Preface,' [11]).

Dryden has been qualified as one of the most enthusiastic of the seventeenth-century British poetic imperialists (Kramer). He not only attributes to himself the virtues of foreign conquest, but claims them on behalf of the noblest of his predecessors, Ben Jonson, who, he says, 'invades Authours like a Monarch, and what would be theft in other Poets, is onely victory in him' (quoted in Kramer 55). On his own behalf, Dryden furnishes an ironic example of the conquest metaphor in the epilogue to *An Evening's Love* (1668, ll. 26–33), where, on being accused of stealing his plot from the French, the narrator reports that the author

> neither swore nor storm'd as Poets do,
> But, most unlike an Author, vow'd 'twas true:
> Yet said, he us'd the *French* like Enemies,
> And did not steal their Plots, but made 'em Prize

But should he all the pains and charges count
Of taking 'em, the Bill so high wou'd mount
That, like Prize-Goods, which through the Office come,
He could have had 'em much more cheap at home. (Dryden 25–6)

And in a version of the same, with more explicit mercantilist overtones: 'If sounding words are not of our growth and manufacture, who shall hinder me to import them from a foreign country? I carry not out the treasure of the nation, which is never to return; but what I bring from Italy, I spend in England: here it remains, and here it circulates; for, if the coin be good, it will pass from one hand to another. I trade both with the living and the dead, for the enrichment of our native language ...' (Dryden, from 'Dedication of the Aeneis' [1697], cited in Steiner 74).

The metaphor continues into the nineteenth century, but seems to divide authors and critics, the first claiming for themselves the act of conquest as a defence against accusations of plagiarism, and the second viewing such claims rather less sanguinely. Both Quérard and the nineteenth-century *Larousse* are sceptical about Dumas's version of the conquest metaphor:

> And Shakespeare and Molière were right, for the man of genius does not steal, he conquers: he makes of the province that he takes an annex of his empire; he imposes on it his laws, he peoples it with his subjects, he extends his golden sceptre over it, and no one dares say, upon seeing his beautiful kingdom: This territory is not part of your rightful heritage.[7]

Dumas extends the metaphor from one of simple conquest to one of full-blown colonization in which, Crusoe-like, the improvement and civilization of the conquered territory legitimize the conquerer's claim to ownership of it. If plagiarism was originally the crime of kidnapping a freeman to press him into slavery, and if colonization is kidnapping on a large scale, it is on this scale that the exertion of superior force is clearly seen as positive: the virtues of territorial conquest and colonization are the political analogies used to shift copying from the category of dishonest theft to one of legitimate appropriation.

'Theorists' of plagiarism continue the metaphor throughout the nineteenth century. Charles Nodier approves the principle that stealing from a modern national author is worse than stealing from any other, and goes on to claim that foreign conquests are justified to the extent that they enrich the national language. The bellicose theme continues: 'Genius has other ways, in truth, to fight a rival nation, but it appears that this way (i.e., plagiarism) is not to be disdained' (*Questions de littérature légale* 6). And Joseph-

Marie Quérard, in his *Supercheries littéraires*, condemns the moral laxness of the times in the following ironic tones: 'Now we have arrived in the nineteenth century. But the writers of this era are too much gentlemen to commit any kind of theft. No one plagiarizes any more, no one steals any more [...], one "conquers"; it's in better taste. [...] Therefore, thanks to the perfect morality of our century, it is not by examples of literary theft the we will continue our survey, but by examples of conquest.'[8] Again, the attack is not against 'conquest' as such but, on the contrary, against the habit of whitewashing literary theft by the ennobling euphemism of 'conquest.'

The tradition of cross-border copying as legitimate conquest survives well into the nineteenth century not only in literary language about borrowing, but also as a practical effect of copyright legislation.[9] It was not until 1838 that Britain and other European countries entered into a series of bilateral copyright treaties which extended protection to foreign works. These agreements were normalized at the Berne Convention in 1887, with the notable exception of the United States, who had traditionally profited from the rampant conquest, more commonly known as piracy, of British works in America, where they were freely reprinted in cheap editions at little cost to the publisher. It was not until America came to realize that such practices were not altogether either in the economic or in the cultural national interests that the tide of conquest was stemmed. In 1891 (Chace Act) the United States passed its own legislation granting rights to foreign works from countries agreeing to reciprocal protection.

STENDHAL: THE CONQUEROR CONQUERED

By the nineteenth century, the distinction between imitation and translation from foreign sources was well established, and lent translation a specific status, such that confusion between the two was not automatically condoned. However, while the traditional aesthetic justification for the practice is outmoded, the legitimacy of imperialism still surfaces in debates about cross-border copying: cross-cultural imitation becomes plagiarism when the source and author of the original are not acknowledged. In a notable instance, Stendhal's 'translation' of the Italian Carpani's *Life of Haydn* was treated with veiled indifference to the crime perpetrated against the foreign author. The controversy between 'Bombet' (Stendhal-Beyle's pseudonym for *La vie de Haydn*) and Carpani lasted from 1815 to 1824 in the form of letters published primarily in *Le Constitutionnel*. In reporting Carpani's denunciation of the plagiarism, *Le Constitutionnel* (13 Dec. 1815) takes an ironic point of view with regard to the Italian's complaints: '"Not only," he says in his letter addressed to M. Bombet, "have you kidnapped my child, but you have gouged out his eyes, cut off his ears, completely ruined his appearance." One could ask this loving father how he was able to recognize such a strangely disfigured child. One must admire here the force of the paternal instinct.'[10]

Carpani's book contains personal anecdotes about the author's experiences with the great composer: Bombet manages to steal from him not only a conversation between Carpani and Haydn, but also a fever, apparently cured by the 'salutary effect of Haydn's music.' Carpani's outrage over the plagiarism was exacerbated by the personal nature of the experiences he recounts, which Bombet systematically, by his unavowed 'translation,' attributes to himself. The Italianate rhetoric of Carpani's letter is described by V. Del Litto as appearing 'not sufficiently serious to be taken seriously by Parisian readers: French taste was unable to discern the severe accents of justified indignation, and almost suspected a mystification.'[11] The ironic and mocking response in *Le Constitutionnel* is evidence of this reaction; the last paragraph of the article is indicative of the lack of gravity that Carpani's denunciation inspired: 'It is difficult to respond to such well-established facts. After an attentive reading of the arguments made by M. Carpani, we do not hesitate to recognize his paternity and we believe we do a useful service to M. Louis-Alexandre-César Bombet in advising him that he should, as a friendly gesture, return to M. Carpani his book, his conversation, and his fever.'[12]

Carpani explains in his letter that he would have been simply amused and somewhat honoured to be so copied by a Frenchman, had it not been that, in the preface to the letters, Bombet insinuates that copies of the original letters had been circulated before the publication of the book, implying, in Carpani's eyes, the possibility of an inversion of the true chronology of the publication, leaving Carpani himself open to the accusations of '*plagiaire, imposteur, menteur*' that are so evidently appropriate to Bombet. Among Carpani's complaints are that Bombet, in his theft-by-translation, has not stolen completely or accurately enough, adding digressions of his own and changing some of the original with the effect of introducing 'errors' into the text: that is, the additions and emendations push the text from legitimate translation into plagiarism. Among many changes of detail, Carpani is also outraged at the emendations made by Bombet in the interests of French sensibilities: where Carpani speaks of the French as 'les maniéristes,' for example, Bombet substitutes 'les Italiens,' thereby attributing what Carpani sees as the 'defects' of French musicians to the Italians (Stendhal 460).

Subsequent to the publication of excerpts of Carpani's two letters in *Le Constitutionnel*, the same newspaper notes a response from Bombet – or perhaps from a friend (Stendhal 471) – where the defence consists principally in returning the accusation of plagiarism against Carpani himself and, significantly, in displacing the question of national origin in favour of the ultimate merit of the book. As the editors of the *Oeuvres complètes* point out, the short piece more resembles an advertisement than a defence, and ends with the declaration: 'All in all, the work merited to be translated into French, if it is Italian; and into Italian, if it is French. M. Bombet's book, original or copy, is available in Paris, *chez* P. Didot, rue du Pont-de-Lodi.'[13]

This notice inspired another response from Carpani, printed in *Le Constitutionnel* in its entirety, in which he challenges Bombet to furnish proof of his allegations. The affair was taking a turn for the ridiculous: in response to Carpani's demand that Bombet himself enter into the fray, a letter was published in *Le Constitutionnel* (1 Oct. 1816), ostensibly written by Bombet's younger brother – most probably by Stendhal's friend Louis Crozet while the former was in Milan (Stendhal 478). In the 'defence,' Bombet *frère* admits that some details of Carpani's *Haydine* were apparently lifted by Bombet, but he justifies the borrowing by arguing that these details are in the realm of 'facts': 'Hume was not a plagiarist of Rapin-Thoiras for having said, after him, that Elisabeth was the daughter of Henri VIII; [...] M. Lacretelle was not a plagiarist of M. Anquetil for having treated, after him, the subject of the war of the Ligue.'[14] Noting that these historians, in repeating history, were able to draw new conclusions, and to renew their subjects by a new treatment, he suggests the test of translating any thirty pages of Carpani's *Haydine* for comparison with the 'same' thirty pages of Bombet: 'Le public jugera' (477), particularly it seems, with regard to the 'graceful style, full of sensitivity without affectation, a style not devoid of the special flair which is, perhaps, the principal merit of M. Bombet's work' ['style plein de grâce, plein d'une sensibilité sans affectation, et qui n'exclut pas le piquant qui, peut-être, est le premier mérite de l'ouvrage de M. Bombet' (Stendhal 477)]. Carpani's work had already been qualified in the letter as 'interminable,' full of 'words and details without interest.'

The affair finally died of its own, Bombet himself refusing to enter the debate. In his *Supercheries,* Quérard recounts a private exchange with Stendhal where the author claims that his publisher, fearing that a French translation of an Italian work would not find 'a single reader,' convinced him to use the pseudonym Louis-Alexandre-César Bombet: 'This beautiful name was admired,' said Stendhal, 'and no one divined the author. Can an anonymous author be a plagiarist?' ['On admira ce beau nom, disait Stendhal, et personne ne devina l'auteur. Un anonyme peut-il être un plagiaire?' (Quérard, *Supercheries*, vol. 1, 547)].

In the Del Litto edition of the *Oeuvres complètes*, which I have been citing, the editor decides that 'the time has come to revise our judgment and to rehabilitate the [*Life of Haydn*]' ['le moment est venu de procéder à une révision du jugement et à la rhéhabilitation du livre' (Stendhal 494)]. He considers that plagiarism indeed occurred, and that if the affair were to take place today, the plagiarist would have been found guilty in court. He goes on to note that Carpani is not Stendhal's only victim, but that others suffered the same fate, these having been enumerated by Paul Hazard in a 1921 article 'Les plagiats de Stendhal,' and that, even then, the list of plagiarisms has not been exhausted: 'An accident of reading will no doubt permit us to lengthen it again by several items' ['Le hasard d'une lecture peut sans doute permettre de l'allonger encore de quelque unités' (495)].[15]

In his attempts to explain Stendhal's plagiarism of Carpani, Del Litto makes reference to Stendhal's political disappointment following the fall of Napoleon and to his disastrous financial situation. He also insists that, rather than undertaking a purely mechanical work of translation-plagiarism, Stendhal 'used the texts of Carpani, Winckler, Sismondi et *tutti quanti*, as an ensemble of materials that he fashioned in his own way. In other words, by isolating his personal contribution, one arrives at the conclusion that the work, far from being a cento, is highly structured such that even the borrowed parts finally melt into a whole *à l'allure bien stendhalienne.*'[16] Del Litto quotes from the manuscript of a future translation of *La Vie* into English, where the author, Richard Coe, reasons that Beyle encountered, in Carpani's work, 'certain basic ideas on the nature of art and music which, from then on, he was to make his own' (502): 'A part of the charm exerted by the *Life of Haydn* emanates precisely from the reciprocal play of two minds so perfectly in harmony (in spite of their apparent quarrels) that it is virtually impossible to attempt a clear separation of ideas: this belongs to Stendhal; that to Carpani.'[17]

Del Litto does not neglect to mention the fact that *La vie de Haydn* was composed after the fall of Napoleon and at the end of his Italian Empire, which lasted from 1805, when he had declared himself king, until 1814 when he was expelled (*La vie* dates from 1815). Del Litto quotes from Stendhal's *Lettre sur l'état actuel de la musique en Italie*: 'The conquest of Italy carried out by means of great actions, first awakened the peoples of Lombardy; next, the exploits of Italy's soldiers in Spain and Russia, her association with the destiny of a great empire, even though this empire met with misfortune [...] all this gave rise in this beautiful country [...] to the thirst for nationhood.'[18]

If the plagiarisms of Stendhal are legion, many are virtually translations: that is, cross-border plagiarisms. Maurevert reports that Goethe, commenting enthusiastically on Stendhal's *Rome, Naples et Florence*, notes in a letter to a friend: 'he knows very well how to use what one reports to him, and, above all, he knows well how to appropriate foreign works. He translates passages from my *Italian Journey* and claims to have heard the anecdote recounted by a marchesina.'[19]

Plagiarism-hunting *chez* Stendhal was largely an activity of the first few years of the twentieth century. Sufficiently armed with the evidence of his methods, later students of Stendhal have turned their attention to the question of why: in particular, why did Stendhal plagiarize Carpani? Jean-Jacques Hamm's answer, situated in a psychoanalytical frame, suggests that Stendhal, in his plagiarisms, was 'reduced to affirming himself through others,' and he cites Lacan's famous phrase: 'Le désir de l'homme, c'est le désir de l'Autre': 'To rewrite, after and with Carpani, the *Life of Haydn*, becomes that grandiose gesture by which the other makes of himself an 'I,' for 'I' can only be an other' ['Récrire, après et avec Carpani, la *Vie de Haydn* devient ce geste grandiose par lequel l'autre se fait je, car je ne saurait être qu'un autre' (Hamm 212)]. Also adopting a psychoanalytical point of view, Schneider arrives at the same conclusion: 'As a true writer, he knew that in what one steals from others, it is always oneself that one reads' ['Ecrivain vrai, il savait que, volant les autres, c'est soi-même qu'on y lit, toujours' (Schneider, 1985 101)]. For Schneider, Stendhal constitutes the exemplary creative plagiarist (as opposed to the pathological plagiarist), revealing the very essence of literature, which is to write 'à la dérobée.'[20]

What is not mentioned in the discussions of Stendhal's plagiarisms is the possible colonizing impulse that led him to a massive pillage of Italian sources. Although his plagiarisms are not limited to the Italian, the first, and the overwhelming majority, of his borrowings are from this language and nation. Stendhal spent many years in Italy, particularly in Milan, and his passion for the Italian culture is well known – as is his obsession with Napoleon and his active role in the imperial endeavour. It is tempting to think, beyond the idiosyncratic psychology attributed to him as a motivation for his plagiarisms, that there may be, as well, a link between the Napoleonic conquest and subsequent loss of Italy, Stendhal's admiration of that culture, and his plagiarisms of its national literature. In place of a conquering army and an imperial conquest, Stendhal proposes a cultural and literary conquest that is, Roman-style, at once emulation and assimilation of a defeated but superior culture. If Stendhal's talent inexorably lay not in invention, but in the rewriting of works and documents that he collected from every corner of Europe, in the recounting of 'le petit fait vrai,' it is not impossible that his pillage of the Italian world is related not only to his admiration for that world, but also to his Napoleonic career.

Stendhal discovers Milan and falls in love, not only with Italy but with an Italian, in 1800, when he travels there with the reserve forces of the victorious Imperial army, which had 'liberated' the city from Austria in 1796. Until 1814, Italy would belong to Bonaparte's Empire. In 1813, Stendhal returns to Milan to recover from the Russian and German campaigns and is still there on the eve of the end of the Empire. After a brief return to

Paris, he finally decides, in 1814, to settle in Milan – without money, his professional and political ambitions at an end. His self-imposed exile lasts seven years. It is during this time that his career as a writer-plagiarist begins: between 1814 and 1818 he composes the *Lives of Haydn* (Carpani), *Mozart* (Winckler), and *Métastase* (Baretti); *L'histoire de la peinture en Italie* (Bossi, Amoretti, Pignott, Lanzi); and *Rome, Naples et Florence*, which owes elements not only to Goethe, but to a number of articles published in the *Edinburgh Review* (Maurevert 167).

In spite of Stendhal's ambiguous and sometimes contradictory opinions about Napoleon, it seems that he is rather constant in his praise of the liberating and progressive influence of the Emperor's conquests in Europe, which had the effect of spreading the ideas born of the French revolution. These salutary effects were especially realized in Italy: 'Because of the government of Napoleon, Italy was able to accomplish, in one leap, three centuries worth of improvement' ['Par le gouvernement de Napoléon, l'Italie sautait à pieds joints trois siècles de perfectionnement ...' (*Rome, Naples et Florence*, 249; quoted in Heisler 72)].

Much has been written about Stendhal's literary method, his desire to be a historian, his 'fear of the blank page,' and there would no doubt be much to gain from a serious psychological study of the origins of his plagiaristic method. Whether he in fact conceived of his works as 'translations,' as the sometimes discrete and general attributions might indicate, whether the 'plagiarisms' were indeed 'involuntary,' as Jean Prévost claims (110) – a thesis that seems hardly defensible – his form of piracy has been consecrated as a method, and as an apprenticeship in genius. Paul Hazard, the exposer of so many of his plagiarisms, lyricizes: 'Lanzi or Carpani as much as you wish, the *Lives of Haydn, Mozart and Metastase*, and *The History of Painting in Italy*, offered nonetheless such a multiplicity of ingenious or profound ideas, and such a personal style, that one would wish, at this price, that many original books had been plagiarized.'[21]

In the context of the question of cultural imperialism and conquest, however, it seems not improbable that an element of the original impulse behind Stendhal's literary conquest of Italian authors and subjects might have been a kind of inversion of the 'liberating' Napoleonic conquest which brought enlightened republicanism to the *Ancien régime* political system of Italy. And the legal and ethical tolerance for cross-border copying, fuelled by a long and not-too-distant tradition of translation-as-creation, contributed to an indifference that left Carpani's justified complaints profoundly unsatisfied. The style of Stendhal's plagiarisms, of which one notable feature is the usurping of the identity of the enunciating subject, is interesting not only for its psychological implications, but also from the point of view of the same conquest-and-substitution process that Copeland has used in describing Roman translations from the Greek. Both gestures enact a radical assimilation of the original text/culture/enunciating subject, not by its repression, but by its simple appropriation by the 'translator.' What is produced in the translation is, on the one hand, an 'I' bereft of its empirical referent and thus fully constituted by its textual apparition but, on the other hand, this 'I' is subsequently informed by the new signature, which in Stendhal's case is, of course, complicated by his multiple pseudonyms. Stendhal steals not only texts, but personalities, memories, experiences, identities – even illnesses. His 'translation' is a conquest in the form of a radical assimilation of the other; but this absorption and eradication enact in turn a profound transformation of the self, which in Stendhal's case amounts to an elimination. The superiority of Italian culture and the inferiority of its social and political situation at the time of the Napoleonic conquest recalls the situation of Greece versus Rome: in this case, captive Italy captured the conquerer Beyle, who made himself over in the image of the conquered. It is significant that Beyle, Napoleon, and the Empire were in fact in the position of the defeated at the moment when he began his plagiarism: by substituting translation/plagiarism for conquest, and at the same time substituting Bombet/Beyle for Carpani, Stendhal enacts a symbolic gesture of conquest which is not without an admission of personal impotence as well as cultural inferiority. Carpani's 'ready-made' life of Haydn furnished him not only with the means to write and the source of an 'I' that he could only discover through the other, but with an access to a cultural identity which he could only acquire through symbolic conquest and assimilation.

POST-COLONIALISM AND REVENGE

Conquest, colonialism, and imperialism have no more gone out of style than has plagiarism but, like plagiarism over the years, they have been discursively transformed and euphemized by metaphors such as 'free trade,' 'the globalization of capital,' 'the new world order,' and 'the free flow of information.' In the literary field, versions of the conquest metaphor still surface, no longer as justifications, but as condemnations of plagiarism. Nowadays, accusations of cultural imperialism challenge the right of an author to appropriate material from one cultural context into another, and defend the authenticity of 'voice' in cultural expression. Cultural artefacts have become the rightful property of the community that produced them; the appropriation of the experience of the 'other,' where this 'other' is inevitably a marginalized or colonized group, is deemed to be a form of imperialism tantamount to illegitimate political domination. At the same time, forms of 'reverse colonialism' – the appropriation of the dominant culture by a minority voice for purposes of 'revenge' or 'criticism' – are considered a legitimate move in a cultural war in which the weaker party can justifiably use means denied the stronger.

In the early days of political and cultural decolonization, the emergence of literatures from former colonies and their penetration of the dominant culture were an integral part of the trend towards a global culture and a breaking-down of the traditional barriers between dominant and dominated. Old values conflicted with right-thinking attempts to raise the cultural products of former colonies to a respectable place in 'World' literature. Léopold Senghor, for example, calls for an international civilization in which the expression of the particular would participate in a universal culture of humanity. Not assimilated but *assimilating*, 'Négritude' is part of a culture of *symbiosis:* 'You will understand, now, why Negro literature written in French is an important contribution to *general literature:* to *Universal Civilization*. Widely understandable, because written in French, it creates the *symbiosis* of two extreme aspects of human Genius. By which fact it constitutes an *integral humanism.*'[22]

The specificity of authentic, indigenous cultural products, the expression of difference from the colonial master rather than deference to him, were highly valued not only by the artists of the emerging nations, but also by liberal Western cultural authorities who celebrated the arrival of national literatures deemed worthy of international status. Always writing in the language of the conqueror, (post-)colonial writers were assigned the task of interpreting indigenous culture for the consumption of the former colonizers, of creating a national culture that was both 'authentic' and accessible to international readers. At the same time, they were required to justify, glorify, and explain their own culture and history to themselves, to create national literary histories from the fund of oral and folkloric traditions that constituted their specificity. Essentially a double effort of translation, the new national literatures had to bridge both a linguistic and a cultural divide. They were assigned the task of recovering an indigenous, oral culture, but expressed in the language of the colonizer and in a literary form able to achieve the appearance of authenticity for both native and Western readers, as well as the standards of readability of European literature.

Occasionally, to the great outrage of the colonizer, a stunning example of 'reverse colonial imperialism' is discovered, as in Yambo Ouologuem's *Le devoir de violence* (1968; *Bound to Violence*, 1971).[23] The novel recounts the epic history of a fictional tribe's evolution from pre-colonial days until a young man's arrival as a student in Paris. In the course of the narrative, Ouologuem traces a history of tribal violence and exploitation that preceded the colonial period, reconstituting the African tribal leaders as precursors of the colonial oppressors. Subsequent to the novel's translation into English in 1971, the author was accused of 'conquering' some not insignificant bits of European literary territory – among them some belonging to Graham Greene and André Schwartz-Bart (many others have since been identified). The offence was great, especially since this 'first truly African novel' had won the Prix Renaudot (1968) in France, its 'authentic Africanness' being an effect not only of the content, but also of the voice of the traditional *griot*, or story-teller. Critics did not hesitate to accuse the author of practising reverse colonialism, of using his plagiarisms to turn the tables on the colonial usurpers of his native Mali. In a full-page exposé in *The Times Literary Supplement*, juxtaposing two pages of text, one from *Bound to Violence* and the other from *It's a Battlefield* by Graham Greene, an anonymous critic comments: 'On its appearance in the United States, *Bound to Violence* was trumpeted as the "first truly African novel," a claim which now looks more than a little sick. Or, is M. Ouologuem on to something: a style of literary imperialism intended as a revenge for the much-chronicled sins of territorial imperialists?' (Anon. 525).

In defence of Ouologuem and his novel, Seth Wolitz explains its authentic Africanness by pointing out that there is more to the contemporary 'authentic African' than the oral and folkloric elements of the noble-savage tradition, which, implicitly, the critique of authenticity entails. According to Wolitz, 'the Africa of contemporary lettered Africans is different from that of the *griots* but just as irreproachably authentic. Never forget that this literature is written by cultured people [*lettrés*] whose linguistic knowledge and whose knowledge of African and Occidental culture are as vast as that of their Occidental critics.'[24] Other defences of Ouologuem's method and novel imply a similar kind of counter-attack against colonialism but attribute to it a more aggressive and defiant intentionality:

> Ouologuem's act violates the national and continental boundaries by which integral bodies of literature are perceived. A 'corpus,' whole unto itself and distinct from all others, is generally assumed in the face-off between Europe, Africa, etc. It is here where dangerous metaphors get their foot in the door, metaphors which Ouologuem explodes: for if one body is distinct from another, one can or must be different, perhaps older and therefore better. [... B]ut *Le devoir de violence* is written in the excrescences, the orifices and the intrusions between European and African literature, by an author without authority. Ouologuem's response to the condition of the African novel (if we can interpret his actions on such a plane) defies the rules of identity and injunction [...] (Miller, 'Trait d'union' 73)

The controversy was fuelled by periodic contributions by Eric Sellin, who has been the most diligent in pursuing and revealing the 'plagiarisms.'

Sellin claims that defenders of the work in terms of imaginative assimilation are themselves guilty of the exploitation of 'European models in a form of reverse cultural imperialism' ('The Unknown Voice of Yambo Ouologeum' 147). In countering the arguments of favourable critics, such as Wolitz, who maintain the use of appropriation for aesthetic ends, he attempts to reverse again the reverse colonialism argument: 'In maintaining that *Le Devoir de violence* is authentically African because it is consistent with the new novel, new-wave film, and the like, critics are merely colonizing Ouologuem's alleged authenticity ... We do not have, as Wolitz proverbially suggests, "new wine in old bottles," but rather old colonialism in a new critic's clothing' (155). Sellin implies that the 'new critics' are imposing foreign, 'new-wave,' and implicitly Occidental aesthetic standards on this apparently inauthentic African novel in order to preserve its Africanness according to Western standards. This argument turns on a rather weak claim, if one credits Ouologuem's own assertion that his intentional allusions participated in such an attempted new aesthetic. Sellin is willing to admit one possible 'authentic' African justification for the plagiarisms:

> the traditional anonymity of the craftsman-artist, whose patron is not posterity but the village or clan, makes the notion of plagiarism absolutely irrelevant [...]
>
> African critics are less nervous than Europeans about plagiarism, feeling no doubt deep in their souls that the writer is a craftsman who owes allegiance to his readership and not to some pantheon or *confrérie* of past writers. In one sense, the tragedy of the Ouologuem affair lies to an equal degree in the European tradition of ownership and the question for private immortality which would cause Mr. Greene or Western critics to care if Ouologuem has borrowed patterns and words from the British novelist.
> (161)

But this 'indigenous' justification for Ouologuem's method is not, in the long run, convincing for Sellin, for presumably Ouologuem knew very well that, regardless of what African oral traditions condoned, he could not get away with 'violating accepted procedure' (162) in the European context. Thus, the only possible argument in favour of authentic Africanness, the recourse to the oral tradition of repetition and the community of property, is ruled inappropriate when carried out in a foreign context that explicitly proscribes such behaviour. Sellin never directly engages the possibility that the 'reverse colonialism' argument might in fact be the most persuasive and legitimizing one; he assumes that reverse colonialism is just as despicable as the original colonialism and, furthermore, is illegitimate when perpetrated on the very territory of the colonizer.

More recent analyses maintain and exploit the 'reverse colonialism' theory of appropriation of colonial discourse for the purposes of deconstruction and criticism. In this context, the use of European texts is seen as a conscious political act:

> It is reasonable to believe that plagiarism is, for Ouologuem, both thing and sign: an act of piracy doubled by the sign of the ironic attitude of an African writer toward the Western text. Plagiarism is then a trope for expressing the abduction [*rapt*] of the body of the white European text [...] It is a metaphor signifying the revenge of the African on the slave-trader who partook in the kidnapping of the slaves, this kidnapping being seen as the physical trace left by the oppressive subject of civilization – understood in this case as the system of thought which refuses the right of difference to the Other.[25]

Understandably, Ouologuem did not himself admit to 'reverse colonial plagiarism.' In self-defence, he compared the technique of his novel to 'the new novel, or even the work of some modern film-makers in which clips from the films of others are inserted' (quoted by K.W. 941). And in an interview with Mel Watkins, Ouologuem declares: 'My novel is not traditional and, although it is based on fact and history, it is not autobiographical. I wrote the book with references to international examples. Afro-American writers have influenced its style and there are Greek and Latin references that are intended to heighten its meaning on a human level. It addresses the problems of all civilizations at specific periods of development; it is not just an African novel' (quoted in Watkins 7).

It is not my aim to decide on Ouologuem's intentions, nor to privilege his defence of his method above the claims of literary critics. It is nevertheless noteworthy that Ouologuem's characterization of the internationalism of his novel echoes Senghor's call for a symbiotic assimilation of the West by Africa, a thesis that his 'plagiarisms' might be seen to have carried out quite literally. The theory of symbiotic assimilation not only finds defenders directly involved in the controversy, but is also generally espoused by much later post-colonial critics. In *Culture and Imperialism* (1993), Edward Said argues against nationalism in the study of World and post-colonial literatures, maintaining that 'no one today is purely *one* thing' (336): 'Once we accept the actual configuration of literary experiences overlapping with one another and interdependent, despite national boundaries and coercively legislated national autonomies, history and geography are transfigured in new maps, in new and far less stable entities, in new types of connections' (317). In a similar vein, Homi Bhabha's theory of a 'Third Space' (1994) defines the 'inscription and articulation of culture's 'hybridity': '[The people of Algeria] are now free to negotiate and translate their cultural identities in a discontinuous intertextual temporality of cultural difference. The native intellectual who identifies the people with the true national culture will be disappointed. The people are now the very principle of "dialectical reorganization" and they construct their culture from the national text translated into modern Western forms of information technology, language, dress' (Bhabha 38).

Was *Le devoir de violence*, in its 'debunking' of cultural and historical myths, and in its 'references to European examples,' an early enactment of contemporary post-colonial theories of cultural hybridity? At least one critic arrives at this argument, and demonstrates that, as a consequence of the political constraints placed on it, post-colonial discourse had assumed an 'artificially unanimous' stance for the needs of a political cause, producing a discourse that had mythologized and homogenized pre-colonial history and identity and that later post-colonial writers needed to expose and denounce. In this sense, Ouologuem would be the first African novelist to demonstrate the interdependence between two discourses traditionally held to be incompatible: the traditional oral and indigenous culture, on the one hand, and the written, Occidental and literate secular culture, on the other (Solongolo 33).

Christopher Miller claims for the novel an even more subtle relationship to its European models. While, on the one hand, the novel 'consciously engages itself in the cross-cultural and interliterary "zone of interferences" between the two continents,' it does so 'not to forge a synthetic response but to exaggerate and undermine the whole tradition we have been reading' (218). Miller posits a subversive tactic that is not *revolutionary* but purely *negative*, a position we explore in the next chapter. *Le devoir* is neither a response to the European Africanist tradition, nor completely separate from that tradition: 'It is a negative response if, by "negative," it is understood that no true contradiction takes place, only a brazen act of trifling with the idols of literary creation, respecting the taboos of neither the African nor the European literary establishment' (218).

I have traced in some detail the evolution of the critical reception of Ouologuem's 'plagiarisms' in order to underline one of the principal lessons of this reception: the intertextual or 'collage' writing that it massively demonstrates is never taken to be an international example of 'postmodern' writing. Whether considered as a positive or negative example of postcolonial writing, *Le devoir de violence* is inevitably an *African* novel. The range of questions asked about it is overwhelmingly dominated by the nature and authenticity of this Africanness, where the utilization of non-African texts is the central piece of evidence, often used as an allegory of other kinds of 'violence' enacted and thematized in the text. The fate of *Le devoir de violence*, its initial success, the tragedy of the controversy and its subsequent importance in post-colonial African literature, are all testimonies to the difficulty, even today, of not being *only one thing*. *Le devoir de violence* either is, or is not, an 'authentic' African novel, and its 'plagiarisms' play an essential role in arguments for and against each interpretation.

The analysis of cross-cultural appropriation as a means of revenge is not an issue confined to literary situations. Departing briefly from my concentration on purely 'literary' plagiarism, it will be useful to explore a controversy that demonstrates some similarities with the one generated by *Le devoir de violence*. In early 1988, in the course of the preparation of Martin Luther King, Jr's collected papers for publication, the scholars of the Martin Luther King, Jr Papers Project (Stanford, Emory, and Martin Luther King, Jr Center for Nonviolent Social Change) made some disquieting discoveries concerning inadequately cited sources in King's doctoral dissertation. *The Journal of American History* (1991) subsequently organized a round table in a special edition devoted to the 'plagiarisms,' in order to understand both his motivations and what impact the discoveries would – or should – have on King's reputation and legacy. Both King's early student papers and his later writings exhibited extensive unacknowledged borrowings that should have been considered insufficiently documented in the academic context. The findings of the Papers Project were that extensive unacknowleged borrowing had indeed taken place, that King consistently received positive evaluations for his work, and that he was aware of academic norms and expectations with respect to citational practices. Without offering a definitive judgment on the question, the editorial team insists that, whatever King's intentions, they presumably met with his professor's expectations: 'That many of King's papers are routine and derivative explications of theological topics suggests that his professors did not expect more originality in such student compositions' (Martin Luther King, Jr Papers Project 28). In the course of the *Journal of American History* symposium, various voices – friends, professors, critics, scholars – express opinions ranging from mild condemnation to whole-hearted disculpation. One line of defence stresses the kind of 'originality' manifest in the ability to compile other's material in a new form for new purposes, as expressed in this interview with one of King's college friends:

> DAVID THELEN: (interviewer): Some people say that originality, the whole point at issue in a discussion of plagiarism, is one of the least valuable qualities for someone whose goal was, like King's, to build a broad consensus by drawing on all sorts of voices and cultures.
>
> CORNISH ROGERS: You're right. For some of us, the originality is how

you put all these things together [...] How you, for your own purposes, graft
things on so that you come up with something new, at least you cause something new to happen as a result of the artful use of what already had been
done and said. ('Conversation between Cornish Rogers and David Thelen'
61–2)

One of the professors involved in the examination of King's thesis
expresses a similar point of view: 'We should see the way in which he
brought all of these [various authors] together into his own personality
and wove them together and then came out as Martin Luther King, Jr.
How many of us are really original anyway? But he was original in the way
in which he brought all these concepts and ideas and attitudes together
and made them a part of himself' ('Conversation between S. Paul Schilling
and David Thelen' 78).

A second line of defence confronts theological with academic conventions and suggests that the African-American Baptist culture was rooted in
an oral tradition of communal learning and repetition, where 'originality'
was less a matter of ideas than of a 'voice,' style, or signature that marked
the orator as having achieved a personal identity (Reagon 118). On the
other hand, the academic theologians refuse to admit that they take a
more lax view with respect to citation and quotation than do other academics ('Conversation between S. Paul Schilling and David Thelen' 79).
King biographer David Levering Lewis dismisses arguments relating to
evangelical, especially African-American traditions, as improbable and at
best irrelevant, since 'Dr. King, of his own volition and intellect, formally
endorsed and claimed to subscribe to the elementary rules of the academy
of learning' (Lewis 82). Lewis's analysis verges on a reverse racism argument: he finds implausible the notion that King's professors were ignorant
of his plagiarisms and impunes to them either 'racial cynicism or paternal-
ism': 'I suspect we have here another case of Dr. Johnson's deplorable apo-
thegm about women preaching and dogs walking on hind legs – that,
distressing as it is to contemplate, Dr. King's professors marveled at his academic performance not because it was "done well; but you are surprised to
find it done at all"' (84). Lewis speculates that, in the face of the racial double standard of his professors, and 'finding himself highly rewarded rather
than penalized for his transparent legerdemain, he may well have decided
to repay their condescension or contempt in like coin' (85). In his introductory essay to the volume, editor David Thelen concludes that 'King's
stilted and unoriginal expressions in graduate school were attempts – indifferent and perfunctory ones – to find a voice that could bridge worlds. The
largest failure of these papers was not that he failed to meet the expectations of the white scholars for whom he was writing by failing to credit his

sources, but that he succeeded too well and thereby failed to find or express his own voice' (20). And in the words of the theologian James Cone: 'But there are a large number of people – and I especially have found that in minority people – who are constantly taught that the only way they can be an intellectual is to be like white people, and thereby to denigrate their own culture and their own self-respect. When that happens, you are urged to try to be somebody else. That's what King did. And I think it also teaches us that integration encouraged him to do that. It has built in it the values of imitating white people. King internalized that' (quoted by Thelen 22).

The arguments, all of which take the moderate and 'objective' line of admitting the 'fact' of the plagiarisms before trying to excuse them, fall roughly into two kinds of justifications: either King knew what he was doing and thought it was acceptable (the proof being his success in his studies and the silence of his professors), or else he knew what he was doing and knew it was wrong, and intended to use the system against itself for his own pragmatic ends (a doctoral degree), as well as, perhaps, for reasons of ideological or political subversion. In both cases, cultural factors are mobilized: either this is what the university system expected of a Black student, or else this is how one Black student chose to react to the expectations of a fundamentally colonial system. In both scenarios, King is a victim of the dominant culture: he was either conforming to expectations thrust upon him by integrationism, which dictated identification with the colonizer, or he was reacting to reverse racism, which held different academic expectations for White and Black students.

The cultural argument about African-American evangelical traditions is a middle ground that tries to justify the 'plagiarisms' as the result of a cultural conflict similar to the one exposed on Ouologuem's behalf, and that runs into the same institutional impasse. Even if 'plagiarism' in the form of repeated discourse is what King's evangelical tradition teaches, one of two conclusions must be reached: he was either posing a kind of cultural revolutionary gesture by importing into the wrong context conventions that he knew were inappropriate, or he was performing a kind of necessary but innocent cultural 'hybridization' that is considered an inevitable strategy of minorities in a dominant culture.

Keith Miller, one of the contributers to the round table, had espoused the theological argument in a 1990 article which predates the plagiarism controversy. In 'Composing Martin Luther King, Jr.,' Miller argues that King's philosophical and theological thinking was less influenced by the European writers whom he himself alleged as the origins of his thought than by little-known theologians of the Black church. As well, 'the black folk pulpit supplied him with the rhetorical assumption that language is a common treasure – not private property – and with a well-established practice of borrowing and voice merging that he adapted to print' (71). Traditionally an oral culture, the Black pulpit tradition 'features ubiquitous and long-lived sermons' (77), where the most common source of a preacher's sermons was those of other preachers. As well as the usual arguments about the importance of repetition in oral cultures, Miller suggests that repetition permits congregational involvement and 'enhances a preacher's standing with an audience': 'In such a context the rhetorical issue is always authority, not originality; appropriateness, not personal expression; the Gospel of Jesus Christ, not the views of an individual speaker. A homilist develops authority by embracing well-loved discourse, creating a voice by melding it with those of previous speakers' (78).

If 'voice-merging' and authoritative repetition are evangelical techniques which not only assured King's position as a preacher, but could be successfully transformed into his political writings and speeches, the same practice in the context of an academic thesis does not meet with the same approval. The general consensus of the round table – not, however, unanimous – is that King's work is his life, and that this life is more than adequate restitution for the pecadillos of an immature Black student in the midst of a White institution.

The many significant differences between Ouologuem and King are too self-evident to enumerate. However, in terms of the conquest theory of plagiarism, there emerges a common ground of cultural conflict that is expressed by participants in both controversies. Whether the 'plagiarisms' are deemed politically and aesthetically intentional, or possibly 'innocent,' that is, devoid of self-conscious and negative intentionality, they are treated as culturally significant. In both cases, copying moves from the realm of the idiosyncratic and condemnable when it can be demonstrated that either the causes or the consequences transcend the personal insufficiencies of failed authorship, and when they can be seen as instances of a larger political contest between dominant and dominated groups. In King's case, the terms of the discussion are not limited to justifying or disculpating the African-American hero, although these are not insignificant elements of the discourse. Rather, a consensus is reached concerning the colonizing effects of integrationism, consequences so devastating that 'even' King was not immune to them. In this scenario, King, as a colonized Black American, is ironically divested of the agency that he was so notable for demonstrating in his subsequent career. Even in the best-case scenario, where the 'plagiarism' is portrayed as being a faithful rendering of a cultural theological authenticity while simultaneously undermining the system by 'getting away with it' – an ambiguous and subversive mimicry – the element of conscious or unconscious racist collusion on the part of his professors is presumed an essential part of the scenario. The possibility is also raised that his instructors and adviser (the latter being now dead) were simply either bad or lazy. In any case, the choice for his professors – between incompetence and reverse racism – is not a comfortable one. The point is that political elements have to be identified in order to make the plagiarism symptomatic of something other than intellectual inferiority and/or dishonesty. Both Ouologuem and King are defended, first, as victims of a colonial history, and, then, to different degrees, as having enacted either a symbolic or an effective victory over the forces of oppression.

. What happened to Ouologuem was comparable to an imaginary situation in which King's 'plagiarisms' had been 'discovered' and punished, perhaps by expulsion, which is the ultimate sanction for serious cases of academic plagiarism. Without wanting to indulge in counter-factual history, one wonders what effect such a discovery would have had on King's career. Ouologuem's novel and his plagiaristic strategies have been somewhat rehabilitated by post-colonial discourse, but too late for the author's career; King's career, which was made in spite of, and independently of, his undiscovered plagiarisms, needs no such rehabilitation. What is apparently needed in King's case is explanation rather than rehabilitation; the notion of colonial mimicry or identification with the colonizer seems sufficiently powerful to supply the needed explanation, particularly as it is one that ultimately renders culpable a systemic, non-personal kind of racism in which both colonizers and colonized are ultimately complicit. For Ouologuem, on the other hand, the evidence requires the premise of a much more self-conscious intentionality, in which the theory of colonial mimicry is raised to the level of an aesthetic strategy entailing either political intentions or effects in order not only to admit the fact of repeated and borrowed discourse, but also, subsequently, to justify it.

A useful counter-example to the cases of Ouologuem and King is that of Alexander Haley, who shares with King, albeit in a different register, a kind of heroic status in African-American culture. I have said that literary works – artistic works in general – rarely end up in court battles because of the expenses involved. Haley and the monumental suit brought against him by Harold Courlander is a notable exception, falling victim to accusations of both plagiarism and fraud, which we have already discussed. In its explanation of the success of Haley's 'hoax,' *The Village Voice* claims that there was nobody and no institution willing to challenge him. In the report of the judge's deliberations, the article claims that he was reluctant to destroy the reputation of the author of *The Autobiography of Malcolm X*, an inspiration for many young Black writers. By his last-minute apology for the unwitting borrowing of three passages from Courlander's *The African*, Haley 'got away with the plagiarism and the hoax, never apologizing, never explaining, never confessing, never feeling the heat, and smearing his few critics as racist or jealous, "gnats," "parasites," and "scorpion"' (Nobile 36). According to the same source, members of the all-white Pulitzer Prize board were affected by reverse racism in their attribution of the award. William McGill, ex-officio of the 1977 board, is cited as saying: 'We were embarrassed by our makeup. We all labored under the delusion that sudden expressions of love could make up for historical mistakes ... Of course, that's inverse racism' (36). Not only the White establishment, but also the Black intellectuals 'recoiled from treating Haley harshly' (37).

Haley's case combines elements of both Ouologuem's and King's: essentially a novelist, Haley had attained immense popular success by the time the charge was brought. His status as 'colonized' is assured not only conventionally by his race, but by his modest origins. Critics deplore, as in King's case, the meniality of attempts to discredit an acknowledged, spectacularly positive role model for African-American youth.

A more recent example of the dangers of cross-cultural borrowing is the controversy generated by Marco Micone's parodic and satiric rewriting of the famous Québécois poem 'Speak White' by Michèle Lalonde (1979). The original dates from 1969 and was read in 1970 at the first 'Nuit de la poésie,' an annual event at which Marco Micone, an Italo-Québécois writer, read, in 1993, his new 'version' of the same poem, 'Speak What.' The original poem was a revolutionary denunciation of the linguistic and economic colonization of the French Québécois by the dominant anglophone minority. A comparison between the colonization of the Québécois and other cultural communities by references to Vietnam, the Congo, Algiers, Little Rock, and Watts extends the notion of oppression beyond the English–French conflict of the Canadian situation into the international context, and the poem terminates with a call for universal solidarity among oppressed peoples: 'we know we are not alone' ['nous savons que nous ne sommes pas seuls'].

Micone's poem, about half the length of the original, starts with the same line: 'il est si beau de vous entendre parler ...' – but where Lalonde's poem cites 'Paradise Lost' and 'Shakespeare,' the neo-Québécois voice shifts the dominant cultural references to national poetic treasures of francophone Québécois culture: 'La romance du vin' (Emile Nelligan) and 'L'homme rapaillé' (Gaston Miron). The poem elaborates a systematic reversal of the role of the Québécois, who are placed in the position of oppressor rather than oppressed. Instead of the voices of the anglophone factory foremen giving orders to the francophone worker, as in Lalonde's poem, Micone's version gives us: 'vous souvenez-vous du vacarme des usines / and of the voice des contremaîtres / you sound like them more and more.' The poem ends with a *détournement* of Lalonde's last line: 'we

are a hundred peoples come from afar / to tell you that you are not alone'
['nous sommes cent peuples venus de loin / pour vous dire que vous
n'êtes pas seuls'].

The new version generated a small but interesting controversy in the
pages of the Montreal newspaper *Le Devoir* when Jacques Lanctôt,
Lalonde's publisher, accused Micone of what the latter interprets as plagiarism: 'M. Jacques Lanctôt wrote that my poem *Speak What* "is borrowed at
all points from Michèle Lalonde's famous *Speak White*, without her – nor
her publisher, in fact – having been consulted." Let's not mince words: M.
Lanctôt is accusing me of plagiarism.'[26] In his own defence, Micone has
recourse to the long tradition of legitimate literary appropriation and
defends his work as an exposé of 'today's Québécois such as transformed
by the presence of immigrants for whom the Francophones now constitute
the dominant group, in spite of the victimism and the jeremiads of a few
whining nationalists.'[27]

In a later and longer defence of the poem, Micone expresses the motivation for his appropriation as being one of promoting 'cultural sharing'
['l'appropriation culturelle comme partage'], in which not only is the
immigrant transformed by his cultural displacement, but reciprocally, the
integrating culture is transformed by the immigrant. This notion of 'sharing' is, however, 'incompatible with nationalist ideology and the ethnocen-
trism of the censors' ['la notion de partage est incompatible avec
l'idéologie nationaliste et l'ethnocentrisme des censeurs'] for whom the
only options for the immigrant are either assimilation or isolation (Micone,
'L'appropriation culturelle comme partage' 311).

A virulent denunciation supporting the accusation of plagiarism was
penned, significantly, by a neo-Québécoise of Greek origin, who qualified
the poem as a 'shameful recuperation' (Vassaramva A9). In his subsequent
response, Micone continues to defend himself in terms of literary tradition, but adds as well the defence of postmodern 'cultural appropriation,'
a practice of decontextualization 'which leads to "a critical moment generating truth"' (R. Richard in *L'Impossible* 1 [Sept. 1992]; quoted in Micone,
'Le p'tit Québec' A9). Writer Marie José Thériault also rises to Micone's
defence in literary terms, which dispense with any legal considerations:
'The poet has the right to appropriate any material which he judges necessary to his work, and Marco Micone has clearly announced the intentions
which governed his explicit borrowing of *Speak White* by Michèle
Lalonde.'[28]

This tempest in a teapot is remarkable for the sensitivity about cultural
material that it manifests. Notably, the reaction was centred not on the
threat to national culture, but on the justification of the appropriation of
this culture for the purpose of its legitimate criticism. Political correctness

seems to be the major concern of those defending the parody. The nationalist francophone Québécois in 1993 is in a sensitive position: on the verge of a referendum that was to take place in October 1995 concerning political separation from Canada, the sovereignist movement was taxed with accusations that, with respect to non-francophone minorities and to Native Canadians living within their borders, Québécois nationalists might be guilty of the same colonial crimes of which they had accused their anglophone oppressors. The voices that are not raised are most notable, as are the arguments that are not made. The offended Graeco-Québécoise speaks in purely aesthetic and ethical terms; the Québécois defence is made in purely aesthetic ones. Only the author himself broaches the question of cultural appropriation, and this argument is not taken up by the parties in the dispute. Michèle Lalonde never entered the fray, and the controversy died its own quiet death, no doubt considered rather trivial by most. But the very fact that it had such a brief life is a sign that many voices decided to avoid the issue altogether. In fact, only a 'neo-Québécois' could have successfully argued the position of the 'victim' without being accused of the colonialist mentality that Micone's poem implies. No literary defenders of the sacrosanct and impervious nature of Franco-québécois literary culture came forward to rise to its defence, and political correctness seems to have been exercised by means of a wise silence.[29]

The question of cultural appropriation has been the focus of several recent plagiarism controversies both in and out of the courts. In these disputes, it is the ethical dimension of cross-cultural borrowing that comes to the fore, as the cases fail to qualify as breach of copyright even though they arouse virulent protests that defend cultural texts as being the inviolable property of a moral person in the form of a cultural group. A notable example was the use by D.M. Thomas of Dina Pronicheva's account of her Holocaust story as recounted in Anatoli Kuznetov's *Babi Yar*. Thomas's appropriation of the first-person narrative by the Holocaust victim was not illegal, but rather, according to some, in bad taste. As one contributor to the controversy in *The Times Literary Supplement* claims, 'no writer has the moral right to take the experience of a real human being and attach it, for his or her own ends, to a made-up character, using the very words of that human being's testimony' (Tennant 412). Another reader characterizes the appropriation as 'opportunist' and criticizes it in aesthetic terms: 'it is the suspicion that the author is cleverly linking disparate materials rather than achieving an organic unity that leads readers into a mistaken attack on the "borrowings" themselves as evidence of imaginative failure' (Frost 412). Although Thomas had made reference on the copyright page to 'use of material from *Babi Yar*,' this disclaimer was deemed insufficient, at least on the part of outraged readers, to justify his borrowing, and the widow of

Kuznetzov complained to the original publishers of *The White Hotel* (Gollancz). Ironically, *Babi Yar* was reissued by Pocket Books and Penguin Books as a result of the success of *The White Hotel* (Hewison 766).

In his own defence, Thomas directly raises the question of voice: his slippage from fiction to documentary was an intentional refusal to indulge in 'some spurious "imaginative re-creation"': 'gradually the only appropriate voice becomes that voice which is like a recording camera: the voice of one who was there [...] The witness's testimony was the truthful voice of the narrative at that point' (Thomas, 'The White Hotel' 383). Recourse to the only 'truthful' voice, the refusal to 'create' a fictive 'eye-witness testimony' was a strategy designed to 'take in the unimaginable which happened' (383). The question that is not explicitly posed in this debate is whether or not his 'appropriation' of the doubly mediated testimony of Dina Pronicheva, independently of acknowledgment and permission, has *given* her, and Holocaust victims in general, a voice, or *deprived* them of one.

Thomas was subsequently accused of having 'adapted' his translation of Pushkin's 'The Bronze Horseman' from two previous translations; in the course of the allegations, innuendos were made about his previous 'plagiarism' (Thomas, 'D.M. Thomas on His Pushkin'). In his self-defence, Thomas points out that 'no one, in fact, ever dared to accuse me of plagiarism in "The White Hotel"; the only debate concerned the artistic validity of using acknowledged eyewitness testimony' (15). Nonetheless, 'plagiarism' and *The White Hotel* are closely linked in the popular imagination, and *The Times Literary Supplement* was moved, in the heat of the debate, to publish a substantial 'symposium' on plagiarism, to which were invited prestigious contributors such as Harold Bloom.

The case of *The White Hotel* never went to court. In other instances, such as in the case of *Un grand pas vers le bon dieu*, by Jean Vautrin, the accuser/ victim fails to convince the courts that a breach of copyright has occurred: copyright law does not have a category for the protection of cultural property and, in this case, the use of a Cajun language dictionary and indigenous folklore was not sufficient to convince the courts that a breach of copyright had taken place, although unacknowledged borrowing clearly had. As the judge ruled, elements of the cultural heritage of a people belong to the public domain and as such are not susceptible to appropriation (P.L. 14).

D.M. Thomas and Jean Vautrin can be dismissed either as legal but opportunistic exploiters of cultural source material, or as innocent victims of overly sensitive cultural paranoids; Micone has articulated an aesthetico-political motivation for his appropriation; the case against Ouologuem was more serious, that is, was taken more seriously by the French and European literary institution. This perceived reverse imperialism appears to have been in very poor taste, according to its accusers, and its effects are sufficient proof that conquest is a virtue only from the point of view of the conqueror. It is also proof, if one is needed, that plagiarism has the pragmatic force to produce significant results: it outraged and disturbed the literary institution to its foundations; it also, not incidentally, ended the career of its perpetrator, a colonized black African. And ironically, its *succès de scandale* has been one of the means propelling this 'failed' example of 'authentic' African literature into an important place in the post-colonial canon.

The discourse of plagiarism-as-conquest has changed its tenor and object over the course of the years since imitation, translation-as-creation and colonial conquest were considered positive cultural norms. Today, 'imperialism' carries with it unremittingly negative connotations as it is transformed from the traditional military realm to those of economy, information, and culture; 'plagiarism,' in this context, is seen as a positive antidote to the evils of cultural imperialism. And the spirit and practice of plagiarism as reverse imperialism extends in postmodern times beyond national or ethnic imperialism into a general critique of power and property in diverse contexts. Whether or not plagiarism can produce the political effects that some postmodern artists intend is difficult to say. But their efforts, as expressed in their discourse, evoke a contemporary reversal of the chauvinistic conquest metaphor that legitimized so much borrowing in the past. With the emergence of theoretical accounts of post-colonial writing, 'plagiarism' has changed its status from a kind of involuntary expression of the effects of colonialism or reverse imperialism, to an explicit and intentional strategy of employing these effects as part of the aesthetic of the work. Whether the theory enables the practice, or whether the practice has generated the theory, what we will see in the next chapter is the emergence of an interpretive community in which 'plagiarism' has achieved not only an aesthetic, but also a politically revolutionary status.

8. Guerrilla Plagiarism

> The aesthetic becomes the guerrilla tactics of secret subversion, of silent resistance, of stubborn refusal.
>
> Terry Eagleton, *The Ideology of the Aesthetic*

Plagiarism and authorship presuppose each other: a generalized kind of 'plagiarism,' no longer recognized as such, as in Borges's 'Tlön,' would be the consequence of the absence of authors, or perhaps of their death. Now that this 'death,' not only of authors, but of the individual humanist subject, has been proclaimed, or at least theorized, it follows that poststructural and postmodern plagiarism would appear to be closely allied with the disappearance of the subject upon which authorship is predicated. 'Plagiarism' might be the necessary or logical form of aesthetic production available to an author who has been deprived of the attributes of subjecthood: as we have seen, only 'non-authors' plagiarize.

The theoretical discourse of poststructuralism and postmodernism assumes a revolution of the humanist and specifically Romantic notion of subjectivity, a breaking-down of the presumed unity and indivisibility of identity, a destabilizing and multiplication of subject positions, as well as an attack on rationalist notions implying the power of mind and subjectivity to order, control, and even understand or interpret experience. In this context, the traditional discourse of authorship is undermined by the impossibility for this new 'non-subject' to actually possess any of the structuring features of individuality or subjecthood that are necessary to effect 'authorship': authenticity, originality, authority, self-expression, and even property can be the attributes of only a full and self-possessed 'subject,' the kind that is often felt to be no longer relevant, or even possible, in the late twentieth century. To the extent that this decomposition is a consequence of late capitalism itself, rather than of theoretical ruminations about it, Huyssen, for one, sees the poststructuralist denial of authorial subjectivity, subsequently adopted by postmodernism, to be asking the wrong questions: 'Isn't the "death of the subject/author" position tied by mere reversal to the very ideology that invariably glorifies the artist as genius, whether for marketing purposes or out of conviction and habit? Hasn't capitalist modernization itself fragmented and dissolved bourgeois subjectivity and authorship, thus making attacks on such notions somewhat quixotic? And, finally doesn't poststructuralism, where it simply denies the subject altogether, jettison the chance of challenging the *ideology of the subject* (as male, white and middle-class) by developing alternative and different notions of subjectivity?' (213). There is no doubt that postmodernism, not only as a theory but as a practice, has evolved in the direction recommended by Huyssen by installing in the place of the universal subject plural, differentiated, shifting, gendered, and decentred subject positions.

If plagiarism presupposes the existence of values such as intellectual property and authorship, a more fundamental presupposition upon which it rests is the notion that individuals possess stable and self-identifiable subjecthood, but which some plagiarists apparently lack. Traditional explanations of plagiarism in the works of writers such as Lowry, Coleridge, and Stendhal appeal to a disturbance of the psychic order that resembles, in many ways, postmodern descriptions of subjectivity. The psychological 'subject' of plagiarism is felt to be somehow aberrant, fissured, divided against itself, fraught with unresolved Oedipal complexes, in brief, 'unstable.' In poststructuralist culture, where the resurgence of imitative modes of creation, appropriation, and recycling of the past have become standard features of various types of aesthetic production, other kinds of explanations emerge: as simulacrum in a process of reproduction of images embedded in a consumer society (Baudrillard); as parody performing a 'critical relation to the "world" of discourse' (Hutcheon 140); and as pastiche, the result of the 'disappearance of the individual subject' and the ensuing 'unavailability of the personal style' (Jameson 16).

The imitative impulse, which appears to have accelerated in the last few decades, has been compared to previous modes of production, from the medieval copyist tradition to the neoclassical aesthetics of imitation. However, in implying a return to former practices, these comparisons inevitably suffer from an essential weakness, in that they ignore the historical position of the latter half of the twentieth century that must necessarily include all of its own past. As Bourdieu has said, 'Never has the structure of the [artistic] field been as present in each act of production' ['Jamais la structure même du champ n'a été aussi présente dans chaque acte de production' (228)]. And, one might add, with respect to poststructuralist and postmodern theories of the subject, never before has theoretical discourse from outside the artistic field itself been so instrumental in shaping that field. The self-consciousness of contemporary appropriation differs from previous artistic imitation principally in that, like the plagiarist who knows what he is doing and that it is wrong, the post-Romantic appropriative artist knows that copying others is not the proper way to be creative, original, or perhaps even legal. It is no longer a matter of the distinction between good and bad imitation, or of the proper and improper application of the rules of imitation; the operative distinction since the Romantic revolution has been between imitation and originality, that is, between copying and not copying.

Rather than a return to a previous aesthetic, the postmodern imitative impulse can be seen as the logical outcome of a subject position that has lost the attributes fundamentally constitutive of the modern notion of authorship. Or, to place postmodern appropriation in a more historical light, if the development of authorship and its modern attributes is seen, as it usually is, as concomitant to the rise of the individual 'subject' throughout the eighteenth century, then the demise of this same subject must entail an accompanying decline of authorship, manifested first of all in the loss of its attributes, of which originality, authenticity, and authority are the most important. This decline can be shown to be, for the most part, highly self-conscious on the part of those artists who practise the most extreme forms of negation of their own authorship. Within a more generalized context of postmodern recycling and appropriation, there exist examples of imitation that are hardly distinguishable from what one would normally consider plagiarism, and which have been threatened with legal sanctions for copyright infringement. The self-consciousness and overtness of these appropriations, of which Kathy Acker's plagiarisms and Sherrie Levine's photographic copies are the best examples, are indications that these practices cannot be qualified as plagiaristic in the aesthetic sense, since they presuppose neither covertness, deceit, nor dishonesty. What is explicitly being claimed in each of these examples of 'aesthetic appropriation' is that some form of 'plagiarism' is the natural or necessary mode of production of the artist as 'non-subject.' In the two cases just cited, lack of subjecthood is postulated as being both a kind of generalized postmodern condition, and the result of a specific political conjuncture, that of the woman artist working in a capitalist and phallocentric culture dominated by the male gaze and the male text. 'Lack of subjecthood' is, in this view, one result of the contradictions of late capitalism: 'This hangover from an older liberal epoch of bourgeois society [the centred, autonomous human subject] is still alive and kicking as an ethical, juridical and political category, but embarrassingly out of gear with certain alternative versions of subjectivity which arise more directly from the late capitalist economy itself' (Eagleton 377).

The self-conscious display of the absence of subjecthood in postmodern artistic productions, the absence of authorship, originality, and authenticity, as well as the flagrant contestation of the institutional and legal apparatus for determining the nature of art and authorship, are intentionally subversive expressions of conceptual precepts which demand to be recognized as such and are what I call 'guerrilla plagiarism.'

Absent subjecthood and guerrilla plagiarism are to be found linked in other contexts as well, notably in post-colonial writing adopting the ideological presuppositions of the decolonialist movement generated in the wake of the Algerian war of independence. In this case, the expression of absent subjecthood by the guerrilla tactics of plagiarism – operating in a somewhat less overt and self-conscious way – produced differing judgments about the nature and intentions of the 'plagiarism.' Both Yambo Ouologuem, and in the Québécois context, Hubert Aquin, explicitly ascribed to theories that had demonstrated the subjectless position of the colonized individual, as well as the castrating effects of domination on the colonized culture, and both produced works involving forms of plagiarism. In Ouologuem's case, the accusation of 'reverse imperialism' is sufficient testimony that his plagiarism could be and was seen as an act of aggression in a colonial war whose battlefield had shifted from the colony, where it was already lost, to cultural and, moreover, metropolitan territory.

The theme of absent subjecthood, implying the impossibility of authorship, is a constant in contemporary instances of plagiarism, whether of the explicit and aesthetic, or more covert and presumably guilty kind. If absent – or disturbed – subjecthood has long been an explanatory tool in discussions of individual cases of 'genius' plagiarists, it is equally powerful in instances where whole communities have come to a belief or realization of their subjectless status. Both postmodern and post-colonial appropriation can be seen as examples of guerrilla plagiarism for their oppositional stance with respect to prevailing aesthetics, as well as to the political ideologies that support those aesthetics. The historical difference between early post-colonialism and postmodern feminism, one perched on the threshold of the postmodern era and enacted from the outside, the other fully participating in advanced postmodernism from the inside, not only accounts for the differing critical reception of plagiarism as a crime, on the one hand, and as a potential aesthetic strategy, on the other, but also accounts for the opposition between covertness, in the earlier instance, and overtness in the latter. In the first instance, guerrilla tactics might be seen as strategic hit-and-run attacks on the subjects of power by the non-subjects of oppression;

in the second, they have become symbols of oppression in an arena that is not – or is no longer – properly a battlefield, but a rather level playing field.

REVOLUTIONARIES AND PLAGIARISTS

> In art, there are only two types of people: revolutionaries and plagiarists. And, in the end, doesn't the revolutionary's work become official, once the State takes it over?
>
> Paul Gauguin[1]

The pragmatic value of plagiarism – the specific contours of uses of plagiarism in constructing and defining power relations – is predicated on the presupposition of the pragmatic possibilities for language in general, and consequently for literature. As Edward Said has said, in the context of comparing the 'discursive situation' to the 'unequal relation between colonizer and colonized, oppressor and oppressed': 'Words and texts are so much of the world that their effectiveness, in some cases even their use, are matters having to do with ownership, authority, power and the imposition of force' (Said 48). Now the revolutionary potential of artistic works has often been disputed, defended, and doubted, both by theoreticians and by practitioners. The perennial conflict between action and reflection, the sword and the pen, has been most intensely felt by writers attempting to infuse their works with the power to translate revolutionary theory and belief into action. Decolonial theory of the 1960s, for example, ascribed a central and necessary role to revolutionary writers, who were called on 'to compose the discourse which expresses the people, to make themselves the mouth-piece of a new reality of action' ['de composer la phrase qui exprime le peuple, de se faire le porte-parole d'une nouvelle réalité en actes' (Fanon 166–7)]. At the same time, the internal contradiction between the institutionalization of art and its revolutionary potential leads Peter Bürger to conclude that 'art as an institution neutralizes the political content of the individual work' (90). In his definition of the avant-garde, Bürger contends that the 'historical avant-garde movements negate those determinations that are essential in autonomous art: the disjunction of art and the praxis of life, individual production, and individual reception as distinct from the former. The avant-garde intends the abolition of autonomous art by which it means that art is to be integrated into the praxis of life' (53–4).

While admitting avant-garde art's revolutionary or negative intentions, Bürger concurs in the widely held belief that these intentions have failed because 'it is art as an institution that determines the measure of political effect avant-garde works can have, and that art in bourgeois society continues to be a realm that is distinct from the praxis of life' (92). However one considers the relationship between avant-garde art and its potential for political or social revolution, Bürger maintains that the historical avant-garde was a 'radical negation of the category of individual creation' (51) and all of its presuppositions, and although 'the political intentions of the avant-garde movements (reorganization of the praxis of life through art) were never realized, their impact in the realm of art can hardly be overestimated. Here, the avant-garde does indeed have a revolutionary effect, especially because it destroys the traditional concept of the organic work of art' (59).

One of the consequences of this revolution was to permanently reorganize the terms of the institution of art so as effectively to negate the possibility of neo– or post–avant-garde revolutionary potential. Using Duchamp's *Ready-Mades* as an example, Bürger points out that a similar gesture today is not a denunciation of the art market but rather an adaptation to it: 'Such adaptation does not eradicate the idea of individual creativity, it affirms it, and the reason is the failure of the avant-gardiste intent to sublate art. Since now the protest of the historical avant-garde against art as institution is accepted as *art*, the gesture of protest of the neo–avant-garde becomes inauthentic. Having been shown to be irredeemable, the claim to be protest can no longer be maintained' (52–3).

As a result, neo–avant-garde art, returning to the gestures and intentions of the historical avant-garde, is fully commensurate with the institution, rather than in radical disjunction with it: 'the neo–avant-garde institutionalizes the *avant-garde as art* and thus negates genuinely avant-gardiste intentions. This is true independently of the consciousness artists have of their activity, a consciousness that may perfectly well be avant-gardiste' (Bürger 58). The relationship between the historical avant-garde and the neo–avant-garde recalls the ineluctable decadence of the moderns with respect to the ancients. Historically dispossessed of access to originality, authenticity and true genius, the moderns were inevitably relegated to a position of imitation and reprise of the always-already-there – as the catalogue of Sherrie Levine's 1993 Philadelphia exhibition 'Newborn' (after Brancusi) explains: 'Her interest in the early moments of [...] modernism reveals her own self-consciousness as an artist working in an inevitable condition of belatedness' (Temkin 11).

Bürger's attachment to considerations of 'genuine intentions' is echoed in the arguments of other critics of the 'neo–avant-garde,' particularly of postmodernist appropriation. Donald Kuspit (1994) maintains that there is a decadent relationship between this phenomenon and 'true' avant-garde art: 'Appropriation art is the death rattle of the avant-garde, or a way of dancing on its grave' (107). The critique is strongly couched in terms that divulge its refusal to engage postmodern art except in modernist terms, to treat 'neo–avant-gardism' as a 'pseudo–avant-gardism.' Kuspit's appropriation artist is inauthentic and does not respect the authenticity of what he [*sic*] appropriates; he is not open to influence or inspiration; he has a 'destructive paranoid-schizoid attitude toward the "parental" art' (107) and suffers a crisis with respect to the purpose of art; he feels that he does not exist as an artist in his own right (106–9). Kuspit sees avant-garde art as a strong assertion of the desire for subjective and emotional wholeness leading to a process of social transformation and healing: 'The denial of the subjectivity implicit in avant-garde art is a particularly important accomplishment of pseudo-avant-garde art, in line with the general denial of subjectivity in modern society' (112). Kuspit relies for the last judgment on Adorno, and quotes, among other evidence, Adorno's statement: 'In art, the true point of reference continues to be the subject' (Adorno 63; cited by Kuspit, 170, n. 32), a point he makes in the context of a critique of Lukacs's attack on modern art. According to Adorno, Lukacs has confused aesthetics and the theory of knowledge, applying the solipsism of bourgeois epistemology to the appearance of the same in art: 'In art, the true point of reference continues to be the subject, whereas in epistemology, solipsism's emphasis on subjectivity is a mere pretence' (Adorno 63).

Kuspit, for his part, confuses the neo–avant-garde reference to subjectivity with its denial. I would concur rather with Adorno in his belief about the continuance of the importance of the reference to the subject and extend this reference into the realm of postmodern appropriative art, while keeping in mind the terms of the 'crisis' of subjectivity that this reference entails. Kuspit's analysis of the 'inauthenticity' of neo–avant-garde is in fact applicable to postmodern appropriative art, but where he sees a kind of failure of authenticity by a self-deluded denial of true artistic feeling and intention, one might see rather a heightened self-consciousness with respect to the conflict between the subject-position of the artist, on one hand, and the imperatives or presuppositions concerning aesthetic production and producer in contemporary society, on the other. It is perhaps true that one of the components of the post-modern reflection on the artist is a 'feeling of not existing as an artist in his [*sic*] own right' (Kuspit 109). However, Kuspit describes the ironic appropriations of the neo–avant-garde art as 'a sad way of avoiding' these feelings, a misreading that is grounded in a firm commitment to the humanist notion of subjecthood. Rather than denial, appropriative art enacts an explicit confrontation and exposure of these feelings, in a gesture that at once asserts the desire for full and present subjecthood, and the social, political and aesthetic impossibility of its existence. Thus Kuspit's assessment of appropriation art's 'most socially constructive achievement,' that is, its 'defeat of avant-garde art's radical expressivity' (113) is based on a misreading of appropriation as a denial of subjectivity, rather than as a statement of subjectivity in crisis.

In the program of revolutionary art as promoted by the decolonial theories of such authors as Memmi and Fanon, true liberation is necessarily preceded by a self-conscious knowledge of the extent of one's submission and dispossession. Authentic subjectivity can only be achieved through the process of fully assuming the (non)-subject position of the oppressed that is the condition of the colonized. For the revolutionary artist, this means, in addition, revealing to one's compatriots the true nature of their oppression in order to bring them to the self-consciousness required for the revolution. It is in this light of self-conscious assertion of the crisis in subjectivity *as crisis* that certain forms of postmodern appropriative art can be considered 'revolutionary.' But whereas the truly revolutionary model proposes the self-consciousness of non-identity as a necessary moment in a dynamic process towards the construction of an authentic identity, the postmodern subject, divided, plural, and always in movement, is not construed as a negative moment in such a reconstructive process. The postmodern subject is rather the realization of a permanent condition of inherent negativity, nonetheless capable of a creative dynamics that is profoundly assertive of its own, albeit negative, subjectivity.

The appropriative work of Mike Bidlo – for example, his painstaking copies of Picasso – has been understood in terms of the examination of the artist's ego in the creative process, and described in a way which evokes a comparison with classical and Renaissance theories of imitation, where the author's identity is subject to a process of *emulation* of the master's soul. Bidlo's art is immersed in the futility of trying to manifest the 'invisible, intangible entity [that] is the soul of the artist whose work he appropriates. To this extent the focus of his attention in actuality is not the external constituents of the original that he chooses to copy but rather the modern master who produced it, or more precisely, the ethereal qualities inherent in the master's inimitable technique – what used to be called the "master's touch" and is now referred to, for lack of a better term, as one's *style*' (Costa 77).

In classical theory, the process of emulation is not a straightforward question of imitation; the imitator must maintain his own individuality and impress the imitation with his own distinctive identity. The goal of emulation is a kind of self-improvement by the assimilation of the soul of genius in which the self and the other are fused in a mutually transformative process resulting in a 'new' work which enhances the virtues of the original by the distinctive filter of the imitating artist. In the comparison between Bidlo's appropriation theory and classical imitation theory, what emerges is a direct reversal on the level of the intention of Bidlo's imitations, on the one hand, and a remarkable similarity in product, on the other. Bidlo's intentions are to eliminate the subjective moment in appropriation, to enact a kind of 'servile imitation' in which the self is completely submerged in the soul of the other. The ironic inevitability, especially for theories maintaining the subjectless nature of postmodern appropriation, is that his own ego 'becomes a necessary component in a process the intent of which is ironically to sublimate the appropriator's own ego in the form of the modern master's persona' (77). As Bidlo himself says: 'The thing about my work is that in a funny way it's always doomed to failure. No matter how hard I try, a work of appropriation can never become the original; I know that when I start painting. Only Picasso can paint *Guernica*, and he could do it once – I can try, but I would have to suppress my ego, and ultimately that's impossible. The intrusion of the ego always gets in the way of my becoming Picasso' (quoted in Costa 77). The inevitable failure of Bidlo's attempts to eliminate all traces of his own ego from his appropriations is a postmodern study in the profoundly subjective – that is, authorial – nature of artistic production.

In the same way, but from the opposite direction, Cindy Sherman's self-portraits have been analysed as an exploration of the artist's 'anti-self.' In a reading that confirms the revolutionary – or psychotherapeutical – program of achieving ideal subjectivity through painful self-consciousness, one commentator of a 1987 retrospective sees in her work an expression of 'the Romantic principle that only through acceptance of the soul's dark side can a person become spiritually whole' (Johnson 49). In Sherman's case, this voyage towards 'spiritual wholeness' involves a dark descent into the 'antimirror' of 'rot and decay – a wasteland of shit' (53). In the tradition of the most revolutionary art, her self-portraiture is seen as a form of psychoanalysis in which she has been seeking 'the worst in herself, and the worst in the American soul': 'Becoming the other, she therapeutically releases the contents of psychic disturbance through the clarifying sanity of a prolifically inventive and witty theatrical, photographic and artistic practice. Thus, she raises into consciousness – into her own personal consciousness *and* into communal consciousness – material that she might tend to repress in herself and that certainly would be repressed by official culture and media' (Johnson 53). Whatever can be said of the subject-position of the postmodern artist, it is difficult to credit the view that this art performs Kuspit's 'sad way of avoiding' the contradictions implied in the (for him) oxymoron 'the postmodern artist.'

The question of whether postmodernism is, or can be, anything like 'revolutionary' or 'oppositional' is traditionally framed in discussions about its relationship to modernism and the avant-garde. The camps are divided according to whether they consider modernism itself as fundamentally revolutionary or reactionary: the ideological fate of postmodernism is determined by one's allegiance to its predecessor.[2] But the question can also be asked as to whether comparisons between postmodernism and the historical avant-garde, ultimately positing its relationship to modernism, are aesthetically or historically justifiable. Proponents of postmodernism, such as Rosalind Krauss, see a historical divide between the two, based on postmodernism's deconstruction of the notions of origin and originality. For Krauss, radical originality is the central postulate of the avant-garde, which perceived originality as 'a literal origin, a beginning from ground zero, a birth' (157). Avant-garde art would be truly solipsistic, proceeding from the myth of absolute self-origin 'safe from contamination by tradition because it possesses a kind of originary naiveté' (157); the postmodern, specifically appropriative critique of the discourse of originality would thus be situated on the other side of the 'historical divide' separating a desire for and belief in originality from its impossibility.

More nuanced positions, such as Andreas Huyssen's, situate postmodernism in a less bipolar relationship to the 'great divide' and postulate both continuities and ruptures between modernism, avant-gardism, and postmodernism; in particular, he calls for the salvaging of the critical and oppositional potential for postmodernism, which, while it may in fact be a condition and even a product of late capitalism, is not thereby necessarily condemned to complete collusion with it: 'If the postmodern is indeed a historical and cultural condition (however transitional or incipient), then oppositional cultural practices and strategies must be located *within* postmodernism, not necessarily in its gleaming façades, to be sure, but neither in some outside ghetto of a properly "progressive" or a correctly "aesthetic" art' (Huyssen 200).

Huyssen sees one of the virtues of postmodernism residing precisely in its ability to counter what he calls the 'modernist litany of the death of the subject by working toward new theories and practices of speaking, writing and acting subjects' (213). For him, the 'death of the subject' is a modernist moment, in so far as poststructuralism is essentially a theory of modernism. If he is right, then postmodernism, including its appropriative strategies, is about something other than the confirmation of late-modernist absent subjecthood.

It is not my purpose to investigate the avant-garde status of appropriative art, or to defend it in terms of authenticity or originality, and even less to enter into the debate about the relationship between modernism and postmodernism that Linda Hutcheon has summarized (1988). In fact, my discussion could just as well dispense with the question of postmodernism altogether, if it weren't that the aesthetic practice of appropriation presupposes the theoretical discourses of poststructuralism and postmodernism. What is rather more interesting is the revolutionary potential of appropriation art, especially those forms of it which cross the uncertain boundary unevenly dividing 'appropriation' from 'plagiarism.' If there is a link between postmodernism and the avant-garde, it is situated perhaps most clearly on the level of intentionality; that is, in the programmatic statements of both avant-garde and appropriative artists with respect to the pragmatic functions of their art. Statements by Sherrie Levine, for example, explicitly evoke the avant-garde aim of the dissolution of the distinction between 'high' and 'low' art: 'I would like you to experience one of those privileged moments of aesthetic negation, when high art and popular culture coalesce. I would like high art to shake hands with its cynical nemesis – kitsch, which in its sentimentality makes a mockery of desire. I would like the meaning of this work to become so overdetermined and congealed that it implodes and brokers a new paradigm' (quoted in Temkin 7).

In the examples of postmodern appropriation/plagiarism I have chosen, aesthetic negation enacts a kind of permanent pre-revolutionary moment whose goal is the examination of the negative condition of the subject, rather than the positive transformation of social, political, or cultural conditions. These efforts could be more properly seen as subversive rather than revolutionary, as purely contestary moments of opposition rather than assertive gestures of revolution. Rather than revolutionaries, one could see postmodern appropriative artists as 'rebels without a cause' – expressing a condition of oppositionality but without the revolutionaries' program for installing a new political or social order of power. In strategically enacting the 'death' of the artistic subject in its humanist form, appropriation performs at the same time the impossibility of non-authorship – the inscription of absent subjecthood on the level of form and content is emphatically reversed on the level of the signature as the name of the artist enters into the processes of aesthetic institutionalization and commodification. Postmodern plagiarism in literature has been approvingly called a kind of 'terrorism'; I prefer to characterize it as a guerrilla tactic of a subversionary movement whose value lies in its pure oppositionality to dominant power – in other words, whose importance lies in the pressure it exerts against the institutions it attacks, but without which it could not exist. As Eagleton has it, 'All "oppositional" identities are in part the function of oppression, as well as of resistance to that oppression' (414).

Bürger has pointed out that the success of the avant-garde has already aestheticized oppositionality to the point where it is conventionally institutional. At the same time, the historical avant-garde has entrenched the value of originality to the point where it coincides with the very notion of art. If the 'original artist cannot copy' (Cocteau), then neither can the artist who copies escape the epithet of originality, as we will see. Postmodern 'plagiarism' is threatened by the same paradox as that of revolutionary art in general; the very fact of its becoming 'art' in the complex of the institutional structure is a necessary negation or neutralization of its revolutionary potential. But Gauguin's distinction between plagiarists and revolutionaries entails that the only true revolutionaries are plagiarists, for only they will ever escape the fate of becoming official in being taken over by the state. Eagleton, for his part, expresses a cynical attitude with respect to the possibility that 'art' can escape recuperation: 'How idealist to imagine that *art*, all by itself, could resist incorporation! The question of appropriation has to do with politics, not with culture; it is a question of who is winning at any particular time. If *they* win, continue to govern, then it is no doubt true that there is nothing which they cannot in principle defuse and contain. If *you* win, they will not be able to appropriate a thing because you will have appropriated them' (p. 372).[3]

What will be clear in what follows is that postmodern 'plagiarism' is enacted with the explicit intent that it *be* revolutionary, and that it perform subversive work with respect to instances of authority that exceed the purely aesthetic: postmodern plagiarism is intended to expose the complex nexus of power relations that are simultaneously aesthetic, political, cultural, social, and economic.

I have already distinguished between covert and overt plagiarism in terms of both the producer's and the receiver's intentionality and argued that it is the receiver's intentionality that is crucial for the determination of the existence of plagiarism, even in the face of explicit claims for or against the intention to plagiarize on the part of the producer. This means that an artist can no more intend to plagiarize and succeed, than she can intend *not* to plagiarize and thereby escape accusations of plagiarism. It is generally considered that a certain level of covertness is required for 'genuine' (negative) plagiarism, while a sufficient level of visibility can negate charges of plagiarism by appealing to the presupposition of intentionality: if the producer intended the receiver to perceive the borrowing, this cannot be a genuine instance of plagiarism. The aesthetic conventionality of appropriation has already been solidly established by the equation between oppositionality and aesthetic value, the latter being independent of judgments about 'artistic merit.' 'Plagiarism' intended for aesthetic revolutionary purposes has also already been assimilated into the infinitely malleable institution as its own salutory moment of self-critique. But appropriation is also subject to the copyright distinction between plagiarism and breach of intellectual property law: aesthetic – or revolutionary – intent is not a defence against legal sanctions. It may be that aesthetic uses of plagiarism may now only be potentially revolutionary in the event that they risk infringing copyright.

Before looking at some instances of guerrilla plagiarism (covert and overt) it will be informative to explore briefly the most radically programmatic example of Gaugin's distinction between plagiarists and revolutionaries, that is, the belief in plagiarism as the last possibility of aesthetic subversion. These manifestations are known as the 'Festivals of Plagiarism,' held in 1988 in London, Glasgow, Braunschweig (Germany), and San Francisco. The festivals included Xerox and video art, as well as 'Free-Form Discussions,' and musical and other performance art spectacles. Stewart Home, the originator of the London festival, produced a pamphlet to advertise and accompany it, entitled *Plagiarism: Art as Commodity and Strategies for Its Negation* (1987) in which he and his collaborators, often adopting pseudonymous or collective names, express their 'left opposition to dominant culture' that 'claims to be "universal" when it is very clearly class based' (Home, *Plagiarism* 3). The text constitutes a manifesto in favour of plagiarism as a weapon against the domination of capital, and against the role played by the 'unique' in capitalist culture in promoting the commodification of 'art.' Plagiarism is placed in opposition to 'postmodernism' which is taxed with being simply a recuperation of actions that might threaten the very constitution of the establishment, a critique that is familiar from Bürger's analyses of the neo–avant-garde. As opposed to 'postmodern appropriation,' which 'falsely asserts that there is no longer any basic reality, the plagiarist recognizes that Power is always a reality in historical society' ('Karen Eliot,' in Home, *Plagiarism* 5).[4] The plagiarist is also dedicated to eradicating the elitist myth of genius, which gained popularity during the triumph of the bourgeoisie: plagiarism is seen as a 'concomitant of Romantic formulations of Genius' (Beard, in Home 6). The commodification of art is determined by the 'concepts of value based in labour time and the difficulty of production, i.e. the political-economic rock of capitalism' that it is the intent of the 'Plagiarist' to subvert (Beard 6). On this basis, 'the forces of order have contrived to make plagiarism of recent texts illegal, making the risk of prosecution a deterent even to the most dedicated plagiarist' (Home 6). In this context, plagiarism is an act of subversion of these forces and its analysis reveals the contradictions inherent in bourgeois society: contradictions based on the value accorded to work time and effort expended in production, for example, that of institutionalized waste. The commodification of art requires that the means of production of art, much less the product, not be available to all: 'Art is a commodity relation, and the admission of art by all onto the market would cause a drastic fall in the rate of profit' ('Bob Jones,' in Home 7).

'Art' is individualistic and emphasizes ownership and creation, whereas plagiarism 'is rooted in social process, communality, and a recognition that society is far more than the sum of individuals (both past and present) who

constitute it' ('Bob Jones,' in Home 7). In the context of bourgeois individualism, art inhibits the 'development of a collective inter-subjectivity which
could transform the world' ('Bob Jones,' in Home 7). A particularly revealing paragraph will serve to capture the spirit and aims of the Festival of Plagiarism:

> It is here, in the creation of new meanings, that we see most clearly the
> divergence between plagiarism and post-modern ideology. The plagiarist
> has no difficulty with meanings, reality, truth. The plagiarist sees no crisis of
> the sign – only the continual transformation of human relationships within
> a social context. When a post-modernist talks of plagiarism they [*sic*] call it
> 'appropriation' (transfer of ownership) in an attempt to maintain the ideo-
> logical role of the artist. As Capitalism sinks further into crisis, it becomes
> increasingly difficult for any 'individual' artist to exude an appearance of
> 'originality.' Reacting to this 'impossible' situation the post-modernist takes
> on a 'corporate' image and 'copyrights' an ill-digested assortment of frag-
> ments. This is in direct contrast to the plagiarist who, rather than accepting
> this stasis, seeks to speed up the process of decay, and opposes both mod-
> ernism AND post-modernism (which are but two stages in the trajectory of
> Capital) with the totality of communist transformation [...]
> Plagiarism deals with the connectedness of things. ('Bob Jones,' in
> Home 8)

   Apart from the leftist rhetoric, one also recognizes echoes of Dadaism
and of the Situationists International, which some of the texts explicitly
invoke, especially in the use of the technique of *détournement* or the displacing of a text into another context where the meaning is changed or undermined, turning itself back on the dominant culture that produced it.
Lautréamont and his surrealistic future are also often invoked: many texts
quote or *détournent* his famous aphorism: 'Plagiarism is necessary. Progess
implies it.'
   A dissenting view from the one expressed above is formulated in another
essay in the 'Festival of Plagiarism' document. Contesting the notion that
plagiarists suffer no crisis of the sign, one contributor puts it this way: 'Perhaps plagiarism becomes useful at a time when the display of "meaningful"
images actually provides evidence of the lack of any "truth." The reality of
so-called post-modern conditions, of the present crisis, consists of a generalized inability to distinguish between meanings which are of any use and
those which are of no use at all. Plagiarism may hammer home this point,
by demonstrating the apparent lack of meaning and by emphasising the
materiality of things as they exist – rather than their evident or supposed
meaning' ('Waldemar Jyroczech,' in Home 25).

Stewart Home concludes the pamphlet with 'A Short Reflection on the Festival of Plagiarism,' where he evaluates the event in terms of his own expectations that 'cultural work can contribute towards social change' (30). The evaluation is largely negative because, first of all, his liberalness in opening the festival to all who applied undercut his ability to make a radical critique, and transformed his intention to reject 'elitist' art into the appearance of striving for its democratization. Second, he made the mistake of soliciting legitimate art spaces in which to hold the exhibitions, thereby attracting artists who sought to gain entry into the art world, rather than to critique it, thus compromising the festival's purpose. Home admits: 'Before holding the Festival I had naïvely imagined that it was possible to use platforms of privilege to make a critique of privilege' (30).[5]

Home's initial disappointment is understandable, and a necessary corollary to his own criticism of the establishment's ability to co-opt or recuperate potentially subversive forces into its relations of power. And yet, what is not clear, is exactly what pragmatic effects Home would envision as constituting 'success' in terms of the goals of the festival. In his short introduction to the pamphlet, Home declares that he hopes that both it and the festival 'will go some way towards demonstrating that there has been an opposition to art since the term took on its modern meaning in the eighteenth century' (3). The consequences of this realization, if one accepts it, are, however, far from evident.

Perhaps this radical attempt at using plagiarism as the last bastion of revolutionary aesthetics remains a marginal event in contemporary aesthetics precisely because of the imperviousness of the aesthetic institution to all of its non-components: there seems to be no median position between the obscurity or invisibility of 'anti-art,' and the diffusing of revolutionary potential by the institutionalization of 'art.' As Eagleton says: '[Anti-art] is not appropriable by the ruling order because – the final cunning – it isn't art at all. The problem with this, however, is that what cannot be appropriated and institutionalized because it refuses to distance itself from social practice in the first place may by the same token abolish all point of purchase upon social life' (371).

The 'Festivals of Plagiarism' attracted little attention, in spite of reviews in various venues, and Home's own analysis reveals the fundamental impasse that the revolutionary impulse encounters in its attempts to produce 'anti-art' as an opposition to institutional forms of power. Indeed, the festival's publications document disagreements expressed by organizers and participants with respect to the revolutionary status of the event. As one of the texts included in the San Francisco publication contends: 'Is copyright being plagiarized and subverted here, or is plagiarism being copyrighted? [...] The challenging of existing authorities and institutions is often only the pretext, the occasion, the means by which alternate authorities and counter-institutions are raised up in their place' ('Professor X,' in Perkins 13). And the 'professor' cites Sherrie Levine, Barbara Kruger, and other appropriationists as a case in point, for they 'derive authority (not to mention money) from their identities as plagiarizers; they claim to contest the commodification of art but only by presenting their contestation as one more set of commodities. And so the post-modernist circus goes round and round milling thru the grinder its spiral of "self-reflexive non-sequiturs"' ('Professor X,' in Perkins 14). This voice also attributes the 'radical nullity of the current, would-be-oppositional culture' to the legacy of the historical avant-garde and its simultaneous and ambivalent submission to the art establishment, on the one hand, and its alliance with the 'authoritarian left,' on the other ('Professor X,' in Perkins 14).

The example of the Festivals of Plagiarism is useful for the explicitness of their politically revolutionary intention, as well as for the internal disputes that underline the difficulty of enacting opposition to the institutions of capital, including the artistic institution. In his evaluation of the 1988 London event, Stewart Home cites a critique levelled against the project by one of its organizers, who claimed that the festival both was 'ignored by the establishment' and 'recuperated by the art world.' Home calls this criticism 'ludicrous since, given the context, these categories are mutually exclusive' (Home 22). While one might suspect that the festivals were more 'ignored' than 'recuperated,' these two fates are probably, in the long run, mutually exclusive. Neither have the revolutionary social and political consequences intended by the organizers of the festivals yet materialized, no doubt because of the degree to which they were able to be ignored, which is only partly a consequence of their ephemeral nature, one of the anti-institutional tactics of the avant-garde. The Festivals of Plagiarism failed both as political and as aesthetic revolution; but the radical difference between the 'failure' of the Festivals of Plagiarism and the alleged 'failure' of the avant-garde is surely a consequence of the latter's ability to be recuperated. The frontiers of the aesthetic institution, as well as the borders between it and larger cultural, social, and political power structures are only successfully permeated and subsequently redrawn by virtue of the cannibalistic nature of the institution, which recognizes no space outside of itself in which to enact the possibility of opposition. Artistic revolution, even that which is radically political in intention, may only hope to succeed if its 'purchase on social life' is sufficient to undermine the autonomy that the historical avant-garde failed to destroy, that is, that it succeed in eliminating the radical separation between the aesthetic and daily life. The inefficacy of the Festivals of Plagiarism may have been due to their rather too exclusive involvement in everyday life, and their lack of involvement with 'art': visitors to the festival were invited to produce Xerox art and participate on all levels of the event, to the point that its organizers claimed that some, at least, were converted from spectators to participants. The ideal of the dissolution of art, which ultimately became confused with its democratization, was the failure of the historical avant-garde; in becoming art, it subsequently had a lasting and revolutionary effect on the institutional structure of the aesthetic world. The Festivals of Plagiarism, on the other hand, in failing to become art, failed absolutely.

Effective oppositional art has been compared to the 'Trojan Horse' (Lippard 341–58). If, in order to defuse subversion, the aesthetic institution is forced to incorporate into itself its most dangerous moments of negativity, then the only true revolutionary position from which to effect aesthetic opposition may be on the inside.

THE NON-SUBJECT AS PLAGIARIST: THE SUBJECT OF COLONIZATION

The question of the revolutionary potential of art and the inevitably allied attempt to produce 'non-art' or 'anti-art' is pertinent to the radical evolution which Québécois literature underwent during the fervent decade of 1960s known as the 'Quiet Revolution.' For a generation of young intellectuals and artists, the cause of political independence for Quebec, its liberation from a colonized present resulting from its colonial history, and the necessity for a new aesthetic direction were inseparably linked. Literature became 'revolutionary,' both in subject and in form, and in conformity with doctrine inherited from Memmi and Fanon, it was invested with the status of a revolutionary weapon, a 'bomb,' a political act. 'Non-poems' (Miron) and 'anti-literature' became the order of the day: the deconstruction of the traditional narrative form, the use of dialect, slang, and blasphemy, as well as the explicit portrayal of subjects formerly censored by the conservative Catholic dominant ideology created a literary and cultural atmosphere that was compared to the acts of terrorism perpetrated by some of the most radical members of the separatist movement. The 'Quiet Revolution' is the origin of the contemporary 'Québécois,' who emerged from 'la grande noirceur'[6] – the great darkness or the 'Dark Ages' – possessed by a desire to assert a national identity free both from the conservatism of its past and the dominance of Anglo-American culture and economy.

It is in this context, in 1968 (the same year as Yambo Ouologuem published his ill-fated novel Le devoir de violence), that Québécois writer Hubert Aquin published his second novel, Trou de mémoire (Blackout). Like his first published work, Prochain épisode (1965), this novel presents a Québécois separatist engaged in a revolutionary struggle for the independence of

Quebec. In *Trou de mémoire*, a sustained analogy between the Québécois character Pierre X. Magnant, and his counterpart from the Côte d'Ivoire, Olympe Guezzo-Quénum, makes explicit the similarities between the colonial condition of Africa and that of Quebec, and the consequences of this colonization for the characters in the novel. Aquin himself adopted the decolonial ideologies promulgated by such writers as Franz Fanon and Albert Memmi. In *Portrait du colonisé* ([1957] 1972), Memmi describes the colonial subject as disempowered and dispossessed; deprived, in fact, of the status of subjecthood.[7] In *Les damnés de la terre* (*The Wretched of the Earth* [1961] 1966), Fanon sees the colonized culture as being condemned, before the revolution, to a culture of 'unqualified assimilation' ['C'est la période assimilationiste intégrale'] in which the only way the colonized can attain a cultural status is to mimic the dominant culture (Fanon, 166). Aquin's explicit engagement with this discourse in *Trou de mémoire* is evident in the identity crises suffered by both his anti-heroes. At the same time, the novel thematizes problems of authorial identity, authenticity, and plagiarism, as each successive narrator glosses and contradicts the former, accusing each other of falsifying the autobiographical discourse that comprises the principal text, of inserting apocryphal writing, and of plagiarism.

Since Aquin's death in 1977, studies of his work have uncovered considerable 'plagiarisms,' both in *Trou de mémoire* and in his subsequent novel *L'antiphonaire* (1969), notably from historical, scientific, or encyclopedic sources. His extra-fictional commentary is explicit, not about 'plagiarism' as such, but about a kind of collage technique of rewriting, so that together with the thematization of these problems in the novel, the practice is easily assimilable to an intentional aesthetic, one that has been characterized as an example of the postmodern in Québécois writing.[8] A central theme in both his novels and essays is the problem of originality, its impossibility and the ineluctable search for it on the part of writers. He arrives at the conclusion that

> the originality of a piece of work is directly proportional to the ignorance of its readers. There is no originality: works of literature are reproductions (which serve a purpose of course in a society with large amounts of spare time to kill and blessed, moreover, with pulp) run off from worn out plates made from other 'originals' reproduced from reproductions that are true copies of earlier forgeries that one does not need to have known to understand that they were not archetypes but simply variants. A cruel invariability governs the mass production of those variants that go by the name of original works. History, too, copies itself. Originality is as impossible there as in literature. Originality does not exist; it is a delusion. ('Occupation: Writer,' in Purdy 51)[9]

Evoking the Mallarmean 'elocutory disappearance of the author,' Aquin also questions the role of authorial subjectivity in the writing – and consequently reading – process:

> I have found that, in contemporary books published in Quebec and elsewhere, the author's presence is all too noticeable. The book ends up being contaminated by the presence of its author, to the point where the whole activity of reading revolves around whether one loves or hates the author's actual person. I have come to the conclusion that what we need is to practice absence, so that books are not lost sight of by virtue of being mired in considerations such as these. I even go so far as to wonder whether the ultimate literary innovation would not be a return to anonymity: anonymous authors for anonymous readers. ('The Disappearance in Language of the Poet [Mallarmé],' in Purdy 111)[10]

This aesthetic has been characterized by Aquin as 'writing in the margins,' and implies a writing subject overdetermined by a complex of cultural influences, whose colonial condition entails the production of a multiplicity of identities, none of which corresponds to the colonized subject's 'authentic' identity: 'Imagine some poor guy suddenly vested with the powers of the many: all at once his most pleasing sensations fade away, his original thoughts grow dull, his subtle tastes melt into thin air' ('The Text or the Surrounding Silence,' in Purdy 119).[11] And between the self and the text there is a necessary mimetism: 'The text is written continuously in the text or in the margins of another text. The self is an intertext, and consciousness of the self a chaotic commentary – marginalia which are sometimes imperceptible but always formative, always originating' ('The Text or the Surrounding Silence,' in Purdy 119).[12]

According to Aquin and his revolutionary colleagues, the 'French Canadian' is a colonized non-subject whose identity is overdetermined by the superimposition of the Canadian present on the French past. However, this double identity is inauthentic; the term 'Québécois' was adopted during the 1960s to describe an authentic subject who is neither Canadian nor French, much less the fusion of these two. And yet Aquin maintains the use of the term 'French Canadian' to denote the dispossession of authentic identity produced by the colonial history of the nation. The French-Canadian author/revolutionary, as imagined by Aquin and incarnated in *Trou de mémoire* in his fictional alter-ego Magnant, was a tormented and essentially impotent non-subject, driven to symbolic acts of erotic violence devoid of truly revolutionary import, and compulsively recording his revolutionary reflections in convoluted and 'anamorphic' prose, analysed within the novel as symptomatic of a complex of psychological disturbances related to various personality disorders.

Aquin expounds a negative theory of subjecthood derived from decolonial theory, but rather than proposing a 'littérature engagée' in the revolutionary sense, he espouses a theory of 'art for art' in which the work becomes the incarnation of the writing subject, the creation of a consciousness which mirrors that of the Québécois author whose identity, as analysed by Aquin, is the equivalent of a vacuum: 'I maintain, against all likelihood, that I am a living writer; and I am going to carry on – insofar as I can follow through on this plan of existence – writing increasingly futile variations on the nothingness of which we writers are the indomitable embodiment. Our endeavour can be compared to an attempt – of uncertain appeal – to give form to an inner vacuity which, by that very fact, we take a certain pleasure in flaunting [...]' ('The Death of the Accursed Writer,' in Purdy 93–4).[13]

The question of plagiarism as it appears thematized in *Trou de mémoire* occupies an ambiguous status: the plagiarized passages could be attributed both to the fictional characters who produce them in the novel, and to the author Aquin. However, the first option is rarely entertained, because of the transgression of the boundaries of fiction implied or required by the notion of a fictional character 'plagiarizing' a text from the 'real' world. But such a transgression is already explicitly part of the fiction, as several of the narrators, two of whom also function as 'editors' of the autobiographical journal within the novel, encumber the text with footnotes to actual texts, notably to psychological studies. The erudition that is woven into *Trou de mémoire*, and sometimes represents wholesale copying, is usually attributed by critics to the real author, and not to his characters. To a certain extent, the question of attribution is immaterial, since the psychological condition of the characters laid out in the novel is clearly to be interpreted as that of the colonized Québécois, a non-identity that the author firmly believed to be his own. Whether attributed to the fictional characters or to the real author, the plagiarism appears as a literal and literary consequnce of the theories of non-identity and cultural imitation expounded by the colonial theorists whom Aquin had studied. While the existence of copied passages in *Trou de mémoire* is indisputable, so that something like 'plagiarism' can be said to be an intentional feature of the novel, what is not clear is whether the relationship between the structure of the colonial identity and the presence of plagiarism were part of Aquin's intentions, or whether this connection is a result of interpretation. If the former were the case, plagiarism would have not only an aesthetic rationalization, confirming the author's often repeated belief in the impossibility of originality, but also a political one: plagiarism would be both an indication and a result of the cultural and personal condition of the colonized non-subject, functioning on the structural level of the novel in the same way as the discourse of authorial instability and inauthenticity – and of plagiarism – functions on the thematic level.

It is at this point that a comparison with Ouologuem becomes interesting. At first glance, the coincidences of the novels' simultaneous year of publication and subsequent success, the themes of colonization, and the presence of plagiarism are about all they have in common. Aquin was pursuing a successful literary career, his novel was awarded the highest Canadian literary prize, the Governor General's Award (refused on political grounds), and there was no suspicion of plagiarism, or at least no discovery of it. Ouologuem, on the other hand, following a similar institutional success, was soundly denounced. And there was an additional piece of evidence uncovered in the African's case that lent credence to the intentionality of his plagiarism, as well as to its possible political motivations. At the time, this evidence contributed to the legitimacy of his accusers' claims; for later readers, it indicates an implicit relationship posited by these 'colonized' or 'postcolonial' writers between plagiarism and their self-consciousness concerning their identity or, as we have seen, non-identity.

In the same year as the publication of *Le devoir de violence*, Ouologuem had produced a collection of polemical essays entitled *Lettre à la France nègre* (1968). One of the 'letters,' addressed to 'Les pisse-copie Nègres d'écrivain célèbres' (165–79),[14] is a humorous and satirical piece of advice to African writers who want to become authors, but who, as Jaucourt would have it, lack the means. This failure is, of course, not attributable to the lack of talent of African writers but implicitly to their colonial condition. First, Ouologuem advises them to stick to the mystery or detective novel, a secondary form of fiction best suited to their subaltern condition (coincidentally, *Trou de mémoire* is a also a kind of detective novel). Second, he develops a system to enable African authors to produce at great speed a large number of successful novels. This is a system of plagiarism, demonstrated in the essay, which involves collecting passages from famous mystery novels and rating them according to the degree of effects of a particular type they are likely to produce, such as violence, eroticism, or suspense. The successful African mystery writer need only call upon such a catalogue of plagiarized passages in order to concoct best-selling novels. This essay was cited in the plagiarism controversy as evidence that in *Le devoir de violence*, Ouologuem had evidently followed his own advice, and that the novel was a cynical product of this plagiaristic system (Sellin, 'Ouologuem's Blueprint' 120). The conclusion is a tempting one, and could be cited as evidence of leaving clues at the scene of the crime, a practice attributed to many allegedly guilt-ridden plagiarists.

Whether or not his plagiarisms in *Le devoir de violence* were an intentional application of this system, whether or not he thought he was plagiarizing, and whether or not these plagiarisms had an aesthetic intent, as he was later to argue, is not part of my study to decide. What Ouologuem's essay does suggest is that the connection between the condition of the colonized writer as non-subject and the necessity of plagiarism was clearly and explicitly present in his imagination. We do not have the psychological evidence required to make judgments about either Aquin's or Ouologuem's personal motivations for engaging in 'plagiarism,' any more than we have evidence about whether their 'true' intentions were indeed plagiaristic, aesthetic, or even political. The coincidence between the two cases is important, however, in allowing us to extend the implications of these 'plagiarisms' beyond their possible individual psychological causes. Without information about the authors' personal intentions, speculation about the use of plagiarism as a kind of guerrilla warfare perpetrated for intentional revenge against the dominant culture must remain merely speculation. What can, however, be concluded is that regardless of their conscious intentions with respect to 'plagiarism,' both Aquin and Ouologuem arrived at the same literary expression of a colonial condition of which it is clear that both were highly conscious, that is which both accepted as culturally true.

Both Aquin and Ouologuem were aware of their subjectless status because of their *engagement* with the same decolonial discourses that proclaimed it, and both had demonstrated their support of the politics and processes of liberation in which their cultures were engaged. Their 'plagiarisms' can be seen less as individual expressions of personal pathologies than as expressions of a cultural and political reality shared by all colonized subjects, as *Lettre à la France nègre* points out. In this way, 'guerrilla plagiarism' could be seen as more than a cultural response to a dominant aggressor whose superior force cannot be countered on the traditional pitched camp battlefield – reverse imperialism. It could also be understood as the inevitable production of a 'non-subject,' that is, a subject dispossessed by colonialism of property, individual identity, originality, authenticity, and most fundamentally of language itself, all of which are culturally presupposed by the function of authorship.

Did Ouologuem's 'guerrilla plagiarism' have a 'revolutionary' effect? In the short term, perhaps not; in any event, Ouologuem was the unqualified loser in the affair. In the longer term, however, the violent reaction to the discovery of the 'plagiarisms' and the furore they caused are a testimony to the power of his transgression. The French literary institution, responsible for awarding the Prix Renaudot and 'authenticating' the Africanness of the novel, was caught short by the deficiency of its own erudition in a way that would have pleased Montaigne. Upon discovering its apparent error in judgment, the institution jumped to its own defence by expelling the offender who had crept into the ranks in sheep's clothing, so to speak, or to reprise another cliché, the jay was stripped of his borrowed feathers. Now, Ouologuem could no more have predicted the stunning success of his novel, than he could have predicted the 'discovery' of his 'plagiarism.' What he probably could have predicted, however, in light of the politics he espoused in *Lettre à la France nègre*, was the violence of the reaction visited upon a Black African who, invited as a visitor into the ranks of the dominant culture, was discovered not only to have perpetrated the theft of the cultural property of his hosts, but to have done it in such a way that he was rewarded for possessing the very riches that he had, apparently, cynically pillaged. One of the fundamental lessons of the Ouologuem case for our discussion of the pragmatic nature of plagiarism is that it pits a dominant culture against an outsider, an 'other,' whose status within that culture is purely a result of leniency, lent for a time and subject to revocation. The largesse of the French literary institution was not unqualified: *Le devoir de violence* was an authentic *African* novel, whose virtues were highly circumscribed by its folkloric and 'primitive' aspects, not the least of which were some pleasingly savage scenes of native violence and sexuality. That some of these authentic Africanisms appeared to be derived from contemporary European literature was intolerable. The expulsion of Ouologuem from the French literary scene was absolute: he never published another work, and *Le devoir de violence* was reissued with the offending passages expurgated.

The question of whether Aquin's plagiarisms constitute guerrilla warfare is less obvious, primarily because he was never accused of plagiarism in his lifetime, and the subsequent discovery of his 'plagiarisms' has not diminished his importance in the Québécois literary institution. Compared with Ouologuem, Aquin was and is very much of an insider on the Québécois cultural and political scene.[15] But, in a way, one could argue that he has achieved what Ouologuem failed to do: if he plagiarized, he certainly 'got away with it,' and reaped advantages in the process. Some of the praise he gleaned for his prose was directly the result of borrowed passages; and the 'plagiarisms' are added proof that the aesthetic of copying he promoted in his extra-fictional writing was translated into real practice.

If Aquin can be qualified as a 'guerrilla plagiarist,' it is not only because of the presence of copied passages in his work, but because of his concern with the importance of guerrilla warfare as revolutionary strategy. He touches on the question in *Trou de mémoire* via a reference to the first battle of the 1837–8 Rebellion in Lower Canada (Quebec), a model for the later revolutionaries of the 1960s. In 'The Art of Defeat: A Matter of Style' (Purdy 67–76; 'L'art de la défaite: considérations stylistiques,' *Mélanges littéraires* 2 [1995], 131–44) he explains that the first and only victory of the rebel forces in Quebec was won by the untrained, badly armed, and unorganized volunteer 'Patriots' on the strength of their guerrilla tactics. It was only when the Patriots succumbed to the fighting style of the superior British troops, and tried to fight a British-style battle to which they were numerically and technically unequal, that defeat became inevitable. Aquin sees the mimetic impulse – the adoption of the style of the oppressor by the oppressed – as symptomatic of the condition of the colonized, whereas guerrilla tactics are an expression of the authentic non-identity of the oppressed. The guerrilla theory of revolutionary war was also adopted by Aquin in his life, as his separatist zeal led him into a series of 'underground' adventures that eventually culminated in his incarceration in a psychiatric institution (Massoutre 148–58).

While both Ouologuem and Aquin explicitly espoused a technique of copying as part of their aesthetic intentions, the discovery of Ouologuem's 'appropriations' became 'plagiarism,' and ended his career, while Aquin's reputation is now guaranteed in spite of those strategies, which are generally considered an integral and positive part of his reputation. Although *Trou de mémoire* elicited much appreciation upon its publication, critics were far from unanimous, and some influential voices condemned the novel's sometimes crude language, and its occasional overbearing and obscure erudition. That the erudite language is partly the result of copying would not have excused the author had it been discovered: it is, of course, impossible to say, but it is probable that a contemporary realization of the presence of borrowed and uncredited discourse in *Trou de mémoire* might have severely damaged the author's reputation.

THE NON-SUBJECT OF FEMINISM

Feminist appropriation of masculine discourses of authority has already been theorized as a 're-appropriative' or 'expropriative' strategy of opposition to phallo(logo)centric structures of all kinds. But the feminist discourse of 'appropriation' is somewhat paradoxical. Hélène Cixous, for example, denounces 'appropriation' as being inauthentic, as it reveals the desire to usurp the master's position, ultimately a phallic move. In place of 'appropriation,' she proposes 'theft':

> Nor is the point to appropriate their instruments, their concepts, their places, or to begrudge them their position of mastery. Just because there's a risk of identification doesn't mean that we'll succumb [...] For us the point is not to take possession in order to internalize or manipulate, but rather to dash through and to [steal-] 'fly.'
> [*Stealing-*] Flying is woman's gesture – [stealing-]flying in language and making it fly. (Cixous 257–8)[16]

Craig Owens, in his analysis of Sherrie Levine's 'appropriations,' prefers the more aggressive and less collusive term 'expropriation': 'Or is her refusal of authorship not in fact a refusal of the role of creator as "father" of his work, of the paternal rights assigned to the author by law? [...] Levine's disrespect for paternal authority suggests that her activity is less one of appropriation – a laying hold and grasping – and more one of expropriation: she expropriates the appropriators' (Owens 182).

The connotations of 'appropriation' insert it within a general economy of property and phallo-capitalist power that feminist discourse explicitly rejects, producing a critical double-bind for the use of 'appropriation' within feminist discourse that may be difficult to circumvent. A similar strategy, motivated by a similar intent, is manifested by Luce Irigaray in *Speculum de l'autre femme,* where she takes on philosophical and psychoanalytical tradition from Aristotle through to Lacan. In a paratextual commentary she inserts a paragraph that is easy to overlook (easier in the French edition than in the English where it is more prominently displayed): 'Precise references in the form of notes or punctuation indicating quotation have often been omitted. Because in relation to the working of theory, the/a woman fulfils a twofold function – as the mute outside that sustains all systematicity; as a maternal and still silent ground that nourishes all foundations – she does not have to conform to the codes theory has set up for itself. In this way, she confounds, once again, the imaginary of the "subject" – in its masculine connotations – and something that will or might be the imaginary of the female.'[17]

Much of the work of feminist 'appropriation' (for lack of a less loaded word) is interpreted – and no doubt intended – to be parodic or deconstructivist: turning masculine discourse against itself, revealing its phallic presuppositions and 'blind spots,' in Irigaray's terms, it enacts a critical transformation of and distance from the appropriated discourse while attempting to avoid succumbing to the fate of identification. In this scenario, 'plagiarism' – the word, at least, but also the practice – could be successfully substituted for 'appropriation' because of the connotations of both theft and impropriety that 'appropriation,' in the current vocabulary of critical discourse, lacks.

Is there a feminist practice that differs from 'appropriation' to the extent that this term is burdened with the double-bind of collusion with a system that is the intended object of feminist critique? An examination of the work of writer Kathy Acker and artist Sherrie Levine will serve to explore this question. What the plagiaristic texts of Aquin and Ouologuem have in common with the explicit postmodern appropriation of Kathy Acker and Sherrie Levine is a theoretical foundation for the strategy that situates it in the context of the problematic identity of the non-subject, in the latter cases, of the specifically feminine non-subject situated within the artistic or literary institution and its dominant masculinist presuppositions.

The radical difference between the post-colonial and the postmodern feminist use of politically motivated 'guerrilla plagiarism' is the overt nature of the more recent uses of copying: in the cases of the post-colonial texts we have examined, the presence of plagiarism was discovered belatedly and was received as an occulted aspect of the texts, rather than as a constitutive element of their initial and explicit signification.

In the case of Acker and Levine, as in postmodern production generally, the political or ideological functions of plagiarism as constitutive of meaning require that they be immediately visible on the surface of the text, and contribute to the initial impact of the work. In these examples, 'plagiarism' is raised to the level of aesthetic strategy. This change of status is an aesthetic decision that does not protect the work from legal sanctions for copyright infraction; it does, however, effectively transform the aesthetic reception of the text such that the use of the term 'plagiarism,' when applied to these productions, is inevitably bracketed by quotation marks. As Acker told her publisher who feared a suit from Harold Robbins, 'I *use* other people's material – I *appropriate* – and this was *not* plagiarism' (McCaffery 74).[18] At the same time, one publication is glossed on the back cover: 'This writing is all fake (copied from other writing). So go away and don't read any of it' (Acker *Hannibal Lecter, My Father*).

Kathy Acker's plagiaristic novels combine a kind of *Bildungsroman* about a young girl's adolescence (some of her female characters are called Kathy) with rewritings of some famous classics (*Don Quixote, Great Expectations*), and some not so classical popular novels such as *The Story of O* and Harold Robbins's *The Pirate*. The absence of linear narrative coherence in her 'novels' and the emphasis on incest, child sex, and prostitution make her writing difficult in more ways than one. She has been threatened with copyright infringement by Harold Robbins's publisher, a threat that was defused by an out-of-court apology, and she has been banned in Germany for immorality, her books being judged dangerous to youth and 'anti-feminist.'

In spite of – or because of – the many difficult aspects of her work, she became an academic hit in the 1980s, and entered the institution by the front door, so to speak, fulfilling teaching engagements in creative writing at important American schools. Her writing is both scandalous and profoundly feminist, notwithstanding the judgment of the German court. The experiences of the women in her novels underline the importance of the body in feminine experience: her characters, in their search for love, are often complicitous in the sexual exploitation of their bodies in a way that exposes the cultural dominance exerted over women. The German decision makes this point without understanding the irony of its condemnation:

[The book] attacks the commercial exploitation of sexuality. The discrimi-

nation of women is condemned in brief sequences. Janey says men
teach women ways they want them to be. Janey, however, is the only
female person who appears in the book; she has an exclusive male
fixation, she has nothing in mind but men, except for her intention to
go to high school.

The novel merely mirrors social problems without being genuinely
creative in any way. It is also remarkable that Kathy Acker who considers
herself a 'feminist' [...] examines less the role of women [in] her novel than
[*sic*] mostly deals with male power and potency. The [newspaper] *Aachener
Illustrierte* in issue No. 2/86 charged her with having no new idea exceeding
or varying traditional male phantasies. ('Immoral,' in Acker *Hannibal Lecter,
My Father* 148)

This is as good a description of the predicament of the female characters
as any: taught by men to have exclusively male fixations, the women in her
novels are subject to male power, potency, and fantasies that are the source
of the commercial and social exploitation of female sexuality.

The use of 'plagiarism' in the novels is linked to problems of authorial
and female identity as well as to aesthetic experimentation in creativity.
Don Quixote, an early novel, opens with the main character, a female Don
Quixote, awaiting an abortion. Acker glosses this episode by explaining
that she started to write *Don Quixote* in a similar situation: 'While I was waiting to have the abortion, I was reading *Don Quixote*. Because I couldn't
think, I just started copying *Don Quixote*. Then I had all these pieces and I
thought about how they fit together. I realized that *Don Quixote*, more than
any of my other books, is about appropriating male texts and that the middle part of *Don Quixote* is very much about trying to find your voice as a
woman' (quoted in Friedman 13). The theoretical link between plagiarism
and authorial female identity is explicit in the epigraph of Part II of *Don
Quixote*: 'Being dead, Don Quixote could no longer speak. Being born into
and part of a male world, she had no speech of her own. All she could do
was read male texts which weren't hers' (Acker 39).

In the interview cited above (Friedman), Acker refers to her fascination
with Sherrie Levine's artistic and photographic copies, which became a
direct inspiration for her work – what she really wanted to produce was a
Sherrie Levine painting. And Levine, for her part, comments on her own
appropriative work in terms very similar to the ones expressed in the epigraph in *Don Quixote*: 'I felt angry at being excluded. As a woman, I felt
there was no room for me. There was all this representation, in all this new
painting, of male desire. The whole art system was geared to celebrating
these objects of male desire. Where, as a woman artist, could I situate
myself? What I was doing was making this explicit: how this oedipal rela-

tionship artists have with artists of the past gets repressed; and how I, as a woman, was only allowed to represent male desire' (Marzorati 96–7).

Kathy Acker links the problem of identity as expressed in plagiarism to schizophrenia, especially as it is formulated in *Anti-Oedipus* (Deleuze and Guattari) as the notion of the 'body without organs,' that which is a machine for attracting desire, having no desire of its own. Schizophrenia is the condition of the subject in, and of, capitalism, a subject that is itself the production of the desiring machines of society, a subject that 'itself is not at the center, which is occupied by the machine, but on the periphery, with no fixed identity, forever decentered, *defined* by the states through which it passes' (Deleuze and Guattari 20). The centre is abandoned by the ego, but something like a 'subject' can nonetheless be discerned: 'It is a strange subject, however, with no fixed identity, wandering about over the body without organs, but always remaining peripheral to the desiring machines, being defined by the share of the product it takes for itself, garnering here, there, and everywhere a reward in the form of a becoming or an avatar, being born of the states that it consumes and being reborn with each new state. "It's me, and so it's mine ..."' (16).

This seems an appropriate description of the female subject as expressed by Acker, as well as of her writing ('the work of art is itself a desiring machine' [32]): the construction of the identity of her female characters is largely a function of the desire of the Other, with all the ambiguity of that formulation; the body of the text is animated by the literary Other that it 'desires' and through which its own desire is expressed. The influence of Lacanian discourse has also been recognized in the work of Sherrie Levine. As interviewer Jeanne Siegel suggests: 'The connection between the Surrealists and Lacanian psychoanalytic theory on identifying with the desire of the Other seems strikingly applicable here. I assume the desire of the father subliminally expressed goes right back to the early rhetoric of your work. And with your polished bronze urinal, *Fountain*, you chose the most notorious Readymade of Duchamp, the quintessential father figure, and turned it into your Readymade *aidé*' (Siegel 19).

The relationship to the expression of the desire of the Other is both parodic and exemplary. On the one hand, it expresses the schizophrenia of the creative subject's inability to recognize or posit her own desire; on the other hand, it underlines a positive moment in the creation of identity. Acker says:

> I became very interested in the model of schizophrenia. I wanted to explore the use of the word I, that's the only thing I wanted to do. So I placed very direct autobiographical, just diary material, right next to fake diary material. I tried to figure out who I wasn't and I went to texts of murderesses. I

just changed them into the first person, really not caring if the writing was good or bad, and put the fake first person next to the true first person.
   I also came to the decision that [the first person] was a false problem because it's a thing that's made. You create identity, you're not given identity per se. What became more interesting to me wasn't the I, it was text because it's texts that create the identity. That's how I got interested in plagiarism. (Acker, *Hannibal Lecter, My Father* 7)

And Sherrie Levine recounts a similar transition in her work, from a debilitating sense of the impossibility of creativity to the integration of the derivative impulse into the work as a constitutive, perhaps 'original,' moment. Speaking of the sense of exclusion that she experienced in the 1950s with respect to the rhetoric surrounding Abstract Expressionism, she says:

It's not that I decided not to paint expressionistically, I just couldn't. I couldn't make that activity feel authentic for myself. Everything I did looked derivative to me [...]
   In fact, these paintings you mention [stripe paintings, checks and chevrons, 1985] were very similar to ones I made in college that embarrassed me. Eventually I decided to embrace the qualities of derivation that the works had. (Levine, quoted in Siegel 16)

The denunciation-by-identification of the position of woman artist as schizophrenic or as non-subject is, however, overlaid with two other levels of critique that are equally explicit in the paratextual commentary of the two authors, as well as in their practice. In the work of both, the position of the woman artist as non-subject participates in a larger phallocentric condition that supports, and is supported by, capitalism and the artistic institution. Acker is explicit about the relationship between the political and the aesthetic, particularly in terms of the structure of ownership in bourgeois society: 'What I have always hated about the bourgeois story is that it closes down. I don't use the bourgeois story-line because the real content of that novel is the property structure of reality. It's about ownership. That isn't my world-reality. My world isn't about ownership. In my world people don't even remember their names, they aren't sure of their sexuality, they aren't sure if they can define their genders' (Acker, *Hannibal Lecter, My Father* 23). The property structure of the bourgeois market economy is also a source of the myth of creativity: 'I suspect that the ideology of creativity started when the bourgeoisie [...] made a capitalistic market place for books. Today a writer earns money or a living by selling copyright, ownership to words. We all do it, we writers, this scam, because we need to earn money, only most don't admit it's a scam. Nobody *really* owns anything' (Acker, 'A Few Notes on Two of My Books' 33). Acker would agree with the critique of her own work expressed by Stuart Home's 'Professor X' in that she recognizes the paradox of the copyrighted plagiarist: 'If I had to be totally honest I would say that what I'm doing is breach of copyright – it's not, because I change words – but so what? We're always playing a game. We earn our money out of the stupid law but we hate it because we know that's a jive. What else can we do? That's one of the basic contradictions of living in capitalism. I sell copyright, that's how I make my money' (Acker, *Hannibal Lecter, My Father* 12).

Sherrie Levine also confronts the question of authorship, though in a less explicitly political but similarly ambiguous way: 'In the beginning, there was a lot of talk about the denial [of authorship and originality] in the work and I certainly corroborated in that reading, but now it's more interesting for me to think about it as an exploration of the notion of authorship. We do believe that there are such things as authorship and ownership. But I think at different times we interpret these words differ- ently. It's the dialectical nature of these terms that now interests me' (Levine, quoted in Siegel 15).

A second level of subversion that the art of copying representations enacts is that of restructuring the notion of representation itself. Both Acker and Levine have recourse to aesthetic justifications for their imitations that seem to contradict the postmodern notion of the simulacrum, in which there is infinite regress to an absent original, and in which representation is not of the world, but of the act of representation itself. This logic both is and is not present in their work. Most readings of both works accept as evident that the copy of a copy foregrounds the elusiveness of the original and of originality in representation, not only bringing to light the (patriarchal and Oedipal) influence that is repressed in the artistic moment, but also calling into question the very nature of representation as a relation between an 'original' and a 'copy.' A case in point is Craig Owen's analysis:

> In postmodernist art, nature is treated as wholly domesticated by culture; the 'natural' can be approached only through its cultural representation. While this does indeed suggest a shift from nature to culture, what it in fact demonstrates is the impossibility of accepting their opposition. This is the point of an allegorical project of Sherrie Levine, who selected, mounted, and framed Andreas Feininger's photographs of natural subjects. When Levine wants an image of nature, she does not produce one herself but appropriates another image, and this she does in order to expose the degree to which 'nature' is always already implicated in a

system of cultural values which assigns it a specific, culturally determined position. (Owens 223)

This reading correctly reflects an important element of the works' critique, that is, that the 'natural original' of artistic appropriation is an a/i/llusion and that 'art' is not properly 'production' but necessarily 'reproduction.' At the same time, both of these artists-as-theorists maintain a theory of representation that is firmly grounded in an origin, that of the 'original' text, photograph, or model that is substituted for the 'natural' world normally taken to be the object of 'legitimate' representation. Kathy Acker compares her 'plagiarisms' to the realist representations of the nineteenth-century novelist: 'What a writer does, in 19th century terms, is that he takes a certain amount of experience and he "represents" that material. What I'm doing is simply taking text to be the same as the world, to be equal to non-text, in fact to be more real than non-text, and start *representing* text' (*Hannibal Lecter, My Father* 13). And in almost identical terms, Levine compares her taking photographs of photographs to other artists taking photographs of 'trees or nudes' (quoted in Buchloch 52). And as Ann Temkin realizes: 'Her decision to remake Duchamp's *Fountain*, a readymade itself, underlined her acceptance of art history as a readymade-in-waiting. Duchamp, of course, had already used his own work in such a manner, in blithe reiteration of his own art history' (Temkin 15).

Rather than nature domesticated by culture, what we have is culture returned to nature. And the artistic artefact becomes the equivalent not only of nature, but of the entire class of undifferentiated natural or artefactual (as opposed to aesthetic) objects that constitute the world and are traditionally available for appropriation by the artist. By taking representations to be the same as the world, the appropriation artist *re*dissolves the aesthetic distance that now exists, for example, between a urinal and *Fountain*, entailing important theoretical consequences not only for representation, but for questions of property and authorship. As a result of becoming itself an object of *representation*, the copied work acquires the status of *original*, assuming a kind of natural primacy in the world, similar to that bestowed on trees and nudes. The re-presentation of an 'original' text or work of art is to treat it not as being once removed from reality, but as *being* reality, as existing in nature as it were, and consequently, as being universally appropriable for subsequent re-presentations.

I do not take this claim that re-presentations constitute reality as an ironic play on Baudrillard's simulacrum: it seems to me a straightforward, rather un-postmodern assertion of the existential primacy of cultural artefacts as existing in the world alongside trees or nudes. It is also not, I think, postmodern recycling in Guy Scarpetta's terms, where appropriation acquires 'a new force in a sort of generalized aesthetic of the "second degree"; [...] what comes back are quotations, and not an originary innocence; a culture and not a nature' ['une force nouvelle: dans une sorte de généralisation de l'esthétique du "second degre"; [...] ce qui revient, ce sont des citations, et pas une innocence originaire; c'est une culture, et non une nature' (381)]. While Scarpetta opposes the primacy of nature and the secondariness of culture, Acker and Levine confuse or equate them. I will not risk the hypothesis that Acker and Levine are not 'postmodernists,' and yet this position could be supported by the shift in Levine's position from a denial of authorship to the assertion of a dialectical relationship in the continuing 'belief' in authorship and ownership.

There is one sense, however, in which the literal representation of a representation, in other words, 'plagiarism,' does participate in the logic of the simulacrum, and which underlines the importance of reception in delineating the status of the work. As in Baudrillard's example of the impossible 'fake' hold-up, where the function of the real reduces everything to some form of reality,[19] there is a simulacrum-like undecidability about Acker's and Levine's 'plagiarism' that was manifestly absent in the reception of *Le devoir de violence,* and which has never been explored in Aquin's work where, as it has been noted, the 'plagiarisms' are normally attributed to the author rather than to his characters. In so far as the works of Levine and Acker represent *representations,* they are either 'genuine' plagiarisms, or else they are merely *(re)presentations of plagiarism,* in the same way that Acker argues that she is 'representing' text. While both have been threatened with copyright suits, the dominant aesthetic reception of their work is overwhelmingly in favour of seeing them as 'fake plagiarism,' rather than as the real thing. This reception returns us to the postmodern impossibility of distinguishing between the *real thing* and its representation. The works of Acker and Levine, being formally identical with plagiarism, do not however succeed in becoming 'real' plagiarism, because· they are assimilated into the representational order. But in order to *represent* plagiarism (rather than describe it), one has to enact it. Whereas Baudrillard's fake hold-up is inevitably recuperated into the 'real,' one could see Acker's and Levine's plagiarisms as being instances of the 'real' inexorably assimilated into the simulacrum of the representational order. The difference between the *impossible staged hold-up* and the *possible staged plagiarism* is situated entirely in the contextual field that conventionally divides the 'real world' from the symbolic. Plagiarism plays both sides against each other in that it confuses and then transgresses distinctions between the real and the simulacrum.

On the one hand, accusations of plagiarism confound the boundaries between the 'real' and the 'symbolic' in so far as they interpret as 'real' a kind of 'hold-up' (theft) that is enacted entirely within the frame of the symbolic. Although it can be seen as the representation of a representation, pure simulacrum, plagiarism nonetheless achieves a powerful entry into the real, the only realm where theft of property and transgressions of ethical or legal norms has any meaning. As Lacan says, 'There is no symbolic property. That is surely the question – if the symbol belongs to everyone, how can things of the symbolic order come to have for the subject this importance, this weight?' ['Il n'y a pas de propriété symbolique. C'est bien la question – si le symbole est à tous, pourquoi les choses de l'ordre du symbole ont-elles pris pour le sujet cet accent, ce poids?' (quoted in Schneider 318)].

On the other hand, the reception of 'plagiarism' as 'aesthetic appropriation' reverses the confusion and finds its revolutionary – in the sense of purely subversive – potential in annulling the dominance of the real over the simulacrum. 'Fake plagiarism' is possible because as the representation of a representation it is excluded from the realm of the real. The paradoxical status of aesthetic productions as property – both as *real* and as *symbolic* – that is, available to all – is exactly what postmodernist appropriation asserts: appropriation threatens and destabilizes the real order of intellectual property laws, and yet Acker and Levine can barely succeed in plagiarizing, because they are received as merely producing simulacra of plagiarisms.

The internal contradictions in their positions make it clear that Acker and Levine both are and are not the 'authors' of their works. To the extent that they hold copyright on their productions, and avoid criminal suits for their copying, they are clearly authors.[20] But clearly, their appropriations situate their work in an arena where 'originality' and 'authority' are not only explicitly contested, but no longer have the kind of currency that allows them to stand as criteria for authorship. Acker's and Levine's own ambiguous position with respect to notions of authority and authorship must be judged in terms of the authority that both have gained within the artistic institution. This position is well circumscribed as a 'revolutionary' moment of transgression of the conventions of 'originality' as well as a contestation of the more formal conventions of legitimate appropriation within the artistic institution. If guerrilla tactics make it sometimes difficult to tell who is winning the war, it seems that many of the advantages are on the side of the artists whose intentional attack on fundamental conventions and institutions of the artistic world has effected, at least in the short term, a transformation of those very institutions.

Of course, in this victory, the institution has also been complicit by espousing the critique and absorbing its critics. By treating the most radical moments of transgression as exemplary moments in a generalized aesthetic of repetition and appropriation characterizing the postmodern ethos, the aesthetic institution can adopt as its own that which appears as a critique: recuperation is a counter-revolutionary move by which the apparatus of legitimation asserts its authority, and defuses the subversive effect. If Acker and Levine are guerrilla revolutionaries, they have succeeded in infiltrating enemy territory, a position which, as we have seen, has been posited as the only effective one for performing oppositional work.

The principal strategy of postmodern 'guerrilla plagiarism' is to confound the aesthetic, ethical, and legal dimensions of originality, undermining the accusation of 'plagiarism' by an outrageous degree of explicitness, achieving 'originality' by an excessive degree of imitation, and slipping through the hands of the law by out-of-court settlements and legal exploitation of the public domain. In the end, guerrilla plagiarists are not real plagiarists, but they might be real revolutionaries. The question in this dangerous game remains: who is being had by whom?

Conclusion: Post-Plagiarism

> The appropriation of imagery from mass media and other sources is, of
> course, a strategy central to postmodern art.
>
> Martha Buskirk, 'Appropriation under the Gun'

APPROPRIATION, COPYRIGHT, AND THE ART WORLD

There is no question that appropriation art, with the success in the 1980s of such artists as Richard Prince, Mike Bidlo, Barbara Kruger, and Sherrie Levine, has now become fully institutionalized as a form of contemporary art. But it has not done so without having generated discussions, both in the art world and in the legal arena, about the contradictions inscribed in the conflict between copyright legislation and the allegedly aesthetic or political uses of the appropriation of social images that, as previously copyrighted commodities, are at the same time private property. Within the art world, the commodification of art is generally considered to be the fundamental point of the critique enacted by appropriative art; the right of artists to appropriate images from the world around them in order to perform their social-critical function is an element of the autonomy of art that its commodification can be argued to jeopardize. To make artistic appropriation subject to the constraints imposed by intellectual-property law is seen as a form of censorship which threatens the artist's right to the freedom of expression protected, in America, under the First Amendment.

The visual arts in the twentieth century have a long history not only of appropriation, but of lawsuits ensuing from such practices: the most notorious cases are those of Rauschenberg, Warhol, and David Salle. More recently, Prince, Levine, and Bidlo have also been threatened with suits. All of these cases have been settled out of court for economic reasons, neither party wanting to spend the time or money involved in pursuing legal action (Morris). The notable exception to this trend is the case of Jeff Koons, who has recently been involved in no fewer than four cases of infringement of copyright, and whose personal financial privilege has made it possible for him to pursue these actions in court, on behalf of the freedom of speech of artists in general.

The artistic community has understandably risen to the defence of the legitimacy of appropriation, and favours a more lenient interpretation of the principle of freedom of expression for the artist. Martha Buskirk, editor of the influential arts criticism review *October*, reacted vocally to the decision against kitsch artist Jeff Koons's right to appropriate a commercially produced photograph. In an article suggestively entitled 'Commodification as Censor: Copyrights and Fair Use' (1992), Buskirk is in the ironic position of having to defend Koons's right to appropriation, even though, as she points out, editors of *October* such as Yves-Alain Bois and Rosalind Krauss had been virulent in their condemnation of Koons, characterizing him and his art as trivial, commercial, exploitative, and self-advertising (105, n. 58). In short, Koons's art is just the kind that gives postmodernism in general, and appropriation in particular, a bad name. While it is clear that Buskirk shares these opinions, she nonetheless sees the decision against Koons as 'rife with ominous implications for the practice of artistic appropriation' (Buskirk, 'Appropriation under the Gun' 37). Although she does not explicitly call for a reorientation of the legal apparatus governing intellectual property, she poses the question of whether 'fine artists [should] be exempt from limitations on copying set up by laws designed to allow creators to exploit intellectual property – laws that fine artists are also able to use to their advantage' (Buskirk, 'Commodification as Censure' 104). In her answer to this question, she attempts to contextualize the practice of appropriation as a neo–avant-garde strategy of the collapsing of the categories of life and art that is, however, held in check by the institutional frame provided by the 'subculture' of the art world. In other words, not all instances of appropriation qualify within that world as 'art.' One of the internally legitimizing structures of the art world is to be found in the signature or proper name that attaches to the work as it 'enters into the art world's institutional network': 'Within that system, the value of the individual work of art is dependent on the name of the artist connected with it; and though the importance of the artist's name is based on the quality associated with his or her previous work, once the artist's name becomes a label given to an oeuvre it can acquire an increasingly abstract value unto itself' (106).

One of the paradoxical consequences of institutionalization is that it is only when the artists themselves become sufficiently well known that they risk becoming subject to legal sanctions:

> There is something of a paradox in the process whereby an artist can become a celebrity on the basis of the use of copyrighted images and mass media-derived strategies while at the same time claiming exemption from the legal limits inherent in their original conditions of production. Warhol's work is largely understood as a critique of the media environment from which he derived both his images and his strategies, and a number of critics have tried to place Koons in that same tradition. But subtle or implied criticism is something that advertisers and others in the mass media are capable of overlooking. This tendency is demonstrated by the number of advertising endorsements Warhol was asked to do [...] (108)

The problem arising from legal disputes involving appropriative art is that 'advertisers and others in the mass media' are not the only ones capable of overlooking 'subtle or implied criticism': 'in dismissing the idea that Koons's work could function as an act of criticism, both courts demonstrated an insistence on unambiguous and pointed criticism, suggesting that works based on nuance, multivalence or ambiguity are less likely to win the day in the legal arena' (Buskirk, 'Appropriation under the Gun' 39).

The rather convoluted point seems to be, that art-institutional conventions should be self-regulating. The value attached to an 'artistic' appropriation perpetrated by Warhol, or even Koons, puts the work into a different category than that of the appropriated work, which is usually, in the contemporary examples available, an instance of a trademark image or else the work of a 'commercial' artist having produced a photograph or other image for commercial purposes. Commercial, in this case, does not mean produced 'in order to accrue a financial profit' – an intention of which Koons has certainly been accused – but concerns the use for which the product was originally intended.[1] As well, the aesthetic value of the signature, as opposed to its simple copyright status, would seem, for Buskirk, to give added protection to works with strong 'signatures,' on the one hand, and added legitimacy to the appropriation of works lacking a strong authorial style, on the other: 'the successful artist establishes his or her sole right to a particular style or method – a "trademark" style – and others who attempt to use the same means are dismissed as mere imitators' ('Commodification as Censure' 107). The consequence of her argument is that Koons's right to appropriation must be protected.

What is considerably more surprising than this defence of appropriation from within the art world is the degree to which the legal profession – or at least some of its members – has also pointed out the discrepancies between accepted artistic practice and the letter of intellectual-property law. The best-known argument was proposed by art historian and jurist John Carlin in an influential 1988 article, 'Culture Vultures: Artistic Appropriation and Intellectual Property Law.' Carlin proposes an expanded interpretation of 'fair use' to apply particularly to the artistic appropriation of commercial images. With reference to the tradition of artistic appropriation, to Guy DeBord's *Society of the Spectacle*, as well as to contemporary theorists such as Lacan and Baudrillard, Carlin subscribes to the postmodern analysis of the ubiquity of the image, the semiotic foundation of contemporary 'nature,' and the fact that in 'the present century culture functions as the ideal artistic referent' (111). In such a context, Carlin argues, 'society needs artists to comment upon corporate imagery in order to balance its monopoly over our sense of social reality. If, as a result of media saturation of contemporary culture, artists almost have to copy protected imagery, the law should remain sensitive to these changes so that its grant of exclusive rights does not interefere with the valid representation of what artists perceive reality to be' (111).

Like Buskirk, Carlin has recourse to Justice Holmes's often quoted principle formulated in a 1903 decision, that 'others are free to copy the original. They are not free to copy the copy. The copy is the personal reaction of the individual upon nature' (Carlin 120). And, like Buskirk, Carlin argues that the enormous changes in the twentieth century since this principle was announced, not only in techniques of mass reproduction, but also in aesthetic theory and philosophy, have entailed the disappearance of the theory of the original, along with its referent, rendering Holmes's argument hopelessly inadequate. Carlin also addresses the question of why some appropriative works escape legal threats while others do not. Rather than relying on the internal logic of an autonomous art world, Carlin's more legalistic answer depends on the copyright law governing 'fair use,' which, according to him, exists when a reproduction is used in 'unique and original works of art, such as painting, sculpture or drawing, but not in multiples like prints and reproductions where Appropriation often is attacked successfully' (129). This distinction, which appears to be a vague rule of thumb rising from business practice, effectively distinguishes between the fragile position of Warhol and Rauschenberg, on the one hand, and the impunity of Johns and Lichtenstein, on the other.

In discussing the aesthetic appropriation of artistic as opposed to commercial images, Carlin defends Sherrie Levine's photographic reproductions, which, although they 'may be unjustified within current interpretations of copyright law, [...] can be justified in terms of recent art history' (137). This reasoning is similar to Buskirk's distinction between the artistic and the commercial uses of appropriation: 'An important difference exists between a commercial artist copying a protected image into something intended for mass reproduction and a "fine" artist copying or using the same image in a unique and original work of art, regardless of the fact that in both instances a profit is realized' (139). In his recommendations for a restructuring of the law in favour of artistic appropriation, Carlin draws one firm line; that is, that there be no grant of freedom to appropriate 'the work of artists currently working and exhibiting their art. This specific limitation would be to avoid direct competition between artists in roughly the same market' (139). In this argument, Sherrie Levine's appropriation of Edward Weston's photographs would be allowed, while David Salle's appropriation of contemporary artists Cockrill and Huges would not be, because Salle's appropriation of their image 'takes from a peer, which could lead to misattribution of the image by the viewing public' (140, n. 134).

Even though we have described Carlin's article at length, we have not done it justice, and it should be read in its entirety by anyone interested in these issues. Although this article remains the most complete – and aesthetically sophisticated – argument in the field, numerous other copyright lawyers and theorists have applied themselves to the question, with similar results. The consensus is generally in favour of expanding the First Amendment defence of freedom of expression, normally excluding visual arts, to include images in which the political message conveyed justifies their status as 'speech':

> The process of appropriation itself acts as a political symbol. As a technique in critical discourse, appropriation defies the very structure that copyright serves to protect. It manifests a rejection of private property in favor of a more communitarian conception of society. Therefore, the act of appropriation itself imparts a political message; it reveals that society (and its legal system) is laden with assumptions that financial incentives promote individual creativity, and that property interests supersede society's right of access to ideas and information. (Krieg 1578–9)

> In order to protect such politically motivated expression, the law should accommodate the appropriation of reproduced images when used for expressive purposes. (1580)

While both the art world and that portion of the legal institution which champions freedom of expression in authors' rights are motivated by admirable impulses in favour of justice and art, there seem to be several underlying paradoxes in their desire to protect politically motivated or 'revolutionary' art from itself. In the first place, legal commentators insist upon the unfortunate paucity of legal decisions about such practices, since the vast majority of them are settled out of court. This situation is deplored because, in the absence of established case law and precedents, it leaves the situation of the artist largely unregulated, subject both to undue restrictions on his or her artistic freedom and to unfair pillaging by other artists. Now, while the implications of copyright law for artists might be a fertile ground for philosophical and theoretical legal speculation, one could suspect these well-intended speculators to be perhaps engaged in tilting at windmills. One must ask what would be gained by reorganizing copyright law to suit existing practices of appropriation. While, on the one hand, a greater 'fit' between the practice and the law might 'legalize' practices that are currently in conflict with the letter of the law, these practices in fact rarely run up against legal obstacles and, when they do, are settled out of court for financial reasons. On the other hand, an improved copyright process recognizing appropriation would presumably provide more vulnerability to legal process for those practices that continue to be judged infractions. There is no evidence that out-of-court settlements are detrimental to anyone but lawyers and legal theory, and the current institutionalization of appropriation has already increased tolerance for it and conventionalized some of its more outrageous moments. There is an unwitting irony in the suggestion that the institution specifically charged with the regulation of private-property rights according to financial incentives, should embrace a critique of those very rights and incentives to the point of 'legalizing' those infractions that it is constituted to control.

But there are more fundamental paradoxes entailed by the idea of 'legitimizing' appropriation. First, both Buskirk's and Carlin's arguments turn on a rather traditional conception of the artist. Although Buskirk's artist is an instance mediated by institutional considerations, she nonetheless subscribes to some rather un-postmodern considerations of individual style and creativity, authorship and ownership. Both defend a simple reformulation of the Romantic/avant-garde genius as the one whose originality imposes its own justification – writes, as it were, its own rules – a traditional privilege here seeking to expand not only aesthetic conventions and practice, but social life itself in the form of a restructuring of the field of intellectual property. The irony of the postmodern defence of aesthetic-property rights is that it mobilizes a strong-author theory as its justification.

A further paradox is situated in the potential effects of such a restructuring of the legal institution under the pressure of oppositional aesthetic practice. Once appropriation-as-oppositionality has been accepted as *aesthetically* legitimate, the only point of appropriation, or 'plagiarism,' as in the extreme form practised by Acker and Levine, is surely in the precariousness of its *legality*. Such a restructuring of copyright law would be the ultimate form of institutional recuperation of the last possibility of 'oppositionality,' which is seen as the motivating principle of this same art. Once the judicial system is amended to admit such practice as legal, there would seem to be no motivation for the continuation or even the existence of the practice. As there may, aesthetically, no longer be any point. Not only has appropriation solidly achieved aesthetic conventionality, but as evidence of the nullifying effects of institutionalization, we can cite Sherrie Levine's evolution from the appropriation of photographic copies, to the adaptation of other forms of art including not only paintings, but objects such as Brancusi's sculptures and Duchamp's Ready-mades in which either there is no copyright, or where the transformative work of appropriation, often involving a change of artistic medium, distances the work from the potential accusation of plagiarism.

The 'plagiarisms' of Acker and Levine emerged at time when aesthetic appropriation, having long been a form of social critique of the aesthetic institution – via Duchamp – and consumer society – via Warhol – was no longer an avant-garde practice. In extending their appropriations to other *aesthetic* objects *qua* art, they turned the critique towards the more internal and sacrosanct presuppositions that still survived within the historical and the neo–avant-garde. Working within a theoretical discourse that simultaneously proclaimed the gendered nature of authorship as well as its death, along with that of the humanist subject and its artistic attributes of authenticity and originality, Acker and Levine simply pushed the logic of these discourses to their literal realization. The consequences of realizing in practice what theoretical discourse proclaimed exposed the contradictions between the ideology of the poststructuralist and postmodernist discourse on subjectivity and the repressed constraints to which this ideology was (is) still subject.

Authors may or may not be dead, but the space of authorship is impossible to maintain as a vacuum: a signature will always fill it up. The plagiarist critique works because of the excessive distance that needs to be travelled in order to read blatant, literal plagiarism as 'real,' even 'original' art. The institutional consequence of 'authorizing' such self-proclaimed 'non-authors' as Acker and Levine is surely a confirmation that where there is art, there is authorship, a condition that still attaches to itself the aura of authenticity, originality, and genius. Plagiarism posits a non-subject as the non-author of non-art; the institution of postmodernism aestheticizes the gesture of subversion, re-creates authorship as a condition of negativity, and authorizes a signature in the place of the absent subject.

APPROPRIATION, POST-AUTHORSHIP AND POST-OWNERSHIP

PoMo Appro – Apropos?
Some guidelines for appropriation:

1 Remember: Appropriation saves time.
2 Appropriate your images from old books and magazines where, chances are, all parties who could make a claim against you are dead or failingly old (ie stiff or infirm).
3 Unfocus the image slightly to avoid the moiré pattern [...]
4 Morph, tweek or otherwise alter the image unrecognizably.
5 Don't alter the image at all; have Italian craftsmen sculpt a simulacrum (not guaranteed to work).
6 Appropriate images from MONDO 2000 – these may already have been appropriated. Let's confuse the trail.
7 Appropriate images from ads in RAY GUN and submit them to MONDO – now it's come full circle – and it's ecologically sound (recycling is *good*).
8 It's hip hop.
9 And finally, this: if *you* take someone else's image it's *appropriation*, or *resonating*, or *recommodification*; if someone takes your image – it's *stealing*.

– appropriated from *MONDO 2000* 10: 2

Much energy has been expended and much excitement created around the rise of electronic means of publication, transmission, and reproduction of all forms of documents, from canonical texts to gallery collections to private communications. International commissions are weighing the pros and cons of contemporary copyright legislation to determine whether the technological revolution is a threat to current copyright legislation (Association littérature et artistique internationale). Questions raised include the notions of originality and authorship, especially for computer-generated and collective or interactive works, but the conclusions reached are generally that there are no reasons in principle requiring significant changes in the spirit or letter of the law. At the same time, enthusiastic supporters of the freedom and unbridled 'democracy,' sometimes called 'anarchy' (with positive connotations), of electronic communications are unqualified in their belief that the Information Highway not only escapes the capacities of current copyright law, but happily does so.

Electronic publication is protected by all the same rights enumerated in the Copyright Act and there seems to be no legal reason to consider electronically produced, reproduced or disseminated work as being different from traditional forms of intellectual property: 'In summary, the Council believes the *Copyright Act* provides sufficient protection for new and existing works, including multimedia works, that are created or distributed in a digital medium. The current legislative and policy framework is sufficiently flexible to provide the means of effectively enforcing copyright on the Information Highway and, at the same time, provide users with reasonable access to protected works' (Information Highway Advisory Council 38).

The problem is, rather, in the application of the law, and the 'Information Superhighway' has been described as a 'mecca for copyright infringement' (Harris 226): 'Effective mechanisms for monitoring illegal access, use, reproduction, and manipulation of copyright works on the Information Superhighway, as well as payment schemes for copyright holders, are not yet in place' (227).

The Canadian Information Highway Advisory Council concurs, stating that it considers that the administrative and technical questions relating to the 'enforcement of copyright and the clearance of rights constitute a priority' (38). At the same time, the council emphasizes the necessity to respect the two founding principles of copyright: 'A balance should be maintained between the rights of creators to benefit from the use of their works and the need of users to access and use those works' (36).

But beyond the technical questions of regulation and enforcement are the more philosophical and aesthetic ones that concern the ways in which this medium will, could, or even should change our standards and expectations about art and intellectual property. Computer-generated creations and transformations of images make Duchamp's moustached Mona Lisa ('L.H.O.O.Q') look crude in comparison; it is worth keeping in mind that copyright originated to face the consequences of a technological revolution and has been constantly evolving under the pressures of new developments. But artists themselves are also subject to the pressures of change: 'The computer represents a threat to the tradition of subjective expression in the same way that the camera did 150 years ago' (Ed Hill, quoted in Dery 75); 'Until artists can imagine a means of using a given technology so that the look of their identity, based in style, can come through, they're not going to embrace it' (Suzanne Bloom, quoted in Dery 75).

The same artists ask questions about the nature of art and the value of originality in the context of the infinitely reproducible and manipulable (76). Other appropriative artists engaged in electronic media see them as admirably suited to the exploration and expression of aesthetic concepts that are at the centre of twentieth-century art: 'My real interest is in the computer's potential for dissolving the barriers holding apart art and artifice, counterfeit and original. As an appropriationist's tool computers are beyond comparison – and a nightmarish disaster for the hoarders of intellectual property (myself included) – although smoothing out the legal speed bumps is going to make fortunes for office blocks of copyright attorneys. By translating knowledge, experience and reality to digital information, originality, truth and even lies become relative concepts (which they always were)' (Paul Mavrides, quoted in Rucker 105).

It is these last questions, rather than those concerning the regulation of copyright infringement, which are at the heart of discussions about the future of authorship and originality and which suggest that, perhaps, we are on the brink of realizing Borges's fiction: is the electronic form of the postmodern era about to introduce another 'post' – the era of 'post-authorship'? 'Appropriation' appears to be neither theft, opportunism, nor plagiarism; it is simply the inevitable consequence of the convergence of technology and ideology. As such, it is seen by some to be a natural evolution, only threatening those species already on the road to extinction.

Wired magazine is a popular forum for the dissemination of electronic ideology, dedicated to the promotion of the Culture of Information (or Information as Culture). Contributors to *Wired*, uniformly practitioners and promoters of the culture in question, are divided, however, on the question of intellectual-property legislation. In a futuristic cyberspace lexicon emanating from a post–intellectual-property twenty-first century, the entry for 'source (v.)' reads:

> to give credit to one's sources of materials, especially those being substantially altered. Sourcing became widespread even before the death of copyright meant that one could source one's materials without fear of being sued for copyright infringement. Some people advocate making sourcing a legal requirement, but because that would obviously be unenforceable and because source data are often unverifiable, this movement has never really gotten off the ground. Accurate sourcing is a point of pride for most artists, and since source lists (or genealogies) can become quite long and complex, a number of ingenious ways of either hiding them or displaying them have been developed. (La Farge 58)

On the other hand, in a note on intellectual property published in the same issue, one reads the following sanguine critique of the intellectual property crisis as industry 'hype':

> People in the computer industry like to think that what they do is unique and historically unprecedented. This largely mistaken belief is the cause for much of the current shrill debate on software patents, with both those who believe patents are crucial to the industry and those who believe patents will cause irreparable harm claiming that the unique nature of software requires sweeping changes in US intellectual property laws. The boring truth is that similar problems have arisen (such as industrial design patents

and music copyrights) and have been solved within the existing framework. The problem isn't the much-maligned patent office, it's people's egos. (Steinberg 120)

One particular area of discursive 'hype' that I would like to consider is that devoted to justifying the practice of free appropriation. The case in defence of appropriation attempts to legitimize it by comparisons between the 'new' situation of electronic information and other past regimes. The rhetorical efficacy of such discourses is undermined from the outset by a double-bind: analogies with the already-known are deemed necessary due to the absolutely 'unique and historically unprecedented' character of electronic information. But this same recourse to the old, a strategy apparently intended both to legitimize 'information' and to render it less threatening to non-specialists, has the obverse effect of familiarizing it, reducing at the same time its absolute otherness, in which its proponents however fervently believe. The electronic age is compared to the American Wild West, to the history of twentieth-century art, and finally to the aesthetic of the Middle Ages.

In a 1994 issue of *Wired*, John Perry Barlow, former rancher and president of the 'Electronic Frontier Foundation,' signs an article entitled 'The Economy of Ideas: A Framework for Rethinking Patents and Copyrights. (Everything you know about intellectual property is wrong).' This text is a fascinating rhetorical justification of piracy as free enterprise and a glorification of the absolute novelty of electronic 'information.' The article asserts the fundamental incommensurability between current American copyright laws and the reality of electronic information as Barlow sees it. He compares, favourably, the electronic world and the Wild West, where laws, unfortunately incompatible with daily reality, were also, fortunately, almost unenforceable. In the face of the apparent inability of intellectual-property law to regulate new forms of information, Barlow enjoys reliving the Utopian state that the outlaw evidently represents for him in his capacity as ex-cowboy. In the purest spirit of American free enterprise, he proposes that the system will regulate itself best if left alone, by which he means it will regulate itself in favour of the most enterprising, who will become, by their audacity and cleverness, the strongest, that is, the richest and, for this reason, the law and the government should not intervene. Barlow's ideal of free access to electronic information is a theory of unbridled capitalism argued from the point of view of the future monopolist.

According to Barlow, the principal obstacle to the assimilation of 'information' to present intellectual property legislation consists in the tradition of investing property in a material, and consequently fixed form, as well as in the idea/expression dichotomy. The law is materialist, and promotes a physical conception of property, presupposing at the same time the separability of idea and expression. The way in which electronic information would circumvent the criterion of material fixation is by its 'dematerialisation,' its detachment from the physical plane. In comparing the transmission of electronic information to 'pure thought,' Barlow proclaims that it is 'now possible to convey ideas from one mind to another without ever making them physical' (88). Since 'information' is pure ether, or energy, or 'thought,' any attempt to regulate it is, according to Barlow, tantamount to the aberration of 'claiming to own ideas themselves and not merely their expression' (88), and represents an attempt to extend intellectual-property rights which Barlow compares to the 'Bad Old Days of property' where ownership was established by force. Today, the winners are still those who can muster the largest armies – of lawyers.

Apparently infected with the *Star Trek* ethic, Barlow even goes so far as to proclaim that 'information' is 'a life form': it is a transformative and generative activity. Digital information, being interactive, can know no fixity or finality, since it is continually in evolution. The instability and fluidity of digital information reminds Barlow of another Golden Age, that of 'oral traditions,' where the text was unstable and the identity of the 'author' disappeared or became multiple, and was considered, in any event, unimportant. The casting of information as an independant life form capable of developing self-regulatory mechanisms appeals to evolutionary common sense overlaid with oblique allusions to the science fiction obsession with the living computer: 'The life forms of information are evolving methods to protect their continued reproduction' (128).

Finally, Barlow's 'information' is distinct from traditional property to the extent that it possesses an intrinsic value that is relational, no doubt, but not commensurate with property since it is not the means to the end of acquiring more or other commodities, itself being the object of value and desire. The essential nature of information-as-value serves to legitimate electronic information, in Barlow's mind, because of its similarity with the august domains of 'politics and academia' where, he informs us, 'potency and information have always been closely related' (127).

In this rhetorical game, Barlow's principal strategy is to constitute 'information' as an utterly unprecedented phenomenon, requiring a new lexicon, whose centrepiece is the word 'information' itself, a term that has the virtue of being both old and new. In Barlow's text, this new life form is both unspecific and endowed with definite imperialistic tendencies: 'information' applies equally to computer programs, to artistic creations, to databases and to conversations and messages distributed on billboards. 'Information' in this special sense is everywhere within the electronic world, and, by implication, nowhere outside of it. The use of the term

'information' is principally effective because in the context of the copyright laws in question, 'information' conceived of in its traditional sense is
specifically not copyrightable: as pure and immaterial thought, 'information' is of the order of the 'idea,' not of the expression of the idea, which
alone can be the object of copyright.

A second rhetorical effect emerging from the term 'information' is to
render inoperative the traditional dichotomy between idea and expression: electronic 'expressions,' being immaterial, seem inseparable from
their content.[2]

Barlow's third strategy is to explicitly misrepresent the nature of intellectual property and the laws governing it. One of the principal points of confusion in his argument comes from the slippage between the legal notions
of 'intellectual property' and common assumptions about 'property' in its
material sense. The value of scarcity attached to traditional property, for
example, would be the opposite in the world of 'information,' where it is
often by means of distribution that value increases. On the other hand, the
value of exclusivity of property is not apparently at risk, only displaced onto
a temporal realm that favours the first comer. As well, 'information' differs
from physical property in that 'information can be transferred without
leaving the possession of the original owner' (89). These 'new' aspects of
'information' betray a wilful obfuscation (if it is not ignorance) since each
one applies equally well to traditional forms of intellectual property that
are by nature immaterial until embodied in a copyrightable form: the ideas
I disseminate are not valued because of their scarcity, but accrue more symbolic value if I am the first 'comer,' and I certainly intend them to be as
widely disseminated as possible, since their transfer to others in no way
deprives me of their enjoyment or their possession. But these apparent
paradoxes, involving questions of exclusivity of ownership, of scarcity, of
dissemination, of value, of reproducibility, and above all of fixity and
immateriality, are all so far from being new in the field of intellectual property law that they constitute in fact the core of discussions about copyright
since the eighteenth century in England, as we have seen.

As we have also seen, modern artists have not waited for the development of electronic media to contravene the laws of intellectual property. If
the definition that Barlow gives of 'information' seems to us to contain
many of the properties of contemporary art, and in so doing, to point to
the fact that 'information' is not as new as he would have us believe, this
feeling is confirmed in two recent essays by the American rhetorician Richard Lanham. Lanham's argument reverses Barlow's and situates the electronic revolution at the *term* of an evolution rather than at its origin.
According to Lanham, 'the computer has fulfilled the expressive agenda of
twentieth-century art' (31); 'often, the electronic screen fulfills an already

existing expressive agenda rather than prophesying a new one' (36). Citing the effects sought by twentieth-century artists since the Futurists, such as interaction with spectators, the role of games and hazard, and a reflection on the status and the function of art, Lanham identifies 'the extraordinary convergence between technological and theoretical pressures. Perhaps we shall find that the personal computer itself constitutes the ultimate post-modern work of art. It introduces and focuses all the rhetorical themes advanced by the arts from Futurism onward' (17). He also discovers that 'Digital expression indeed fulfills the postmodern aesthetic, but also a much larger movement that comprehends and explains that aesthetic – a return to the traditional pattern of Western education through words [...] Digital expression, in such a context, becomes not a revolutionary technology but a conservative one [...] Its perils prove to be the great but familiar perils that have always lurked in the divided, unstable, protean Western self' (51). Rehearsing roughly the same list of qualities as Barlow attributes specifically to 'information,' Lanham demonstrates that 'clearly every stage of this [electronic] revolution has been predicted by the post-modern visual arts' (45).

Lanham's panygeric is no less transparent than Barlow's, especially in his desire to reconstruct the electronic media as predestined at least by the history of twentieth century art, if not by the entire history of Western rhetoric, which is in fact what he would like to argue. And Lanham is not alone in his vision of the electronic world as participating in an aesthetic and philosophical teleology that expresses a continuity with the past. To return to the pages of *Wired*, a doctoral student in medieval art history discovers analogies between the electronic world and the scribal anarchy of the Middle Ages where 'authors saw themselves as engaged in a common project: the search for knowledge, or during their free time, mutual entertainment' (Zorach 50): 'From today's tensions over copyright infringement, it is clear that the impulse toward creation-by-copying, in the medieval fashion, is alive and well. If we cannot all agree on the legal implications of copying technology, we can at least celebrate some of the freedom of the "new medieval" aesthetics ...' (50). Her article ends with the idealistic hope that the informational elitism of the Middle Ages will not be reproduced in this electronic return to the scribal aesthetic.

All of these discourses, and their celebration of appropriation as a form of transgression, imply that the anti-proprietary moment appears to be ephemeral. If Barlow exults in the contradictions between electronic information and the conventions of intellectual property, it is because he knows that this moment is fleeting: the fun of the outlaw is that of knowing that he is in the right place at the right time to profit from the momentary disarray of the institutions of control that will eventually reassert themselves.

In the same way, Sherrie Levine's art, perhaps the most radical of the appropriative trend of the 1980s, was also fleeting and more easily managed by the institution. Her appropriations, being closer to the conventional cases that the law was used to regulating, were more easily disciplined. But the contradiction between practice and the institution, which was essential to the conception of her appropriations, is the victim of a second form of discipline: that of the normalization of the gesture within art-institutional discourse itself. In this particular case of aesthetic appropriation, the radical move was in turn appropriated by the discourse of the institution which has made of it a new norm: like Duchamp's *Fountain* (Levine has also made her own 'Fountain') Levine's appropriations have become exemplary of a moment in contemporary high culture, rather than its opposite, participating in what Bourdieu, following Marcel Mauss, describes as an act of *collective misrecognition:*

> The artist who puts her name on a ready-made article and produces an object whose market price is incommensurate with its cost of production is collectively mandated to perform a magic act which would be nothing without the whole tradition leading up to her gesture, and without the universe of celebrants and believers who give it meaning and value in terms of that tradition. The source of 'creative' power, the ineffable *mana* or charisma celebrated by the tradition, need not be sought anywhere other than in the field, i.e. in the system of objective relations which constitute it, in the struggles of which it is the site and in the specific form of energy or capital which is generated there. (81)

With the exception of software products, legal cases involving electronic intellectual property and especially artistic works generated by electronic means are as yet sufficiently rare not to have placed insurmountable pressure on the legal institution. But some theorists, less confident than copyright jurists about the capacity of contemporary copyright laws to embrace the new media, predict a radical change in the future. In *The Electronic Media and the Transformation of the Law* (1989), M. Ethan Katsh also uses the analogy of the Middle Ages to insist on the differences between the presuppositions of laws based on print and those which should govern the new technologies:

> The redefinition of copyright is inevitable because much more of the act of creation in the future will involve working with copied information. (176)

> The new media are revolutionizing the means of producing works and, more slowly, changing the form in which works appear. While the copying

capability of the new media is widely recognized, we will only slowly become aware of the proliferation of new creative, artistic and literary forms [...] Copyright law currently states that it applies to creative works in all media, but we should recognize that it has had to deal with only very few modes of producing a copyrightable work. The new processes of creation will pose a challenge for language as well as law as more hybrid forms appear. (180)

At law, the notions of authorship, of originality and of intellectual property are statutory creations and not natural entities tending towards an ideal state that their continual evolution might one day allow them to attain. It suffices that the law decree otherwise for the definitions of author, owner, and property to change. But in what direction, and by the force of what necessity? Given the paucity of actual cases trying the limits of these laws, it is possible that such questions will remain, for the time being, at the level of speculation.

What seems unlikely, however, is that the combined force of postmodern theory, appropriation practice and the possibilites of technology will succeed in ushering in a new era of 'post-ownership,' although it is possible that some contemporary artists have already adopted a practice of 'post-authorship.' The issues raised by electronic media again underline the essential difference between plagiarism and copyright infringement. Clearly, post-modern appropriative artists and the proponents of the freedom of electronic 'information' are relatively unconcerned with 'originality,' or even with notions of propriety or integrity with respect to the use of intellectual property; they are, however, much concerned with the economic value of this property in a way similar to that expressed by Kathy Acker's declaration that she is forced to copyright her productions against her ideological preferences, in order to make a living.

We have defined plagiarism as a crime perpetrated against authors, and infringement of copyright as a crime against owners. In the history of this dichotomy, it is plagiarism/authorship that appear to be constant and ancient, the capacity of ownership of copyright being a new addition to the quality of authorship during the eighteenth century. If 'authors' were invented in the eighteenth century, it is strictly in terms of this additional privilege of economic rights accruing to possession. Nowadays, the distinction between 'author' and 'owner of copyright' may not be purely semantic: whereas the author is always the first owner of the copyright of what she or he produces, there often follows swift and effective transfer of the control over published material to the publisher. However, the proliferation of the ideology of 'appropriation' and of postmodern electronic 'information' may point us to the return of the distinction between authorship and ownership, plagiarism and copyright. If contemporary appropriation artists participate freely in an aesthetic of 'post-authorship,' they are not yet ready nor willing, it appears, to enter the Utopia of 'post-ownership.'

Will the proliferation of electronic media change the face of authorship and intellectual property? Will we inhabit 'Tlön'? Will ownership be the new death of the author such that only economic rights will be of any interest to producers of 'information'? Has 'plagiarism' as a crime against authors already disappeared, been completely subsumed by questions of ownership? In spite of the evidence of current trends, some scepticism might be permitted in the face of the antiquity and durability of the concept and practice of authorship itself, independently of sanctions and protections of a legal and economic nature.

In a world, as yet only science-fiction, in which electronic information is the universal standard and the anarchic Utopian dream of information as a free commodity has been harnessed by corporate and government interests, it is possible to imagine that the condition of authorship will become increasingly reduced to ownership as the fundamental inviolable right of intellectual workers. And that authorship, an unalienable right of paternity – or maternity – and propriety over intellectual products, will not survive the onslaught of technology. But in order to imagine a future in which authorship is no longer an attribute of intellectual producers, one would have to imagine, with Borges, the disappearance not only of authors, but of plagiarism; or, more correctly, the unlikely disappearance of charges and accusations of plagiarism.

Notes

PREFACE

1 'Dictionnaire où l'on trouve classés dans l'ordre alphabétique des écrivains de langue française qui, par suite des emprunts qu'ils semblent avoir faits dans les oeuvres d'autres auteurs, sont ou pourraient être considérés comme des pilleurs occasionnels ou systématiques, des copieurs sournois, des compilateurs laborieux, des imitateurs sans vergogne, des vaniteux de la plume, en un mot, des plagiaires' (Chaudenay).
2 Since the writing of this study was completed, two new important works appeared that have not been taken into account here: Lise Buranen and Alice M. Roy, eds., *Perspectives on Plagiarism and Intellectual Property in a Postmodern World* (Albany: SUNY Press, 1999), and Hélène Maurel-Indart, *Du plagiat* (Paris: Presses universitaires de France, 1999).
3 See Martineau for a discussion of such writers as Blaise Cendrars and the OuLiPo group, who inhabit the margins between plagiarism and literary borrowing.

INTRODUCTION

1 While becoming a literary author is not, itself, independent of other criteria (for example, the author's position in a related institution, such as academia), it remains true that the price of membership is the creation – and subsequent publication or other dissemination – of a work of literature, however this distinction is achieved.
2 See, with respect to the Russian formalists, Tynianov, 'De l'évolution littéraire,'

and Eikhenbaum, 'La théorie de la "méthode formelle"' (Todorov). Chlovsky in particular coined the theory of the 'ligne cadette' (the 'junior branch'), in which the canonized or traditional literary forms are constantly submitted to pressure from lower-order literary forms that in turn, may achieve canonization, only to be submitted to the same dynamic process of evolution.

Bourdieu formulates a similar theory: 'It goes without saying that [...] change in the space of literary or artistic possibles is the result of change in the power relation which constitutes the space of positions. When a new literary or artistic group makes its presence felt in the field of literary or artistic production, the whole problem is transformed, since its coming into being, i.e. into difference, modifies and displaces the universe of possible options; the previously dominant productions may, for example, be pushed into the status either of outmoded [*déclassé*] or of classic works' ('The Field of Cultural Production' 32).

Bourdieu explicitly distances himself, however, from the Russian formalist tradition by enlarging the field of conflicting positions outside of the discourse field itself, to include the 'balance of forces between social agents who have entirely real interests in the different possibilities available to them as stakes and who deploy every sort of strategy to make one set or the other prevail' (34).

3 'En fait, ces retours sont toujours *apparents*, puisqu'ils sont séparés de ce qu'ils retrouvent par la référence négative (quand ce n'est pas l'intention parodique) à quelque chose qui était lui-même la négation (de la négation de la négation, etc.) de ce qu'ils retrouvent. Dans le champ artistique ou littéraire parvenu au stade actuel de son histoire, tous les actes, tous les gestes, toutes les manifestations sont, comme dit bien un peintre, "des sortes de clins d'eoil à l'intérieur d'un milieu" : ces clins d'oeil, références silencieuses et cachées à d'autres artistes, présents ou passés, affirment dans et par les jeux de la distinction une complicité qui exclut le profane, toujours vouée à laisser échapper l'essentiel, c'est-à-dire, précisément les interrelations et les interactions dont l'oeuvre n'est que la trace silencieuse. Jamais la structure même du champ n'a été aussi présente dans chaque acte de production' (*Les règles de l'art* 228).

4 'ANNE: "Will you have a glass of brandy?"

OMAR: "You know I'm a good moslem"' (Sperber and Wilson, *Relevance* 79).

5 It is not my intention to reduce the highly developed areas of literary theory and criticism mentioned, and many others not mentioned, to subcategories of literary pragmatics. But this field, ever since it was dubbed the 'garbage can of linguistics' (Bar-Hillel; Mey, *Pragmatics* 12ff) – into which everything not belonging to pure linguistics was dumped – has responded by a reciprocal imperialistic tendency. The pragmatic approach is most useful in creating a space in which questions deriving from discourse analysis, reader reception, sociocriticism (etc.) can be formulated in terms of a coherent problematic.

6 This distinction is not intended to suggest that the two realms of the symbolic and market value of goods are separate, but that the two values can exist separately. As Bourdieu says: 'Symbolic goods are a two-faced reality, a commodity

and a symbolic object. Their specifically cultural value and their commercial value remain relatively independent, although the economic sanction may come to reinforce their cultural consecration' ('The Market of Symbolic Goods' 113).

7 Ken Adachi, a noted book reviewer for the *Toronto Star*, committed suicide shortly after the revelation of a plagiarism that was not the first in his career. The report of his death clearly links the suicide to the plagiarism, apparently on the basis of the timing (see Allemang).

8 'Définissons donc le plagiat proprement dit, l'action de tirer d'un auteur (parti- culièrement moderne et national, ce qui aggrave le délit) le fond d'un ouvrage d'invention, le développement d'une notion nouvelle ou encore mal connue, le tour d'une ou plusieurs pensées; car il y a telle pensée qui peut gagner à un tour nouveau; telle notion établie qu'un développement plus heureux peut éclaircir; tel ouvrage dont le fond peut être amélioré par la forme; et il seroit injuste de qualifier de plagiat ce qui ne seroit qu'une extension ou un amendement utile' (Nodier, *Questions de littérature legale* 36–7).

9 'Qu'est-ce donc proprement qu'un *plagiaire?* C'est un homme, qui voulant à quelque prix que ce soit s'ériger en auteur, & n'ayant pour cela ni le génie, ni les talens nécessaires, copie non-seulement des phrases, mais encore des pages & des morceaux entiers d'autres auteurs, & a la mauvaise foi de ne les pas citer; ou qui, à l'aide de quelque légers changemens dans l'expression ou de quel- ques additions, donne les productions des autres pour choses qu'il a imaginées & inventées, ou qui s'attribue l'honneur d'une découverte faite par un autre' (Jaucourt, 'Plagiaire,' in Diderot, *Encyclopédie* 680).

1: WHAT IS AN (ORIGINAL) AUTHOR?

1 'Nous savons maintenant qu'un texte n'est pas fait d'une ligne de mots, dégag- eant un sens unique, en quelque sorte théologique (qui serait le message de l'Auteur-Dieu) mais un espace à dimensions multiples, où se marient et se con- testent des écritures variées, dont aucune n'est originelle: le texte est un tissu de citations, issues des mille foyers de la culture [...] [L]'écriture ne peut qu'imiter un geste toujours antérieur, jamais originel; son seul pouvoir est de mêler les écritures, de les contrarier les unes par les autres, de façon à ne jamais prendre appui sur l'une d'elles [...]' ('La mort de l'auteur' 65).

2 'Ce n'est pas le plagiat qui fait le plagiaire, c'est le fait qu'on soit plagiaire ou écrivain vrai qui qualifie l'emprunt: influence ou plagiat. Un grand auteur reste auteur. Il ne sauroit avoir plagié les médiocres [...] Seuls les médiocres peuvent être réputés plagiaires, en tout cas aux yeux de l'histoire littéraire' (Schneider 97, 98).

3 'Ceux-là continueront obstinément à reconnaître le plus pur esprit stendhalien dans des pensées de Robertson, ou du docteur Johnson, ou de vingt autres; ils continueront même à admirer l'extrême nouveauté de la théorie des milieux

appliquée aux arts ou aux lettres; quand même on leur montrerait à l'évidence qu'elle se trouve chez tous les bons auteurs du xviiie siècle, à commencer par l'abbé Dubos, ils ne se déjugeront pas [...] Si on prétend découvrir dans les livres de la loi stendhalienne quelques interpolations, on devient hérétique et blasphémateur. Comment oser parler, dès lors, de plagiats?' (Hazard, 'Les plagiats de Stendhal' 347).

4 The gendered nature of the plagiarist is, surprisingly, not merely a feature of non–gender-inclusive discourse. Schneider also insists – albeit indirectly – on the Oedipal-masculine nature of plagiarism, and his examples of true authors and great plagiarists are all men. The only women discussed are Marguerite Duras, not a 'real' plagiarist, and Régine Desforges, not a 'true' author. For a discussion of the female playwright and plagiarist during the Renaissance, see Rosenthal, whose premises about the social construction of authorship are close to our own.

5 For Nelson Goodman, on the contrary, authenticity constitutes an element of aesthetic quality: 'the fact that we cannot tell our two pictures apart merely by looking at them does not imply that they are aesthetically the same' (109); however, knowledge of authorship is a constitutive feature of our ability to distinguish between aesthetic features: 'since the exercise, training, and development of our powers of discriminating among works of art are plainly aesthetic activities, the aesthetic properties of a picture include not only those found by looking at it but also those that determine how it is to be looked at' (111–12). On Vermeer and Van Meegeren, see, in particular, Werness and Lessing.

6 On the question of fakes in general see 'Fakes and Forgeries' in Eco; 'Art and Authenticity' in Goodman; Grafton; Haywood.

2: ORIGINATING DISCOURSE

1 This is largely a classical concept. For much Renaissance and neoclassical poetics, the ancients had achieved perfection and could not be improved upon, only approximated, by perfecting one's style to match that of the model. The degree of 'generous rivalry' permitted to the poet is the source of considerable dispute during the Renaissance.

2 The traditional theory of the complete submission of the medieval author to the *auctoritas* of the divine or ancient *auctor* has recently become a suject of much debate and revision. My point is simply to recall how authorship and authority have been intimately and continually linked, a relationship that continues into the present.

3 Piracy, on the other hand – the theft of manuscripts – and forgery – the purloining of entire texts and their re-presentation under false signatures – were both practised: 'However, the theft of words is not unknown in this culture, but it is situated on the margins of literature and is more related to forgery than plagiarism.

In hagiography, for example, while certain compilers [...] distinguish carefully in the margins of the manuscript between borrowed texts (often with indications of the source) and those they have themselves produced, others do not hesitate to copy whole passages and to hide their theft: in this way, the author of the anthology of the *Miracles of Notre-Dame de Chartres* borrowed word for word a text of 468 lines from Gautier de Coinci [...] One can find in this case pecuniary considerations: it is a case of propaganda for the financing of the cathedral [...] [T]he ends justify any means *ad majorem Dei gloriam*' ['Pourtant le vol des mots n'est pas inconnu dans cette culture, mais il se situe en marge de la littérature et relève plus de la pratique du faussaire que du plagiaire. En hagiographie, par exemple, alors que certains compilateurs [...] distinguent soigneusement, en marge du manuscrit, les textes qu'ils empruntent (avec souvent indication de la source) de ceux qu'ils ont eux-mêmes produits, d'autres n'hésitent pas à copier intégralement et à dissimuler leur larcin: ainsi l'auteur du recueil des *Miracles de Notre-Dame de Chartres* a emprunté mot à mot un texte de 468 vers à Gautier de Coinci [...] On retrouve là des considérations pécuniaires: il s'agit d'une oeuvre de propagande pour le financement de la cathédrale. [...] [T]ous les moyens sont bons *ad majorem Dei gloriam*' (Kunstmann 141–2).]

4 With reference to these lines, T. Cave points out that, although it is important not to invest the notion of 'self-expression' with the Romantic connotations of 'emotional experience,' one must not underestimate its importance: 'it is a formulation virtually absent from classical and medieval rhetoric, and marks a shift the magnitude of which is hard to measure' (42). In particular, by conjoining the deictic pronoun and reflexive verb, 'self-identity is thereby enacted syntactically as both the origin and the object of discourse' (43).

5 'Le référent encore vivace auquel Montaigne tentait d'échapper était le grand homme, l'*auctoritas* qui lui accorderait une identité [...] Montaigne refusait l'épreuve et la garantie de la tradition mais il n'en connaissait pas de nouvelle' (Compagnon 311).

6 'On voit dans tout son livre un caractère original qui plaît infiniment: tout copiste qu'il est, il ne sent point le copiste; et son imagination forte et hardie donne toujours le tour original aux choses qu'il copie' (Malebranche, quoted in Compagnon 313).

7 'Il y a donc une façon d'imiter les modèles qui, sous couleurs d'en éterniser les prestiges, vise en fait à s'en débarrasser. On ne reprend les archétypes que pour en user, en épuiser les réserves, dans l'espoir de déboucher ailleurs, si possible' (Delègue 94).

8 'Je n'ay jamais leu Aristote, et ne sçay point les regles du theatre, mais je regle le merite des pieces selon le plaisir que j'y recoy. Celle-cy a je ne sçay quoy de charmant dans son accident extraordinaire [...] Je ne m'enquiers point de ce qui est pris de l'Autheur Espagnol, ou de ce qui n'en est pas, c'est le Cid entier que je defends, et non point Corneille; et il m'importe fort peu si c'est traduction ou

invention; en fin je declare que c'est en gros une piece for agreable, dont les pensées sont extraordinaires et picquantes, et les incidents sensibles et divertissans' ('Le jugement du Cid; composé par un Bourgeois de Paris, Marguillier de sa Paroisse' [Charles Sorel?], Gasté 231–2).

9 '[...] en fin apres la confession que vouz avez faite, que le Cid a desja esté mis en Poëme dramatique, il ne vous peut rester autre gloire que celle d'estre Plagiaire, et de rimer puerilememt apres trente ans d'estude. Vous dites pourtant que l'on ne vous reproche que soixante vers de larcin en une piece de deux mille: ceux qui ont leu l'original entier, asseurent qu'il n'y a pas un mot en vostre ouvrage qui ne soit tiré de l'Espagnol [...]' (Gasté 308).

10 'Vous m'avez voulu faire passer pour simple Traducteur, soubs umbre de soixante et douze vers que vous marquez sur un ouvrage de deux mille; Et que ceux qui s'y cognoissent n'appelleront jamais de simples traductions: Vous avez declamé contre moy, pour avoir teu le nom de l'Autheur Espagnol, bien que vous ne l'ayez appris que de moy, et que vous sçachiez fort bien que je ne l'ay celé à personne, et que mesme j'en ay porté l'original en sa langue à Monseigneur le Cardinal Vostre Maistre et le mien: En fin vous m'avez voulu arracher en un jour ce que pres de trente ans d'estude m'ont acquis' (Gasté 149)

11 'Pour me faire croire ignorant, vous avez tasché d'imposer aux simples, et avez avancé des maximes de Theatre de vostre seule auctorité, dont toutesfois quand elles seroient vrayes, vous ne pouriez tirer les consequences cornuës que vous en tirez: Vous vous estes fait tout blanc d'Aristote et, d'autres Autheurs que vous ne leutes et n'entendites peut estre jamais, et qui vous manquent tous de garentie: Vous avez fait le Censeur Moral, pour m'imputer de mauvais exemples: Vous avez épluché jusques a en accuser un de manque de cezure: Si vous eussiez sceu les termes du mestier dont vous vous meslez, vous eussiez dit qu'il manquoit de repos en l'Emistiche' (Gasté 148–9).

12 'Neantmoins la naïveté et la vehemence de ses passions, la force et la delicatesse de plusieurs de ses pensées, et cet agréement inexplicable qui se mesle dans tous ses defaux luy ont acquis un rang considerable entre les Poëmes François de ce genre qui ont le plus donné de satisfaction. Si son Autheur ne doit pas toute sa reputation à son merite, il ne la doit pas toute à son bonheur, et la Nature lui a esté assez liberale, pour excuser la Fortune si elle luy a esté prodigue' (Gasté 417).

13 'Dès lors [à travers le dix-huitième siècle] que les théories esthétiques remettent en question la théorie de l'imitation et que, par conséquent, on reconnaît que le poète puisse trouver en lui sa matière, le terme d'invention (pris dans son sens étymologique et rhétorique) ne suffit plus, et c'est progressivement le terme de 'creation' qui s'imposera pour finalement se substituer à lui' (Jacinthe Martel 41).

14 'La nouveauté apportée par le XVIIIe siècle, ce sera la préférence accordée à l'expression directe, immédiate, fidèle et sincère du sentiment et des idées. Le

fait d'emprunter des images, des schémas formels, des structures existantes sera considéré comme une entorse à cette sincérité' (Mortier 134–5).

15 'L'originalité prend ici un caractère presque existentiel; elle se confond avec l'*authenticité.* Imiter, c'est être inauthentique, faux, mensonger' (Mortier 82).

16 'Quelques génies puissants créent ou découvrent; après eux, et les yeux fixés sur les chefs d'oeuvre, des esprits d'une moindre trempe créent des oeuvres similaires, originales encore en quelque point et qui ne sont pas des *imitations,* mais dont ils n'auraient pas eu l'idée sans leurs devanciers. Après ceux-ci, l'*imitation* devient servile et tombe de degré en degré jusqu'au plagiat' ('Imitation,' Larousse 582).

17 See, especially, the introduction to *Biographia Literaria* (Coleridge, vol. 7, pt i).

18 Hartman and Ricks concur in their assessment of Coleridge's 'Romantic' condition. According to Hartman, Fruman 'assigns to private morals or psychic mystery faults that have to do more with the ethics of the literary market-place of the time [...] He fails to see that Coleridge is not a special case, that his charlatanism is hardly of a perplexing or freaky kind. Is not every claim to fame or authority, especially in the modern period, shadowed by imposture?' (36). Ricks concurs: 'Why was [*sic*] forgery and plagiarism so rife in that era, and not just in Coleridge?' (32). 'Romanticism, though committed to the new, was weighed down with a crippling sense of the old, of the burden of that past which seemed to have said all that is worth saying' (33). Fruman responds: 'The reasons why so great a genius as Coleridge was almost incapable of acknowledging his sources with any candor are not to be found in vague generalities about Romanticism, which in any case operated on everyone, but in his own desperately driven and insecure nature' ('Originality, Plagiarism, Forgery, and Romanticism' 48).

In this dispute, it is clear that, for all concerned, Coleridge, a 'charlatan,' in fact 'plagiarized,' the only question at issue being why, or whether or not his actions should reflect badly on his genius. While this genius is felt to be personal, Ricks and Hartman defend his 'plagiarism' in institutional or general 'spirit of the age' terms. The question not raised in the discussion is why Coleridge, among the many potential plagiarists of the time to which all contributors to the discussion allude, should be particularly susceptible to charges of plagiarism.

19 For some pertinent contributions to this debate, see Roof and Wiegman.

3: OWNING DISCOURSE

1 It has been suggested to me that the translation also dispenses with a subtle play on words generated by multiple meanings of 'liber,' which include, as well as 'book,' the sense of 'free' as in a free man, and, more rarely, 'child,' thereby activating the three meanings of 'plagium' already cited. But my Latinist author-

ity refuses such a reading on grammatical grounds, the free play of signifiers presumably not being an art much practised at the time.

2 This is a common post-Lacanian assumption. In Grosz's explication of Lacan, 'the subject cannot be considered the agent of speech; it is (through) the Other (i.e. the unconscious) that language speaks the subject. The subject is the effect of discourse, no longer its cause' (98).

To quote another interpreter of Lacan: 'Not only is the *subject not the cause of language but the subject is caused by language.* Which means that the subject who comes into being through language participates in it only in the sense of an effect; an effect of language which brings the subject into existence [...]' ['Non seulement *le sujet n'est pas cause du langage, mais il est causé par lui.* Ce qui veut dire que le sujet qui advient par le langage ne s'y insère que sur le mode d'un effet; un effet du langage qui le fait exister [...] (Dor 137)].

3 'Citer comme plagier est prendre à l'autre sans lui demander son avis, mais dans le plagiat, on demeure dans une sorte de violence pré-oedipienne, à l'intérieur d'une fusion ou d'une relation duelle. L'effacement du nom propre de l'auteur témoigne d'un conflit oedipien esquivé ou mal engagé, et d'un repli vers le pré-oedipien. Le nom du père n'a pas eu lieu. La question du père est probablement l'un des aspects essentiels de la pyschologie du plagiaire. Absence de père, filiations falsifiées, les écrivains sujets au plagiat [...] ont souvent, caché dans leur histoire, un rapport problématique au père' (Schneider 282).

4 The passage in Grimarest is 'Cyrano de Bergerac [...] was then received into the meetings and conversations which Gassendi would hold with the persons I have just named. And as this same Cyrano was very eager of knowledge, and because he had a powerful memory, he profited from everything, and made himself a storehouse of good things from which he drew advantage in the future. There-fore, Molière did not hesitate to place in his works several ideas that Cyrano had already employed in his. I am permitted, said Molière, to take back my posses-sions [*reprendre mon bien*] wherever I find them' (Grimarest [1705] 1955, p. 39).

5 'Molière, en embellissant ses larcins, avoit acquis le droit de dire: "Cela est bon, cela m'appartient, il est permis de prendre son bien où on le trouve"' (Cailhava, *Etudes sur Molière* 273; quoted in Bonvallet 239).

6 For a similar reading to ours, see Chaudenay, who concludes: 'I therefore with-draw this plagiarism from Molière and give it to Cyrano [...] In any case, Molière has a sufficiently large number of plagiarisms to his name that we need not lengthen the list' (204).

7 'Un Auteur qui remonte jusques aux sources, et qui vérifie tous les Passages que d'autres ont alleguez, devient un Possesseur légitime. Il est en droit de ne citer que les Ecrits originaux qu'il a consultez; on serait injuste de le nommer Plagi-aire, sous prétexte qu'il rapporte les mêmes choses que d'autres. Je croi pour-

tant que la bonne foi, l'équité, la gratitude, demanderoient que l'on reconnût les obligations qu'on a aux Ecrivains qui nous ont montré les sources. Quand donc un Auteur est convaincu en sa conscience, que s'il n'eût point lu les Dissertations de quelques Modernes qui ont cité les anciens Auteurs, il eût ignoré à qui il se faloit adresser pour connoitre les Autoritez originales, il feroit très bien d'apprendre au public le bon office que ces Modernes lui ont rendu. Aiant fait cela dans une Préface, il peut citer de son chef tous les Anciens qu'il consulte, et agir en véritable propriétaire. Disons en passant que les Ecrivains qui se font une Religion de citer jusques aux Chapitres, et auz pages, à l'égard de toutes les choses qu'ils empruntent de leur prochain, son plus honnêtes que politiques. Ils négligent les intérêts de la vaine gloire, il se depouillent du plaisir d'être citez; car ils facilitent de telle sorte la vérification, qu'il n'y a guère d'Ecrivain qui ne la fasse lors qu'il a besoin des mêmes preuves, ou des mêmes faits qui se trouvent dans leurs Livres: après quoi il se contente de citer l'ancien Auteur. Mais s'ils alleguoient de belles choses sans dire où ils les prennent, en se contentant de marquer le nom des témoins, on n'oseroit guère débiter ces mêmes choses que sous leur autorité, à moins qu'on ne fût de la première volée. Ils se verroient donc aux marges d'une infinité de Livres; on leur feroit long tems cet honneur' (Bayle, 'Nihusius,' *Dictionnaire historique et critique* 2098–9).

8 'Cette traduction *subreptice* est un véritable plagiat, un vol caractérisé, quand elle n'est pas accompagnée d'une déclaration formelle, ou d'une déclaration implicite, comme celle qui résulte de la conformité du titre même, et l'on n'en a jamais jugé autrement' (Nodier, *Questions de littérature légale* 2, note 1).

9 'Le compilateur, puisant des idées, des notions et des faits à diverses sources parfois inconnues ou oubliées, les rassemble, les confronte, opère un tri et rend accessible à chacun des connaissances auxquelles seuls pourraient prétendre des spécialistes.

'Bien entendu, un compilateur qui ne cite pas ses sources n'est plus un compilateur, il est tout simplement un plagiaire. C'est un compilateur qui vous le dit' (Chaudenay 22).

10 'Il est vrai que j'ai pris dans *Le Sublime* quelques renseignements. Mais vous oubliez de dire que *Le Sublime* n'est pas une oeuvre d'imagination, un roman; c'est un livre de documents dont l'auteur cite des mots entendus et des faits vrais. Lui emprunter quelque chose, c'est l'emprunter à la réalité' ('Letter to Auguste Dumont,' the director of *Le Télégraphe*, in Zola, *Correspondance* 548).

11 'Jusqu'à présent on m'a accusé de mentir dans *L'Assommoir*: voilà maintenant qu'on va me foudroyer, parce qu'on s'aperçoit que je me suis appuyé sur les documents les plus sérieux. Tous mes roman sont écrits de la sorte; je m'entoure d'une bibliothèque et d'une montagne de notes, avant de prendre la plume. Chercher mes plagiats dans mes précédents ouvrages, Monsieur, et vous ferez de belles découvertes' (Zola, *Correspondance* 548).

12 This history has been treated many times by legal and literary specialists alike.

David Saunders's *Authorship and Copyright* (1992) is an accessible survey of
Anglo-American and Continental developments in copyright, written with an
eye to the literary implications of these developments and their interaction with
contemporary literary theory. Two other recent publications, Paul Goldstein's
Copyright's Highway (1994) and *Authors and Owners* by Mark Rose (1993), also furnish contemporary histories of authorship as it is related to copyright.

13 'Il faut bien le comprendre, le respect de règles d'ordre éthique n'influe pas sur
le droit d'auteur, même s'il peut permettre de conclure à la bonne foi du cher-
cheur. Rappelons-le, la bonne foi d'un contrefacteur est sans conséquence
quant à la violation du droit de produire ou de reproduire une oeuvre, quoique
cette bonne foi puisse influer sur l'attribution de dommages-intérêts' (Tamaro,
Le droit d'auteur 101).

14 Birrell (114–17) alerted us to this source; the citation is from the original rather
than from Birrell's edited version.

15 'Maintenant, depuis deux siècles, l'homme a créé une nouvelle et immense propriété. Dans cette propriété, tout émane de l'homme; seul il a créé l'encre, il a
créé le papier; la pensée imprimée procède de lui, là tout est de lui. C'est une
valeur qui ne s'appuie que sur elle-même, une valeur anthropomorphe, car un
auteur y met sa vie et son âme et ses nuits. C'est précisément cette propriété
qu'on lui contesterait! c'est celle-ci qui donnerait lieu à l'exhérédation des
familles sans indemnité! Le *droit* est plein de précautions pour l'or et pour la
terre, pour les meubles acquis par le travail matériel ou commercial; il y a onze
cents articles dans le Code pour ces propriétés, et il n'en existe pas un seul pour
saisir, dans les caprices de ses transmissions et de ses stipulations, la propriété
créée par le travail intellectuel [...] [L]e contrat littéraire est livré à tout le
vague des déterminations judiciaires sans règle, et les juges tordent les cas pour
les faire rentrer dans le lit du Code' ('Sur les questions de la propriété littéraire
et de la contrefaçon,' 1836, in Balzac, 1956, 300–1).

16 'La législation n'est pas seulement arbitraire sur certains points; elle est incom-
plète et obscure sur d'autres. Ainsi la question de savoir s'il existe un droit
d'auteur en vertu de la Common Law, c'est-à-dire en dehors de la loi écrite,
n'a jamais été décidée et a soulevé des contestations à plusieurs reprises' (Recht
24–5).

17 'Le privilège accordé à l'auteur a pour effet de récompenser son travail, son
activité créatrice et qu'il est perpétuel. Il ne peut être confondu avec le privilège
accordé à l'éditeur, dont l'objet est de l'indemniser de ses frais et ne peut
dépasser la vie de l'auteur' (Recht 33).

18 'Cependant, je n'ai pas donné que mon travail manuel, j'ai donné mon cerveau,
j'ai donné mon coeur, j'ai donné ma vie. Et c'est pour cela qu'on nous fait le
grand honneur de nous exproprier, en invoquant l'utilité publique, la cause de
l'humanité tout entière' ('La propriété littéraire,' 1896, in Zola, *Correspondance*
762).

4: READING THE READER

1 'C'est le jugement des lecteurs qui arrache un livre à ses influences et en font simplement un livre, vrai, même s'il n'est pas neuf. Le plagiat se juge donc à ses effets. La réalité des emprunts cède le pas aux considérations esthétiques' (Schneider 102).

2 'Peu à peu, le plagiat est redevenu, réhabilité sous le nom savant d'intertextualité, quelque chose qui n'est plus une fatalité mais un procédé d'écriture parmi d'autres, parfois revendiqué comme le seul' (Schneider 48).

3 'Or quant à ceux qui sont si grans ennemis de toute traduction, à leur bon commandement; mais que cependant ilz ne perseverent point à desrober (qu'ilz appellent imiter) plusieurs vers, et périodes des anciens poètes, lesquels vers, sentences et périodes toutes entières ilz s'attribuent; car ilz ne sauroient si bien se couvrir de ce qu'aucuns poètes renommez ont fait de semblable, que cependant lon ne les puisse et lon ne les doive à bon droit renvoyer au jugement que fait Aristophance devant le roy Ptolémée, et à la punition que le dict roy fait de tels cinges de Poëtes plagiaires' (Fontaine, quoted in Raymond 58).

   Raymond qualifies this as an attack on Ronsard and the *Deffence et illustration*. According to him, both Du Bellay and Ronsard are secretly indebted to Fontaine, whom Raymond qualifies as an industrious poet and Latinist who 'could have affirmed that the innovators merely pushed to the extreme ideas which had been his for a long time' ['ce familier des Latins aurait pu affirmer que les novateurs poussaient seulement à l'extrême des idées qui étaient depuis longtemps les siennes' (56)].

4 'En effet, l'on peut dérober à la façon des Abeilles, sans faire tort à personne; mais le vol de la Fourmi, qui enlève le grain entier, ne doit jamais être imité' (*Petits traités en forme de lettres. Ecrites à diverses personnes*, Lettre cxxxix, 'Des scrupules de grammaire,' in *Oeuvres*, 3 ed [Paris II, 1052], II: 1052; quoted in Welslau 105).

5 'Le geai paré des plumes de paon'
   Il est assez de geais à deux pieds comme lui,
   Qui se parent souvent des dépouillles d'autrui,
   Et que l'on nomme plagiaires.
   Je m'en tais; et ne veux leur causer nul ennui:
   Ce ne sont pas là mes affaires.
   (La Fontaine, Fable ix, Bk 4).

6 '[...] sonde diligemment son Naturel, & se compose à l'immitation de celuy, dont il se sentira approcher de plus pres. Autrement son immitation ressembleroit à celle du Singe' (Du Bellay, Part II, ch. 3).

7 'Et vous voulez que moi, plagiaire des plagiaires de Sterne –
   Qui fut plagiaire de Swift –
   Qui fut plagiaire de Wilkins –

Qui fut plagiaire de Cyrano –
Qui fut plagiaire de Reboul –
Qui fut plagiaire de Guillaume des Autels –
Qui fut plagiaire de Rabelais –
Qui fut plagiaire de Morus –
Qui fut plagiaire d'Erasme –
Qui fut plagiaire de Lucien – ou de Lucius de Patras – ou d'Apulée – car on ne sait lequel des trois a été volé par les deux autres, et je ne me suis jamais soucié de le savoir ...
Vous voudriez, je le répète, que j'inventasse la forme et le fond d'une livre! le ciel me soit en aide! Condillac dit quelque part qu'il seroit plus aisé de créer un monde que de créer une idée.' (Nodier, *Histoire du Roi de Bohême* 26–7).

The work, of which one of the major themes is that of literary imitation, not only was itself a pastiche, but became itself the object of numerous pastiches (see Boisacq-Generet 32–8).

8 'Au total, c'est une question toute particulière de savoir s'il est permis à l'éditeur d'un ouvrage quelconque de s'enrichir des travaux d'un émule, dont il détruit du même coup la propriété, fût-ce à l'avantage des sciences; question, dis-je, qui me semble moins du ressort de la critique littéraire que de celui de la conscience morale' (Nodier, *Questions de littérature légale* 39–40).

9 '[...] il me semble que j'ai fait assez bien voir que les palmes de la littérature avoient pu souvent être livrées à des hommes dénués de délicatesse et d'honneur, qui ne regardoient la carrière du talent que comme un des chemins de la fortune' (Nodier, *Questions de littérature légale* 152–3).

10 'Les exemples de grands génies que de grands torts ont flétris sont infiniment rares, et il seroit à souhaiter qu'ils n'existassent pas, au prix même des beaux ouvrages que nous serions obligés d'y perdre' (Nodier, *Questions de littérature légale* 154).

11 'Quelle nécessité, nous dira-t-on peut-être, de démasquer tant de gens? Mais une très-grande: celle d'aplanir, autant que possible, la difficulté d'écrire l'histoire littéraire de notre époque: de faire disparaître de ses archives la confusion qu'on y a jetée. Lorsque les industriels biographes surchargent chaque jour nos dictionnaires historiques de pygmées littéraires, dont la postérité aura à rejeter les titres, laisserions-nous encore à celle-ci la rude tâche de s'enquérir de personnages imaginaires? C'est cette considération qui nous a déterminé à ôter le masque de la plus grande partie des littérateurs qui occupent actuellement le public' (Quérard, *Supercheries,* vol. 1, 3–4).

12 'La dignité des lettres a disparu. Depuis 1830 surtout, la littérature, en général, n'est plus une mission chez les écrivains contemporains. Ecrire est devenu un négoce, un moyen de parvenir, un moyen d'argent: à partir de l'époque où tout homme n'a plus dû avoir de considération qu'en raison de son argent, l'homme de lettres n'a pas voulu rester au-dessous d'épiciers et de marchands

de peaux de lapins, devenus électeurs et éligibles: l'intelligence a voulu lutter avec la richesse' (Quérard, *Supercheries*, vol. 1, 71).

13 'C'est un livre qui renferme des révélations très-piquantes. C'est peut-être un livre méchant; mais la faute doit moins m'en être imputée qu'à notre époque; j'ai eu tant de fraudes et tant de traits de charlatanisme à dévoiler! ce livre est néanmoins d'un honnête homme' (Quérard, *Supercheries*, vol. 1, 3).

14 'Les oeuvres du passé ne sauraient être comprises et jugées que par ceux qui savent le passé. Voilà le domaine de la critique professionnelle' (Thibaudet 68).

15 The distinction works aphoristically in French: 'Avant le xixe siècle il y a des critiques [...] mais il n'y a pas la critique' (Thibaudet 7).

16 'C'est une sorte de crime littéraire, pour lequel les pédans, les envieux, et les sots ne manquent pas de faire le procès aux écrivains célèbres. *Plagiat* est le nom qu'ils donnent à un larcin de pensées, et ils crient contre ce larcin comme si on les volait eux-mêmes, ou comme s'il était bien essentiel à l'ordre et au repos public que les propriétés de l'esprit fussent inviolables' (Marmontel 859).

17 'Pourquoi donc les pédans, les demi-beaux-esprits, et les malins critiques, sont-ils plus scrupuleux et plus sévères? Le voici. Les pédans ont la vanité de faire montre d'érudition, en découvrant un larcin littéraire; les petits esprits, en reprochant ce larcin, ont le plaisir de croire humilier les grands; et les critiques dont je parle, suivent le malheureux instinct que leur a donné la nature, celui de verser leur venin' (Marmontel 862).

18 'Rien n'est plus commun dans la république des lettres [que le plagiat]; les vrais savans n'y sont pas trompés; ces vols déguisés n'échappent guère à leurs yeux clairvoyans' (Diderot, *Encyclopédie* 680).

19 'Tous les hommes qui nous apparaissent à diverses époques dominant le plus leur siècle, ces hommes tiennent à leur génération et aux générations précédentes, non par des fils invisibles, mais par des liens puissants et forts que l'on aperçoit facilement dès qu'on veut s'en donner la peine' (Lalanne 119; quoted in Larousse, 'Plagiat' 1109).

20 'Le titre d'auteur original à ce délicieux ouvrage [...] a été sottement, je dirais presque avec ingratitude, contesté à Le Sage par ces demi-critiques, qui s'imaginent découvrir un *plagiat* dès qu'ils peuvent apercevoir quelque espèce de ressemblance entre le plan d'un bon ouvrage et celui d'un autre de même nature traité plus anciennement par un écrivain inférieur' (Scott, quoted in Larousse, 'Plagiat' 1109).

21 '[C]'est la critique, en leur prêtant [aux grands auteurs] l'appui de son désintéressement, qui a comme assuré au delà d'eux la durée de leurs oeuvres et de leur réputation' (Brunetière, 'Critique' 414).

22 Mallon has documented the case of the prolific but unfortunately plagiaristic career of Jayme Sokolow in the Texas Tech History department; and Martin Luther King, Jr's 'plagiarized' thesis has also been debated within an academic context (see *infra*, chapter 7).

23 The controversy has been explored in a recent issue of the *Journal for Information Ethics*, on which the following account is based.

5: READING THE ACT

1 'Au sens moral, le plagiat désigne un comportement réfléchi, visant à faire usage des efforts d'autrui et à s'approprier mensongèrement les résultats intellectuels de son travail. Le plagiat au sens strict se distingue de la cryptomnésie, oubli inconscient des sources, ou de l'influence involontaire, par le caractère conscient de l'emprunt et l'effacement des sources. Il est malhonnête de plagier. Le plagiaire sait que ce qu'il fait ne se fait pas' (Schneider 38)
2 See Donald Bruce's *De l'intertextualité à l'interdiscursivité* for a recent history of intertextuality.
3 'il y a intertextualité obligatoire, lorsque la signification de certains mots du texte n'est ni celle que permet la langue ni celle que demande le contexte, mais le sens qu'ont ces mots dans l'intertexte. C'est l'inacceptabilité de ce sens dans la langue ou dans le contexte qui contraint le lecteur à une présomption, à l'hypothèse d'une solution offerte dans un homologue formel du texte qu'il essaie de déchiffrer. L'intertexte, par conséquent, n'est pas un objet de citation, c'est un objet *présupposé*' (Riffaterre 9).
4 'Je puis [...] traquer dans n'importe quelle oeuvre les échos partiels, localisés et fugitifs de n'importe quelle autre, antérieure ou postérieure. Une telle attitude aurait pour effet de verser la totalité de la littérature universelle dans le champ de l'hypertextualité, ce qui en rendrait l'étude peu maîtrisable; mais surtout, elle fait un crédit, et accorde un rôle, pour moi peu supportable, à l'activité herméneutique du lecteur [...]. J'envisage la relation entre le texte et son lecteur d'une manière plus socialisée, plus ouvertement contractuelle, comme relevant d'une pragmatique consciente et organisée' (*Palimpsestes* 16).
5 Cited in an unpublished letter to Louis-Georges Carrier, Aquin Archives, Edition critique de l'oeuvre d'Aquin, Université du Québec à Montréal.
6 'Ses habitudes de papeterie, de reliure, son goût du cahier continu, ont contribué à ses plagiats involontaires. Il est difficile de disloquer un long texte qu'on a copié d'un seul tenant' (Prévost 110).
7 'l'écrivain tue en lui le plagiaire [...]. Travail qu'on verra prendre la forme d'une appropriation, d'un style, un peu comme la sexualité normale tient à, et de, la sexualité perverse par la façon spécifique de s'en détacher, en la transposant, la répétant, la contredisant, à travers une structuration symbolique, celle de l'Oedipe' (Schneider 34).
8 'Il est vrai, pour me consoler, que j'ai du moins cette ressemblance avec Shakespeare et Molière, que ceux qui les ont attaqués étaient si obscurs, qu'aucune mémoire n'a conservé leur nom' (cited in Quérard, *Supercheries*, vol. 1, 73).
9 'Parody is not specifically mentioned in the [Canadian] *Copyright Act* however

certain parodies would be allowed under Canadian law, depending on the particular circumstances [...] In the United States, parody is considered a form of criticism and falls under the fair use provision' (Harris 127).

10 'Je suis comme la pie voleuse. Je ramasse à droite et à gauche tout ce qui me plaît pour l'entasser dans mon nid. Le problème, c'est de remuer toutes ces choses hétéroclites jusqu'à ce qu'il en sorte un livre' (Chaudenay 284). The quotation is from the interview with Tournier in J.-L. de Rambures, *Comment travaillent les écrivains* (Paris: Flammarion, 1978), 163.

11 'Bravo! Voilà le talent doublé d'une solide franchise qui coupe court à tout soupçon d'appropriation littéraire clandestine. Ceux qui avaient cru faire des trouvailles en filtrant *le Roi des aulnes* au tamis de Flaubert en seront pour leurs frais' (Tournier, in Chaudenay 284).

12 See, for example, the discussion on the protection of the fictional character in Canadian law in Goudreau, 'La protection du personnage en droit canadien.'

13 'Il faut s'entendre sur le mot *plagiat*, et ne pas confondre le larcin de la pensée et du style avec l'usage de ce fonds commun, de ces banalités inévitables auxquelles l'intelligence la plus originale est condamnée, comme le corps l'est aux lois du mouvement, qu'il ait les proportions de l'Apollon du Belvédère ou celles de Thersite. Un imbécile prétendait un jour que Voltaire le copiait, parce qu'il terminait ses lettres, ainsi que lui, par *votre très-humble et très-obéissant serviteur*. Il ne manque pas, en effet, de petits esprits qui n'ont ni idée, ni talent, et qui s'imaginent qu'on s'estime assez peu pour leur faire des emprunts. Ces pauvres gens oublient qu'on n'emprunte qu'aux riches' (Quérard, *Supercheries*, vol. 1, 70).

14 'Un esprit soucieux uniquement des lettres ne s'intéresse pas à de telles contestations [i.e. accusations of plagiarism]. Il sait qu'aucun homme ne peut se flatter raisonnablement de penser quelque chose qu'un autre homme n'ait pas déjà pensé avant lui. Il sait que les idées sont à tout le monde et qu'on ne peut dire: "Celle-ci est mienne" [...] Il sait enfin qu'une idée ne vaut que par la forme et que donner une forme nouvelle à une vieille idée, c'est tout l'art, et la seule création possible à l'humanité' (France 538–9).

15 'Et le lecteur remarquera sans aucun doute que, dans cette analyse, Sardou trouve le moyen de raconter tout le *Barbier de Séville* sans prononcer une seule fois le nom de Figaro qui en est le protagoniste' (Maurevert 222).

16 This genealogy is an excellent example of the literal transmission of 'knowledge' in encyclopedia. Although Quérard mentions Lalanne and D'Israeli, and Lalanne acknowledges D'Israeli, the passage contains five paragraphs they both cite textually from their source without quotation marks, and seamlessly integrated into their own prose. They both claim that the 'details' of the case are drawn from their respective sources, whereas in fact it is not only the historical 'facts,' but the expression itself, which is copied from D'Israeli.

17 Richesource's original text is cited by both Lalanne and Quérard: 'de changer ou déguiser toutes sortes de discours, composés par [des orateurs] ou sortis

d'une plume étrangère, de telle sorte qu'il devienne impossible à l'auteur lui-même de reconnaître son propre ouvrage, son propre style, et le fond de son oeuvre, tant le tout aura été adroitement déguisé' (Lalanne 147–8; Quérard, *Supercheries*, vol. 1, 74–5).

18 '... une oeuvre originale ne repose jamais sur des bases "frauduleuses" ...' (Tamaro, *Le droit d'auteur* 44);

'... il faut apporter quelque chose de distinct ou de différent de ce qui préexiste sous la même forme ...' (44);

'... il existe des situations où une personne tenterait de déguiser l'emprunt à une oeuvre antérieure. Il s'agit de la notion d'imitation déguisée. Et il y a imitation déguisée d'une oeuvre lorsque l'on cherche frauduleusement à en reprendre une partie importante' (68).

19 'La création de Lamartine, qui n'est peut-être pas négligeable, a consisté à substituer le *vous* au *me*, puis à replacer ce bel alexandrin dans un ensemble où il resplendit en effet' (Bydlowski 84).

6: PROFIT PLAGIARISM

1 The story goes like this: 'A crew of hirelings were said to be busily engaged in the Library of Congress making synopses of all the unproduced plays copyrighted by obscure authors. The synopses were forwarded to the New York office of the ring, where monitors scanned Broadway openings for similarities. When they hit on a likely quarry, they'd communicate with the copyright owner of the prior script, buy his rights for a pittance, and launch their suit against the show.

'Another syndicate, it was reported, made a practice of procuring worthless unpublished songs. The syndicate would submit a song to a music publisher, taking care to establish direct access. The composition would be rejected. The blackmail boys would then lie in wait until the publisher had a hit. They'd fabricate a new number closely resembling the hit, declare that it was the song they had originally sent to the publisher, and pounce on the victim with an infringement action.

'Many a defendant paid blood money to be let off. The few doughty ones who put up a fight and won had good reason to be rueful about their victory. Contemplating their depleted purses, they could understand why it's so often said that in a plagiarism set-to, the defendant never wins' (Lindey 267).

2 'Thomas's use of *Babi Yar* seems opportunistic in a way characteristic of the novel as a whole [...] It is the suspicion that the author is cleverly linking disparate materials rather than achieving an organic unity that leads readers into a mistaken attack on the "borrowings" themselves as evidence of imaginative failure' (Frost 412).

'One of the many damaging aspects of the Karlinsky/McDowell prosecution is that it suggests that my book [Thomas's translation of Pushkin's *The Bronze Horsemen*] [...] has been thrown together opportunistically. In fact, the translations were written over three years' (Thomas, 'D.M. Thomas on His Pushkin' 22).

3 'Certains écrivains, comme Leconte de Lisle, vont jusqu'à voir dans le succès immédiat "la marque d'une infériorité intellectuelle." Et la mystique christique de l'"artiste maudit," sacrifié en ce monde et consacré dans l'au-delà, n'est sans doute que la transfiguration en idéal, ou en idéologie professionnelle, de la contradiction spécifique du mode de production que l'artiste pur vise à instaurer. On est en effet dans un monde économique à l'envers: l'artiste ne peut triompher sur le terrain symbolique qu'en perdant sur le terrain économique (au moins à court terme), et inversement (au moins à long terme)' (Bourdieu, *Les règles de l'art* 123). A similar discussion is found in 'The Field of Cultural Production, or: The Economic World Reversed,' Bourdieu, *The Field of Cultural Production* 29–73).

4 'non pas de créer des produits d'une grande valeur et d'une haute originalité, mais de produire le plus abondamment possible et au meilleur marché [...] on voit rarement des industriels se livrer à des études et à des recherches [...] il faut aller vite en besogne' (Larousse, 'Imitation').

5 'Il faut bien se résigner aux habitudes nouvelles, à l'invasion de la démocratie littéraire comme à l'avènement de toutes les autres démocraties. Peu importe que cela semble plus criant en littérature. Ce sera de moins en moins un trait distinctif que d'écrire et de faire imprimer. Avec nos moeurs électorales, industrielles, tout le monde, une fois au moins dans sa vie, aura eu sa page, son discours, son prospectus, son *toast*, sera *auteur*. De là à faire un feuilleton, il n'y a qu'un pas. [...] Quoi de plus honorable, de plus digne d'intérêt que le travail assidu (fût-il un peu hâtif and lâché) d'un écrivain pauvre, vivant par là et soutenant les siens?' ('De la littérature industrielle' [1839], in Sainte-Beuve, 1992, 206).

6 'Du moment, d'ailleurs, qu'il y a production d'une richesse dans la société, il y a un possesseur, et il est juste que la richesse produite ne se trompe point, qu'elle n'aille point presque entière à qui l'a moins méritée. [...] Ces questions complexes étaient peut-être contenues dans votre programme: elles resteront longtemps encore proposées; nous aimons à espérer qu'elles se résoudront peu à peu, et dans un sens qui ne sera pas défavorable, en définitive, à l'honneur des Lettres, ni à l'émancipation de l'esprit' ('Rapport fait par M. Sainte-Beuve [1856], in Sainte-Beuve, 1992, 249–50).

7 'Depuis que l'art et la littérature, qui ne menaient jadis l'écrivain ou l'artiste qu'à la considération, le mènent à la fortune, et que les lettres ou la peinture sont devenues des 'carrières' comme le commerce ou l'administration, nombre de gens s'y sont jetés qui n'y voient que des affaires à brasser et de l'argent à gagner. Il importe qu'on les connaisse, et c'est à la critique qu'il appartient de les dénoncer' (Brunetière, 'Critique' [1880–1892], 1925, vol. ix, 59).

8 Zola's defence of money as a positive artistic value could be understood in terms of the same strategy of self-legitimation that Bourdieu attributes to his defence of his 'popularity':

> novelists could only realize profits equivalent to playwrights by reaching 'the general public,' that is, according to the negative connotations of the expression, by exposing themselves to the discredit attached to commercial success. Thus, Zola, whose novels achieved the most compromising success, could probably only escape, at least in part, the social fate to which his large print runs and his trivial subjects destined him, by transforming 'commercial,' a 'vulgar' and negative expression, into the term 'popular,' an expression charged with all the positive prestige of political progressivness. This transformation was made possible by the role of social prophet which had been imparted to him within the literary field and for which he had become recognized thanks to his militant [social] commitment [...]
>
> [les romanciers ne peuvent réaliser des bénéfices équivalents à ceux des auteurs de théâtre qu'à condition d'atteindre 'le grand public', c'est-à-dire, comme l'indiquent les connotations péjoratives de l'expression, en s'exposant au discrédit attaché au succès commercial. C'est ainsi que Zola, dont les romans ont connu la plus compromettante fortune, n'a sans doute dû d'échapper, en partie, au destin social que lui assignaient ses grands tirages et ses objets triviaux qu'à la conversion du 'commercial', négatif et 'vulgaire', en 'populaire', chargé de tous les prestiges positifs du progressisme politique; conversion rendue possible par le rôle de prophète social qui lui a été imparti au sein même du champ et qui lui a été reconnu bien au-delà grâce au concours du dévouement militant [...] (Bourdieu, *Les règles de l'art* 169)].

9 'Ensuite, ayez le respect de l'argent, ne tombez pas dans cet enfantillage de déblatérer en poètes contre lui; l'argent est notre courage et notre dignité, à nous écrivains, qui avons besoin d'être libres pour tout dire; l'argent fait de nous les chefs intellectuels du siècle, la seule aristocratie possible. Acceptez votre époque comme une des plus grandes de l'humanité, croyez fermement en l'avenir, sans vous arrêter à des conséquences fatales, le débordement du journalisme, le mercantilisme de la basse littérature' ('L'argent dans la littérature,' in Zola 85).

10 'Il faudrait étudier le cas prodigieux de Balzac, si l'on voulait traiter à fond la question de l'argent dans la littérature. Balzac fut un véritable industriel, qui fabriqua des livres pour faire honneur à sa signature. Accablé de dettes, ruiné par des entreprises malheureuses, il reprit la plume, comme le seul outil qu'il connût bien et qui pût le sauver. Voilà la question de l'argent posée avec carrure. Ce n'est pas seulement son pain de tous les jours que Balzac demande à ses livres; il leur demande de combler les pertes faites par lui dans l'industrie.

La bataille dura longtemps, Balzac ne gagna pas une fortune, mais il paya ses dettes, ce qui était déjà bien beau. Nous sommes loin, n'est-ce pas? du bon La Fontaine, rêvant sous les arbres, s'asseyant le soir à la table des grands seigneurs, en payant son dîner d'une fable. Balzac [...] n'a pas cherché dans les lettres que de la gloire, il y a trouvé de la dignité et de l'honneur' ('L'argent dans la littérature,' in Zola 63).

11 'Ainsi la technique habile de Dumas, soit à la scène soit dans le roman, ne peut en aucun cas combler les lacunes laissées par le manque de travail profond, la rapidité d'exécution et surtout l'absence de vision originale qui, pour Balzac, à juste titre, marque l'oeuvre d'art véritable' (Delattre 303).

12 'il a besoin de *ne rien faire*, pour faire quelque chose en son art. Il faut qu'il ne fasse rien d'utile et de journalier pour avoir le temps d'écouter les accords qui se forment lentement dans son âme, et que le bruit grossier d'un travail positif et régulier interrompt et fait infailliblement évanouir' (Vigny 30).

13 'Very early on, M. Alex. Dumas knew how to calculate the financial profits which, with intelligence, could be made from a literary production that later, in 1857, M. Dumas qualified as "merchandise." Another *maréchal* of literature, M. Hon. de Balzac, has been accused of having on several occasions reproduced short stories that his readers already knew. M. de Balzac found in M. Alex Dumas as clever a speculator as himself.' ['De très bonne heure M. Alex. Dumas sut calculer les profits pécuniaires qu'avec de l'intelligence on pouvait retirer d'une production littéraire, que plus tard, en 1847, M. Dumas a qualifié de marchandise. On a reproché à un autre maréchal de la littérature, M. Hon. de Balzac, d'avoir maintes fois reproduit des Nouvelles que ses lecteurs connaissaient déjà. M. de Balzac a trouvé en M. Alex. Dumas un aussi habile spéculateur que lui (Quérard, *Supercheries*, vol. 1, 1093).]

14 'Le fait de traduire le sujet d'un livre ou d'une oeuvre littéraire quelconque en pièce de théâtre, et réciproquement, [...] sans le consentement exprès et par écrit de l'auteur, constitue un plagiat' (Balzac, *Oeuvres complètes*, vol. 23, 715).

15 'De plus, je ne peux pas, je ne dois pas, je ne veux pas subir la dépréciation qui pèse sur moi par les marchés de Sue, et par le tapage que font ses 2 ouvrages, je dois faire voir, par des succès *littéraires*, par des chefs-d'oeuvre, en un mot, que ses oeuvres en détrempe sont des devants de cheminée, et exposer des Raphaël à côté de ses Dubufe [bourgeois portraitist despised by Balzac]. Vous me connaissez assez pour savoir que je n'ai ni jalousie ni aigreur contre lui, ni contre le public! Dieu merci, mes rivaux sont Molière et Walter Scott, Lesage et Voltaire, et non pas ce Paul de Kock en satin et à paillettes; mais [...] il s'agit de payer 120 000 fr. de dettes, d'avoir sa case et une vie décente, ce qui, pour un homme comme moi, à 45 ans, est une nécessité, et si je n'envie rien de ce triomphateur à mirliton, vous me permettez de déplorer qu'on lui paye ses volumes 10 000 fr. tandis que je n'obtiens que 3 000 des miens. Or, en frappant deux grands coups, en étant littéraire, de grand style et plus intéressant, en étant vrai, si

j'éteins à mon profit cette *furia francese*, qui se porte aux *Mystères* [*de Paris*. E. Sue] [...] je puis trouver 200 000 fr. pour 10 volumes des *Scènes de la vie militaire*, et j'ai du pain' (Balzac, *Lettres à Madam Hanska*, vol. 2, 510–11).

16 'On pourrait, ce nous semble, reprocher a bon droit, à M. de Balzac, d'avoir fait souvent un livre nouveau par la réunion d'esquisses ou d'études connues depuis long-temps: de semblables moyens sont trop fréquemment employés par les libraires pour faire acheter aux bibliophiles une seconde, une troisième fois, un livre qu'ils possèdent déjà; mais chez le littérateur, ils ne doivent pas être excusés' (Quérard, *La littérature française contemporaine*, vol. 1, 140).

17 'Voici encore cinq volumes à la publication desquels, nous aimons à le croire, M. de Balzac est resté étranger. Qu'est-ce que le *Livre des Douleurs*, sinon une nouvelle édition du *Livre mystique*, lequel n'était lui-même que la réunion de deux ouvrages qui avaient été réimprimés quatre et cinq fois [...] En vérité M. de Balzac devrait bien s'opposer à ce dégoûtant mercantilisme' (Quérard, *La littérature française contemporaine*, vol. 1, 145).

18 'Par malheur, [...] se laissa prendre à l'amorce des gros bénéfices, et comme son nom était une excellente enseigne pour la librairie, il répondit par des productions hâtives aux offres souvent considérables des éditeurs [...] On a tant de fois et si durement reproché à M. Dumas ce qu'on appelle son industrialisme littéraire, que nous n'insisterons point sur ce fait. Mais en admettant, comme on le dit, que M. Dumas achète ses romans tout faits, qui passent sous son nom, est-ce lui seul qu'il faut blâmer, et le mercantilisme des vendeurs n'est-il pas aussi condamnable que le sien?' (Quérard, *La littérature française contemporaine*, vol. 3, 335).

19 'Tout cela est bel est bon; mais M. Dumas ne fera croire à personne qu'il est permis à un écrivain de copier textuellement des pages entières écrites par d'autres, et de les donner comme siennes au public' (Quérard, *La littérature française contemporaine*, vol. 3, 338).

20 The documentation in the *Village Voice* article is extensive, and relies heavily on interviews with first-hand participants in Haley's career. No print sources are given for the documentation, except the blanket reference to the Haley Papers Collection, and the information cannot be verified.

21 'The other day I chanced upon such a borrowing. I had languished along behind some French words, words so bloodless, so fleshless and so empty of matter that indeed they were nothing but French and nothing but words. At the end of a long and boring road I came upon a paragraph which was high, rich, soaring to the clouds. If I had found a long gentle slope leading up to it, that would have been pardonable: what I came across was a cliff surging up so straight and so steep that I knew I was winging my way to another world after the first half-a-dozen words. That was how I realized what a slough I had been floundering through beforehand, so base and so deep that I did not have the heart to sink back into it' (Montaigne, 'On Educating Children,' Bk I, 26, 165).

22 'Aussitôt que le vote fut acquis, l'un d'entre eux, ne pouvant réprimer plus
   longtemps sa joie, sortit son téléphone portatif devant certains de ses collègues
   médusés afin d'annoncer directement la nouvelle à la principale intéressée'
   (Assouline 10).

23 'Accusée preuves en main, confrontée aux documents, elle ne répond jamais
   sur le plagiat mais à côté. Hors sujet en quelque sorte. Mais elle le fait avec une
   telle constance que ça en est vraiment suspect. Il n'en fallait pas plus pour
   s'immerger dans son oeuvre' (Assouline 10–11).

24 'A la limite, la biographie de l'auteur incriminé importe peu (et la qualité de
   l'éditeur encore moins). C'est le principe et non la personne qui est en cause.
   Par le passé, *Lire* a deja eu l'occasion de dénoncer haut et fort des plagiats com-
   mis par des auteurs venus d'horizons différents' (Assouline 8).

7: IMPERIAL PLAGIARISM

1 Eric Cheyfitz (1991) has studied the relationship between translation and colonization from a contemporary point of view, insisting on the violence of translation in the history of European imperialism, particularly in the British
  encounter with Native Americans. His study is an example of the evolution of
  the metaphor of conquest and the context of the politics of translation. See
  also, with respect to Anglo-Indian colonization and translation, T. Niranjana,
  Siting Translation: History, Poststructuralism and the Historical Context.

2 In the prologue to *Adelphi*, Terence rails against 'unfair critics' who, as well as
  accusing him of hiring ghost writers, claim that he has copied his play. The
  defence is that *Adelphi* is based on a Greek play of Diphilus subsequently remade
  by Plautus into the *Commorientes*. Terence claims that he has adopted for his own
  play a portion which Plautus has left out: 'This portion he (i.e. the poet, Terence)
  has adopted in the *Adelphi, and* has transferred it, translated word for word. This
  new *Play* which we are about to perform; determine *then* whether you think a theft
  has been committed, or a passage has been restored to notice which has been
  passed over in neglect' (Terence 200–1). And similarly in the Prologue to the
  Andrian: 'Now I beseech you, give your attention to the thing which they impute
  as a fault. Menander composed the Andrian and the Perinthian [i.e., Terence's
  Andrian is a translation of Menander's *Perinthian*]. He who knows either of them
  well will know them both; they are in plot not very different, and yet they have
  been composed in different language and style. What suited, he (i.e., Terence,
  the Poet) confesses he has transferred into the Andrian from the Perinthian, and
  has employed them as his own. These parties censure this proceeding; and on
  this point they differ *from him,* that Plays ought not to be mixed up together. By
  being *thus* knowing, do they not show that they know nothing at all? For while
  they are censuring him, they are censuring Naevius, Plautus, *and* Ennius, whom
  our *Poet* has for his precedents [...]' (Terence 5–6).

3 'Et certes, comme ce n'est point chose vicieuse, mais grandement louable
  emprunter d'une Langue étrangère les sentences, et les mots, et les approprier
  à la sienne: aussi est-ce chose grandement à reprendre, voyre odieuse à tout
  Lecteur de libérale Nature, voir en une mème langue une telle Immitation [...]'
  (Du Bellay, *Deffence*, Bk I, ch. 8).

4 'Prendre des anciens et faire son profit de ce qu'ils ont écrit, c'est comme
  pirater au delà de la ligne; mais voler ceux de son siècle, en s'appropriant leurs
  pensées et leurs productions, c'est tirer la laine aux coins des rues, c'est ôter les
  manteaux sur le pont Neuf' (La Mother le Vayer, quoted in Larousse, 'Plagiat'
  1108). Both Diderot (1765) and Nodier (1828) cite these passages from Scudéry
  and La Mothe Le Vayer.

5 'Je crois que tous les auteurs conviennent de cette maxime, qu'il vaut mieux
  piller les anciens que les modernes, et qu'entre ceux-ci il faut épargner ses com-
  patriotes, préférablement aux étrangers [...] Tous les plagiaires, quand ils le
  peuvent, suivent le plan de la distinction que j'ai alléguée; mais ils ne le font pas
  par principe de conscience. C'est plutôt afin de n'être pas reconnus. Lorsqu'on
  pille un auteur moderne, la prudence veut qu'on cache son larcin' (Bayle,
  'Ephore'; quoted from Nodier 5).

6 Mercantilist theory was developed by French economists such as Montchrestien
  (1575–1621) and Laffemas (1545–1612). Colbert (1619–1683) was strongly influenced by their doctrines and put into practice their theory, one that promoted,
  in terms of external relations, the notion of the finality of wealth in the world
  measured by the existence of precious metals, especially gold. Mercantilism was
  a theory of economic growth based not on the expansion of sovereignity over
  foreign territory or populations, but on the acquisition of wealth by its transfer
  into the metropolitan power. The ideology of conquest thus inspired saw the
  establishment of foreign territories primarily as a source of commercial supply
  and profit. Colonization, in the sense of permanent settlement supported by
  agricultural self-sufficiency, was merely a derivative of the necessity to guarantee
  the commercial viability of the system. The system is centripetal in the sense
  that the flow of goods and wealth into the metropolitain power must necessarily
  exceed the expense required to maintain the colony.

7 'Et Shakespeare et Molière avaient raison, car l'homme de génie ne vole pas, il
  conquiert; il fait de la province qu'il prend un annexe de son empire: il lui
  impose ses lois, il la peuple de ses sujets, il étend son sceptre d'or sur elle, et nul
  n'ose lui dire, en voyant son beau royaume: "Cette parcelle de terre ne fait
  point partie de ton patrimoine"' (Dumas, 'Comment je devins auteur dramatique'; quoted in Quérard, *Supercheries*, vol. 1, 72–3).

8 'Nous voici arrivé au dix-neuvième siècle. Mais les écrivains de cette époque
  sont trop gentilshommes pour se permettre tel larcin que ce soit. On ne plagie
  plus, on ne vole plus [...]; on *conquiert*, c'est meilleur ton; [...] Ce n'est donc
  plus, grâce à la parfaite moralité de notre siècle, par des exemples de vols

littéraires que nous continuerons notre rapide aperçu, mais bien par des con-
quêtes' (Quérard, *Supercheries*, vol. 1, 72–3).

9 The following account is summarized from Brown and Denicola 725–40.

10 ' "Non seulement, dit-il dans sa lettre adressée à M. Bombet, vous m'avez enlevé
mon enfant, mais vous lui avez arraché les yeux, coupé les oreilles, gâtés les
formes." On pourrait demander à ce tendre père comment il a pu reconnaître
un enfant si étrangement défiguré. Il faut admirer ici la force de l'instinct paternal' (Stendhal 452).

11 'trop peu sérieuses pour être prises au sérieux: le goût français y cherchait
vainement l'accent sévère de la juste indignation, et flairait presque une mystification' (Stendhal 451).

12 'Il est difficile de répondre à des faits aussi positifs. Après une lecture attentive
des raisons alléguées par M. Carpani, nous n'hésitons pas à reconnaître sa
paternité et nous croyons servir utilement M. Louis-Alexandre-César Bombet en
lui conseillant de restituer amicalement à M. Carpani son livre, sa conversation
et sa fièvre' (Stendhal 454).

13 'Du reste, l'ouvrage méritait d'être traduit en français, s'il est italien; en italien,
s'il est français. Le livre de M. Bombet, original ou copie, se vend à Paris, chez
P. Didot, rue du Pont-de-Lodi' (Stendhal 471).

14 'Hume n'était point le plagiaire de Rapin-Thoiras pour avoir dit, après lui,
qu'Elisabeth était fille de Henri VIII; [...] M. Lacretelle n'était point le plagiaire
de M. Anquetil pour avoir traité, après lui, le sujet de la guerre de la Ligue'
(Stendhal 476).

15 A short summary of the most notable plagiarisms is found in Chaudenay; a
longer account is to be found in Maurevert.

16 'il s'est servi des textes de Carpani, Winckler, Sismondi et *tutti quanti*, comme
d'un ensemble de matériaux qu'il a façonnés à sa manière. En d'autres termes,
en isolant son apport personnel, on arrive à la conclusion que l'ouvrage, loin
d'être un centon, est fortement structuré, de sorte que même les parties
empruntées finissent par se fondre dans un ensemble à l'allure bien stendahli-
enne' (Del Litto, in Stendhal 500).

17 'Une partie du charme qu'exerce la *Vie de Haydn* émane justement du jeu récip-
roque de deux esprits si parfaitement accordés (en dépit de leurs apparentes
querelles) qu'il est virtuellement impossible de chercher à repartir nettement
les idées: ceci est à Stendhal, cela est à Carpani' (Stendhal 502).

18 'La conquête de l'Italie opérée au moyen d'actions qui avaient de la grandeur,
réveilla d'abord les peuples de la Lombardie; dans la suite, les exploits de ses
soldats en Espagne et en Russie, son association aux destinées d'un grand
empire, quoique cet empire ait eu du malheur [...] tout a fait naître dans ce
beau pays (...) la soif d'être une nation' (Stendhal 505).

19 'il sait très bien mettre en oeuvre ce qu'on lui rapporte, et surtout il sait très
bien s'approprier les écrits étrangers. Il traduit des passages de mon *Voyage en*

Italie, et affirme avoir entendu raconter l'anecdote par une marchesina' (Maurevert 166).

20 In the context, *à la dérobée,* nowadays meaning 'in a covert manner,' recovers its older literal meaning: *dérober* = to steal.

21 'Lanzi ou Carpani tant qu'on voudra, les *Vies de Haydn, Mozart et Métastase,* et l'*Histoire de la peinture en Italie,* n'en offraient pas moins une telle multiplicité d'idées ingénieuses ou profondes, et un style si personnel, qu'on souhaiterait que beaucoup de livres originaux fussent plagiés, à ce prix' (Hazard, *La vie de Stendhal* 128).

22 'Vous comprenez, maintenant, pourquoi la littérature nègre d'expression française est une contribution importante à la *littérature généralisée:* à la *Civilisation de l'Universel.* C'est que, communicable par le fait qu'elle est écrite en français, elle fait la *symbiose* des deux aspects extrêmes du Génie humain. Par quoi elle est *humanisme intégral'* (Senghor, 'La littérature africaine d'expression française,' *Liberté* 1, 402).

23 See the summary of the scandal in Sellin, 'The Unknown Voice of Yambo Ouloguem; Miller, *Blank Darkness;* and Randall, 'Appropriate(d) Discourse.'

24 'L'Afrique des lettrés africains contemporains est différente de celle des griots mais d'une authenticité aussi irréprochable. N'oublions jamais que cette nouvelle littérature est écrite par des lettrés dont les connaissances linguistiques et culturelles africaine et occidentale sont aussi vastes que celles de leurs critiques occidentaux' (Wolitz 134).

25 In this context, the connotations of 'rapt' are not completely captured by the notion of 'abduction' or 'kidnapping.' As in the English 'rape' whose archaic meaning is the 'action or an act of carrying away a person, esp. a woman, by force,' *rapt* originally included the contemporary sense of 'rape.' 'Il est raisonnable de penser que le plagiat est pour Ouologuem à la fois chose et signe: acte de piraterie doublé du signe de son attitude ironique d'écrivain africain devant le texte occidental. Le plagiat est alors la figuration du rapt du corps du texte albo-européen [...] Il est une métaphore signifiant la revanche de l'Africain sur le négrier qui s'est livré au rapt des esclaves, le rapt étant vu comme la trace physique du sujet opprimant de la civilisation – entendue dans ce cas comme le système de pensée qui refuse à l'Autre le droit à la différence' (Bouygues 3).

26 'M. Jacques Lanctôt écrivait que mon poème *Speak What* "est calqué en tous points sur le célèbre *Speak White* de Michèle Lalonde, sans que celle-ci – ni l'éditeur, d'ailleurs – ait été consultée." N'ayons pas peur des mots: M. Lanctôt m'accuse de plagiat' (Micone, 'Speak What,' *Le Devoir,* 12 Jan. 1994 A7).

27 'le Québécois d'aujourd'hui tel que transformé par la présence des immigrants pour qui les francophones constituent désormais le groupe dominant nonobstant le victimisme et les jérémiades de quelques "nationaleux"' (Micone, 'Speak What,' 1994). 'Nationaleux' is a derogatory deformation of *nationaliste,* which is difficult to render in English.

28 'Le poète a le droit de s'approprier tout matériau qu'il juge nécessaire à son oeuvre, et Marco Micone a clairement énoncé les intentions qui ont présidé à son emprunt non dissimulé du *Speak White* de Michèle Lalonde' (Thériault A9).

29 The role of the neo-Québécois in the political and cultural fabric of Quebec remains a sensitive issue. At the time of the 1995 referendum on sovereignty, Jacques Parizeau, the leader of the Parti Québécois whose sovereigntist platform was defeated, caused a scandal by blaming the defeat on the 'ethnic vote,' that is, on the non-francophone and immigrant population who voted in the majority in favour of continuing the federalist status quo. He was denounced by members of his own party as well as by many other voices in the province.

8: GUERRILLA PLAGIARISM

1 *The Writings of a Savage*, 107; cited (incorrectly) in Kuspit 111.

2 The postmodernist debate is much more complex than this opposition implies. However, postmodernism itself is not my object, and the discussions surrounding its definition and evolution are far too extensive to be treated here. My goal here is simply to suggest some of the positions with respect to which postmodern appropriation can be seen to be 'revolutionary,' or not. A useful overview of the subject is offered by Bertens, *The Idea of Postmodernism*.

3 It may be unnecessary to note that 'appropriation,' here, means 'recuperation,' not the aesthetic of appropriation art that I have been discussing.

4 In another text signed 'Karen Eliot' ('Orientation for the Use of a Context and the Context for the Use of an Orientation,' Home 9), one reads the following: 'Karen Eliot is a name that refers to an individual human being who can be anyone. The name is fixed, the people using it aren't. The purpose of many different people using the same name is to create a situation for which no one in particular is responsible and to practically examine western philosophical notions of identity, individuality, value and truth.' The 'authors' cited in quotation marks are pseudonyms for Home or his co-organizer Ed Baxter.

5 In a subsequent account, Home declares that he considers the London Festival a success, both for him personally, and on the administrative level, it having been entirely engineered without funding (*The Festival of Plagiarism* 21).

6 'La grande noirceur' refers to the 'reign' of the arch-conservative premier of Quebec, Maurice Duplessis, who died in 1959. But the ideology of 'conservation' dates as far back as the middle of the nineteenth century. French-Canadian nationalism promoted an isolationism intended to perserve the religious, linguistic, and cultural identity that was threatened by the dominant North American and Anglo-Canadian context. The goal of the Liberal government that took power in 1960 was the political, social, and economic restructuring of Quebec, to bring the society 'into the 20th century.'

7 *Portrait du colonisé* was re-edited for the Québécois market in 1972, accompanied

by a text entitled 'Les Canadiens français sont-ils des colonisés?' in which Memmi responds to questions by students from the *Haute école commerciale* in Paris. To their objections that the Québécois are not colonized because of their prosperity and because they are themselves part of a colonial nation who subjugated the Native peoples, Memmi responds: 'All domination is relative. All domination is specific. It is obvious that one is not dominated in the absolute, but always with respect to someone, in a given context' ['Toute domination est relative. Toute domination est spécifique. Il est évident que l'on n'est pas dominé dans l'absolu, mais toujours par rapport à quelqu'un, dans un contexte donné' (Memmi 139)].

8 See J. Paterson, *Moments postmodernes dans le roman québécois* (Ottawa: Les Presses de l'Université d'Ottawa, 1990). Paterson does not discuss 'plagiarism' among the postmodern strategies she analyses in *Trou de mémoire*.

9 '[...] l'originalité d'un écrit est directement proportionnelle à l'ignorance de ses lecteurs. Il n'y a pas d'originalité: les oeuvres sont des décalques (fonctionnels, cela va de soi, dans une société à haute consommation de loisirs et dotée, par surcroît, de pulpe) tirés de contretypes oblitérés qui proviennent d'autres "originaux" décalqués de décalques qui sont des copies conformes d'anciens faux qu'il n'est pas besoin d'avoir connus pour comprendre qu'ils n'ont pas été des archétypes, mais seulement des variantes. Une invariance cruelle régit la production sérielle des variantes qu'on a accoutumé de nommer des oeuvres originales. L'histoire décalque, elle aussi. L'originalité y est aussi impossible qu'en littérature. L'originalité n'existe pas, c'est un leurre' ('Profession: écrivain,' in Aquin, *Point de fuite* 47).

10 'Dans les livres contemporains québécois et autres, j'ai trouvé que l'auteur est décidément surprésent. Le livre se trouve, en fin de compte, contaminé par la présence de son auteur à tel point que le jeu, quand on lit, consiste à aimer ou à détester la personne même de l'auteur. J'en viens à préconiser une pratique de l'absence de telle sorte que les livres ne deviennent pas indiscernables à force d'être englués. A la limite, je me demande si la grande innovation littéraire ne serait pas de revenir à l'anonymat ... A lecteurs anonymes, auteurs anonymes ...' ('La disparition élocutoire du poète' [Mallarmé],' in Aquin, *Mélanges littéraires*, vol. 1, 248–9).

11 'Imagine un pauvre type investi soudain par le multiple: d'un seul coup ses sensations privilégiées se dissolvent, ses pensées originales s'émoussent, ses goûts subtils s'évaporent' ('Le texte ou le silence marginal,' in Aquin, *Mélanges littéraires*, vol. 1, 537).

12 'Le texte s'écrit continuellement dans le texte ou le long des marges d'un autre texte. Le moi est un intertexte, la conscience du moi un commentaire désordonné – marginalia parfois indiscernable mais pourtant toujours formante, instauratrice' ('Le texte ou le silence marginal,' in Aquin, *Mélanges littéraires*, vol. 1, 537–8).

13 'Je maintiens, contre toute vraisemblance, que je suis un écrivain vivant et –
dans la mesure où je puis donner suite à ce projet d'existence – je vais aussi
continuer à écrire des variantes toujours plus inutiles du néant dont nous, les
écrivains, sommes l'invincible incarnation. Notre entreprise peut se comparer
à une tentative plus ou moin séduisante pour donner une forme à la vacuité
intérieure que, par le fait même, nous étalons non sans quelque plaisir ...' ('La
Mort de l'écrivain maudit,' in Aquin, *Mélanges littéraires*, vol. 1, 206).

14 This title defies my abilities of translation. 'Nègres' is French for 'ghost-writer';
in the context the capital 'N' refers equally to race: Ouologuem's essay suggests
that 'Nègres' are inevitably subject to the anonymous, subaltern condition of
'ghost writers for famous authors' ('écrivains célèbres'). 'Pisse-copie' is a neolo-
gism, implying perhaps the speed with which ghost-writers must produce copy
('copie' refers to student papers at school as well as to the copy as plagiarism);
the essay refers to producing novels 'à la chaîne' – in assembly-line fashion.

15 The question of Aquin's position in the cultural and political scene of the day is
somewhat relative. Although from a historical point of view he appears at the
centre of both the political and the cultural movements of the 1960s and 1970s
in Quebec, it is clear that he saw his own position as being very much on the
margins of a culture that was itself marginal. Despite his institutional literary
success, he was not able to secure for himself a stable position in either the cultural or the political institutions of influence, and his suicide (1977) was preceded both by a writer's block and by unfulfilled expectations that the new
Québécois (pro-independence) government would call upon him to occupy a
post in the Ministry of Culture.

16 I have 'corrected' the translation by Keith Cohen and Paula Cohen, who note
the importance of the play on words between 'theft' and 'flight' (*vol*) but do not
systematically maintain the ambiguity.

17 'Les références précises sous forme de notes ou de guillemets indiquant la citation auront souvent été écartées. La/une femme occupant par rapport à l'élab-
oration théorique une fonction à la fois de dehors mutique soutenant toute
systématicité et de sol maternel (encore) silencieux dont se nourrit tout fonde-
ment, elle n'a pas à s'y rapporter de manière déjà codée par la théorie. Confon-
dant ainsi, une fois de plus, l'imaginaire du "sujet" – dans ses connotations
masculines – et ce qui serait, sera peut-être, celui du "féminin"' (Irigaray 458).

18 The distinction among copying, appropriation, and plagiarism seems unstable
for Acker, and shifts according to whether she is referring to an aesthetic or a
legal context, as is the case in this quotation. Three years earlier she says: 'When
I copy, I don't appropriate. I just do what gives me most pleasure: write' (Acker,
'A Few Notes on Two of My Books' 34).

19 Baudrillard suggests that simulation is more threatening to the apparatus of
repression than actual violence, since the second 'only upsets the order of
things, the right of property, whereas the other interferes with the very prin-

ciple of reality' (266). His example of the impossible fake hold-up goes as follows: 'Go and organize a fake holdup. Be sure to check that your weapons are harmless, and take the most trustworthy hostage, so that no life is in danger (otherwise you risk committing an offense). Demand ransom, and arrange it so that the operation creates the greatest commotion possible – in brief, stay close to the "truth," so as to test the reaction of the apparatus to a perfect simulation. But you won't succeed: the web of artificial signs will be inextricably mixed up with real elements (a police officer will really shoot on sight; a bank customer will faint and die of a heart attack; they will really turn the phony ransom over to you) – in brief, you will unwittingly find yourself immediately in the real, one of whose functions is precisely to devour every attempt at simulation, to reduce everything to some reality – that's exactly how the established order is, well before institutions and justice come into play' (267).

20 Levine has renounced the practice of photographic reproductions and has turned to the appropriation or adaptation of artistic works in the public domain. She has declared that she does not intend knowingly to infringe copyright.

CONCLUSION: POST-PLAGIARISM

1 In the case of Rauschenberg's appropriation of Morton Beebe's photograph of a diver, the original had been used as an advertisement for the Nikon camera company; in the case of Warhol's appropriation of 'Flowers,' the original photograph had appeared in *Modern Photography* as an advertisment for Kodak; the appropriation of journalistic photos is also the subject of many disputes. In general, appropriation for non-commercial (aesthetic) purposes is more legitimate than copying for purely commercial ends. See Morris, 'When Artists Use Photographs,' and Carlin, 'Culture Vultures.'

2 The idea/expression dichotomy is in fact a major source of disagreement and discussion among intellectual-copyright jurists, especially in the context of computer-software protection: 'With source and object code being copyrightable, the courts have now shifted to a second generation of software copyright issues. The two major legal issues are the degree of copying protected by the statute and the idea/expression dichotomy ... Under the second major legal issue of the idea/expression dichotomy under copyright law, defendants typically justify their actions by alleging that the plaintiff's copyright is protecting the idea, rather than the expression, of the source and object code. This would make the copyright void. Plaintiffs naturally allege that their copyright is only one expression of the idea and is thus legal under the Copyright Act' (Soma 57–8).

Works Cited

Acker, Kathy. *Don Quixote, which was a dream*. New York: Grove, 1986.
- 'A Few Notes on Two of My Books.' *The Review of Contemporary Fiction* 9.3 (1989): 31–6.
- *Hannibal Lecter, My Father*. Ed. Sylvère Lotringer. Native Agents Series. New York: Semiotexte, 1991.
Adams, J.K. *Pragmatics and Fiction*. Amsterdam: John Benjamins, 1985.
Aden, John M., ed. *The Critical Opinions of John Dryden: A Dictionary*. Nashville: Vanderbilt UP, 1963.
Adkins, Nelson F. '"Chapter on American Cribbage": Poe and Plagiarism.' *Papers of the Bibliographical Society of America*. 42 (1948): 169–210.
Adorno, Theodor W. *Aesthetic Theory*. Trans. C. Lenhardt. Ed. G. Adorno and R. Tiedemann. London and Boston: Routledge, 1984.
Alberge, Dalya, and Ben MacIntyre. 'French Novel Written Off as Copy of Okri's Booker Winner.' *Times* 26 Nov. 1996.
Allemang, John. 'Award-winning *Star* Columnist Found Dead.' *Globe and Mail* 11 Feb. 1989: A11.
Amis, Martin. *The Rachel Papers*. 1973. Harmondsworth: Penguin, 1984.
Anon. 'Something *New* Out of Africa?' *Times Literary Supplement* 5 May 1972: 525.
Aquin, Hubert. *Mélanges littéraires*. Ed. Claude Lamy and Jacinthe Martel. 2 vols. Bibliothèque québécoise. Montreal: Leméac, 1995.
- *Point de fuite*. 1971. Ed. Guylaine Massoutre. Bibliothèque québécoise. Montreal: Leméac, 1995.
- *Prochain épisode*. 1965. Ed. Jacques Allard. Bibliothèque québécoise. Montreal: Leméac, 1995.
- 'Le texte ou le silence marginal.' Aquin, *Mélanges littéraires*, 1: 535–9.

- *Trou de mémoire.* 1968. Ed. Janet Paterson and Marilyn Randall. Bibliothèque québécoise. Montreal: Leméac, 1993.
- *Writing Quebec: Selected Essays by Hubert Aquin.* Edited with an introduction by A. Purdy. Trans. P. Gibson, R. Joshee, A. Purdy, and K. Shouldice. Edmonton: U of Alberta Press, 1988.

Arnold, Matthew. 'The Function of Criticism at the Present Time.' 1865. *Essays in Criticism: First Series.* Ed. Sister T.M. Hoctor. Chicago and London: U of Chicago P, 1968: 8–30.

Association littéraire et artistique internationale. *Information et le droit d'auteur.* Cowansville: Les éditions Yvon Blais, 1989.

Assouline, Pierre. 'L'affaire Beyala rebondit.' *Lire* Feb. 1997: 8–11.

Bainbridge, David I. *Intellectual Property.* London: Pitman 1992.

Balzac, Honoré de. *Lettres à Madame Hanska.* Ed. Roger Pierrot. Vol. 2. Paris: Éditions du Delta, 1968.

- *Oeuvres complètes.* Vol. 3, *Oeuvres diverses.* Paris: Club de l'Honnête homme, 1956.

Bar-Hillel, Yehoshua. (1971). 'Out of the Pragmatic Waste-basket.' *Linguistic Inquiry* 2 (1971): 401–7.

Barlow, John Perry. 'The Economy of Ideas: A Framework for Rethinking Patents and Copyrights in the Digital Age (Everything you know about intellectual property is wrong).' *Wired* 2.03 (Mar. 1994): 84–6, 88–90, 126–9.

Barthes, Roland. 'The Death of the Author.' 1968. *Image, Music, Text.* New York: Hill & Wang, 1997

- 'La mort de l'auteur.' 1968. *Essais critiques IV: Le bruissement de la langue.* Paris: Seuil, 1984: 61–6.

Baudrillard, Jean. 'The Precession of Simulacra.' 1983. Wallis 253–81.

Bayle, Pierre. *Dictionnaire historique et critique.* Rotterdam: R. Leers, 1697.

- *A General Dictionary Historical and Critical.* Trans. John Peter Bernard. Vol. 7. London: Thomas Virch and John Lockman, 1738.

'Becoming Martin Luther King Jr.: Plagiarism and Originality, A Round Table.' *Journal of American History* 78 (June 1991)

Benstock, Shari. 'At the Margins of Discourse: Footnotes in the Fictional Text.' *PMLA* 98. 2 (Mar. 1983): 204–25.

Bertens, Hans. *The Idea of the Postmodern: A History.* London and New York: Routledge, 1995.

Bhabha, Homi. *The Location of Culture.* London: Routledge, 1994.

Birrell, Augustine. *Seven Lectures on the Law and History of Copyright in Books.* 1899. New York: Augustus M. Kelley; Rothman Reprints, 1971.

Blair, Hugh. 'A Critical Dissertation on the Poems of Ossian.' 1763. *The Poems of Ossian.* Trans. James Macpherson. Boston: Phillips, Sampson & Co., 1850. 88–188.

Bloom, Harold. *The Anxiety of Influence.* New York: Oxford UP, 1975.

Bloom, Harold, et al. 'Plagiarism – A Symposium.' *Times Literary Supplement* 9 Apr. 1982: 413–15.

Boisacq-Generet, Marie-Jeanne. *Tradition et modernité dans L'Histoire du Roi de Bohême et de ses sept châteaux de Charles Nodier.* Paris: Honoré Champion Editeur 1994.

Bonvallet, Pierre. *Molière de tous les jours.* Paris: Le Pré aux clercs, 1985.

Borges, Jorge Luis. *Ficciones.* 1956. Ed. Anthony Kerrigan. New York: Grove Press, 1962.

Bosco, Monique. 'Ce "cochon de payant" de lecteur.' *Maclean's* 8. 6 (1968): 47.

Boswell, James. *Life of Johnson.* 1799. Oxford: Oxford UP, 1965.

Bourdieu, Pierre. *Distinction: A Social Critique of the Judgement of Taste.* Trans. Richard Nice. 1979. Cambridge, MA: Harvard UP, 1984.

– *The Field of Cultural Production.* Ed. Randal Johnson. New York: Columbia UP, 1993.

– 'The Field of Cultural Production.' 1983. Bourdieu, *The Field of Cultural Production,* 29–73.

– 'The Market of Symbolic Goods.' 1983. Bourdieu, *The Field of Cultural Production.* 112–41.

– 'The Production of Belief: Contribution to an Economy of Symbolic Goods.' 1983. Bourdieu, *The Field of Cultural Production.* 74–111.

– *Les règles de l'art: genèse et structure du champ littéraire.* Paris: Seuil, 1992.

Bouygues, Charles. 'Yambo Ouologuem, ou le silence des canons.' *Canadian Journal of African Studies* 25 (1991): 1–11.

Bowers, Neal. *Words for the Taking: The Hunt for a Plagiarist.* New York: Norton, 1997.

Boyd, Herb. 'Plagiarism and the *Roots* Suit.' *First World* 2.3 (1979): 31–3.

Bray, Robert. 'Reading between the Texts: Benjamin Thomas's *Abraham Lincoln* and Stephen Oates's *With Malice toward None.*' *Journal of Information Ethics* 3.1 (1994): 8–24.

Brown, R.S., and R.C. Denicola. *Cases in Copyright.* 5th ed. Westbury, NY: Foundation Press, 1990.

Bruce, Donald. *De l'intertextualité à l'interdiscursivité.* Toronto: Paratexte, 1995.

Brunetière, Ferdinand. 'Critique.' *La grande encyclopédie.* Paris: H. Lamirault, 1886–92.

– 'La critique.' *Études critiques sur l'histoire de la littérature française.* 1880–92. Paris: Hachette, 1925.

Bruns, Gerald. 'The Originality of Texts in a Manuscript Culture.' *Comparative Literature* 32.2 (1980): 113–29.

Buchloch, Benjamin. 'Allegorical Procedures: Appropriation and Montage in Contemporary Art.' *Art Forum* Sep. 1982: 43–4, 46–56.

Bürger, Peter. *The Theory of the Avant-Garde.* Trans. Michael Shaw. Theory and History of Literature Series. Vol. 4. Minneapolis: U of Minnesota P, 1984.

Burlingame, Michael. 'A Sin against Scholarship: Some Examples of Plagiarism in Stephen B. Oates's Biographies of Abraham Lincoln, Martin Luther King Jr., and William Faulkner.' *Journal of Information Ethics* 3.1 (1994): 48–57.

Buskirk, Martha. 'Appropriation under the Gun.' *Art in America* Jun. 1992: 37, 39, 41.

– 'Commodification as Censor: Copyrights and Fair Use.' *October* 60 (1992): 83–109.

Bydlowski, Michel. 'Plagiats, supercheries et mystifications littéraires.' *Quai Voltaire* 1 (1991): 83–92.

Camden, Lord. 'Cases of the Appelants and Respondents in the Cause of Literary Property, Before the House of Lords.' *The Literary Property Debate: Six Tracts, 1764–1774*. 1774. Ed. Stephen Parks. New York and London: Garland Reprints, 1975.

Carlin, John. 'Culture Vultures: Artistic Appropriation and Intellectual Property Law.' *Columbia–VLA Journal of Law and the Arts* 3 (1988): 103–43.

Carroll, D. Allen, ed. *Greene's Groatsworth of Wit: Bought with a Million of Repentance.* Attributed to Henry Chettle and Robert Greene. 1592. Medieval and Renaissance Texts and Studies. Binghamton: Center for Medieval and Early Renaissance Studies, 1994.

Carruthers J. '*Gondos* v *Hardy et al.'* *Ontario Reports.* 16 July 1982, 38 O.R. (2d): 555–77.

Cave, Terence. *The Cornucopian Text.* Oxford: Clarendon Press, 1979.

Chaudenay, Roland de. *Dictionnaire des plagiaires.* Paris: Perrin, 1990.

Cheyfitz, Eric. *The Poetics of Imperialism: Translation and Colonization from The Tempest to Tarzan.* New York and Oxford: Oxford UP, 1991.

Cixous, Hélène. 'The Laugh of the Medusa.' *New French Féminisms.* Ed. Elaine Marks and Isabelle de Courtivron. New York: Schocken, 1981. 245–64.

Cocteau, Jean. *L'appel à l'ordre.* Paris: Stock, 1948.

Coleridge, Samuel Taylor. *Biographia Literaria.* 1983. Vols. 8–9 of *The Collected Works of Samuel Taylor Coleridge.* Ed. J. Engell and W. Jackson Bate. London: Routledge and Kegan Paul; Princeton: Princeton UP. 14 vols., 1969–93.

Compagnon, Antoine. *La seconde main.* Paris: Seuil, 1979.

'Conversation between Cornish Rogers and David Thelen.' *Journal of American History* 78:1 (1991): 41–62.

'Conversation between S. Paul Schilling and David Thelen.' *Journal of American History* 78:1 (1991): 63–80.

Copeland, Rita. 'The Fortunes of "Non verbum pro verbo."' *The Medieval Translator.* Ed. Roger Ellis. Cambridge: D.S. Brewer, 1989. 15–35

Corneille, Pierre. *Oeuvres complètes.* Vol. 1. Paris: Gallimard, 1980.

Costa, Robert. 'Bidlo's Monstrous Eggs.' *Arts Magazine* 62 (Apr. 1988): 76–7.

Craig, D.H., ed. *Ben Jonson: The Critical Heritage (1599–1798).* London and New York: Routledge, 1990.

Culler, Jonathon. 'Presupposition and Intertextuality.' *Modern Language Notes* 91 (1976): 1380–96.

Dauber, Kenneth. *The Idea of Authorship in America.* Madison: U of Wisconsin P, 1990.

Deforges, Régine. *La bicyclette bleue.* Paris: Ramsay, 1985.

Dejevsky, Mary. 'Prize Battle Strips Academy of All Honour.' *Independent* (London) 27 Jan. 1997, International section: 9.

Delattre, Guy. *Les opinions littéraires de Balzac.* Paris: PUF, 1961.

Delègue, Yves. *Le royaume d'exil: le sujet de la littérature en quête d'auteur.* Paris: Obsidiane, 1991.

Deleuze, Gilles, and Félix Guattari. *Anti-Oedipus: Capitalism and Schizophrenia.* 1972. Trans. R. Hurley, M. Seem, and H. Lane. Minneapolis: U of Minnesota P, 1992.

Delfau, Gérard, and Anne Roche. *Histoire, littérature: histoire et interprétation du fait littéraire.* Paris: Seuil, 1977.

Dery, Mark. 'Art Goes High Tech.' *ArtNews* 92.2 (Feb. 1993): 74–83.

Diderot, Denis. *L'encyclopédie ou dictionnaire raisonné des sciences, des arts et des métiers.* Paris: Briasson, David, Le Breton, Durand, 1761–5.

– 'Lettre historique et politique adressée à un magistrat sur le commerce de la librairie.' 1764. *Oeuvres complètes.* Vol. 5. Ed. Roger Lewinter. Paris: Le Club français du livre, 1969. 300–81.

D'Israeli, Isaac. *Curiosities of Literature.* 1791–3. New York: Garland, 1971.

Do, Tess. 'Aux prises avec les prix: les Femmes du prix Fémina.' Diss. U of Western Ontario. 1998.

Dor, Joël. *Introduction à la lecture de Lacan.* Vol. 1: *L'inconscient structuré comme un langage.* Paris: Denoël, 1985.

Douglas, John. *Milton vindicated from the Charge of Plagiarism brought against him by Mr. Lauder, and Lauder himself convicted of several forgeries and gross Impositions on the Public.* London: A. Millar, 1751.

Dryden, John. *The Prologues and Epilogues of John Dryden: A Critical Edition.* Ed. William B. Gardner. New York: Columbia UP, 1951.

Du Bellay, Joachim. *Deffence et illustration de la langue française.* 1549. Geneva: Slatkine Reprints, 1972.

Dubois, Jacques. *L'institution de la littérature.* Bruxelles: Fernand Nathan, Editions Labor, 1978.

Dupriez, Bernard. *Gradus: les procédés littéraires (Dictionnaire).* Paris: Union générale d'éditions, 1980.

Dunton, Chris, and M+G Reporters. 'Beyala Doesn't Need to Steal.' *Mail and Guardian* 5 Dec. 1996. <http://mg/art/reviews/96dec/rvbeyala.html>.

Dutton, Denis, ed. *The Forger's Art: Forgery and the Philosophy of Art.* Berkeley, Los Angeles, London: U of California P, 1983.

Eagleton, Terry. *The Ideology of the Aesthetic.* Oxford: Blackwell, 1990.

Eco, Umberto. *The Limits of Interpretation.* Bloomington, Indiana: Indiana UP.

– *The Open Work.* Trans. Anna Cancogni. Cambridge, MA: Harvard UP, 1989.

Eliot, T.S. *Selected Essays.* 1932. London; Faber & Faber, 1969.

Enfield, William. 'Observations on Literary Property.' *The Literary Property Debate. Eight Tracts, 1774–1775.* Ed. Stephen Parks. New York and London: Garland, 1974.

Epstein, Jacob. *Wild Oats.* Boston and Toronto: Little, Brown, 1979.

Erasmus. *Dialogus Ciceronianus.* 1528. Trans. Betty Knott. *Collected Works of Erasmus (CWE).* Vol. 28. Ed. A.H.T. Levi. Toronto: U of Toronto P, 1986. 342–448.

– *The Praise of Folly.* Trans. Hoyt Hopewell Hudson. Princeton, NJ: Princeton UP, 1970. Also trans. Betty Radice. *CWE.* Vol. 27. 1986. 77–153.

Fanon, Frantz. *The Wretched of the Earth.* 1961. New York: Grove P, 1966.

Ferriar, John. *Illustrations of Sterne with Other Essays and Verses.* London: Cadell and Davies, 1798; New York: Garland, 1971.

Fisher, Murray, Ed. *Alexander Haley: The Playboy Interviews.* New York: Ballantine, 1993.

Fiske, George C. *Lucilius and Horace: A Study in the Classical Theory of Imitation.* Studies in Language and Literature no. 7. Madison: U of Wisconsin P, 1920.

Flamand, Paul. 'Letter to the Editor.' *Research in African Literature* 4.1 (Spring 1973): 129. (Contains excerpt of Letter from A. Schwartz-Bart to P. Flammand, editor Editions Seuil, 16 Aug. 1968.)

Foucault, Michel. 'The Subject and Power.' 1982. Wallis 417–32.

– 'What Is an Author?' 1969. *Language, Counter-memory, Practice.* Ed. Donald. F. Bouchard. Ithaca, NY: Cornell UP, 1977. 113–38.

France, Anatole. 'Apologie pour le plagiat.' 1892. *Oeuvres complètes.* Vol. 7:. *La vie lit-téraire,* 3d and 4th ser. Paris: Calmann-Lévy, 1926.

Françon, André. *Le droit d'auteur: aspects internationaux et comparatis.* Cowansville, PQ: Éditions Yvon Blais, 1993.

Friedman, Ellen. 'A Conversation with Kathy Acker.' *The Review of Contemporary Fiction* 9.3 (1989): 12.

Frost, David. 'The White Hotel.' *Times Literary Supplement* 6 Apr. 1982: 412.

Fruman, Norman. *Coleridge: The Damaged Archangel.* New York: Braziller, 1971.

– 'Originality, Plagiarism, Forgery, and Romanticism.' *Centrum* 4.1 (1976): 44–9.

Gallays, François. 'La lecture de la justice.' Vandendorpe 189–98.

Gasté, Armand. *La querelle du Cid: Pièces et pamphlets publiés d'après les originaux.* Paris: H. Welter Libraire-Éditeur, 1898.

Gauguin, Paul. *The Writings of a Savage.* Ed. Daniel Guérin. Trans. Eleanor Levieux. New York: Viking P, 1978.

Genette, Gérard. *Palimpsestes.* Paris: Seuil, 1982.

Goldstein, Paul. *Copyright's Highway: From Gutenberg to the Celestial Jukebox.* New York: Hill & Wang, 1994.

Goudreau, Mistrale. 'La protection du personnage en droit canadien.' Vanden-dorpe 215–29.

Goodman, Nelson. *Languages of Art: An Approach to the Theory of Symbols.* Indiana and Cambridge: Hackett Pub Co. 1976.

Grace, Sherrill. 'Respecting Plagiarism: Tradition, Guilt and Malcolm Lowry's "Pelagiarist Pen."' *English Studies in Canada* 18.4 (Dec. 1992): 461–82.

Grafton, Anthony. *Forgers and Critics: Creativity and Duplicity in Western Scholarship.* Princeton, NJ: Princeton UP, 1990.

Grimarest, Jean Léonor Le Gallois de. *La vie de M. de Molière.* 1705. Ed. Georges Mongrédien. Paris: Michel Brient, 1955.

Grosz, Elizabeth. *Jacques Lacan: A Feminist Introduction.* London and New York: Routledge, 1990.

Hamm, J.J. 'Stendhal et l'autre du plagiat.' *Stendhal Club* 91 (15 Apr. 1981): 203–14.

Hargrave, Francis. *An Argument in Defence of Literary Property.* 1774. New York: Garland P, 1974.

Harris, Lesley Ellen. *Canadian Copyright Law.* Toronto and Montreal: McGraw-Hill Ryerson, 1995.

Hartman, Geoffrey. 'Coleridge, the Damaged Archangel.' *New York Times Book Review* 12 Mar. 1972: 7, 32.

Haywood, Ian. *Faking It: Art and the Politics of Forgery.* New York: St Martin's Press, 1987.

Hazard, Paul. 'Les plagiats de Stendhal.' *Revue des deux mondes* (1921): 344–64.

– *La vie de Stendhal.* Paris: Gallimard, 1927.

Heisler, Marcel. *Stendhal et Napoléon.* Paris: Nizet, 1967.

Hertz, Neil. 'Two Extravagant Teachings.' *The End of the Line: Essays on Psychoanalysis and the Sublime.* New York: Columbia UP, 1985. 144–59.

Hewison, Robert. 'Behind the Lines.' *Times Literary Supplement* 16 July 1982: 766.

Home, Stewart, ed. *Art as Commodity and Strategies for Its Negation.* Calendar and texts of the London Festival of Plagiarism, 7 Jan.–28 Feb. 1988.

– *The Festival of Plagiarism.* London: Sabotage, 1989.

– ed. *Plagiarism: Art as Commodity and Strategies for Its Negation.* London: Aporia, 1987.

Horace. *The Art of Poetry.* Trans. Daniel Bagot. Edinburgh and London: Blackwood, 1880.

– *Epistles.* Ed. Roland Mayer. Cambridge and New York: Cambridge UP, 1994.

– *The Works of Horace.* Trans. C. Smart. London: G. Bohn, 1859.

Hutcheon, Linda. *A Poetics of Postmodernism: History, Theory, Fiction.* New York and London: Routledge, 1988.

Huyssen, Andreas. *After the Great Divide: Modernism, Mass Culture, Postmodernism.* Bloomington: Indiana UP, 1986.

'Information for Alexander Donaldson and John Wood against John Hinton.' 1773. *The Literary Property Debate: Six Tracts, 1764–1774.* Ed. Stephen Parks. New York and London: Garland, 1975.

Information Highway Advisory Council. *Connection Community Content: The Challenge of the Information Highway.* Ottawa: Ministry of Supply and Services Canada, 1995.

Irigaray, Luce. *Speculum of the Other Woman.* Trans. Gillian C. Gill. Ithaca, NY: Cornell UP, 1985.

– *Speculum de l'autre femme.* Paris: Éditions de Minuit, 1974.

Jameson, Frederic. *Postmodernism, or the Cultural Logic of Late Capitalism.* Durham, NC: Duke UP, 1992.

Johnson, Ken. 'Cindy Sherman and the Anti-Self: An Interpretation of Her Imagery.' *Arts Magazine* 62.3 (Nov. 1987): 47–53.

Jonson, Ben. *Ben Jonson's Literary Criticism.* Ed. James D. Redwine Jr. Lincoln: U of Nebraska P, 1970.

Katsh, M. Ethan. *The Electronic Media and the Transformation of the Law.* Oxford: Oxford UP, 1989.

Kozak, Ellen M. 'Towards a Definition of Plagiarism: The Bray/Oates Controversy Revisited.' *Journal of Information Ethics* 3.1 (1994): 70–5.

Kramer, David. *The Imperial Dryden: The Poetics of Appropriation in Seventeenth-Century England.* Athens and London: U of Georgia P, 1994.

– 'Onely Victory in Him: The Imperial Dryden.' *Literary Transmission and Authority.* Ed. J. Brady and E. Miner. Cambridge: Cambridge UP, 1993. 55–78.

Krauss, Rosalind. 'The Originality of the Avant-garde.' *The Originality of the Avant-garde and Other Modernist Myths.* 1985. Cambridge, MA: MIT P, 1989. 151–70.

Krieg, Patricia A. 'Copyright, Free Speech and Visual Arts.' *Yale Law Journal* 93.8 (July 1984): 1565–85.

Kunstmann, Pierre. 'Oecuménisme médiéval et *actoritas*: Art et liberté de la copie.' Vandendorpe (1992): 133–42.

Kuspit, Donald. *The Cult of the Avant-garde Artist.* Cambridge: Cambridge UP, 1994.

K.W. 'In Defence of Yambo Ouologuem.' *West Africa* 2875 (21 July 1972) 939, 941.

La Farge, Antoinette. 'Cylex. The Official Lexicon, 17th Edition, 2020.' *Wired* 2.05 (May 1994): 54, 56–8.

LaFollette, Marcel. *Stealing into Print: Fraud, Plagiarisms and Misconduct in Scientific Publishing.* Berkeley: U of California P, 1992.

La Fontaine, Jean de. *Fables choisies mises en vers.* 1668. Ed. Georges Couton. Paris: Garnier Frères, 1975.

Lalanne, Ludovic. *Curiosités littéraires.* Paris: Paulin, 1845.

Lalonde, Michèle. 'Speak White.' *Défense et illustration de la langue Québécoise.* Paris: Seghers/Laffont, 1979.

Langbaine, Gerard. *Momus Triumphans; or The Plagiaries of the English Stage.* 1688 [1782]. Pub. no. 150. Berkeley: William Andrews Clark Memorial Library, U of California, 1971.

Lanham, Richard. *The Electronic Word: Democracy, Technology and the Arts.* Chicago: U of Chicago P, 1993.

Larousse, Pierre. *Grand dictionnaire universel du 19ème siècle.* Paris: Administration du Grand dictionnaire universel, 1866[–70].

Lessing, Alfred. 'What's Wrong with a Forgery.' 1964. Dutton 58–76.

Lewis, David Levering. 'Failing to Know Martin Luther King, Jr.' *Journal of American History* 78.1 (1991): 81–5.

Levinson, Stephen C. *Pragmatics.* Cambridge: Cambridge UP (Cambridge Textbooks in Linguistics), 1983.

Liebaert, Alexis. 'Nous somes tous des faussaires.' *L'événement du jeudi* 20–26 Feb. 1997: 64–95.

Lindey, Alexander. *Plagiarism and Originality.* New York: Harper, 1951.

Lippard, Lucy. 'Trojan Horses: Activist Art and Power.' Wallis 341–58.

Lucas, André. 'Plagiat et droit d'auteur.' Vandendorpe 199–213.

Mallon, Thomas. *Stolen Words: Forays into the Origins and Ravages of Plagiarism.* New York: Ticknor & Fields, 1989.

Mani, Laure. 'Calixte [*sic*] Beyala: Mongo Beti condamne la romancière.' *Cameroun Actualité* 18 Apr. 1998 <http://www.iccnet.cm/cam_actu/culture/c980481.htm>.

Mansfield, Lord. 'Speeches or Arguments in the Cause of Millar against Taylor.' 1769. *The Literary Property Debate: Seven Tracts, 1747–1773.* Ed. Stephen Parks. New York and London: Garland, 1974.

Marmontel, Jean-François. *Elemens de littérature.* 1787. *Oeuvres complètes.* Vol. 4. Geneva: Slatkine Reprints, 1968 (reimpression of 1819–20 edition).

Martel, Jacinthe. 'De l'invention. Eléments pour l'histoire lexicologique et sémantique du concept: xvième–xxème siecles.' *Etudes françaises* 26.3 (1990): 29–49.

Martel, Jean-Pierre. '*Trou de mémoire*: oeuvre baroque. Essai sur le dédoublement et le décor.' *Voix et images du pays* 8 (1974): 67–104.

Martial. *Epigrams.* 2 vols. Trans. W. Ker. London: Heinemann; Cambridge, MA: Harvard UP, 1961.

Martin Luther King, Jr Papers Project. 'The Student Papers of Martin Luther King, Jr: A Summary Statement on Research.' *Journal of American History* 78.1 (1991): 23–31.

Martineau, Yzabelle. 'Le faux littéraire.' Diss. McGill University, 1995.

Marzorati, Gerald. 'Art in the (RE)Making.' *Artnews* 85.5 (May 1986): 91–9.

Massoutre, Ghyslaine. *Itinéraires d'Hubert Aquin: chronologie.* Bibliothèque québécoise. Montreal: Leméac, 1992.

Matthews, Brander. *Pen and Ink: Papers on Subjects of More or Less Import.* New York and London: Longmans, Green, 1888.

Maurevert, Georges. *Le livre des plagiats.* Paris: Arthème Fayard et Cie, 1922.

McCaffery, Larry. 'Reading the Body: Interview with Kathy Acker.' *Mondo 2000.* (1992): 73–7.

Meltzer, Françoise. *Hot Property: The Stakes and Claims of Literary Originality.* Chicago and London: U of Chicago P, 1994.

Memmi, Albert. *Portrait du colonisé suivi de 'Les Canadiens française sont-ils des colonisés?'* 1966. Montreal: Éditions étincelle, 1972.

Merton, Robert K. *On the Shoulders of Giants: A Shandyean Postscript.* 1965. Chicago and London: U of Chicago P, 1993.

Mey, Jacob. *Pragmatics: An Introduction.* Oxford and Cambridge, Blackwell, 1993.

Micone, Marco. 'L'appropriation culturelle comme partage.' *Recyclages: économie de l'appropriation culturelle.* Ed. W. Moses. L'univers des discours. Montreal: Les Éditions Balzac, 1996. 307–14.

– 'Le p'tit Québec.' *Le Devoir* 3 Feb. 1994: A9.

– 'Speak What.' *Jeu* 50 (1989): 84–5.

– 'Speak What.' *Le Devoir* 12 Jan. 1994: A7.

Miller, Christopher. *Blank Darkness: Africanist Discourse in French.* Chicago and London: U of Chicago P, 1985.

– 'Trait d'union: Injunction and Dismemberment in Yambo Ouologuem's *Le devoir de violence.*' *Esprit Créateur* 23.4 (Winter 1983): 62–73.

Miller, Keith. 'Composing Martin Luther King, Jr.' *PMLA* 105:1 (Jan. 1990): 70–82.

Minnis, Alistair. *Medieval Theory of Authorship: Scholastic Literary Attitudes in the Later Middle Ages.* Aldershot: Scolar, 1988.

Mitchell, Margaret. *Gone with the Wind.* New York: Macmillan, 1936.

Montaigne, Michel de. *The Essays of Michel de Montaigne.* Trans. and ed. M.A. Screech and Allen Lange Harmondsworth: Penguin, 1991.

Morawski, S. 'The Basic Functions of Quotation.' *Sign, Language and Culture.* La Haye: Mouton, 1970. 690–705.

Morris, Gay. 'When Artists Use Photographs: Is It Fair Use, Legitimate Transformation or Rip-off?' *Artnews* 80.1 (Jan. 1981): 102–6.

Mortier, Roland. *L'originalité: une nouvelle catégorie esthétique au siècle des lumières.* Geneva: Librairie Droz, 1982.

Moss, Sidney P. *Poe's Literary Battles.* Durham, NC: Duke UP, 1963.

Nesselroth, Peter W. 'Lautréamont's Plagiarisms.' *Pre-text, Text, Context: Essays on Nineteenth-Century Literature.* Ed. Robert L. Mitchell. Columbus: Ohio State UP, 1980.

Niranjana, Tejaswini. *Siting Translation: History, Poststructuralism and the Colonial Context.* Berkeley: U of California P, 1992.

Nobile, Philip. 'Uncovering *Roots.*' *The Village Voice* 23 Feb. 1993: 21–38.

Nodier, Charles. *Histoire du Roi de Bohème et de ses sept châteaux.* 1830. Les Introu-vables. Paris: Éditions d'aujourd'hui, 1977.

– *Questions de littérature légale. Du plagiat, de la supposition d'auteurs, des supercheries qui ont rapport aux livres.* Paris: Crapelet, 1828.

Oates, Stephen B. '"A Horse Chestnut Is Not a Chestnut Horse"': A Refutation of Bray, Davis, MacGregor, and Wollan.' *Journal of Information Ethics* 3.1 (1994): 25–41.

Ouologuem, Yambo. *Le devoir de violence.* 1968. Trans. as *Bound to Violence.* Paris: Seuil, 1971.

– *Lettre à la France nègre.* Paris: Editions Edmond Nalis, 1968.

Owens, Craig. 'The Allegorical Impulse: Toward a Theory of Postmodernism.' Wallis 203–35.

– 'The Discourse of Others: Feminists and Post-modernism.' *Beyond Recognition: Representation, Power and Culture.* Ed. S. Bryson, B. Kruger, L. Tillman, and J. Weinstock. Berkeley: U of California P, 1992. 166–90.

Pagnini, M. *Literary Pragmatics.* Bloomington: Indiana UP, 1987.

Pasco, Allan, H. *Allusion: A Literary Graft.* Toronto: U of Toronto P, 1994.

Paterson, Janet. *Moments postmodernes dans le roman québécois.* Ottawa: Les Presses de l'Université d'Ottawa, 1990.

Paull, H.M. *Literary Ethics.* London: Thornton Butterworth, 1928.

Perkins, Stephen, ed. *The Festival of Plagiarism.* San Francisco: Plagiarist, 1989.

Perri, Carmila. 'On Alluding.' *Poetics* 7 (1978): 289–307.

Picoche, Jacqueline, ed. *Dictionnaire étymologique du français.* Paris: Usuels du Robert, 1979.

P.L. 'Jean Vautrin n'est pas un plagiaire.' *Le Monde* 25 Jan. 1991: 14.

'Plagiarism: Part I.' *Journal of Information Ethics* 3.1 (1994).

Poe, Edgar Allan. *The Works of Edgar Allan Poe.* Vol. 6. Ed. E.D. Stedman and G.E. Woodberry. New York and Pittsburgh: Colonial Company, 1903.

Pope, Alexander. *Literary Criticism of Alexander Pope.* Ed. Bertrand A. Goldgar. Regents Critics Series. Lincoln: U of Nebraska P, 1965.

Prévost, Jean. *La création chez Stendhal.* Paris: Mercure de France, 1959.

Prieto, Luis U. 'Le mythe de l'original.' *Poétique* 81 (Feb. 1990): 3–19.

Putnam, George Haven. *Authors and Their Public in Ancient Times.* New York: Cooper Square, 1967.

Quérard, Joseph-Marie. *La littérature française contemporaine.* 3 vols. Paris: Maisonneuve et Larose, 1827–44.

– *Supercheries littéraires dévoilées.* 3 vols. 1845–53. Paris: G.P. Maisonnevue et Larose, 1964.

Quincey, Thomas de. 'Letter to the editor of the *Edinburgh Saturday Post.* Nov. 3.' 1827. *New Essays by De Quincey. His Contributions to the* Edinburgh Saturday Post *and the* Edinburgh Evening Post, *1827–28.* Ed. Stuart M. Tave. Princeton, NJ: Princeton UP, 1966.

Quint, David. *Origin and Originality in Renaissance Literature: Versions of the Source.* New Haven and London: Yale UP, 1983.

Randall, Marilyn. 'Appropriate(d) Discourse: Plagiarism and Decolonization.' *New Literary History* 22.3 (1991): 525–41.

– 'The Context of Literary Communication: Convention and Presupposition.' *Journal of Literary Semantics* 17.1 (Apr. 1988): 446–53.

– 'Critiques et plagiaires.' Vandendorpe 91–104.

– 'Le faux et le vraisemblable: le cas du faux Chanel.' *Proteé* 22.3 (Fall 1994): 65–71.

– 'Le présupposé d'originalité et l'art du plagiat: lecture pragmatique.' *Voix et images* 44 (Winter 1990): 196–208.

Raymond, Marcel. *L'influence de Ronsard sur la poésie française (1550–1585).* Geneva: Droz, 1965.

Reagon, Bernice Johnson. '"Nobody Know the Trouble I See" or; "By and By I'm Gonna Lay Down My Heavy Load."' *Journal of American History* (1991): 111–19.

Recht, Pierre. *Le droit d'auteur: une nouvelle forme de propriété. Histoire et théorie.* Paris: Librairie générale de droit et de jurisprudence; Gembloux: J. Duculot, 1969.

Rees, Abraham. 'Plagiary.' *Cyclopaedia or Universal Dictionary of Arts, Sciences and Literature.* London: Longmans, Hurst, Rees, Orme and Brown, 1819.

Ricks, Christopher. 'The Moral Imbecility of a Would-be Wunderkind.' Rev. of *Coleridge: The Damaged Archangel* by Norman Fruman. *Saturday Review* 15 Jan. 1972: 31–3, 49.

Riffaterre, Michael. 'La trace de l'intertexte.' *La Pensée* 215 (Oct. 1980): 4–18.

Roof, Judith, and Robyn Wiegman. *Who Can Speak? Authority and Critical Identity.* Urbana: U of Illinois P, 1995.

Ronsard, Pierre. *Odes.* Ed. C. Guérin. Paris: Editions du Cèdre, 1952.

Rose, Mark. 'The Author as Proprietor: Donaldson vs Becket and the Genealogy of Modern Authorship.' *Representations* 23 (Summer 1988): 51–85.

– *Authors and Owners: The Invention of Copyright.* Cambridge, MA: Harvard UP, 1993.

Rosenthal, Laura. *Playwrights and Plagiarists in Early Modern England.* Ithaca, NY: Cornell UP, 1996.

Roy, Mario. 'Emprunts étonnants dans le dernier Paul Ohl.' *La Presse* 10 Jan. 1992: 1, 2.

Rucker, Rudy. 'You Can't See Your Own Eyes: The Compassion of St. Lucy and the Art of Paul Mavrides.' *Mondo 2000* 10 (n.d.): 96–105.

Said, Edward. *Culture and Imperialism.* New York: First Vintage, 1994.

– *The World, the Text and the Critic.* Cambridge, MA: Harvard UP, 1983.

Sainte-Beuve, Charles-Augustin. 'De la littérature industrielle.' 1839. *Pour la critique* 197–222.

– *Pour la critique.* Ed. Annie Prassoloff and José-Luis Diaz, Paris: Gallimard, 1992.

– 'Rapport fait par M. Sainte-Beuve.' 1856. *Pour la critique* 243–50.

Saunders, David. *Authorship and Copyright.* London and New York: Routledge, 1992.

Scarpetta, Guy. *L'impureté.* Paris: Bernard Grasset, 1985.

Schneider, Michel. *Voleurs de mots.* Paris: Gallimard, 1985.

Schulte, Rainer, and John Biguenet, eds. *Theories of Translation: An Anthology of Essay from Dryden to Derrida.* Chicago: U of Chicago P, 1992.

Sellin, Eric. 'Ouologuem's Blueprint for *Le devoir de violence.*' *Research in African Literatures* 2.2 (Fall 1971): 117–20.

– 'The Unknown Voice of Yambo Ouologuem.' *Yale French Studies* 53 (1976): 137–62.

Senghor, Léopold. *Liberté 1: Négritude and Humanisme.* Paris: Seuil, 1964.

Shaw, Peter. 'Plagiary.' *The American Scholar* 51.3 (Summer 1982): 325–37.

Siegel, Jeanne. 'The Anxiety of Influence – Head On. A Conversation between Sherrie Levine and Jeanne Siegel.' *Sherrie Levine.* Zurich: Kunsthalle, 1991, 14–21.

Smith, Barbara Herrnstein. *Contingencies of Value: Alternative Perspectives for Critical Theory.* Cambridge, MA; Harvard UP, 1988.

Smith, Paul. *Discerning the Subject.* Minneapolis: U of Minnesota P, 1988.

Solongolo, Aliko. 'Fiction and Subversion: *Le devoir de violence.*' *Présence africaine* 120 (1981): 17–34.

Soma, John T. *Computer Technology and the Law.* 1993 Cumulative Supplement. Colorado Springs: Sheppard's McGraw Hill, 1993.

'Speeches or Arguments of the Judges of the Court of King's Bench in the Cause of Millar against Taylor.' 1769. *The Literary Property Debate: Seven Tracts, 1747–1773.* New York: Garland, 1974.

Sperber, Dan, and Deirdre Wilson. 'Mutual Knowledge and Relevance in Theories of Communication.' *Mutual Knowledge.* Ed. N.V. Smith. London: Academic Press, 1982.

– *Relevance.* Cambridge, MA: Harvard UP, 1986.

Stalnaker, R.C. 'Pragmatics.' *Semantics of Natural Languages.* Ed. D. Davidson and G. Harman. Dordrecht: Reidel, 1972. 380–97.

Steinberg, Steve G. 'Hype List.' *Mondo 2000* 10 (n.d.): 120.

Steiner, T.R., ed. *English Translation Theory, 1650–1800.* Amsterdam: Van Gorcum, Assen, 1975.

Stendhal. *Vies de Haydn, Mozart et Metastase. Oeuvres complètes.* Vol. 41. Ed. Victor Del Litto and Ernest Abravanel. Geneva: Slatkine Reprints, 1986.

Sterne, Laurence. *The Life and Opinions of Tristram Shandy, Gentleman.* 1759–67. Boston: Houghton Mifflin, 1965.

St Onge, K.R. *The Melancholy Anatomy of Plagiarism.* Lanham, MD: University Press of America, 1988.

Tamaro, Normand. *Le droit d'auteur, fondements et principes.* Montreal: Presses de l'Université de Montréal, 1994.

– *1995 Copyright Act.* Trans. C. Mcguire. *Statutes of Canada Annotated.* Scarborough: Carswell, 1995.

Temkin, Anne. *Sherrie Levine. Newborn.* Catalogue. Philadelphia Museum of Art, 1993.

Tennant, Emma. 'The White Hotel.' *Times Literary Supplement* 9 Apr. 1982: 412.

Terence. *The Comedies of Terence and the Fables of Phaedrus.* Trans. H.T. Riley. London: George Bell and Sons, 1891.

Thelen, David. 'Becoming Martin Luther King, Jr.: An Introduction.' *Journal of American History* (1991): 11–22.

Thériault, Marie José. 'Des mensonges enrobés de vérité.' *Le Devoir* 3 Feb. 1994: A9.

Thibaudet, Albert. *Physiologie de la critique.* 1930. Paris: Nizet, 1971.

Thomas, D.M. 'D. M. Thomas on His Pushkin.' *New York Times Book Review* 24 Oct. 1982: 15, 22.

– *The White Hotel.* Harmondsworth: Penguin, 1971.

– 'The White Hotel.' *Times Literary Supplement* 2 Apr. 1982: 383.

Todorov, Tsvetan. *Théorie de la littérature: textes des formalistes russes.* Paris: Seuil, 1965.

Trésor de la langue française. Paris: CNRS, Gallimard, 1988.

Vandendorpe, Christian, ed. *Le plagiat.* Ottawa: U of Ottawa P, 1992.

Van Dijk, Teun, ed. *Pragmatics of Language and Literature.* Amsterdam: North Holland, 1976.

Vassaramva, Theodora. 'Speak Whatever.' *Le Devoir* 28 Jan. 1994: A9.

Vautrin, Jean. *Un grand pas vers le bon Dieu.* Paris: Grasset, 1989.

Viala, Alain. *Naissance de l'écrivain.* Paris: Minuit, 1985.

Vigny, Alfred de. 'Dernière nuit de travail.' *Chatterton.* Paris: Didier, 1967.

Vitruvius. *The Ten Books of Architecture*. Trans. Morris Hicky Morgan. New York: Dover, 1960.

Wadsworth, Frank W. *The Poacher from Stratford: A Partial Account of the Controversy over the Authorship of Shakespeare's Plays*. Berkeley and Los Angeles: U of California P, 1958.

Wallis, Brian, ed. *Art after Modernism: Rethinking Representation*. New York: New Museum of Contemporary Art; in association with David R. Godine, Publisher, Boston, 1984.

Walsh, William. *Handy-book of Literary Curiosities*. 1892. Detroit: Gale, 1966.

Watkins, Mel. 'Talk with Ouologuem.' *New York Times Book Review* 7 Mar. 1971: 7, 34.

Welslau, Erich. *Imitation und Plagiat von der Renaissance bis zur Revolution*. Romanistik nr 8. Bernsberg. Schauble Verlag, 1976.

Werness, Hope. 'Hans Van Megeeren *fecit*.' Dutton 1–57.

White, Harold Ogden. *Plagiarism and Imitation during the English Renaissance*. 1935. New York: Octagon, 1973.

Wimsatt, W.K. *The Verbal Icon*. Lexington: U of Kentucky P, 1954.

Woodmansee, Martha. *The Author, Art, and the Market: Rereading the History of Aesthetics*. New York: Columbia UP, 1994.

Woodmansee, Martha, and Peter Jaszi, eds. *The Construction of Authorship: Textual Appropriation in Law and Literature*. Durham and London: Duke UP, 1994.

Wolitz, Seth. '"L'art du plagiat," ou, une brève défense de Ouologuem.' *Research in African Literatures* 4.1 (Spring 1973): 130–4.

Wollan, Laurin A., Jr. 'Plagiarism and the Art of Copying.' *Journal of Information Ethics* 3.1 (1994): 58–64.

Yates, Sir Joseph. 'Speeches or Arguments of the Judges in the Court of King's Bench in the Cause of Millar against Taylor.' 1769. *The Literary Property Debate: Seven Tracts, 1747–1773*. Ed. Stephen Parks. New York and London: Garland P, 1974.

Young, Edward. *Conjectures on Original Composition*. 1759. New York and London: 1970.

Zangrando, Robert L. 'A Crying Need for Discourse.' *Journal of Information Ethics* 3.1 (1994): 65–9.

Zola, Emile. *Emile Zola: Correspondance*. Vol. 2. Ed. B.H. Bakker. Montreal: Les presses de l'Université de Montréal; Paris: Éditions du Centre National de la Recherche scientifique, 1980.

– *L'encre et le sang*. Ed. Henri Mitterand. Brussells: Éditions complexe, 1989.

– 'La propriété littéraire (*Le Figaro*, 25 avril 1896).' *Oeuvres complètes*. Ed. H. Mitterand. Paris: Cercle du livre précieux, 1980. 762–7.

– 'Letter to Auguste Dumont, Paris, 16 March.' 1877. *Emile Zola: Correspondance*. Vol. 2. 548–9.

Zorach, Rebecca E. 'New *Mediae*val Aesthetic: Learning from the Nerds of the Middle Ages.' *Wired* 2.01 (January 1994): 48, 50.

Index

Académie française 45–7, 113, 120, 184,
187; Prix de l', 184
Acker, Kathy xiv, 29, 145–6, 220, 242–
51, 259, 297n18
acknowledgment, discreet 140–7
Adachi, Ken 273n7
adaptations 45, 139
Aesop 60, 103
aesthetic intentions 130, 138, 152; and
adaptations 139; claims to 145–7;
and discreet acknowledgment 140–7;
and 'divine ventriloquism' 139; and
great authors 139–40; and thematic
clues 143–6; and translations 139
allusion xi, 128–31, 143
Amis, Martin (*The Rachel Papers*) 182–3
appropriation 3; aesthetics of 8, 9, 22,
220; and copyright law 253–60; as
critique 206, 214, 216, 221, 242; 253–
9; of cultural material 208, 213–15;
for commercial purposes 256–7,
298n1; electronic means of 260–9;
and feminism 241–7; and plagiarism 101, 146, 228, 229, 241–3, 250;
and post-colonialism 202–8, 221; and

post-modernism 220–9, 234, 242–51,
260–9; of public property 68, 70–1,
94; and revolution 227–8; of
voice 56, 216. *See also* borrowing;
copying; imitation; plagiarism; theft
appropriation art 63, 223–5, 241–51;
and copyright law 253–60; as critique
206, 221, 253–9
Aquin, Hubert 132, 144; *Trou de mémoire* 144, 151, 234–7, 240–1, 297n15;
as colonized writer 221, 234–41; compared to Ouologuem 238–40
Arnold, Matthew 118–19 .
*Association littéraire et artistique
internationale* 93
authenticity 3, 7, 15, 28; and authority
51, 54–5; and authorship 28, 33–5,
48, 57; of identity 236; and originality
35, 48, 51, 56, 57; of voice 56, 210,
216, 244
author: anonymous 198, 236; *auctor*
34–6, 51; colonized 202–13; death
of 24, 56, 57, 59, 218, 259; failed or
'non' 18, 20, 160, 161, 163, 183; gendered nature of 27, 242, 245, 259,

274n4; 'great' ('true') 3, 23, 26–8, 36, 53–5, 116, 139–40, 161; modern 6, 56–9, 65, 78, 220; originality of 26, 28, 48–9, 68, 163. *See also* authorship
author-function 20, 24–6, 57–9
authority: *auctoritas* 33–6, 39, 42; and authenticity 51, 54–5; and authorship 28, 29, 33–6, 57, 250; crisis of 28–9, 176–7; of individual 39; of reader 29; of repetition 36, 211
authority-to-speak 59
authorship: attributes of 20, 23–31, 36, 57–9, 188, 218; *auctoritas* 33, 34, 36; and authenticity 28, 33–5, 48, 57; and authority 28, 29, 33–6, 57, 250; and copyright laws 77–8, 93; definition of 57–9; dualist notion of 93; modern 6, 56–9, 78, 220; Montaigne and 39–43; negation of 219–20, 242, 247, 249–50; Oedipal theory of 26, 244–5; and ownership 65–6, 77–8, 81, 85, 93–5, 269; and postmodernism 218–21, 226; and propriety 60–7, 77–8, 81. *See also* author
authorship, history of: in antiquity 32–5, 60–7; in Middle Ages 32, 34–6; in Renaissance 32–4, 36–43; in seventeenth century 43–8; in eighteenth century 48–51; in twentieth century 6, 55–7, 59. *See also* author
author's rights (*droit d'auteur*) 92–3; versus copyright 80–1; economic rights 79, 166; limited versus perpetual term rights 81–95; patrimonial versus moral rights 76, 79–80, 91, 93; versus plagiarism 76, 78, 85, 95; statutory versus common law rights 80–1, 83, 85, 88, 92. *See also* copyright
avant-garde art: 222–4, 226–8

Balzac, Honoré de 90–1, 164–71
Barlow, John Perry 263–5

Barthes, Roland ('The Death of the Author') 23–4, 57
Baudrillard, Jean 248, 249, 297n19
Bayle, Pierre 70–1, 102, 107, 193
Berne Convention 80, 91, 93, 196
Beti, Mongo 186
Beyala, Calixthe 183–8
Beyle, Henri. *See* Stendhal
Bhabha, Homi 206–7
Bidlo, Mike 225–6
Bloom, Harold (*Anxiety of Influence*) 26, 55, 64
Boileau, Nicolas ('L'art poétique') 44
Bombet, Louis Alexandre-César. *See* Stendhal
Borges, Jorge Luis ('Pierre Menard, Author of Don Quixote') 4; ('Tlön') 60, 218, 269
borrowing 103; good versus bad 119, from reality 74; unacknowledged 31, 41, 185, 208. *See also* appropriation; copying; imitation; plagiarism; theft
Bourdieu, Pierre xii, 7, 9, 10, 100, 163, 177, 178, 219–20, 267, 271nn2, 6
Bowers, Neal 137
Bray v *Oates* 122–5
breach of copyright. *See* copyright: infringement of
Brunetière, Ferdinand 119, 166
Bürger, Peter 222–3, 228–9
Buskirk, Martha 254–5

cento 105, 138
Chatteron, Thomas 30, 33, 163
Chatteron (Vigny, Alfred de) 163, 167
Chaudenay, Roland de viii, ix, 72–3, 146
Chaucer 34, 35
Cicero 38
Cixous, Hélène 241
cliché 73, 147, 148
Coleridge, Samuel Taylor 52–5, 135,

136, 139, 141, 277n18; *Biographia literaria* 52, 54, 139, 141–2

colonialism. *See* colonization; conquest, post-colonialism

colonization: and Martin Luther King, Jr 210; versus mercantilism 196, 292n6; non-subject of 234–41; and plagiarism 195, 202–15, 234–41; and Quebec 234–8, 295n7; and reverse colonialism 202–8; and translation 191–3, 194, 291n1. *See also* conquest; post-colonialism

Compagnon, Antoine 42

compilation viii, 35, 72–3, 107–13; *compilator* 35; and dictionaries 72–3, 107–8; and plagiarism 72–3, 109–13

conquest: and plagiarism 189–202, 211; and translation 189–96; 200–2. *See also* colonization; post-colonialism

context. *See* pragmatic context

conventions: discursive 11; transgression of 3, 7, 12, 13, 46, 144, 237, 250

copy (n.) 29, 30; versus original 30, 64, 247–8

copying 3, 17, 18, 72; of ideas versus expression 147–50; versus imitation 29, 31; of (in)significant and (in)substantial materials 150–3; intentionality of 127, 138; of obscure sources 151–2; and piracy 94; by significant enhancement 155; of well-known sources 146; 152–3. *See also* appropriation; borrowing; imitation; plagiarism; theft

copyright: Anglo-American versus Continental 80, 91, 93; and appropriation 253–60; and authorship 77–8, 93; versus author's rights 80–1; and digital technology 64, 260–9; and freedom of expression 253–9; history of British 75–89; history of French

89–93; infringement of 4, 19, 76–8, 247, international 173–96; versus plagiarism 61, 75–9, 85; and private property 67; and public property 72. *See also* author's rights

Corneille, Pierre (*Le Cid*) 4, 45–7, 120, 153

counter-accusations 134–5; 185–7

critic 113–27; versus artist 118, 177; contemporary 120; Montaigne on 114–15; pedantic 114–16; versus plagiarist 114; professional 111, 117–19; role of 114, 165–6; 'true' 116

criticism 113–27; academic 117–19; functions of 118–19, 166; institutionalization of 114, 117; journalistic 117

cryptomnesia 127, 133; Beyala and 185; Montaigne and 41–2

Defoe, Daniel 84

Deforges, Régine (*La bicyclette bleue*) 140, 141, 146, 154–5, 274n4

dictionaries: as plagiarism 107–10; of plagiarism 107, 109–13. *See also* compilation

Diderot, Denis 17, 90; *Encyclopédie* 17, 107–9, 116

digital technology: and appropriation 260–9; and ideas versus expression 74; and new medieval aesthetic 266

discourse: as linguistic act 10–13; literary 11–12, 13, 25, 67; as property 14, 25, 63, 65, 67–8

discourse analysis 10

D'Israeli, Isaac 149, 285n16

'divine ventriloquism' 139

Donaldson v *Beckett* 83, 92

Donne, John 128

droit d'auteur. *See* author's rights; copyright

Dryden, John 30, 134–5, 148, 194–5

Du Bellay, Joachim 44, 104, 192, 281n4

Ducasse, Isidore 144. *See also* Lautréamont
Dumas, Alexandre (père) 140, 167–71, 195
Duras, Marguerite 274n4

Eliot, Thomas Sterne 119
Epstein, Jacob (*The Wild Oats*) 182–3
Erasmus, Desiderius: *Ciceronianus* 37–9; *The Praise of Folly* 160
ethics, literary 55, 65, 184

fake 30; hold-up (Baudrillard) 249, 297n19; plagiarism 249; writing 146
Fanon, Franz 222, 235
feminism: and appropriation 241–7; (non)-subject of 241–6
'Festivals of Plagiarism' 230–4
Foucault, Michel 8, 20; ('What Is an Author?') 24–6, 56, 57
France, Anatole 148–9
fraud 15, 18, 36, 48, 63; and *Roots* 179–81
freedom of expression: versus copyright laws 63, 253–9

Genette, Gérard 130
Goldsmith, Oliver 128
Gondos v *Hardy* 155
Greene, Graham (and Yambo Ouologuem) 204
Greene, Robert (*Groatsworth of Wit*) 104
guilt, denial of: via aesthetic intentions 137–47; via counter-accusation 134–6; via lack of intentionality 132–4; via legal copying 147–55; via psychological incompetence 135–7

Haley, Alexander 132–3, 212–13; *Roots* 179–81
Hazard, Paul 27, 199, 201
historical writing: as

intertextuality 123–4; and plagiarism 122–5
history: as plagiarism 235; as public domain 71, 123, 198
Horace 103, 162
horizon of expectations 13, 100
Huyssen, Andreas 219, 227

ideas, as property 83–6, 94, 147
idea versus expression 67, 72–4, 85, 147–50, 263–5, 298n2
identity: discursive construction of 40, 58, 246; female 244–6; individual 9; Montaigne and individual 38, 50–1; overdetermined 236, and ownership 71. *See also* subject; subjecthood
imitation: Cicero on 38; versus copying 29, 31; disguised 150; Erasmus on 37–9; filial metaphor of 64–5; of foreign cultures 190–1; Horace on 33; Montaigne on 39–43; versus plagiarism 67–8; proper 6, 32, 34, 36–8; servile 6, 33, 37, 44, 50, 226; and transformation 32, 37, 38, 40, 68; and translation 36, 64, 72, 106, 191; Young on 49–51. *See also* appropriation; borrowing; copying; originality; plagiarism; theft
imitation, colonial. *See* mimetism, colonial
imitation, history of: in antiquity 32–6, 67–9, 225; in Middle Ages 32, 34–5; in Renaissance 34–44, 69; in seventeenth century 44–7, 69–71; in eighteenth century 47–51, 71; in nineteenth century 51–5, 72; in twentieth century 55–7 (*see also* appropriation; appropriation art)
imperialism, cultural. *See* conquest; colonization; post-colonialism
industrialism, literary 111–12 160–81; Balzac versus 164–71; economy

of 162; Haley and 179–81; Poe versus 171–8; victims of 170, 181

industrialist, literary 162–3, 169; versus author 163, 170; Balzac as 165–71; Dumas as 167–71

industry: versus genius 164, 171; and imitation 164; versus work 164, 167–8

influence, literary: anxiety of 26, 53, 64; Oedipal theory of 64–5; patriarchal model of 64–5; versus plagiarism 117

institution: academic 7, 14, 113–14, 131; artistic 222–3, 229, 250–1, 254–6; authority of 188; literary 6–8, 16, 114, 147, 163, 239–40; as phallocentric 242, 246

intellectual property 3, 14, 15, 76–7, 80–1, 85, 88; and digital technology 260–9; metaphysical view of 81, 87; versus real property 80–1, 83–5, 87–8, 91. See also property; ownership

intentionality: of author 24; of author and reader viii, 11–13, 29, 104, 126–7, 130–1, 145, 155, 159, 185, 229; of Coleridge 53–4; lack of 42, 100, 132–4; of plagiarist 126–7, 130; presupposition of 11. See also reader; reception

intentional fallacy 11

intentions: communicative 11–12; contest of 131; guilty or fraudulent 53–4, 126–7, 131; of plagiarist 20, 127, 160. See also aesthetic intentions

intertextuality xi, xiv, 27, 105, 121, 128; and historical writing 123–4; and identity 236; and plagiarism 101; theories of 129–30

Irigaray, Luce (The Speculum of the Other Woman) 142–3, 242

Johnson, Samuel 87
Jonson, Ben 102, 105, 161–2, 194

judgment. See intentionality; reader; reception; value

King, Jr, Martin Luther 208–12
kleptomania 136
Koons, Jeff 254–5
Kristeva, Julia 129
Kuspit, Donald 223–5

Lacan, Jacques 200, 250, 278n2
La Fontaine, Jean de 103
Lalanne, Ludovic 116, 149, 285n16
Lalonde, Michèle ('Speak White') 213–15
Lamartine, Alphonse de 153–4
Langbaine 134, 194
language, as public property 148, 211–12, 216
Lanham, Richard 265–6
Larousse, Pierre (Dictionnaire universel) 27, 51–2, 109, 164, 195
Lautréamont, le comte de 151,171. See also Ducasse, Isidore
Levine, Sherrie 220, 223, 228, 241–51, 256, 257, 267, 298n20
literariness 12, 16, 121
literary communication 11
literary property. See intellectual property; property
literary transmission: Oedipal theory of 64; as patriarchal 64–5, 116
literature: autonomization of 6, 117, 162, 166, 177; construction of 8; popular versus 'high' 162, 177–8; and money 166–7, 288n8. See also institution, literary
literature, postcolonial. See postcolonialism
literature, postmodern. See postmodernism
Longfellow, Henry Wadsworth 171, 173, 174

Mallon, Thomas ix, 143–4, 182–3
Marmontel, Jean-François 115
Martial 62–3, 65–6
Maurevert, Georges (*Le livre des plagiats*)
    112, 149, 199
Memmi, Albert 225, 235, 295n7
memory. *See* cryptomnesia
mercantilism 196, 292n6
Merton, Robert 133–4, 135, 152
Micone, Marco ('Speak What')
    213–15
Millar v *Taylor* 83
Milton, John 48–9
mimetism, colonial 172–3, 210–12, 235,
    241; as subversion 210–11
mimicry, colonial. *See* mimetism
Molière 69–70, 278n4
Montaigne, Michel de 36, 39–43, 114–
    15, 128

Newton, Isaac 135
Nodier, Charles 16–17, 107, 109, 110,
    164, 195
note-book syndrome 132–3, 182

Oedipal theory: of authorship 26, 244–
    5; of plagiarism 26, 137, 182–3, 219,
    274n4
Ohl, Paul 132
oral tradition: African 205; African-
    American Baptist 209–11
original (n.): versus copy 30–1, 247–8
originality 3, 7, 15, 34, 145; and authen-
    ticity 35, 48, 51, 56–7; and authorship
    28, 52, 57; and avant-garde 227; cri-
    tique of 247, 250; impossibility of xii,
    117, 120, 148, 152, 235, 237, 247. *See
    also* imitation
originality, history of: medieval 36;
    Renaissance 36–43, seventeenth
    century 43–7; eighteenth century
    47–51; nineteenth century 51–5,

twentieth century (*see* appropriation;
    avant-garde art; postmodernism)
Ossian 30, 44–5
Ouologuem, Yambo 120, 145, 161,
    211–12, 221, 238–40; compared to
    Aquin 238–40; *Le devoir de violence*
    120, 145, 161, 203–8, 240; *Lettre à la
    France nègre* 145, 238, 240
ownership 15, 28, 77; and authorship
    65–6, 77–8, 81, 85, 93–5, 269; of
    ideas/knowledge 83–6, 94, 147; and
    individuality 71. *See also* intellectual
    property; property

palimpsest, historical writing as 122
palimpsestic syndrome 133–4
parody 142, 213, 219, 242
parvenu 112, 161–3, 169; Beyala as
    183–8; Epstein as 182–3; Poe
    versus 171–8
Pasco, Allan 129–30
pastiche 142, 219
pedantry 42, 43, 46, 114–15, 140; of Poe
    173. *See also* critics
pedants. *See* pedantry
piracy 4, 30, 77, 79, 83, 91, 94, 160–1,
    171–3, 274n3
plagiarism: in academia 121–5, 208–11;
    aesthetic functions of xi, xiv, 6, 229,
    237, 241, 250; and appropriation 101,
    146, 228, 229, 241–3, 250; and coloni-
    zation 195, 202–15, 234–41; and
    conquest 189–202, 211; versus
    copyright 61, 75, 77–9, 85; criteria
    for xi, 15, 20, 126–7, 219; definitions
    of vii, 14–20; discursive construction
    of x, xi, 19; dictionaries of 107, 109–
    13; etymology of 61–3, 102; 'Festivals
    of Plagiarism' 230–4; and imitation
    67–8; versus influence 116–17; in lit-
    erature 3–6; metaphors for 62–4, 79,
    101–6, 189 (*see also* conquest); non-

literary 5, 14; Oedipal theory of 26,
137, 182–3, 219, 274n4; political functions of 207, 210–11, 213, 217, 221,
230–51, 259; and postmodernism 6,
218, 220–1, 228–9, 242, 243; and
power vii, x, 120, 190, 195, 211, 239;
versus quotation 65; as reverse colonialism 203–6, 217, 239; studies of
vii–x, 10; thematized xi, 143–6, 235,
237. *See also* appropriation; borrowing; copying; imitation; theft
plagiarism, history of xii, xiv, 3, 4, 14,
99; in antiquity 60–7; in Renaissance
43; in seventeenth century 43–8; in
eighteenth century 48–51; in nineteenth century 51–5; in twentieth
century 55–6
plagiarism, pragmatic. *See* pragmatic
plagiarism
plagiarist: definition of 17, 18; as failed
or non-author 18, 20, 26, 27, 52, 160,
161,163, 218; female 184–8, 241–6;
male 27, 274n4; as great writer 112,
173; as non-subject 218–19; as non-
subject of colonization 234–1; as
non-subject of feminism 241–7; as
psychological subject 19–20, 219; psychology of 19–20, 26, 53, 186, 200–1,
219, 237, 239; as revolutionary 229–
51; as victim 170, 181, 216
Poe, Edgar Allen 29, 171–8
Pope, Alexander 106, 115, 157–8
post-authorship 268–9
post-colonialism: and plagiarism 202–
17, 221, 238–41; and reverse colonialism 202–4; and Quebec 213, 234–8.
See also colonization, conquest
postmodernism 218–30; aesthetics
of 75, 218–20, 224; and appropriation 220–9, 242–51, 260–9; and
authorship 218–21, 226; as critique
227; and digital technology 265–6;

and plagiarism 6, 218, 220–1, 228–9,
242, 243; as revolutionary 226–7, 229;
subjectivity and 218–21, 225–7
post-ownership 268–9
poststructuralism 219; and
authorship xiv, 218–21
power: language and 222; literature
and 8, 162, 172; plagiarism and vii,
x, 120, 190, 195, 211, 239
pragmatic context 12–13; 190
pragmatic plagiarism vii, viii, xi, 4, 8,
18, 146, 217, 222, 240; theory of 3–4,
131
pragmatics 8–14; contextual viii, 12–13;
literary 13, 272n5
presuppositions xiv, 4–5, 9, 10, 11, 12,
20; of intentionality 56; of originality
128,145
profit: as unearned advantage 17, 18,
159; economic 87–8, 90–1, 111, 131,
159–60, 162, 166; economic versus
symbolic 163, 288n8; symbolic 89,
159, 160, 166
profiteer. *See* parvenu; industrialist
property 15, 67–80; and Balzac 90–1;
and Diderot 90; discourse as 14, 25,
63, 65, 67–8; ideas or knowledge as
83, 84, 86, 94; versus propriety 77–9,
81, 91; public versus private 67–75,
95; symbolic 250. *See also* intellectual
property; ownership
propriety: and authorship 60–7, 76–9,
81; precopyright 79; versus
property 77–9, 81, 91
psychological (in)competence 18, 23,
135–7; and Neal Bowers 137; of
Coleridge 136; and kleptomania 136;
and Oedipal complex 137
public domain. *See* property

Quérard, Joseph-Marie 111–12, 148,
149, 167–70, 196, 198, 285nn16, 17

'Querelle des anciens et des modernes' 44, 46, 71
Quiet Revolution (Quebec) 234
Quincey, Thomas de 116–17
quotation: and Montaigne 42, 128; and originality 128; and ownership 70–1, 128; versus plagiarism 65. *See also* sources

racism: and Beyala 183, 185, 187; and Haley 180, 213; and King 209–12
reader 13, 19, 20, 24; as authority viii; role of 11, 99–102, 131, 155. *See also* intentionality; reception
reception vii, xi, xii, 9, 11–13, 19, 99. *See also* intentionality; reader
recycling. *See* repetition
Rees, Abraham (*Cyclopaedia*) 108
repetition xi, 3, 4, 9, 13; as aesthetic quality 99; authoritative 36, 211; as inevitable xi, 3, 100, 113, 121, 140; and plagiarism 13, 100, and postmodernism 248–9
representation: of plagiarism 249; and postmodernism 247–9; of representation 247–9. *See also* simulacrum
revolution 207, 210, 213; and postmodern art 222–29; 234, 250; and decolonial theory 222, 225; and plagiarism 229–51; and Quebec 234, 236. *See also* subversion; transgression
revolutionary: as plagiarist 229–51
Richesource, Professor 149–50, 285–6n17
Riffaterre, Michael 129
Ronsard, Pierre 192, 281n3
Russian Formalists 7, 271n2

Saïd, Edward 206, 222
Sainte-Beuve, Charles Augustin 164–5
Sardou, Victorien 149
schizophrenia 245–6

Schneider, Michel viii, 26, 65, 99, 101, 133, 137, 200, 274n4
Schwartz-Bart, André 120, 204
Seneca 69
Senghor, Léopold 203
self-consciousness: of artist 224, 226; of authorship 58, 220, 224; of lack of subjecthood 225, 239, 244–5; of plagiarism 126–7, 220
Shakespeare, William xiv, 33, 104, 105, 161–2
Sherman, Cindy 226
Sidney, Philip (*Defense of Poetry*) 71
significant enhancement 18, 45, 146; and ideas 154–5; and repetition 153–4
simulacrum 219, 247–50, 297n19
sincerity, literary. *See* authenticity
Société des gens des lettres 90, 165, 168
sources, attribution of 66, 70–1, 128, 140–1, 262. *See also* quotation
Statute of Anne 82–3, 88
Stendhal 27, 132, 196–202
Sterne, Laurence 143, 144
St Onge, K.R. 18, 23
structuralism: and author 24, 25; and authorial intentions 126
subject: of colonization 221, 225, 234–41; discursive construction of 19; of feminism 241–6; and postmodernism 225–7
subjecthood, absence of 218–21, 224–8, 236, 239, 241–6; attributes of 218–19; denial of 224, 237
subversion 210, 211; and plagiarism 230–4, 247; versus revolution 228; in postmodern art 221, 247. *See also* revolution; transgression

Terence 106, 291n2
theft 14, 15, 17, 18, 50; metaphors for 105; in antiquity 60–7. *See also*

appropriation; borrowing; copying; imitation; plagiarism
Thibaudet, Albert 114, 118
Thomas, D.M.: *The White Hotel* 140, 145, 215–16, 286n2; *The Bronze Horsemen* 286n2
Thomasius, Jacques 107
Tournier, Michel 146
transformation 94; of artistic institution 250; and imitation 32, 37, 38, 40, 68; metaphors of 38, 40, 103; Montaigne on 40–2; and work 94. *See also* imitation
transgression: of institution 239, 250; of literary conventions 3, 7, 12,13, 46, 144, 237, 250. *See also* revolution; subversion
translation: of ancients versus moderns 92–3; and *Le Cid* 45–6; and colonization 191–3, 194, 291n1; and Coleridge 139; and conquest 189–96, 200–2; of foreigners versus nationals 191–3; and imitation 36, 64, 72,106, 191; versus invention 44; Latin theory of 188–92; and national improvement 191, 193; and plagiarism 168,

196–7, 199; and Stendhal 196–202
tu-quoque-ism. *See* counter-accusations

Valéry, Paul 27
value: aesthetic 9, 99, 100; economic 87–8, 90–1, 111, 131, 159–60, 162, 166; judgments of 4, 9, 10; symbolic 89, 159, 160, 166; symbolic versus economic 163, 272n6, 288n8. *See also* profit
Vautrin, Jean (*Un grand pas vers le bon Dieu*) 216
Vitruvius 66, 102
voice: appropriation of 56, 216; authenticity of 56, 210, 216, 244
voice-merging 211

Wired 262–3, 266
work: versus industry 164, 167–8; and transformation 94

Young, Edward (*Conjectures on Original Composition*) 49–51, 71

Zola, Emile 74, 93, 166–7, 178, 288n8